Deterrence and Incapacitation: Estimating the Effects of Criminal Sanctions on Crime Rates

Alfred Blumstein, Jacqueline Cohen,
and Daniel Nagin, *Editors*

PANEL ON RESEARCH ON DETERRENT
AND INCAPACITATIVE EFFECTS

Committee on Research on Law
Enforcement and Criminal Justice
Assembly of Behavioral and Social Sciences
National Research Council

NATIONAL ACADEMY OF SCIENCES
Washington, D.C. 1978

NOTICE: The project that is the subject of this report was approved by the Governing Board of the National Research Council, whose members are drawn from the Councils of the National Academy of Sciences, the National Academy of Engineering, and the Institute of Medicine. The members of the Committee responsible for the report were chosen for their special competences and with regard for appropriate balance.

This report has been reviewed by a group other than the authors according to procedures approved by a Report Review Committee consisting of members of the National Academy of Sciences, the National Academy of Engineering, and the Institute of Medicine.

Prepared under Contract #J-LEAA-006-76 from the National Institute of Law Enforcement and Criminal Justice, Law Enforcement Assistance Administration, United States Department of Justice. Points of view or opinions stated in this document are those of the author and do not necessarily represent the official position or policies of the United States Department of Justice.

Library of Congress Cataloging in Publication Data

National Research Council. Panel on Research on Deterrent and Incapacitative Effects.
Deterrence and incapacitation.

"Papers provided basic material for a two-day conference convened at Woods Hole, Massachusetts, on July 19–20, 1976."
Includes bibliographies.
1. Punishment in crime deterrence—Congresses. 2. Punishment—Congresses. 3. Criminal behavior, Prediction of —Congresses. I. Title.
HV8680.N37 1977 364.6'01 77-27082
ISBN 0-309-02649-0

Available from:

Printing and Publishing Office
National Academy of Sciences
2101 Constitution Avenue, N.W.
Washington, D.C.

Printed in the United States of America

PANEL ON RESEARCH ON DETERRENT AND INCAPACITATIVE EFFECTS

Members

ALFRED BLUMSTEIN (*Chairman*), School of Urban and Public Affairs, Carnegie-Mellon University

FRANKLIN M. FISHER, Department of Economics, Massachusetts Institute of Technology

GARY G. KOCH, Department of Biostatistics, School of Public Health, University of North Carolina, Chapel Hill

PAUL E. MEEHL, Department of Psychology, University of Minnesota

ALBERT J. REISS, JR., Department of Sociology, Yale University

JAMES Q. WILSON, John Fitzgerald Kennedy School and Department of Government, Harvard University

MARVIN E. WOLFGANG, Center for Studies in Criminology and Criminal Law, University of Pennsylvania

FRANKLIN E. ZIMRING, Department of Law and The Center for Studies in Criminal Justice, University of Chicago

SAMUEL KRISLOV, *Ex Officio* (Chairman, Committee on Research on Law Enforcement and Criminal Justice), Department of Political Science, University of Minnesota

Staff

JACQUELINE COHEN, Carnegie-Mellon University

DANIEL NAGIN, Duke University

Contents

Preface

The Panel on Research on Deterrent and Incapacitative Effects was established in response to a vigorous national debate over the appropriate role of criminal sanctions in reducing the high crime rates of the 1970s. A new element introduced into the debate was recent research results purporting to demonstrate that the deterrent and incapacitative effects of criminal sanctions could produce significant and quantifiable benefits in terms of reduced crime rates. The research results were put forth by advocates of various policy positions for use in policy decisions. Indeed, they represented an important step forward in the discussion of crime-control policy: questions were being addressed in empirical terms as well as in the more traditional ideological terms.

The technical complexity of the statistical and analytical studies precluded an adequate assessment of their validity by the decision makers involved, few of whom had extensive training in such methodologies. Thus, the Panel was convened to provide an objective assessment of the scientific validity of the technical evidence, focusing on both the existence and the magnitude of any crime-reducing effects. Since the process of assessment would inevitably identify gaps in current knowledge, the Panel was also asked to identify directions for future research.

Such an assessment is a complex research task that requires familiarity with the use and the limitations of the methodologies involved in the studies, expertise in the diverse disciplines represented in the analyses, and knowledge of the behavior of the institutions in the criminal justice system and the data they generate. In order to incorporate the range of disciplinary and methodological expertise necessary for such an assessment, members of the Panel were drawn from the disciplines of political science, sociology, psychology, economics, criminology, and law and from the methodological areas of statistics, econometrics, and operations research.

Despite the ideological controversy over the subject matter involved, it is important to note that all the Panel's deliberations focused exclusively on questions of scientific validity. This reflected the Panel's view of its task as one of assessing and reporting on the quality of the evidence, and not as one of prescribing a sanctioning policy.

In its review of the evidence, the Panel was conservative in its willingness to accept evidence with flaws or important errors. This is consistent with the notion that "scientific evidence" should require a rigorous standard of proof. Such a standard is necessary for that evidence to retain its integrity and to ensure its special credibility when it does have valid information to contribute. The assumptions on which any such results are based must be carefully scrutinized in order to assess the validity of the conclusions derived. For these reasons, the Panel had to probe deeply into those assumptions.

An important contribution to the work of the Panel was provided by a number of papers commissioned by the Panel and incorporated in this volume. These papers included literature reviews (by Daniel Nagin on studies of deterrence through analysis of natural variation, by Franklin Zimring on field experiments, by Jacqueline Cohen on models of incapacitation, and by John Monahan on approaches to predicting individuals' future criminality), reanalyses of data that had already been reported and published (by Walter Vandaele on noncapital sanctions and by Lawrence R. Klein, Brian Forst, and Victor Filatov on capital sanctions), and some papers laying out possible future research agendas (by Franklin M. Fisher and Daniel Nagin on simultaneous econometric models and by Charles Manski on individual-choice models).

These papers provided basic material for a two-day conference convened at Woods Hole, Massachusetts, on July 19-20, 1976. Participants at that conference (listed in the Appendix) used the commissioned papers as a basis for their discussions on the validity of the available evidence and on directions for future research. The conference provided valuable guidance to the Panel in developing its conclusions and its report.

A draft of the Panel's report was distributed for comment to more than 50 persons, including many of those whose work is discussed in the report. Many of the responses contained valuable suggestions, and all the contributions were appreciated, especially those from Albert Biderman, Barbara Boland, Jan Chaiken, James Davis, and Kenneth Wolpin.

Since the Panel was associated with the Committee on Research on Law Enforcement and Criminal Justice of the National Research Council's Assembly of Behavioral and Social Sciences, the membership of the Panel was approved by that Committee; the Committee was kept informed of the work of the Panel; and the Committee's Chairman, Samuel Krislov, actively participated in the Panel's deliberations. Members of the Committee also had the opportunity to comment on the draft of the Panel's report. The report, however, is solely the responsibility of the Panel.

The Panel would like to express its appreciation for the work of its two staff analysts, Daniel Nagin of Duke University and Jacqueline Cohen of Carnegie-Mellon University, for their significant efforts in reviewing the literature and in helping to develop this report. Jane Beltz at Carnegie-Mellon University provided vital secretarial support to the Panel. We would also like to express our appreciation to the staff of the Assembly: the Associate Executive Director, Lester P. Silverman, and the Study Director of the Committee on Research on Law Enforcement and Criminal Justice, Susan O. White, provided useful support and assistance; Eugenia Grohman provided valuable aid in the final editing of the report; and Christine L. McShane prepared the volume for production.

ALFRED BLUMSTEIN, *Chairman*
Panel on Research on Deterrent
and Incapacitative Effects

REPORT OF THE PANEL

Summary

This report focuses narrowly on attempts to estimate what are called the "deterrent" and "incapacitative" effects—in terms of crimes averted—of criminal sanctions:

Deterrence is the inhibiting effect of sanctions on the criminal activity of people *other than* the sanctioned offender.

Incapacitation is the effect of isolating an identified offender from the larger society, thereby preventing him or her from committing crimes in that society.

Two aspects of the Panel's task should be emphasized. First, the Panel was not asked to make recommendations to either increase or decrease the use of imprisonment or other sanctions. Any such choice involves weighing the crime-reduction benefits of sanctions against the many costs involved, and the Panel has not attempted to assess those costs; instead, it has focused only on the benefits, in terms of crimes averted, associated with different sanctions. Second, in evaluating the crime-reduction benefits of sanctions, the issue is not whether the Panel believes these benefits to be large or small, but rather the scientific validity of the available evidence.

ASSESSMENT OF THE EVIDENCE ON DETERRENCE

The hypothesis underlying deterrence derives from the general proposition that human behavior can be influenced by incentives. This leads to the specific prediction that increases in the severity of the penalties or the certainty of their imposition on offenders who are detected will reduce crime by those who are not directly sanctioned. It is argued that, in response to the resulting perceived risk of sanctions, at least part of the population is dissuaded from committing some criminal acts. Thus, all theories of deterrence predict a negative association between aggregate crime rates and sanctions, with levels of sanctions measured either by severity or by risk. The sanction risks usually studied in analyses of deterrence are apprehension, conviction, imprisonment, or execution (all conditional on committing a crime), and sanction severity is usually measured by prison sentence length or time served.

There are three major kinds of research designs for estimating the magnitude and statistical significance of the deterrent effect: experiments, quasi-experiments, and analyses of natural variation. Because of practical, scientific, and ethical constraints, the opportunities for experiments are rare. Quasi-experiments are more common; typically, such studies have examined statutory changes in sanctions (*e.g.*, the abolition of capital punishment) or a clearly defined change in enforcement policy (*e.g.*, a crackdown on speeding violators). The most commonly used approach for measuring deterrent effects is the analysis of the natural variation in crime rates and sanction levels across different units of observation. These analyses interpret a negative association between sanction levels and crime rates (*i.e.*, when sanction levels are high, crime rates are low, and vice versa) as an indication of a possible deterrent effect.

THE EVIDENCE ON NONCAPITAL SANCTIONS: ANALYSES OF NATURAL VARIATION

Taken as a whole, the reported evidence consistently finds a negative association between crime rates and the risks of apprehension, conviction, or imprisonment. The Panel's task is to assess the degree to which the observed association is found *because* the higher sanction levels reduced the amount of crime committed. If the association is found to reflect deterrence, the Panel's task is then to assess the accuracy of the magnitude of the estimated effect.

Sources of Bias

There are three primary obstacles to interpreting the finding of a negative association in analyses of natural variation as valid evidence that sanctions indeed deter crime: (1) the error in measuring crimes; (2) the confounding of incapacitation and deterrence; and (3) the possibility that the level of crime affects sanctions in addition to sanctions deterring crime, which is known as a simultaneous relationship.

Error in Measuring Crimes The sanction measure most commonly used in studies of deterrence is the risk of being sanctioned for a crime, for example, the risk of apprehension or of imprisonment. In most analyses, these measures are defined as the ratio of the number of times the sanction is imposed to the number of offenses known to the police (*e.g.*, the number of arrests divided by the number of offenses). The number of offenses then appears in both the numerator of the crime rate (offenses per population) and the denominator of the sanction variable.

Data on known offenses are the result of citizens' reports to the police or of the police discovering offenses on their own and of those reports then being recorded in official crime statistics. Because of the way the sanction risk and the crime rate are defined, any variation in the reporting or recording rates in different jurisdictions could cause a negative association, even in the absence of a deterrent effect.

Confounding of Deterrence and Incapacitation Imprisoning offenders produces an incapacitative effect as well as a deterrent effect. The incapacitation of those offenders who are imprisoned will thereby reduce crime even in the absence of any deterrent effect. For sanctions having incapacitative effects, then, a negative association between crimes and sanctions reflects the combined effects of deterrence and incapacitation, rather than a deterrent effect alone.

Simultaneous Effects Any negative association between crime and sanctions could also be interpreted as reflecting an inverse causal effect, whereby jurisdictions impose lower sanctions because they have higher crime rates. Such an inverse causal effect of crimes on sanctions may arise because the criminal justice system resources (*e.g.*, police, prosecutors, prisons) become overburdened by the increased amount of crime and hence less able to deal with new offenders. Another explanation for such an inverse effect may be an increased tolerance for criminality in those jurisdictions where crime is more common, as reflected, for example, in a reduction in the average sanctions imposed for a particular type of crime. In either case, crimes and sanctions are then simultaneously related.

The statistical procedures for isolating the deterrent effect in a simultaneous relationship require critical prior assumptions called "identification restrictions." These generally involve assuming that certain factors *do not* influence the crime rate directly, but *do* affect one or more of the other simultaneously related variables (such as sanction levels). If these assumptions are seriously in error, the estimated effect may contain large errors reflecting contamination by the simultaneous effects.

The arguments for and against simultaneity differ appreciably, both in substance and persuasiveness, for different sanctions. Thus, in assessing the evidence, the Panel examined the different sanctions separately and examined each from the perspectives of both the assumption of simultaneity and the assumption of nonsimultaneity. Those assessments involved both the validity of the alternative assumptions and our assessment of the research results under each assumption.

Summary of the Evidence

Analyses of natural variation, with few exceptions, find a negative association between crime rates and noncapital sanction risks, controlling for other presumably causal determinants of crime. Any conclusion that these negative associations reflect a deterrent effect, however, is limited principally by the inability to eliminate other factors that could account for the observed relationship, even in the absence of a deterrent effect.

The most important such factor is the possibility that crime rates influence sanctions as well as vice versa; that is, that there is a simultaneous relationship between crimes and sanctions. If this is so, simultaneous estimation methods are required to isolate the deterrent effect. If simultaneous effects are appreciable, then substantial questions remain about whether the simultaneous analyses have successfully isolated the deterrent effect in the simultaneous relationships.

The extent to which simultaneity is an issue may vary with the kind of sanction employed. The likelihood that sanctions and crime are simultaneously determined is probably greatest for imprisonment, less for conviction, and least for arrest. The extent to which simultaneity does exist has rarely been investigated. Until we have a clearer understanding of simultaneity, however, we believe that caution should be exercised in interpreting the available results as establishing a deterrent effect, and especially so for the sanction of imprisonment.

For those sanctions for which simultaneous effects are probably not appreciable, the deterrence estimates resulting from the nonsimultaneous analyses suffer from the bias introduced by error in measuring crimes; this bias forces a negative association even in the absence of deterrent effects. However, since it is unlikely that the observed negative association can be wholly attributed to measurement error for all crime types, the analyses based on an assumption of nonsimultaneity do offer some credible evidence of the existence of a deterrent effect. The estimates of the magnitude of that effect, however, are likely to be seriously in error because of the bias.

In summary, therefore, we cannot yet assert that the evidence warrants an affirmative conclusion regarding deterrence. We believe scientific caution must be exercised in interpreting the limited validity of the available evidence and the number of competing explanations for the results. Our reluctance to draw stronger conclusions does not imply support for a position that deterrence does not exist, since the evidence certainly favors a proposition supporting deterrence more than it favors one asserting that deterrence is absent. The major challenge for future research is to estimate the magnitude of the effects of different sanctions on various crime types, an issue on which none of the evidence available thus far provides very useful guidance. The research program developed in this report is intended to facilitate these efforts.

THE EVIDENCE ON NONCAPITAL SANCTIONS: EXPERIMENTS AND QUASI-EXPERIMENTS

Controlled experiments are relatively rare; quasi-experiments are far more common, usually taking advantage of abrupt changes in the law or in the actual application of sanctions when these occur. The best examples of controlled experiments in deterrence are the test of the crime-control effectiveness of preventive patrol by police in Kansas City, the San Diego field-interrogation experiment, and the study of the effectiveness of different strategies to reduce income tax evasion. Quasi-experimental studies are available on the effect of changes in penalties for drunk driving, drug use and sales, bad checks, and abortion. The deterrent effects of changes in enforcement or patrol practice have also been examined for speeding, for crime on the subway in New York City, and for crime in general.

The results of the experimental and quasi-experimental studies are mixed: some find evidence of significant deterrent effects and others find no evidence of measurable changes in crime rates. In most cases, however, the research designs suffer from a variety of remediable flaws, which undermine confidence in the results; all too often, other factors can be identified to account for findings of either an effect or of no effect.

When the flaws in a particular study have been identified, that line of research is much more likely to be dropped rather than to be replicated with the flaws corrected. As a result, there is a proliferation of unique studies examining a wide variety of intervention strategies. Because most of the studies are not comparable, the results are usually limited to the specific crime types examined and the specific crime control tactics invoked, and they are often restricted to the particular experimental locale. Therefore, no general conclusions can be drawn from the evidence available at this time from experimental and quasi-experimental studies on deterrence.

THE EVIDENCE ON CAPITAL SANCTIONS: THE DETERRENT EFFECT OF CAPITAL PUNISHMENT ON HOMICIDE

Early empirical efforts to test the deterrence hypothesis for capital punishment typically took three forms: the comparison of the homicide rates in contiguous jurisdictions, some of which had abolished capital punishment; the examination of time-series data on homicide rates within a jurisdiction during the years before and after the abolition of capital punishment; and the comparison of the homicide rates in a jurisdiction just before and after the imposition of a death sentence or an execution. While all these studies failed to find evidence of a deterrent effect, they suffered from a number of methodological weaknesses; the most serious flaw was the general failure to control adequately for the variety of demographic, cultural, and socioeconomic factors that influence homicide rates. Examining "similar" contiguous states or the same jurisdiction over short time periods represents some effort to hold these factors constant; however, when dealing with rare events like homicides and executions (where the numbers are quite small), the crudeness of the controls could mask any effects that may exist. In addition, there were no controls for the effects of noncapital sanctions in reducing homicides.

In contrast, a recent analysis of time-series data for 1933-1969, in which homicides and executions were aggregated for the entire United States, claims to find a deterrent effect for executions. A number of reanalyses of these data have shown those findings to be sensitive to minor technical variations in the analysis, which either reversed the direction of the presumed effect or greatly reduced its magnitude.

The findings of the analysis are particularly sensitive to the time period included and result largely from the fact that, during 1962-1969, executions ceased and homicides increased; however, the increase in homicides was no more than increases in other crimes. Thus, to conclude that a deterrent effect exists, one must assume, first, that the steady rise in homicides over this eight-year period was caused at least in part by the decline in executions and, second, that the two steady trends in executions and homicides were not generated either independently or by some common third cause, which might also account for the rise in other crimes. If one makes those assumptions, then statistical analyses contribute no further information to the test of the deterrence hypothesis.

In summary, the flaws in the earlier analyses finding no effect and the sensitivity of the more recent analysis to minor variations in model specification and the serious temporal instability of the results lead the Panel to conclude that the available studies provide no useful evidence on the deterrent effect of capital punishment.

Our conclusion about the current evidence does not imply that capital punishment should or should not be imposed. The deterrent effectiveness of capital punishment is only one consideration among many in the decision regarding the use of the death penality—and, in that decision, those other considerations are likely to dominate the inevitably crude estimates of the deterrent effect.

ASSESSMENT OF THE EVIDENCE IN INCAPACITATION

Incapacitation involves removing an identified offender from society at large, thereby reducing crime by physically preventing that offender from committing crimes in society. The incapacitative effect of a sanction refers exclusively to that preventive effect and does not include any additional reduction in crime due to deterrence or rehabilitation.

There are fewer problems in inferring the existence of effects from incapacitation than there are in establishing the existence of a deterrent effect. As long as there is a reasonable presumption that offenders who are imprisoned would have continued to commit crimes if they had remained free, there is unquestionably a direct incapacitative effect.

Models exist for estimating the incapacitative effect, but they rest on a number of important, and as yet untested, assumptions. Using the models requires adequate estimates of critical, but largely unknown, parameters that characterize individual criminal careers. The most basic parameters include estimates of individual crime rates and of the length of individual criminal careers as well as of the distribution of both of these parameters across the population of criminals. Because the crimes an individual commits are not directly observable, these parameters are extremely difficult to estimate. Data are also needed on the chance of an individual being sent to prison, which involves the probabilities of apprehension, conviction, and sentence, and on the time actually served in prison; estimates of these variables are more readily determined, and they vary across jurisdictions.

While the currently limited models and parameter estimates cannot be relied on for exact numerical calculation of incapacitative effects, they are useful for relative comparisons. They can be used in this limited way to explore the implications for crime and prison populations of changes from present incapacitation policies. Such explorations reveal that the expected incapacitative effect of any change in imprisonment policy is quite sensitive to the current value of the individual crime rate and to the current value of imprisonment policy variables. When the current rate of imprisonment per crime and the individual crime rate are low, the percentage increase in prison population needed in order to achieve a given percentage reduction in crime is large. Since the high-crime-rate jurisdictions that are most likely to be looking to incapacitation to relieve their crime problems also tend to have relatively lower rates of time served per crime, they can expect to have the largest percentage increases in prison populations to achieve a given percentage reduction in crime.

RECOMMENDATIONS FOR RESEARCH AND PROGRAM MANAGEMENT

RESEARCH ON NONCAPITAL SANCTIONS: ANALYSES OF NATURAL VARIATION

In order to assess the importance of simultaneity, much more attention should be given to establishing which kinds of criminal justice system behaviors are indeed affected by the level of work load. For example, the relationships between the proportion of charges that are dismissed by prosecutors and prosecutorial case load should be examined.

In order to pursue simultaneous analyses, it is important to identify the most important determinants of the sanction variables. These could include police deployment strategies, judicial decisions limiting police discretion, programs oriented at improved prosecutorial management, and legislation prescribing sentences. Those factors that affect sanction levels, without affecting the crime rate directly or being affected by crime rates, are important candidates for use as identification restrictions in simultaneous estimation.

More deterrence analyses should use a time series of cross-sectional data. Analyses of deterrence in the United States have been limited to cross-sectional data because reports of prison commitments and the actual length of imprisonment (*i.e.*, time served) are published sporadically rather than annually. To make time-series analyses possible, data on commitments and time served by crime type should be collected and published on an annual basis. Also, these data should be disaggregated to smaller jurisdictions within states.

Foreign data bases represent potentially rich sources of time-series data on crime rates and sanction levels. In addition to their potential as data sources, analyses of such data will also provide a basis for assessing the generality of results derived solely from United States data.

As an alternative to the aggregate studies that constitute the bulk of the deterrence literature, a fruitful approach might focus on the effects of sanctions on individual criminal behavior. Increased attention should be given to developing both methods and data bases that would make the study of individual criminal behavior possible.

Analyses of more narrowly defined criminal acts should be pursued to provide insight into the deterrability of specific kinds of criminal behavior.

RESEARCH ON NONCAPITAL SANCTIONS: EXPERIMENTS AND QUASI-EXPERIMENTS

Most of the flaws encountered in experimental research on deterrence are remediable through the use of more careful research designs. Since most of the research opportunities in deterrence arise from legislatively or administratively imposed changes in sanctioning, improved designs will often require an increased awareness of changes before they occur. One mechanism for improving the quality of such research would involve creating a panel with both operational and technical expertise to identify opportunities for experiments and advise on the formulation and execution of study designs. We recommend that the National Institute of Law Enforcement and Criminal Justice organize such a panel and support it with internal staff assistance.

The panel should seek out significant changes in policies or operations so that it can act as a clearinghouse to promote studies of these natural experiments as the opportunities arise. Examples of policy changes that might be profitably studied include the variety of career offender programs and the efforts to decriminalize offenses (either legislatively or *de facto* through changes in enforcement).

RESEARCH ON CAPITAL SANCTIONS

A major part of the problem with current knowledge is the extremely broad categories used in studies on capital sanctions. Future research should involve much more intensive analysis of data that are disaggregated into finer categories. Disaggregation should separate the different types of homicide (*e.g.*, those subject to the death penalty from those that are not), find smaller and more homogeneous units of observation (preferably cities), and use time intervals like days or weeks in order to observe the short-term response to capital sentences or executions.

Opportunities for "interrupted time-series" studies of the effect of capital punishment on homicide will be possible if various states reinstitute the death penalty in the wake of recent Supreme Court decisions. If such research is pursued, adequate baseline data establishing the recent trends in capital crimes must be collected. Furthermore, attempts to assess effects should distinguish among the various manifestations of the capital punishment threat, such as the probability of execution for a homicide, the number of capital sentences or executions per year, and the media coverage given to capital sentences or executions.

In undertaking research on the deterrent effects of capital punishment, however, it should be recognized that the strong value content associated with decisions regarding capital punishment and the high risk associated with errors of commission make it likely that any policy use of scientific evidence in this area will impose extremely severe standards of proof; nonexperimental research, to which the study of the deterrent effects of capital punishment is limited, almost certainly will be unable to meet those standards of proof. Thus, the Panel considers that research on the deterrent effects of capital sanctions is not likely to provide results that will or should have much influence on policy makers.

RESEARCH ON INCAPACITATION

Further model development is necessary to reflect more accurately variations in patterns of individual criminal activity. Research should be directed at identifying variations as the offender ages or accumulates a criminal record and any relationships between individuals' crime rates and their likelihood of being apprehended, their career length, and other variables characterizing individual criminal careers. In addition, research on the sequence of crime types committed during a criminal career ("crime-switching") should be pursued in order to determine the degree to which incarcerating a robber also prevents the burglaries that offenders might commit.

It is also important to measure the extent to which offenders' criminal activity persists in the community even after they are incapacitated. This may occur because of replacement of the criminal activity of an imprisoned offender by recruitment from an illegitimate labor market or because of the continued activity of a group of offenders (such as gangs) from which the imprisoned offender was removed. If such patterns are prevalent, they significantly reduce the anticipated incapacitative effect. The patterns of recruitment and persistence for criminal networks should be explored.

Good empirical estimates of the model parameters are essential for reliably estimating the incapacitative effect. The most immediate empirical investigations should be directed at estimating the individual crime rate and the length of a criminal career. These estimates should be disaggregated by crime type and demographic group and should reflect the statistical distribution of the parameters. Two approaches to estimation can be pursued, one involving analysis of recorded arrest histories (police "rap sheets") and the other using self-reports obtained from offenders.

Current estimates of the sanctioning variables can be obtained from criminal justice agency records. These will have to be augmented, however, to reflect the ways the different parts of the criminal justice system respond to changes in their environments. It is necessary to know, for example, to what extent judges and prosecutors increase their use of dismissals when mandatory-sentence laws are passed. Information on the kind and degree of this adaptive response is needed to assess the net incapacitative effect if anticipated gains from increased sanction levels in one part of the system are offset by compensating decreases elsewhere.

This research program will depend critically on securing rich data bases documenting the progress of individual criminal careers, including the crime types and dates of all arrests, convictions, and sentences. Longitudinal samples like the FBI's Careers in Crime file, appropriately augmented by juvenile data and better data on time served, are needed. A survey of self-reported criminality for a subsample of such a file would provide needed data on undetected crimes.

MANAGEMENT AND ORGANIZATION OF A RESEARCH PROGRAM

Common Data Needs

There is a fundamental need for various standard data items that can best be collected centrally. Such common data bases would include two important classes of information. First, cross-sectional, time-series information on crimes and on the processing of suspects, defendants, and offenders by the criminal justice system; these data are important for studies of deterrence. Second, longitudinal information on criminal-career histories of individuals; these data are essential for estimation of incapacitation effects.

To serve these data needs, a central depository of all research data collected by persons undertaking research on the criminal justice system should be maintained by the National Institute of Law Enforcement and Criminal Justice. It should be a condition of federal research support that the data collected be submitted to that depository at a reasonable time after completion of the research projects.

Accessibility of Data

After research findings are published, the need for verification and replication requires open access to the details of the data used. Published results should, as a minimum, report an essential summary of the raw data from which the published results are derived or make the data readily available.

Peer Review

To promote more successful research on crime and the effects of sanctions, the National Institute of Law Enforcement and Criminal Justice should establish a committee of methodological and substantive research experts to review proposals relating to deterrence and incapacitation.

Introduction

The Panel on Research on Deterrent and Incapacitative Effects was established in response to a growing national debate over the appropriate policies for controlling crime. At the time the Panel was established, at the end of 1975, the nation was faced with both overcrowded prisons and an increasing crime rate. There were 250,000 people in state and federal prisons, a new high in U.S. history. At the same time, the Federal Bureau of Investigation (FBI) reported that police departments had recorded a total of 11.3 million index crimes,[1] which was also a new high.

As the nation was trying to grapple with the two problems of a high crime rate and crowded prisons, the long-standing debate over the proper approach to crime control was becoming markedly more complex. The traditional ideological positions arguing for more versus less punishment were augmented by the introduction of the results of research studies that purported to estimate the deterrent and incapacitative effects of alternative sanction policies.

These studies often involve complex analytical methods that are built upon a series of theoretical or methodological premises and assumptions. Those assumptions are not always stated, and they are not

[1]Index crimes are those offenses included in the FBI index of crime. Prior to 1973, they were murder and nonnegligent manslaughter, forcible rape, robbery, aggravated assault, burglary, larceny ($50 or more), and motor vehicle theft. Subsequently, all larceny has been included regardless of the value of the property involved.

readily apparent to an audience not deeply familiar with the particular method used in the study. This problem is particularly severe in the field of criminal justice, where the key decision makers—lawyers, judges, and legislators—are typically not well trained in such research techinques. Thus, the Panel was convened in order to provide an objective technical assessment of the studies of the deterrent and incapacitative effects of sanctions on crime rates. The Panel was also asked to identify gaps in knowledge and thereby provide some guidance for future research.

The Panel has focused its attention on policy options available within the criminal justice system. Thus, we did not try to address the many issues related to crime prevention through the reduction or elimination of the social causes of crime, however important those approaches might be as general matters of social policy. Furthermore, although the criminal justice system seeks to control crime in three ways—rehabilitation, deterrence, and incapacitation—this report focuses on the latter two, deterrence and incapacitation.[2]

Deterrence is here limited to the effect of a sanction in inhibiting the criminal activity of people other than the sanctioned offender. Sanctions are imposed on those people who commit crimes and are arrested, convicted, and punished: deterrence is the effect of those sanctions on others.[3] The presumption is that individual behavior is at least somewhat rational and responds to incentives—in particular, to the negative incentives inherent in the sanctions of the criminal justice system.[4] A further presumption is that differences in sanctions are

[2]A Panel on Research on Rehabilitative Techniques has been established under the auspices of the Committee on Research on Law Enforcement and Criminal Justice to investigate the issues related to rehabilitation.

[3]This effect is often characterized as "general deterrence" to distinguish it from "special deterrence," which refers to the effect of the punishment on the person punished. In this report, we focus only on general deterrence, since we view special deterrence as closely related to rehabilitation, a subject outside the scope of this Panel. The broad subject of deterrence and its relationship to crime and punishment has been treated by many authors in law, philosophy, sociology, and psychology, among them Andenaes (1966), Pincoffs (1966), Acton (1969), Campbell and Church (1969), Cohen (1971), Walker (1971), Zimring and Hawkins (1973), and Gibbs (1975).

[4]Empirical deterrence research examines the relationship between the level of sanctions and crime. The presumption under the deterrence hypothesis is that potential criminals are inhibited by the desire to avoid punishment. There is no empirical basis, however, for distinguishing deterrence from other interpretations of the same behavioral response, such as the normative validation or moral definition effects of punishment. Thus, no attempt is made in this report to distinguish among the alternative interpretations of the internal psychological mechanisms by which sanctions discourage crime; all of the effects are included in what we refer to as the "deterrent effect" of sanctions.

somehow perceived by the population of potential criminals. Thus, if deterrence works, one should be able to detect shifts in overall crime-committing behavior as a result of shifts in the risk of the imposition of sanctions or in the severity of the sanctions imposed.

Incapacitation refers to the effect of simply isolating identified offenders from the larger society, thereby preventing them from committing crimes in that society. This is often done in a traditional high-security prison, but it is also accomplished in a minimum-security institution, a local jail, or a work farm. The effect is direct; it is associated with the people incarcerated. The fundamental problem is, first, knowing how much crime the people who are incapacitated would have committed if they had remained free, and, second, knowing how much of that crime will be committed anyway, by someone else. Thus, estimating incapacitative effects involves an attempt to assess the unobserved crime-committing behavior of individual criminals.

It should be emphasized that the Panel was not asked to make recommendations to either increase or decrease the use of imprisonment or other sanctions. Any such choice involves weighing the crime-reduction benefits of sanctions against the many costs involved, among them the custodial costs in prison, lost earnings, the welfare costs created, and the many other human costs associated with one group of people punishing another group. The Panel has not attempted to assess any of these costs; it has focused its attention on only one side of the equation, namely, the benefits, in terms of crimes averted, associated with imprisonment or other forms of sanction. This focus illuminates some of the components in the consideration of the appropriate role of sanctions, but the final decision on punishment policy is left to the political process, which is the appropriate arena for making the very difficult and complex trade-offs between the social costs of punishment and the benefits of crimes averted.

Another important point must be stressed here. In our evaluation of the crime-reduction benefits of sanctions, the issue is not whether the Panel believes these benefits to be large or small, but rather, whether the scientific validity of the available evidence is high or low. If that validity is high, then the evidence would be more compelling than any individual beliefs on the matter. If the validity is low, however, then the available evidence should have no more weight than the informed judgments of any lawyer, judge, police chief, or social worker. In this event, as long as the validity is low, science cannot contribute much to policy decisions on the use of criminal sanctions. The focus of this report, therefore, is on the scientific validity of the available evidence and on directions for improving the quality of that evidence.

The next section presents our assessment of the available evidence on deterrence. Following a brief review of the principal methodological approaches to the study of deterrence, the report first examines the most extensive body of literature, that using nonexperimental studies of natural variation in sanctioning to infer deterrent effects for noncapital sanctions. The report next examines field experiments and other quasi-experimental approaches to measuring deterrent effects for noncapital sanctions. Finally, the report examines the evidence concerning the deterrent effect associated with capital punishment. In each part, the assessment is followed by research recommendations intended to fill current gaps in knowledge or methodology.

The third section presents the Panel's assessment of the evidence on the estimation of crimes averted through incapacitation, concluding with a discussion of potential research directions.

The final section deals with organizational and managerial issues related to carrying out the research recommended in the report.

Deterrence

The hypothesis underlying general deterrence derives from the general proposition that human behavior can be influenced by incentives. This leads to the specific prediction that increases in the severity of penalties or the certainty on their imposition on offenders who are detected will reduce crime by those who are not directly sanctioned.

Individual theories of deterrence differ in their characterization of how people perceive sanctions, how they process information on sanctions, how they weigh different aspects of penalties (such as the certainty of imposition in contrast to the severity), and on the kinds of people and the kinds of behavior most responsive to changes in sanctions. Additionally, these theories of deterrence are frequently embedded in larger theories of criminality, which differ in the emphasis given other factors affecting crime, such as economic opportunities, social alienation, habit formation, and moral environment.

Fundamentally, however, all theories of general deterrence are based on the premise that sanctions are negative inducements and that their imposition on detected offenders serves to discourage at least some others from engaging in similar pursuits. Thus, all theories of deterrence predict a negative association between aggregate crime rates and sanction levels, with sanction levels measured either by sanction severity, by sanction risk, or both; all tests of a deterrence hypothesis search for that negative association.

Although deterrence is a phenomenon reflecting individual behavior, attempts to measure it have been limited to studies involving groups or using aggregate data.[5] This results from the almost total absence of detailed data on: (1) individual criminal activities; (2) the availability of alternatives to crime; and (3) individual perceptions of sanctions. Deterrence research ordinarily uses aggregate statistics reflecting the behavior of an entire population, with separate regions or jurisdictions (such as precincts or states) as the units of observation. The research tends to assume, first, that the sanctions in each jurisdiction are uniformly applied throughout the jurisdiction and, second, that the actual, measured sanction levels accurately reflect the population's perceptions of the threat of these sanctions.[6] The sanctions that have most commonly been studied in such analyses are the risks of apprehension, conviction, imprisonment, or execution (all conditional on committing a crime), and the severity as measured by sentence length or time served.

There are a variety of research designs for estimating the magnitude and statistical significance of the deterrent effect. These approaches can be broadly categorized as controlled experiments, quasi-experiments, and analyses of natural variation.

From a scientific perspective, controlled experimentation is the ideal approach to test for any effects, including those of deterrence. The technical problems involved in conducting such experiments are familiar problems in experimental design: they require finding and isolating comparable groups to serve as experimental and control groups, measuring appropriate response variables (*e.g.*, crime rates), maintaining the treatment level for the experimental groups, ensuring that the members of the control group are unaffected by the treatment, and collecting enough observations so that the experiment will have sufficient statistical power to distinguish a null effect from the hypothesized magnitude of the treatment effect.

Controlled experiments are rare in deterrence research; they are typically limited to tests of the deterrent effect of policing strategies. The infrequent use of controlled experiments is a reflection of the

[5]An exception to this is the income tax study by Schwartz and Orleans (1967), which examined the effect of informing selected individuals of the potential sanctions for tax violation. This device of targeting the sanction threat on specific individuals is generally not employed in deterrence research, largely because of the difficulty of experimentally manipulating that threat ethically and with credibility.

[6]To the extent that the perceived threat of sanctions differs from actual sanction levels, the deterrent effects of the former may be quite different from those of the latter. Most of the available deterrence research, however, examines only the deterrent effects of actual sanction levels because of the difficulty of measuring perceptions directly. The determinants of perceptions of sanctions is an issue that should be addressed in future research.

practical, legal, and ethical obstacles: the costs in time and money of mounting social experiments are considerable; operating agencies in the criminal justice system are generally hesitant to function under the rigid controls required for experiments; and ethical and legal constraints limit the degree to which similar offenders can be treated differently solely for the purposes of obtaining experimental knowledge.

Analyses of quasi-experiments are more common in deterrence research. Typically, these analyses have examined the deterrent effect of an identifiable social intervention by government. The interventions studied include statutory changes in sanctions (*e.g.*, the abolition of capital punishment or the escalation of mandatory penalties as in the New York Second Felony Offender Law and the British Road Safety Act) or a clearly defined change in enforcement policy (*e.g.*, a crackdown on speeding violators). The best examples of these analyses follow the design of controlled experiments as closely as possible. The population affected by the intervention is regarded as the "control" group before the intervention and the "experimental" group after, and outcome variables are compared before and after the intervention (*i.e.*, interrupted time-series analysis). If possible, populations similar to the "experimental" population, but presumed to be unaffected by the intervention, are identified and act as "quasi-control" groups; the response variables are measured before and after the intervention for both the "experimental" and the "quasi-control" populations.

The third, and most commonly used, approach in deterrence research is the analysis of natural variations in crime rates[7] and sanction levels that occur across geographical units (cross-sectional) or over time (longitudinal). These analyses examine whether the variations in sanction levels are associated with variations in the crime rate. A negative association, *i.e.*, crime rates are high when sanction levels are low or vice versa, is regarded as an indication of a possible deterrent effect. The types of statistical methods used in these analyses vary considerably in technical complexity, ranging from contingency tables or zero-order correlations to complex econometric techniques.

In evaluating the evidence, analyses of the deterrent effect of noncapital sanctions are considered separately from those concerned with capital punishment. For noncapital sanctions, we consider, first, analyses of natural variations and, second, the results from experimental and quasi-experimental studies. The evidence on capital punishment is reviewed in the final part of this section.

[7]Throughout this discussion of deterrence, the crime rate refers to the rate of crimes known to and officially recorded by the police.

NONCAPITAL SANCTIONS: ANALYSES OF NATURAL VARIATION

Typically, analyses of natural variation have employed cross-sectional data on crime rates and sanction levels. The data derive primarily from U.S. sources;[8] the unit of observation is generally the state, although Standard Metropolitan Statistical Areas (SMSAS), cities, counties, and municipalities have also been used. The index crime rate (aggregate or crime-specific) or some other closely related category is used as the measure of the crime rate. Sanction levels have been estimated with a variety of measures, including: (1) the risk of police apprehension, which is measured by the clearance rate[9] or by the ratio of arrests to reported offenses; (2) the risk of conviction, which is the ratio of convictions to reported crimes; (3) the risk of imprisonment, which is the ratio of prison commitments to reported crimes; and (4) the severity of prison punishment, which is usually measured by mean or median time served.

Using a variety of statistical techniques, sometimes controlling for the variety of other factors that influence crime rates, many investigators[10] have examined the association of crime rates with sanction levels. With few exceptions, the evidence indicates that crime rates are negatively associated with the risks of apprehension, conviction, and imprisonment.[11] The results on the association between crime rate and time served in prison are more equivocal; several analyses have found such an association, but many others have not.

The specific task confronting the Panel was to assess the degree to which the observed negative association can be interpreted as reflecting a deterrent effect: that is, the degree to which we can conclude that the association is found because the higher sanction levels caused fewer people to commit crimes or reduced the rate at which active criminals commit crimes. Furthermore, if the association is found to reflect deterrence, the accuracy of the estimated magnitude of the effect would then have to be assessed.

[8]Two analyses, one using Canadian data (Avio and Clarke 1974), and one using English data (Carr-Hill and Stern 1973), have also been reported.

[9]The clearance rate is the proportion of reported crimes that are "solved" by the police. Since most crimes are "solved" by arresting a suspect, clearance rates are frequently used as measures of the probability of apprehension.

[10]The details of these analyses are discussed in Nagin (in this volume).

[11]An analysis by Forst (1976), which did not find a negative association between crime rate and imprisonment risk, is an important exception.

There are four major obstacles to interpreting the finding of a negative association as valid evidence that sanctions do deter crime: (1) possible common third causes; (2) error in measuring crimes; (3) confounding the effects of incapacitation with those of deterrence; and (4) the possibility of a simultaneous relationship between crimes and sanctions.

SOURCES OF BIAS

Common Third Causes

Because of the absence of any control over the process in analyses of natural variation, nonexperimental analyses are particularly vulnerable to criticism. In particular, a negative association between crimes and sanctions might be produced by some common third cause that influences crimes and sanctions in opposite directions. It may be, for example, that juveniles have appreciably higher crime rates than adults and are also treated more leniently by the courts. Significant variations in the proportion of juveniles in the population across the units of observation could thereby produce a negative association between crime rates and sanction levels.

Statistical procedures exist to control for the effects of such potential third causes, and many of the analyses have included controls for a variety of socioeconomic and demographic differences among the populations in the units of observation. But the possibility of still unknown third causes exists in any statistical analysis of nonexperimental data, and it will always be troublesome in explaining phenomena as complex and heterogeneous as those labeled as "crime," especially when no demonstrable theory of causation exists. While there is the possibility that as yet unknown and so untested third causes exist, this is not a sufficient basis for dismissing the observed negative association as spurious in view of the fact that many of the analyses have included some of the more obvious possible third causes and they still find negative associations between sanctions and crimes.

Error in Measuring Crimes[12]

Many of the sanction variables used are intended to measure the risk of being sanctioned for a crime (*e.g.*, the risk of apprehension). In most analyses, these measures are defined as the ratio of the number of

[12]This problem is discussed at greater length in papers by Nagin; Fisher and Nagin; and Klein, Forst, and Filatov (in this volume).

times the sanction is imposed to the number of offenses known to the police (*e.g.*, the number of arrests divided by the number of known offenses). The number of known offenses then appears in both the numerator of the crime rate (known offenses per population) and the denominator of the sanction variable.

Data on known offenses are the result of citizens reporting crimes to the police or the police discovering crimes on their own, and those offenses then being recorded in official crime statistics. Because of the way the sanction risk and the crime rate are defined, any variation in the reporting or recording rates across the units of observation could cause a negative association, even in the absence of a deterrent effect.

This problem of measurement error can be seen in a simple example (see Figure 1). Consider a number of jurisdictions, each with identical populations (N), the same true number of crimes (C), and the same volume of sanctions imposed (S). If the true crime rate per population (C/N) is plotted against the true sanction risk (S/C), all the jurisdictions will be located at the same point (S/C, C/N), indicated by a circle in Figure 1. Now suppose there is variation in the rates of reporting and recording crimes among jurisdictions. Using the recorded number of crimes in these jurisdictions, the observed crime rates will all be lower than C/N, and the sanction risks will all be higher than S/C. Figure 1

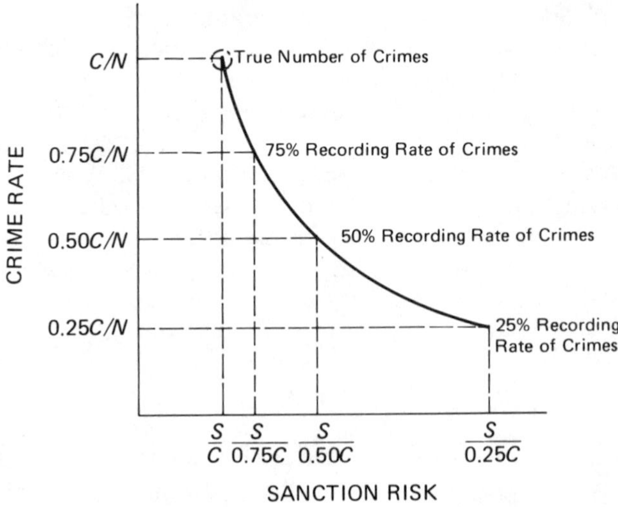

FIGURE 1 The role of measurement error in the level of crime in inducing a negative association between the crime rate (C/N) and the sanction risk (S/C).

indicates the observed rates for several different recording rates; as can be seen, the variation in the error in measuring crimes induces a spurious negative association between the crime rate and the sanction risk in these otherwise identical jurisdictions.

Confounding Deterrent and Incapacitative Effects[13]

For some sanctions, such as imprisonment, the imposition of the sanction results in an incapacitative effect as well as a deterrent effect. During periods of incarceration, an individual is physically prevented from committing crimes (in the general society), thereby reducing the crime rate even in the absence of any deterrent effect. For these incapacitative sanctions, then, a negative association between crimes and sanctions reflects the combined effects of deterrence and incapacitation, rather than of a deterrent effect alone.

Simultaneous Effects—The Identification Problem[14]

Any negative association between crimes and sanctions could also be interpreted as reflecting an inverse causal effect: jurisdictions impose lower sanctions because they have higher crime rates. Such an inverse causal effect of crimes on sanctions may arise because the criminal justice system resources (*e.g.*, police, prosecutors, prisons) become overburdened in dealing with an increased amount of crime and hence less effective in pursuing offenders.[15] Another explanation of such an inverse effect is that an increased tolerance for criminality may develop in those jurisdictions where crime is more common, as reflected, for example, by a reduction in the average sanctions imposed for a particular type of crime.[16] When this inverse effect is operating in addition to the deterrent effect, crime and sanctions are said to be "simultaneously" related, and it is then necessary to separate the two effects in order to isolate the deterrent effect.

Mathematically, a simultaneous relationship is expressed as a set of two or more "structural" equations, one for each of the simultaneously

[13]See Nagin (in this volume) for a more detailed discussion of this problem.

[14]For a more technical discussion of the identification problem, see Fisher (1966), Nagin (in this volume), and Fisher and Nagin (in this volume).

[15]This resource-saturation hypothesis is frequently found in the deterrence literature; see, for example, Ehrlich (1973) and Carr-Hill and Stern (1973).

[16]This explanation is suggested in Blumstein and Cohen (1973) and Blumstein, Cohen, and Nagin (1976) as one basis for their hypothesis that there are stable levels of punishment in a society.

related variables. Statistical procedures exist for estimating the mutual effects of simultaneously related variables such as crimes and sanctions; however, for these simultaneous estimation procedures to be able to isolate a particular effect, such as the deterrent effect, one must make critical assumptions called "identification restrictions."

Identification restrictions take the form of *a priori* assumptions about the behavior of the simultaneous relationship. Most commonly, the restrictions involve assuming that certain factors affect one or more of the simultaneously related variables—but not all of them. To estimate the deterrent effect, for example, the restrictions typically involve assuming that some factors affect sanctions but not crimes. The exclusion of one or more variables from one of the equations in the simultaneous relationship aids in the "identification" of that equation.[17] However, choosing which variable to exclude cannot be determined from the data involved in estimating the simultaneous relationship. That choice is an assumption that must be based on external considerations. If the assumptions to exclude certain variables are seriously in error, then the estimated effects for the identified relation may contain large errors reflecting contamination by the simultaneous effects.[18] The central role of identification in estimating the effects of simultaneously related variables is illustrated in the example (pp. 27–29).

Identification is not a minor technical issue. If a system is not properly identified, completely erroneous conclusions can be drawn from the estimated relationship. In the example developed (see inset), improper identification restrictions would result in construing the negative effect of crime on the clearance rate as evidence of deterrence, even when no deterrence is present.

Allowing for the possibility of a simultaneous relationship between crime rates and sanction levels thus appreciably complicates interpreting the available evidence on deterrent effects. Unfortunately, the hypothesis that crime rates influence sanction levels has received only limited empirical attention when its effect could not be interpreted as a

[17]The excluded variables may be "exogenous"—variables other than those involved in the simultaneous relationship—or they may be "predetermined"—values of the simultaneously related variables determined in prior periods.

[18]Improper identification has repercussions beyond the estimates of the effects for the simultaneously related variables. The estimated structural effects for all the variables in the misidentified relation are similarly in error. For example, if the crime rate function is misidentified, the estimated coefficients of exogenous variables, such as unemployment or poverty level in the structural equation for crime, are also inconsistent and therefore also inappropriate for assessing the causal impact of these variables on crime.

Example of the Indentification Problem in Simultaneous Systems

Consider the case where the crime rate (C) and the clearance rate (S) as the sanction variable are simultaneously determined. Such a relationship might be expressed by the following two equations:

$$C = a + bS \tag{E-1a}$$

$$S = c + dC \tag{E-1b}$$

where C is the crime rate, S is the clearance rate, and a, b, c, and d are the system's parameters, which are to be determined.[19]

For C and S mutually determined in this way, only a single equilibrium point (C_0, S_0) will be observed (Figure E-1).[20] This point, however, does not provide sufficient information for distinguishing the two equations, E-1a and E-1b, that produced the point from any other pair of equations that might also pass through that point. Thus, the data alone are insufficient for estimating equations E-1a and E-1b. A simple regression of either C on S or S on C will generate biased and inconsistent[21] estimates of the parameters.

Now suppose that average sentence, T, is suspected to have an effect on crimes, but is *known* to have *no* effect on clearances. Equation E-1a could then be respecified as:

$$C = a + bS + eT \tag{E-1a$'$}$$

Additionally, assume that:

$e < 0$[22] (*i.e.*, reflecting a deterrent effect of average sentence);
$d < 0$ (*i.e.*, more crime leads to a lower clearance rate); and
unbeknownst to us, clearances (S) indeed have no effect on crime (*i.e.*, $b = 0$).

[19]These relations also contain stochastic disturbance terms reflecting the effect of other causal determinants not included in the defined relationships. In order to simplify the discussion, these disturbance terms are suppressed throughout.

[20]The same argument holds when the relations in E-1a and E-1b contain stochastic disturbance terms. Then, however, the observations will be scattered around the point (C_0, S_0).

[21]An estimator is said to be "consistent" if its probability limit exists and equals the true parameter value. Intuitively, this amounts to saying that with a sufficiently large sample, the parameter can be estimated with any desired precision (with high probability). An estimator that is inconsistent will also generally be biased in small samples. The converse, however, is often not the case.

[22]An assumption of $e > 0$ would do just as well; an assumption, however, of $e = 0$ would leave both equations unidentified as before.

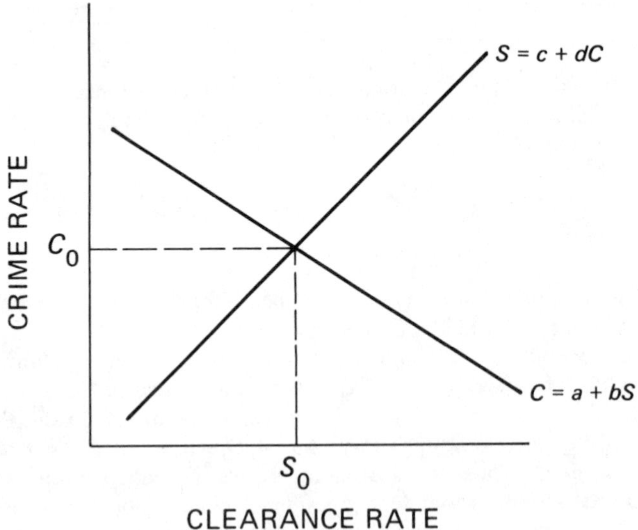

FIGURE E-1 A simplified model of a simultaneous relationship between crimes (*C*) and sanctions (*S*).

Figure E-2 presents equation E-1a′ for three different values of T. Consistent with the assumption of $e < 0$, for any given value of S, C is smaller for larger values of T.

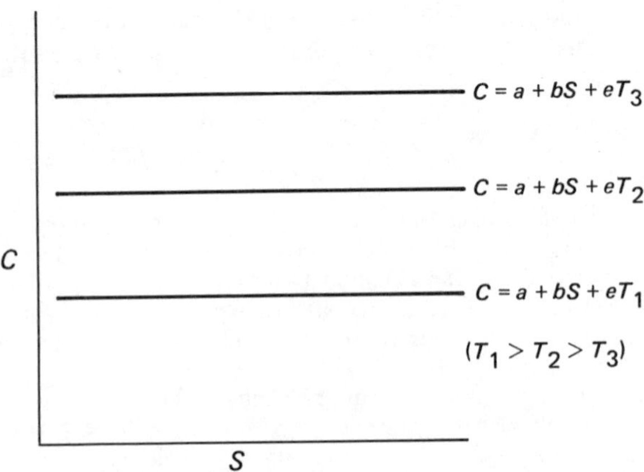

FIGURE E-2 The crime rate (*C*) as a function of the clearance rate (*S*) and the average sentence (*T*) in a simplified model of a simultaneous relationship between crimes and sanctions.

Superimposing equation E-1b on equation E-1a′ yields Figure E-3. The crime function now "sweeps" along the clearance function and the three points—(S_1, C_1), (S_2, C_2), and (S_3, C_3)—represent the equilibrium values of C and S for the three values of T. If these three equilibrium points were observed and connected, then equation E-1b would be uniquely determined. This illustrates the role of T in identifying the clearance function.

The crime function still cannot be estimated because *it* is not identified. The clearance function is identified only because of the *a priori* exclusion of T from this function. This exclusion makes sense because there is no reason to assume that sentences directly affect clearance rates.

If, however, it were arbitrarily (and, in this example, erroneously) assumed that sentence, T, affected clearance rates and not crime rates, then the mechanics of simultaneous estimation would have yielded an estimate for the deterrent effect, b, in the crime rate function. That estimate, however, would be identical to the one obtained by drawing a line through the three equilibrium values of C and S in Figure E-3. Thus, the estimated relation would actually be the relationship describing the behavior of clearance rates and not crime rates; in this event, it would be erroneously inferred that b is negative when it is actually zero.

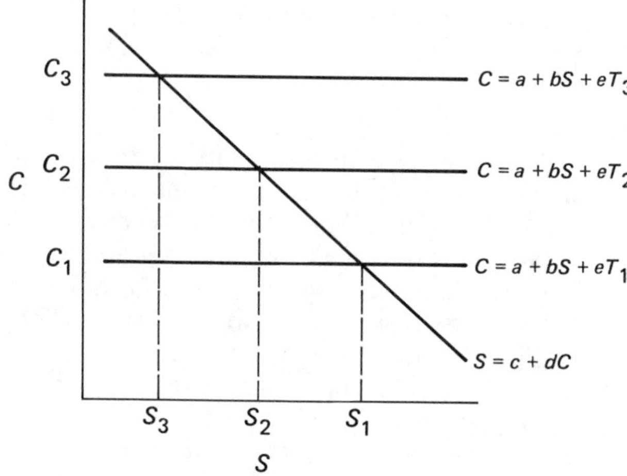

FIGURE E-3 The identifying role of T in a simplified model of a simultaneous relationship between crimes and sanctions.

deterrent effect. If the effect of crime rates on sanction levels is assumed to be small, then nonsimultaneous estimation techniques are appropriate, and a major obstacle to interpreting a negative association as a deterrent effect is overcome.

The arguments for and against the assumption of simultaneity differ appreciably, both in substance and persuasiveness, for different sanctions. Therefore, in assessing the evidence, the Panel examined the different sanctions separately and examined each sanction from the perspective of an assumption of simultaneity and from an assumption of nonsimultaneity. In making its assessments, the Panel found it necessary to judge the validity of the alternative assumptions and of the research results under each assumption.

The remainder of this section thus presents the Panel's assessment of the evidence on the deterrent effects of noncapital sanctions for each of those sanctions under each of the two assumptions about simultaneity. In this section, the sanctions are discussed in the order of apprehension risk, imprisonment sanction (imprisonment risk and time served), and conviction risk. In addition, a number of studies that have explored the relationship between police resources and their presumed deterrent effect are also reviewed.

THE EVIDENCE ON THE DETERRENT EFFECT OF THE APPREHENSION RISK

An Assumption of Simultaneity

One model of police behavior assumes that resources (*e.g.*, personnel and equipment) play a key role in determining the effectiveness of the police in apprehending criminals. This model predicts that the apprehension risk is positively related to police resources and that increases in resources will enhance the apprehension risk by applying more resources to the solution of each crime. Likewise, holding resources constant, increases in crime will decrease the level of police resources that can be devoted to the solution of each crime and thereby reduce the apprehension risk. Thus, for a given level of resources, changes in the crime rate will inversely affect the apprehension risk.

This model additionally assumes that resources allocated to the criminal justice system in general, and to the police in particular, will be positively affected by the crime rate, with increases in crime resulting in local governments' allocating larger budgets to police departments. The increase in expenditures will thereby increase the resources per crime, which will in turn increase the apprehension risk.

From this perspective, there are causal interactions among crime

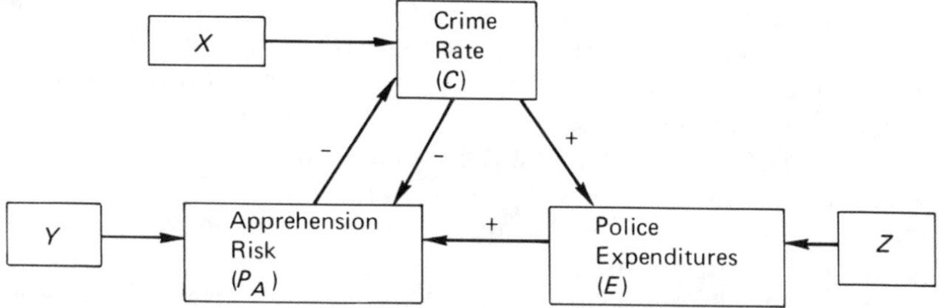

FIGURE 2 The causal interconnection of crime rate, apprehension risk, and police expenditures: a simultaneous model.

rates, apprehension risk, and police resources. We can denote levels of police resources (usually measured as expenditures) by E, the total crime rate by C, and the apprehension risk by P_A. Then, the postulated causal interconnections can be characterized mathematically as:

$$C = f(P_A, X) \tag{1a}$$

$$P_A = g(C, E, Y) \tag{1b}$$

$$E = h(C, Z) \tag{1c}$$

where X, Y, and Z are sets including any other variables specified as causal factors. These might include socioeconomic and demographic factors, measures of community attitudes, and total municipal budgets.

Figure 2 depicts the causal links in this mathematical model, including the exogenous sets of variables X, Y, and Z, which influence C, P_A, and E, respectively. Two arrows directly link the crime rate and the apprehension risk. The apprehension risk has a deterrent effect on crime, and, for any given level of resources, increased crime reduces the apprehension risk.[23] The crime rate also has an indirect effect on the apprehension risk, through its effect on police expenditures: this effect is positive, whereas the direct one is negative.

If either of the effects of the crime rate on the apprehension risk is large, simultaneous equation estimation methods must be used. In

[23]Increased crime rates may also decrease the risk of apprehension indirectly through the inverse effect of crime on prosecutors. If prosecutors pursue cases less vigorously when crime rates increase, perhaps because of the increased drain on their resources, the police may respond by being less inclined to make arrests, especially for marginally criminal activities.

order to estimate the deterrent effect of the apprehension risk, the crime rate function (the crime equation) must be identified. This can be achieved by excluding variables from the crime rate function that are included in the apprehension risk function or the police expenditures function. The validity of any of these exclusions—and of the resulting deterrence estimates—rests upon the validity of the assumption that the excluded variables neither directly influence, nor are themselves influenced by, the crime rate.

Four kinds of identification restrictions have been used in the studies that were reviewed by the Panel:[24] the variables excluded from the crime equation have been (1) socioeconomic or demographic measures, (2) crime rates for types of crime other than the one under investigation, (3) police expenditures per capita, and (4) public-finance variables.

There is no reasonable basis for using the first kind of identification restriction.[25] It is simply not plausible to assume that variables measuring population characteristics will affect apprehension risk or police expenditures but will have no effect on crime rates. In analyses using such identification restrictions, no rationale is provided for the exclusion; it is simply introduced as a mechanical process.

The second kind of identification restriction has been used in analyses examining the effect of apprehension risk on individual crime types (*e.g.*, robbery rates or burglary rates). These analyses have assumed that the crime rates for crime types other than the one under investigation affect either the apprehension risk for the crime type under investigation or police expenditures. For example, if the analyst is primarily interested in examining variations in robbery rates, the rates for all other property crimes might be included as determinants of the apprehension risk for robbery and of police expenditures, presumably because of their impact on police resources. Since the crime rates of these other crime types are omitted from the specification of the crime rate function of interest, this amounts to assuming that none of the factors leading to variations in these other crime rates (beyond those already included in the analyses as specifically affecting the crime type under investigation) directly affect commission of the crime type being examined. It does not seem likely that individual crime types, especially the index crimes, are in fact products of such distinct processes.

[24]Phillips and Votey (1972), Carr-Hill and Stern (1973), Vandaele (1973), Avio and Clarke (1974), and Pogue (1975).

[25]See Nagin (in this volume) and Fisher and Nagin (in this volume) for a more detailed assessment of the difficulties with these identification restrictions.

The third category of identification restrictions uses police expenditures per capita as an omitted variable from the crime equation; this would achieve identification only if police expenditures per capita were unaffected by the crime rate. Expenditure levels, however, are likely to be a function of the crime rate.

Some investigators have addressed this problem by specifying a three-equation model involving all three of the variables depicted in Figure 2—crime rate, apprehension risk, and police expenditures. Then, variables related to public finance (*e.g.*, municipal tax revenues) can be included among the variables in the expenditures equation and reasonably omitted from the crime equation. This approach to identifying the crime equation was used by Pogue (1975). His results, however, are clouded by his finding that police expenditures had no influence on the apprehension risk. Without the causal link between expenditures and apprehension risk (depicted in Figure 2), variations in expenditures will have no influence on the crime rate, and the expenditures function provides no help in identifying the crime rate function.

In summary, all of the identification restrictions used in the available simultaneous analyses of the deterrent effect of apprehension risk are, for different reasons, unsatisfactory. In the absence of valid restrictions, the estimates of the deterrent effect are themselves questionable. Thus, if there is a strong mutual causal interaction among the crime rate, the apprehension risk, and police expenditures, one must conclude that the available analyses have not yet successfully estimated the deterrent effect of the apprehension risk.

An Assumption of Nonsimultaneity

If valid identification restrictions are employed, an analysis that allows for simultaneity is more general than one that does not, since it provides a consistent estimate of the actual deterrent effect whether or not there is a simultaneous relationship. Indeed, if the apprehension risk function were validly identified, the estimated simultaneous relationship might reveal that the effect of crime on the apprehension risk is negligible.

In the absence of such plausible identification restrictions on the apprehension function, however, the estimated simultaneous relationship provides no useful evidence on the question of whether or not the crime rate affects the apprehension risk. Thus, without an independent source of evidence on the issue of simultaneity, adopting the nonsimultaneous assumption must rest on the plausibility of the arguments for nonsimultaneity. If a plausible case can be made for this assumption,

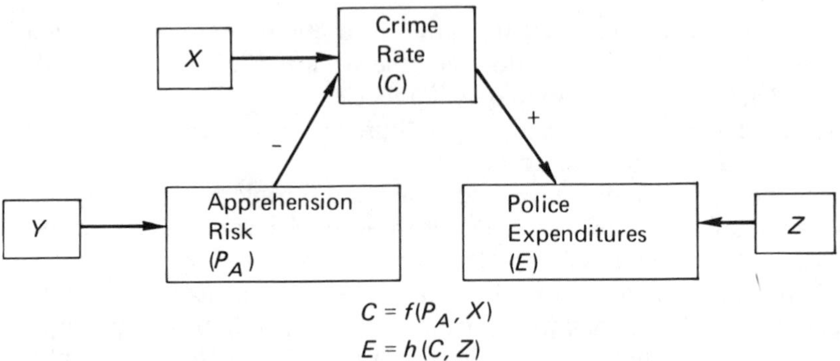

FIGURE 3 The causal interconnection of crime rate, apprehension risk, and police expenditures: a nonsimultaneous model.

then a significant obstacle to interpreting the negative association between crime rates and apprehension risk is avoided, and one can look to the deterrence conclusions based on nonsimultaneous estimation methods such as ordinary least-squares regressions.

One argument for a simultaneous relationship is the theory that the level of resources available for the solution of each crime (E/C) is an important determinant of the apprehension risk. If a strong argument can be made that the apprehension risk is unaffected by the level of police resources (at least over the observed range of E/C), then the nonsimultaneous position would have some support. If this argument is valid, then declining levels of resources per crime (E/C) will not affect the apprehension risk, and both the negative and positive effects of crime on apprehension would disappear. Figure 3 illustrates this nonsimultaneous model. The positive effect of crimes on expenditures may or may not remain; either way, the crime rate has no effect on the apprehension risk.

It can be argued that the apprehension risk is largely determined by the administrative policies governing police operations and that this is a matter of management style and not particularly influenced by crime rate.[26] This management style might be reflected in such policies as police deployment strategies and the incentives offered for making arrests. For example, in departments where the law enforcement aspect of policing is emphasized, there are likely to be increased incen-

[26]This argument is developed, for example, in Wilson (1968) and Wilson and Boland (1976).

tives for making arrests, resulting in a more aggressive pursuit of enforcement activities. This is likely to lead to increased contacts between the police and suspects, thereby increasing the apprehension risk in these departments. From this perspective, professional standards and organizational incentives, rather than the level of police resources, are the predominant determinants of the apprehension risk.

The argument that levels of police resources play only a minor role in determining the apprehension risk can also be justified on other grounds. Most apprehensions are made by the police either at the scene of the crime, in direct pursuit from the scene, or after a positive identification by a witness (Greenwood *et al.* 1975). Furthermore, work load studies of police indicate that the time spent making apprehensions represents only a small proportion of the patrolman's duty time (Blumstein and Larson 1970). Because apprehensions absorb so little of total police resources, the argument that the level of these resources will not have an appreciable effect on the apprehension risk also has some indirect empirical support. Thus, if the crime rate only affects the apprehension risk through the saturation of police resources, the argument that the apprehension risk is not affected by the crime rate has considerable merit.

However, there may be reasons unrelated to the saturation of police resources for a simultaneous effect. For example, in high-crime-rate jurisdictions, the police may choose to ignore minor criminal behavior, even when a legal arrest could be made. This reluctance to make arrests for minor crimes might reflect an increased community tolerance for minor criminality resulting from a greater concern for more serious crime.[27] The police may also react to a reduction in prosecutions that may result from an increase in crime. If prosecutors' resources are strained by the impact of more crime, they might respond by choosing not to prosecute the less serious cases. Because of the high dismissal rate, the police in turn may diminish their arrest rate for these minor crimes.

Unfortunately, the available U.S. data do not permit us to rule out either of these effects of crime rates on apprehension risk. Thus, while the argument for nonsimultaneity between crime rates and apprehension risk is plausible, the question of simultaneity remains unresolved at this time.

If the relationship is indeed nonsimultaneous,[28] the principal obsta-

[27]See Blumstein and Cohen (1973) for an elaboration of this argument.

[28]Nonsimultaneous studies have been reported by Kobrin *et al.* (1972), Sjoquist (1973), Tittle and Rowe (1974), and Logan (1975). These studies are examined in greater detail in Nagin (in this volume).

cle to interpreting the observed negative association between crime rates and apprehension risk as reflecting deterrence is the error in measuring crimes. This bias is caused by variation in the reporting or recording of crimes, which induces a negative association because the number of known offenses appears in both the numerator of the crime rate and the denominator of the apprehension risk.[29]

The extent of the bias is a function of the variation in reporting and recording across observations. If that variation is small, the bias is small; if the variation is large, the bias can be substantial. There is no question that variation exists. The only question is the magnitude of that variation and the degree to which the observed negative association can be attributed to that variation.[30]

The evidence on the magnitude of the measurement error bias is limited. Data are needed on the nature of variations in the reporting and recording process in different jurisdictions. The National Crime Panel survey of criminal victimization in 26 U.S. cities was designed in part to provide this information, but analyses of the survey data have raised serious questions about the survey's own vulnerability to measurement error (National Research Council 1976). For example, the proportion of minor crimes in a city's overall crime rate is negatively related to the overall crime rate, suggesting that surveyed individuals in high-crime-rate cities were less likely to report minor crimes to interviewers. Such differential underreporting is a source of measurement error in the victimization surveys.

Two studies have attempted to gauge the magnitude of the measurement error problem.[31] Using different approaches they examine the

[29]It should be noted that this measurement error problem is not included among the obstacles under an assumption of simultaneity. When simultaneous estimation methods are employed, the possibility of relations between crime rates and sanction risk other than that due to deterrence is explicitly allowed for. The measured sanction risk is thus not assumed independent of variations in the unobservable factors affecting crime, including variations in crime reporting. This obviates the crime-measurement problem in a simultaneous formulation.

[30]See Nagin (in this volume) for a formal demonstration of the effects of measurement error.

[31]Using the National Crime Panel (NCP) city victimization data, Wilson and Boland (1976) found a negative and significant association between NCP rates for serious robberies and apprehension risk (as measured by the ratio of officially recorded robbery arrests to the NCP serious robbery rate). They attempted to circumvent the measurement error problem by replacing the apprehension risk with a surrogate variable that does not include crimes in its measurement.

Wilson and Boland argue that where there are "professional" police departments there will be higher apprehension risks. Using a categorical variable indicating whether a city's police department is "professional," they analyzed the association between "profes-

potential impact of measurement error on robbery rates and burglary rates. Their conclusions suggest that the measurement error problem varies with crime type. Measurement error appears to be a significant factor in the observed negative correlation between burglary rates and the apprehension risk for burglary, but is considerably less of a factor for robbery rates and the apprehension risk for robbery.

The magnitude of the error in measuring crimes remains a problem, but it is unlikely that the consistently observed negative association between crime rates and apprehension risk can be wholly attributed to measurement error in all cases. If one assumes that simultaneous effects are negligible, the consistent finding of a significant negative association between crime rates and apprehension risks in nonsimultaneous analyses may well suggest that the apprehension risk does deter crime. However, due to the measurement error problem, considerable uncertainty remains about the magnitude of that effect.

THE EVIDENCE ON THE DETERRENT EFFECT OF IMPRISONMENT SANCTIONS

An Assumption of Nonsimultaneity

Several analyses examining the deterrent effect of the imprisonment sanctions (the imprisonment risk given a crime and the time served by those imprisoned) have used statistical procedures that are appropriate only if the relationship between crime rates and imprisonment sanctions is not simultaneous.[32] These analyses consistently find a negative and significant association between the crime rate and the imprisonment risk, but generally do not find a significant association between the crime rate and time served.

---

sionalism'' and the NCP crime rates. Professional cities were still found to have significantly lower serious robbery rates. They conclude from this analysis that the negative association between NCP robbery rates and apprehension risks cannot be wholly attributed to the error in measuring crimes.

Using a different approach, Cook (1977) correlated NCP burglary rates with the ratio of burglary clearances reported by the police to NCP burglaries and found no significant association. The correlation of the Uniform Crime Report (UCR) burglary rate with the ratio of burglary clearances to UCR burglaries was found to be negative and significant. Cook argues that since the NCP data are ''less error prone'' than the UCR data, the observed negative association using the UCR data can be wholly attributed to measurement error, at least for burglary.

[32]Gibbs (1968), Gray and Martin (1969), Tittle (1969), Chiricos and Waldo (1970), Bean and Cushing (1971), Logan (1971, 1972), Kobrin *et al.* (1972), and Antunes and Hunt (1973); see Nagin (in this volume) for a more detailed description of these analyses.

The results for time served may be partially explained by distortions in the data resulting from charge reductions. Some preliminary evidence is available that suggests that in cases involving charge reductions, judges sentence convicted offenders on the basis of the original charge and not on the basis of the reduced charge (Hagan 1974 and Wilkins *et al.* 1976). For example, a person originally charged with robbery but convicted of larceny is likely to receive a longer sentence than a person originally charged with and convicted of larceny. This phenomenon would overstate the time served for less serious crime types. If charge reductions occur more frequently in high-crime-rate jurisdictions (perhaps because of increased plea bargaining), this would tend to neutralize any negative effect between time served and the crime rate for specific crimes.

Even when a negative association is found between the imprisonment risk and the crime rate, assuming that the simultaneous effects are indeed small, there are two obstacles to concluding that this association reflects deterrence. First, since reported crimes are included both in the numerator of the crime rate and the denominator of the measure of the imprisonment risk, the error in measuring crimes is responsible for some part of the negative association. Second, the negative association between crime rates and imprisonment sanctions must be interpreted as reflecting the combined effects of deterrence and incapacitation, rather than deterrence alone. These two issues are certainly troublesome. However, some cautiously affirmative conclusions about deterrence might be entertained, as was suggested with the apprehension risk, if it were not for the implausibility of the assumption that crime rates and imprisonment sanctions are not simultaneously related.

It is difficult to argue that crime rates will not affect either the imprisonment risk for a crime or the time served in prison. The imprisonment risk for committing a crime has two components: the apprehension risk given commission of a crime and the imprisonment risk given apprehension. Even if only one of these components is affected by the crime rate, the composite measure, the imprisonment risk given commission of a crime, will be simultaneously affected.

While it can reasonably be argued that crime rates do not affect the apprehension risk, it is difficult to argue that crime rates do not affect the imprisonment risk after apprehension. Unlike the police, who spend only a small portion of their time apprehending criminal suspects, prosecutors and judges are predominantly involved in processing criminal cases. The level of crime thereby has a very direct impact on prosecutors' and judges' case loads. By all accounts, these officials' work loads are generally heavy, particularly in high-crime-rate jurisdictions. Furthermore, overburdened judges and prosecutors have ample discretion for reducing a backlog of cases: charges can be dismissed or reduced; cases can be pursued less vigorously or prepared with less care; plea bargains can be offered that are more attractive to defendants; and pressures can be brought by corrections officials to reduce the number of convicted offenders sentenced to prison or jail. Additionally, congestion in prison can be relieved by parole boards granting more early releases, thereby reducing the time served. Each of these actions represents a response to increasing crime rates by reducing the risk of imprisonment given apprehension or the time served by those imprisoned.

The Panel finds that these arguments for simultaneity between crime rates and imprisonment sanctions are sufficiently persuasive that the results deriving from nonsimultaneous analyses cannot be validly interpreted as estimates of the deterrent effects of the imprisonment sanctions. The probable effect of the crime rate on the risk of imprisonment or on time served must be taken into account.

An Assumption of Simultaneity

Two analyses have focused on the deterrent effect of imprisonment sanctions using a simultaneous model. In these analyses, the imprisonment risk, measured by the number of prison commitments per crime, is assumed to be simultaneously affected by crime rates while time served is not.[33] Using 1960 data from a cross-section of states, Ehrlich (1973) estimated the deterrent effect of imprisonment risk and time served for each of the index crimes individually and for the aggregate index crime rate. He consistently found negative associations, and, with few exceptions, the estimated effects were more than twice their asymptotic standard error.[34] Using 1970 data from a cross-section

[33]The assumption that time served is unaffected by the crime rate is dubious. If prisons are filled to capacity, higher crime rates may lead to shorter sentences—either to relieve the pressure on capacity or because higher crime rates may lead to a greater tolerance for crime. On the other hand, higher crime rates may lead to longer sentences if society "cracks down" on crime. In either case, a simultaneous model must be considered.

[34]When ordinary least-squares regression is used in nonsimultaneous estimation, the significance levels of estimates can be found from the standard tables. In such cases, if degrees of freedom are reasonably adequate, estimates that are twice their standard error are statistically significant at roughly the 5-percent level. With simultaneous estimation, however, small sample distributions are not generally known, and significance levels in small samples cannot be computed. In such cases, estimates that are approximately twice their standard error are significant at the 5-percent level only asymptotically as the number of degrees of freedom becomes very large.

of states, Forst (1976) estimated the deterrent effect of the two imprisonment sanctions for the aggregate index crime rate and found no effect.[35]

There are two primary obstacles to interpreting Ehrlich's results as a reasonably unambiguous demonstration of the deterrent effects of the imprisonment sanctions.[36] First, the negative effect is at least partly a reflection of the incapacitative effects of imprisonment. If Ehrlich's estimates were consistent estimates of the combined incapacitative and deterrent effects of imprisonment, then up to 50 percent of the negative association between the aggregate index crime rate and the two imprisonment sanctions might be attributed to incapacitation (see Nagin, in this volume). Thus, his estimated effect cannot readily be attributed solely to deterrence.

Second, and more fundamentally, Ehrlich's estimates may not even be consistent estimates of the total imprisonment effect (combining the incapacitative and deterrent effects) because of the implausibility of his identification restrictions. In Ehrlich's model, crime rates, the imprisonment risk, and police expenditures per capita are simultaneously related. To obtain identification, Ehrlich's model assumes that demographic composition, urbanization, and economic conditions affect the imprisonment risk or police expenditures but do not affect crime rates. However, the strong interconnections among the many socioeconomic and demographic correlates of the crime rate make it difficult to determine which among them do or do not have a causal association with crime. Furthermore, it is simply not plausible to assume that none of the variables used by Ehrlich for identification causally affects crime, while also assuming that each does influence either the probability of imprisonment, or police expenditures per capita, or both.

In a search for results based on more plausible identification restrictions, the Panel commissioned a reanalysis of the data used by Ehrlich (see Vandaele, in this volume). The difficulty of finding good identification restrictions, especially among the limited set of variables that were available, was evident in that reanalysis. Many of the revised formulations suffered from the same problems as Ehrlich's original specification. The one that was most plausible identified the crime function by excluding the prior year's expenditures on police from the crime function. Using that exclusion, Vandaele was unable to find evidence of a

[35]Other studies (Vandaele 1973, Avio and Clarke 1974, and Swimmer 1974) have included the imprisonment risk or time served among the sanctions in a simultaneous analysis, but the imprisonment variables are not determined simultaneously in these analyses.

[36]Measurement error is not a problem when simultaneous estimation is used (see the discussion of the nonsimultaneous analysis of apprehension risk).

deterrent effect for crimes against the person (homicide, assault, and rape) although the deterrent effect for crimes against property did persist.

For the exclusion of prior year's police expenditures to properly identify the crime function, two requirements must be met: (1) the prior year's police expenditures must not directly affect the crime rate, and (2) it must not be affected by the crime rate. The first criterion is met if police expenditures affect crime only insofar as the expenditures affect the apprehension risk but not the crime rate directly. For example, if increased police expenditures are used for more police officers and if their presence—rather than their improved performance in apprehension—deters crime, then the first criterion would be violated. Regarding the second criterion: although there is little doubt that crime rates do influence police expenditures, the effect can occur no earlier than the current period. Thus, the validity of using police expenditures per capita to achieve identification rests crucially on the validity of using a lagged variable (last year's expenditures) rather than a contemporaneous one.

The fact that last year's expenditures are influenced by the crime rate last year (or in some earlier year) imposes an additional requirement if the exclusion of the expenditures variable from the crime function is to be validly used as an identification restriction: the stochastic disturbance terms in the relationships must not be "serially correlated."[37] The disturbance term in each relationship includes all those factors affecting the dependent variable, but not explicitly included in the specification. If the disturbances are correlated over time, then they are said to be "serially correlated."

In an analysis using data from a cross-section of states, serial correlation will occur if the variables that are not accounted for in the statistical model tend to be consistently higher over time in some states and lower in others. The magnitude of this serial correlation determines the size of the error it causes. In cross-sectional data, appreciable serial correlation is very likely.[38] Thus, confidence in the Vandaele reanalysis is limited by the questionable validity of the assumption that the disturbance terms are not serially correlated.

In reaching a conclusion on the deterrent effect of the imprisonment sanctions, Forst's (1976) failure to find a deterrent effect with 1970 data must also be considered. Forst specified a state's crime rate and imprisonment risk as simultaneously related, and its police expenditures per capita are specified as a function of the prior year's crime rate.

[37]See Fisher and Nagin (in this volume) for the bases behind this requirement.
[38]Fisher and Nagin (in this volume) develop this issue more fully.

Forst identifies the crime function by omitting from the crime function the current year's police expenditures and a categorical variable indicating whether a state is southern or not.

No rationale is provided for assuming that "southernness" affects the imprisonment risk but not the crime rate. However, a reanalysis of Forst's data, using only the police expenditures variable as an omitted identifying restriction, resulted in a similar null effect.

Like the Vandaele analysis, the validity of the results from the reanalysis of Forst's 1970 data rests on the validity of the assumptions regarding serial correlation necessary to use the exclusion of police expenditures as an identifying restriction. If those assumptions are not seriously in error, then one of the two studies that excludes police expenditures for identification supports the deterrence hypothesis for property crimes only, and the other does not support it. If those assumptions are incorrect, however, the results tell us no more about the combined deterrent and incapacitative effect of imprisonment than do results based on nonsimultaneous estimation techniques. Since convincing arguments can be made that there is substantial serial correlation, the necessary assumption for using the police expenditure identification is seriously in error (see Fisher and Nagin, in this volume).

Assuming that there is a simultaneous relationship between crime rates and imprisonment sanctions, the Panel concludes that, because the potential sources of error in the estimates of the deterrent effect of these sanctions are so basic and the results sufficiently divergent, no sound, empirically based conclusions can be drawn about the existence of the effect, and certainly not about its magnitude.

THE EVIDENCE ON THE DETERRENT EFFECT OF THE CONVICTION RISK

The paucity of published data on convictions has limited the number of analyses of the deterrent effect of the conviction risk.[39] Nevertheless, the small body of evidence generally finds a negative and statistically significant association between crime rate and conviction risks. The

[39]The definition of the conviction risk varies among analyses. Sjoquist (1973), Kobrin *et al.* (1972), Avio and Clarke (1974), and Carr-Hill and Stern (1973) estimate the conviction risk as a ratio of convictions to charges. Each of these analyses includes a measure of the apprehension risk and treats the conviction risk as exogenous. Blumstein and Nagin (1977), in an analysis of the deterrent effect of sanctions on draft evasion, measure conviction risk by the proportion of defendants convicted at trial. Orsagh (1973) measures the conviction risk as the ratio of convictions to crimes and is the only one who treats the conviction risk as simultaneously related to the crime rate.

issues in interpreting this evidence are largely identical to those addressed for the other sanctions.

An Assumption of Nonsimultaneity

As with all measures of the sanction risk in a nonsimultaneous formulation, the negative association partly reflects the measurement error problem. However, the principal difficulty in interpreting the negative association observed in the nonsimultaneous analyses is the likelihood of a simultaneous relationship. While the argument for nonsimultaneity for the conviction risk is appreciably weaker than it was for the apprehension risk, it is not without merit. It might be argued, for example, that prosecutors adapt to increased work loads principally by offering reduced prison sentences or probation in return for guilty pleas from those who could be convicted in court anyway. If this were the only effect, the impact of increased crime on sanctions would be limited to the postconviction penalties (the imprisonment risk given conviction and the time served given imprisonment), and crimes and conviction risks would not be simultaneously determined. In this event, the negative association could be cautiously interpreted as reflecting a deterrent effect.

The effect of work loads, however, need not be limited to influencing postconviction imprisonment sanctions. Increased crime rates might also reduce the conviction risk given a crime if there is an increased propensity for overworked prosecutors to lose cases either because of hasty preparation or because of an increase in the proportion of cases dropped before trial.

On the other hand, increased work loads might increase the use of plea bargaining; this could result in increased convictions from guilty pleas (but with less severe punishment) or in fewer convictions on the original charge because of charge reductions. While the magnitude of these and related effects of the crime rate on the conviction risk is problematic, the existence of any of them would require the use of simultaneous techniques.[40]

[40]Blumstein and Nagin (1977), who find a negative and significant association between draft-evasion rates and conviction risks, argue that sanction levels and draft-evasion rates were not simultaneously related because the offense is narrowly defined and because the prosecution of draft-evasion defendants was given priority treatment. Nevertheless, even if their assumption of nonsimultaneity for this unique crime is correct, their finding of a deterrent effect cannot readily be generalized to index crimes because, as they point out, the decision to evade the draft was likely to be "rational" (draft evaders were well informed of the sanction risk and they had considerable opportunity to ponder their evasion decision), and their socioeconomic characteristics and prior criminal records differ substantially from those of the typical individuals who commit index crimes.

An Assumption of Simultaneity

Only one analysis (Orsagh 1973) has estimated the deterrent effect of the conviction risk in the context of a simultaneous model; the estimated deterrent effect was negative and significant. However, Orsagh's identification of the crime function is based on the exclusion of police expenditures. As argued in the discussion cf imprisonment sanctions, excluding police expenditures is not likely to be a satisfactory identification restriction. Therefore, the evidence for the effect of the conviction risk under an assumption of simultaneity is still limited and inconclusive; it cannot yet support an affirmative conclusion that the conviction risk has a measurable deterrent effect.

Considerable uncertainty surrounds the interpretation of the evidence for the effect of the conviction risk. An assumption of nonsimultaneity for this effect is less convincing than it was for the effect of the apprehension risk, and the only simultaneous analysis available uses an inappropriate identification restriction. Therefore, no conclusion on the evidence of a deterrent effect of the conviction risk is yet warranted.

RELATIONSHIP BETWEEN POLICE RESOURCES AND CRIME

A major rationale for increasing police resources (*e.g.*, more dollars, reflected in more officers or more patrol cars) derives from the theory that more resources will enhance the crime-control effectiveness of the police. Increases in police resources may increase the actual apprehension risk by increasing police officers' ability to detect and apprehend offenders. For example, additional expenditures on the implementation of a computer-based information system of known offenders might improve police effectiveness and thus increase the actual apprehension risk. Alternatively, increased levels of police resources may increase the visibility of the police in the community (through increased numbers of officers and patrol cars) without having any measurable effect on the actual apprehension risk. This increased visibility could deter potential offenders who mistakenly assume that the apprehension risks are indeed increased.

Three studies (McPheters and Stronge 1974, Swimmer 1974, and Greenwood and Wadycki 1973) have examined the crime-reducing effect of police resources using cross-sectional data on cities or Standard Metropolitan Statistical Areas. In all of these analyses, police resources and the crime rate are assumed to be simultaneously determined. When police resources are measured by the annual expenditures on the police, the estimated effect of police resources is negative and more than twice its asymptotic standard error,[41] which is consistent with the hypothesis that police resources have a crime-reducing effect. However, when police resources are measured by the number of police officers, the estimated effect is positive.

The principal criterion for evaluating these results is the plausibility of the model specifications, particularly the restrictions used to identify the crime function. In all three analyses, at least one of the variables omitted from the crime function is an accounting measure (either the total municipal budget or the per capita property tax revenues). The mutual relationship between this accounting measure and the crime rate is likely to be minimal, especially since other variables reflecting city size (*e.g.*, population) and wealth (*e.g.*, a measure of the relative incidence of poverty incomes) are included as explicit determinants of the crime rate. The use of such a restriction to achieve identification is thus plausible.

In two of the analyses (Greenwood and Wadycki 1973 and Swimmer 1974), however, other variables—the geographical size of the city in one and median family income in the other—are omitted from the crime function. Controlling for population, geographical size measures the population density: since it is difficult to see how increased density would influence the demand for police resources without also having an effect on the crime rate, the exclusion of geographical city size from the crime function is probably inappropriate. Likewise, since median family income probably affects the crime rate, it cannot be used as an omitted identifying variable. The results of these two analyses are thus questionable.[42]

The one analysis (McPheters and Stronge 1974) that uses plausible identification restrictions finds a highly significant negative effect of police expenditures on crime. While this suggests that increased police resources do have an inhibiting effect on crime, the conclusion must still be regarded as tentative since the result derives from only one study.

Furthermore, that analysis relies on total expenditures as a measure of the level of police resources. To the extent that increases in resources are converted to higher salaries, to pensions, or to fringe benefits, they are not likely to affect either police performance or visibility.

[41] See footnote 34.

[42] Using an incorrect restriction to achieve identification results in specification error and hence inconsistency in the estimates. This is true even if some of the restrictions used are correct and would be sufficient to identify the crime equation if used alone.

The use of theoretically more meaningful variables—such as the number of units on patrol—would be a more satisfying measure of the impact of police resources on crime. From the analysis, it is also impossible to identify how much of the effect is due to increases in the actual apprehension risk and how much is due to changes in the perceived risk. An analysis that also includes the actual apprehension risk as a determinant of crime would permit a separate determination of the sources of the effect.

SUMMARY OF THE EVIDENCE ON DETERRENCE FROM ANALYSES OF NATURAL VARIATION

Analyses of natural variation, with few exceptions, find a negative association between crime rates and noncapital sanction risks, controlling for other presumed determinants of crime. Any conclusion that these negative associations reflect a deterrent effect, however, is limited principally by the inability to eliminate other factors that could account for the observed relationship even in the absence of a deterrent effect.

The most important factor is the possibility that crime rates influence sanctions, as well as vice versa; this affects different types of sanctions to varying degrees. For the imprisonment risk, results purporting to show a deterrent effect are the least reliable because the argument that imprisonment sanctions and crime rates are simultaneously related seems very compelling. On the other hand, the likelihood of simultaneity seems less compelling for sanctions at the earlier stages of the criminal process, with simultaneity less likely for the conviction risk and still less likely for the apprehension risk. If simultaneity is likely, simultaneous estimation methods must be used to isolate the deterrent effect. For those analyses that have used simultaneous estimation methods, however, substantial questions exist about whether they have successfully isolated the deterrent effect.

For those types of sanctions for which simultaneous effects are *not* likely to be appreciable, the results from nonsimultaneous analyses suffer from the bias that is introduced by error in the measurement of crime. That bias has the effect of forcing a negative association even in the absence of deterrent effects, but, since it is unlikely that the observed negative association can be wholly attributed to measurement error, the nonsimultaneous analyses do offer some credible evidence of the existence of a deterrent effect. The estimates of the magnitude of that effect, however, are likely to be seriously in error.

While we cannot yet assert that the evidence proves the existence of deterrent effects, it is important to recognize that, in the extremely difficult task of measuring a phenomenon as complex as deterrence, the accumulation of analyses amassed to date represents a significant step forward. Our reluctance to assert that the evidence warrants an affirmative conclusion regarding deterrence derives from the limited validity of the available evidence and the number of competing explanations for the results.

It is also important to recognize that our reluctance to draw stronger conclusions does not imply support for a position that there are no deterrent effects: the evidence certainly favors a proposition supporting deterrence more than it favors one asserting that deterrence is absent. Furthermore, the Panel is convinced on *a priori* grounds that criminal sanctions do influence at least some criminal behavior by some individuals. The major challenge for future research is to estimate the magnitude of the effects of different sanctions on different crime types, an issue on which none of the evidence available thus far provides very useful guidance. The research program developed below is directed toward that challenge.

RECOMMENDATIONS FOR RESEARCH

The recommended research program is designed to address principally the basic issue of simultaneity, the problem of error in measuring crime, and the confounding of deterrence with incapacitation, which limit the reliability of estimates of deterrent effects from analyses of natural variation; it also suggests other topics for research on deterrence that may be fruitful.

The Issue of Simultaneity

Analyses of the Effect of Crime on Sanctions Because of the difficulties in finding plausible identification restrictions, the simultaneity obstacle is perhaps the most difficult to overcome. Knowledge of the effect of crime on the behavior of the criminal justice system is still extremely limited. Sanction levels reflect a variety of activities within the criminal justice system, including the apprehension efficiency of police, the decisions of prosecutors to pursue cases, the actions of judges and juries in deciding guilt, the actions of judges in sentencing a person to prison and establishing the length of that sentence, and the actions of parole boards in determining actual time served.

There have been a limited number of attempts to assess the impact of work loads and crime-type mix on the decision-making of officials in the criminal justice system;[43] much more attention should be given to pursuing these issues in order to establish which kinds of criminal justice system actions are indeed affected by level of input.[44] As an example of such an analysis, one might examine the relationship between the prosecutorial case load and the prosecutor's exercise of discretion in dismissing cases or reducing charges in exchange for guilty pleas.

Such studies, however, should go beyond the office directly affected. Because of the likelihood of strong interdependencies among the different activities of the criminal justice system, studies of the impact of crime on sanctions should be done from the perspective of the full system whenever possible. A study that focuses only on prosecutors is likely to overlook the impact of changes in prosecutors' work load on the activities of the police or of judges, but these effects outside prosecutors' offices are as important as any that may be identified within those offices.

For those sanctions that are affected by crime rate, studies of the sanctioning process may well result in finding plausible means for identifying the crime rate function. While the seeming dearth of untainted identification restrictions may reflect the fact that none exist, it is certainly as likely that it simply reflects our ignorance of the determinants of sanctions.

For example, a potentially fruitful source of identification restrictions consists of variables characterizing the institutional practices that affect sanction decisions within the criminal justice system: police deployment strategies that are not apparent to the public may affect crime only through their effect on apprehension probability; judicial decisions limiting police discretion may have a similar effect; programs to improve prosecutorial management and judicial decisions affecting evidentiary rules or time delay to trial may affect conviction probability but not crime directly; similarly, for corrections, early-release programs or legislative action to restrict sentencing discretion may directly affect time served in prison but not crime directly. Such analyses may reveal that these and other determinants of sanction levels can be plausibly assumed neither to affect the crime rate directly nor to be affected by crime rates.[45]

[43]Included among these studies are Green (1961), Feeley (1975), and Levin (1977).

[44]Such an examination of the sanctioning process may also be useful in providing insights into the problems of implementing policy changes.

[45]It must be noted, however, that identifying restrictions cannot be manufactured. If the process generating the data is truly one that leaves the crime function unidentified, then persistent attempts to produce identifying restrictions because of the desire to estimate the deterrent effect will only produce different kinds of error. Even if all such attempts

Thus, a major research commitment should be directed at learning the determinants of sanctions within the criminal justice system. This is not simply an academic matter of finding out what factors influence discretion. It is a necessary step in determining the nature of the relationship between crimes and sanctions—knowledge that is necessary in order to manipulate those sanctions to achieve deterrence or any other desired policy effect.

Correction for Errors Due to Serial Correlation and the Use of Alternative Data Sets While research on the effects of crime on sanctions is necessary, research on deterrence should certainly not halt in anticipation of results from that research. One approach is to pursue deterrence analyses that identify the crime function by excluding variables measuring criminal justice system expenditures (*e.g.*, police budgets). While previous estimates of the deterrent effects from such analyses are invalid because of serial correlation among the disturbances in the model, methods are available to correct the inconsistency in these parameter estimates. Since those methods require that the same variables be analyzed over time, time-series, cross-sectional data should be used in analyses of deterrence.

Analyses of deterrence in the United States have been limited to cross-sectional data because reports of prison commitments and actual length of imprisonment (*i.e.*, time served) are published sporadically rather than annually. To make time-series analyses possible, data on commitments and time served should be collected by crime type and published on an annual basis. Additionally, the present statewide data should be modified so that comparable annual data on crimes, arrests, charges or indictments, and convictions are available for smaller jurisdictions within states, and these data should be supplemented with annual data on imprisonments and length of sentence for these jurisdictions. This will require using comparable definitions and reporting formats throughout the criminal justice system.

Foreign data bases also represent potentially rich sources of time-series data on crime rates and sanction levels. A number of European countries have developed extensive data collection systems that have been operating for many years.[46] In addition to providing rich sources of time-series data, analyses of foreign data also provide a basis for

---

found a "deterrent" effect, no conclusion would be warranted unless some of them used validly based identification restrictions.

[46]A recent study by Wolpin (1976) addresses the deterrence question using time-series data on crime and sanctions in England and Wales.

assessing the generality of results derived initially from United States data alone.

The Problem of Error in Measuring Crime

A variety of approaches should be considered to correct for the negative association induced by error in measuring crime.[47] One approach is to use two separate data sources to estimate the number of crimes, one for the crime-rate variable and the other for the sanction variable. For example, the two different data sources could be the National Crime Panel victimization survey and the Uniform Crime Reports of offenses known to the police. If the errors in the two different crime estimates are uncorrelated, then no negative association will be forced.[48]

The Confounding of Deterrence with Incapacitation

One way to isolate the deterrent effect of imprisonment is to estimate the incapacitative effect and subtract it from estimates of the combined effects of deterrence and incapacitation. The incapacitation models reviewed in Cohen (in this volume) provide an initial basis for separating the incapacitative effect, but those models require further development to be applicable in crime-specific analyses of deterrence. In their current form, the models are only suitable for estimating the incapacitative effect for the aggregate of all crimes. Unless offenders specialize in a specific crime type, incarcerating them for one crime type will also prevent any other crime types they might commit. The models also assume that the crimes of incarcerated offenders do not persist during their incarceration (*e.g.*, through replacement by new recruits or the presence of multiple offenders per crime). Methods for dealing with these problems remain to be developed.

Other Topics for Research

Individual-Choice Models As an alternative to the aggregate studies that constitute the bulk of the deterrence literature, a fruitful approach might focus on the effects of sanctions on individual criminal behavior

[47]As noted earlier, this problem is less serious for simultaneous than for nonsimultaneous analyses.

[48]Any correlation between the measurement errors in the two different data sources, however, could bias the results, and the implications of such a relationship should be analyzed.

and then aggregate these effects over the population.[49] Any individual's choices have a negligible effect on the level of aggregate criminal opportunities or on the operation of the criminal justice system, so that simultaneity is not an issue. Thus, in principle, estimates of deterrent effects should be readily obtainable from observations of individual criminal behavior.

The primary impediment to empirical analyses of individual criminal behavior has been the absence of suitable data on individuals' sanction risk and on alternative opportunities available to them. A secondary obstacle has been lack of an adequate causal model of criminal behavior. Increased attention should be given both to developing methods and data bases that would make the study of individual criminal behavior possible and to developing causal models of criminal behavior that would make such analyses meaningful.

Disaggregation of Crime and Criminal Types With few exceptions, analyses of natural variation have examined the association between crime rates and sanction levels for very broad categories of crimes and criminals. For example, each of the index crimes used in most of the analyses can cover activity that ranges from the acts of a predatory stranger or a professional criminal to a youthful escapade or a misunderstanding among acquaintances that got out of hand. At this level of aggregation, the behavior involved and the nature of the participants, their beliefs about possible sanctions, and the actual sanctions they may face are all much too diverse to be subsumed under a homogeneous concept of deterrence.

Furthermore, even if the observed negative associations reflect deterrence, many questions remain unanswered: for example, how is the presumed deterrent effect distributed between reductions in the rate at which new recruits enter criminal careers and the rate at which active offenders commit crimes? Analyses should be directed at assessing the proportion of recruits among detected offenders and at examining how recidivism rates are affected by the introduction and implementation of laws that are especially severe on repeat offenders. Examination of the consequences of crackdowns on career criminals should also provide some useful insights into this question.

[49]The potential of and problems associated with individual-level analysis are discussed in detail in Manski (in this volume). Witte (1976), using individual data on a population of prison releasees, found some evidence of a negative association between recidivism rates and sanction risks. More importantly, Witte's analysis demonstrated the feasibility of using individual data to estimate deterrent effects when suitably rich information on individual criminal behavior is available.

Analyses of more narrowly defined criminal acts might also provide insights into the deterrability of specific kinds of criminal behavior. For example, such analyses might examine whether laws that limit the availability of guns, or increase the sanctions imposed when a gun is used in a crime, deter criminal activity, or whether offenders merely substitute another weapon or physical force as a means of intimidation. While such narrowly focused analyses will provide evidence of only limited generalizability, an accumulation of such detailed evidence could provide an empirical base for developing a more general theory that explains differences in the deterrability of certain kinds of behavior in certain individuals under certain circumstances.

Alternative Model Specifications Almost all analyses of deterrence have posed models that focus on the deterrent effect of particular sanctions. Because of the substantive interests of the analyst or of data limitations, a model may consider only police functions (like arrest or clearance rates) or it might be concerned with the effects of the imprisonment sanctions (the probability of imprisonment given an offense and the time served). This selective attention to individual sanctions amounts to assuming that only those sanctions explicitly included in the model have a significant deterrent effect. To the extent that an omitted sanction is an important determinant of crime and is related to the included sanction, the resulting estimates may reflect the confounded effect of all the sanctions and not only the separate effect of the included sanction. To resolve this ambiguity and indicate the sanctions that are most important for deterrence, future analyses of aggregate data should specify models that include various sanctions.

Alternative model specifications might also consider lagged relationships between crimes and sanctions instead of the current contemporaneous formulations. In a system as large as that of criminal justice, there are bound to be substantial delays in the transmission of information. Even after the necessary information is obtained, further delays are likely before the relevant behavior is modified. As a result, both the deterrent effect of sanctions on crimes and any accommodation of sanctions to changes in the level of crime will not occur instantaneously. If these response delays are short compared to the typical reporting interval of one year, contemporaneous models are adequate, but if the response delays are as long as a year or if reporting intervals can be shortened to be comparable to the response time, models using lagged effects should be developed.

Perceptions of Sanctions Most of the studies of natural variation have used objectively measured sanctions to estimate sanction risk.

This may be the easiest way to measure those variables, but it is not necessarily the most appropriate: it is the perceptions of these risks by potential offenders that are most relevant to deterrence. Thus, a research effort should be directed at determining public perceptions of criminal sanctions. The research should address: (1) which manifestations of the sanctions are most relevant (*e.g.*, the objective risks, the experiences of friends and acquaintances with the criminal justice system, the display provided by the media); (2) the accuracy of perceptions; and (3) how those perceptions might be influenced. This research should be focused on those population groups most likely to comprise marginal criminals—neither the confirmed criminals nor the confirmed noncriminals.

NONCAPITAL SANCTIONS: EXPERIMENTS AND QUASI-EXPERIMENTS

THE EVIDENCE ON DETERRENT EFFECTS

Using various levels of control, a number of studies have adopted an experimental approach to examine the deterrent effects of different sanctioning measures.[50] The principal sanctions investigated include increases in legislated penalties (usually jail or prison terms) for convicted offenders and various tactics to enhance apprehension risk (including variations in police deployment schemes and investigation techniques).

The particular sanction investigated plays a central role in determining the parameters that characterize the research design. For example, studies involving legislative changes in penalties are usually targeted at individual crime types, with drunken driving being the crime type usually studied. In these studies, the jurisdictions are generally defined by legislative boundaries, typically nations or states.

When examining the effect of changes in police tactics, the expected effect on crime is generally diffuse, and changes in either overall crime rates or selected target-crime rates might constitute evidence of a deterrent effect. The jurisdiction studied is defined by the jurisdictional boundaries of the police force, usually a city.

The research method employed in any given instance is also largely determined by the sanction under investigation. Because due process and equity considerably limit opportunities for controlled experiments,

[50]See Zimring (in this volume) and Zimring and Hawkins (1973) for reviews of the details of most of these studies.

studies of the deterrent value of variations in penalties typically employ a quasi-experimental design, usually an interrupted time series. By contrast, strategies related to the apprehension risk are more amenable to controlled experiments involving police tactics.

Even for changes in the apprehension risk, however, controlled experiments are relatively rare. In those that are available, the jurisdiction under study is usually subdivided into independent policing areas (*e.g.*, precincts or patrol beats). These areas are then assigned to the experimental or control conditions by some random process or by matching on a variety of socioeconomic and demographic variables. The best examples of controlled experiments in deterrence are the test of the crime-control effectiveness of preventive patrol by police in Kansas City (Kelling and Pate 1974), the San Diego field interrogation experiment,[51] and the study of the effectiveness of different strategies to reduce income tax evasion (Schwartz and Orleans 1967).

Quasi-experiments are far more common, usually taking advantage of abrupt changes in the law or in the application of sanctions. Studies are available on the effect of changes in penalties for drunk driving (Robertson *et al.* 1973, Ross 1973, 1975, Ross *et al.* 1970, Shover and Bankston 1973, U.S. Department of Transportation 1974), drug use and sales (Association of the Bar of New York 1975-1976, California State Assembly Office for Research 1968), bad checks (Beutel 1957, Zimring 1968), and abortion (Zimring 1972). The deterrent effects of changes in enforcement or patrol practice have also been examined for speeding (Campbell and Ross 1968, Glass 1968), crime on the subway in New York City (Chaiken *et al.* 1974), and crime in general (Press 1971, Mitre Corporation 1976).

A typical quasi-experimental design involves an interrupted time series comparing measures of the target behavior before and after the change. In a well-designed study, both the base and study periods are long enough to detect important trends in the data, and a number of alternative outcome variables are considered to provide independent measures of an effect. Whenever possible, comparison sites are also selected to provide independent data on time trends, a procedure that increases the statistical reliability of the design.

The results of experimental and quasi-experimental studies of deterrence are mixed, with some finding evidence of significant deterrent effects and others finding no evidence of measurable changes in crime rates. In most cases, however, the research designs suffer from a vari-

[51]"Field interrogation" is a contact initiated by a patrol officer who stops and questions a citizen on the street because of the officer's suspicion about the citizen's possible involvement in a crime; the experiment is reported in Boydstun (1975).

ety of flaws, many of which are remediable, that undermine confidence in the results. All too often, other factors can be identified to explain positive or negative findings, and thus the analyses fail to provide any valid evidence on deterrent effects.

Some studies are less vulnerable to criticisms of their methodology: the study of the impact of harsh penalties for drunk driving provided by the British Road Safety Act of 1967 (Ross 1973, Ross *et al.* 1970), the San Diego field interrogation experiment (Boydstun 1975), and the study of the deterrent effect of the criminal abortion law in Hawaii (Zimring 1972). Even these studies, however, report mixed findings on the existence of deterrent effects. For the drunk driving and field interrogation studies, the level of crime noticeably decreased with increases in the level of a sanction (the potential penalty in one case and the police patrol tactic in the other), and this was documented in a reasonably unambiguous fashion. In contrast, removing criminal sanctions for abortions had no measurable impact on the incidence of abortions. The mixed findings in these studies probably reflect the wide variation in the degree to which changes in sanction policies influence the incidence of different kinds of criminal behaviors. Enforcing speed limits, for example, may produce much more dramatic effects than special alcohol safety enforcement projects.[52] A large variation in effect can reasonably be expected across the broad spectrum of behaviors labeled as "criminal."

METHODOLOGICAL ISSUES

Failure to Maintain Experimental Conditions

One of the difficulties with experimental research in an operating system is the almost inevitable incompatibility between the objectives of the researchers and those of the officials of the system. The implementation of an experiment usually requires active cooperation from the people who are carrying out the daily activities of the system. Without this cooperation, the stated policy changes may not be reflected in actual changes in the system's activities. This was a problem in the implementation of the drunk driving provisions of the British Road Safety Act of 1967, where the police and magistrates did not change

[52]Studies of the effects of enforcement on speeding include Road Safety Laboratory (1963), Munden (1966), and Institute for Research in Public Safety (1971). Results of research on special alcohol safety projects are reported in U.S. Department of Transportation (1972, 1974), Shover and Bankston (1973), Robertson *et al.* (1973), Ross (1975), Zador (1976), and Johnson *et al.* (1976).

their behavior regarding arrest or conviction behavior in accord with the provisions of the Act.

Experiments may also be poorly designed so that the experimental conditions do not adequately represent the policy alternatives under investigation. The Kansas City preventive patrol experiment has been criticized on this ground. In this case, the reactive beats (those ostensibly without any preventive patrol) continued to experience considerable police visibility because of patrols on the perimeter of the beats, patrol cars crossing the reactive beats to get to other beats, and normal responses to calls for service within reactive beats (Larson 1975). All of these factors considerably reduced the actual differences in treatment between the experimental and control beats.

The Power and Sensitivity of Statistical Tools

Many experimental studies suffer from a failure to adequately measure the treatment variables. This problem is most common for variables measuring the level of sanctioning behavior and includes a failure to identify specifically the sanction being examined or to monitor the frequency with which a penalty is imposed or an enforcement tactic pursued. Because of the strong possibility that intended changes in sanctions are not in fact realized, it is as important to measure actual sanctioning behavior as to measure the dependent variable, *i.e.*, the crime rate. These measurements permit an evaluation to distinguish between a finding of no effect that is due to no real change in the sanctions (which says very little about deterrence) and one due to the absence of differential deterrent effects for different sanction levels.

Many studies also fail to collect adequate baseline data on the experimental variables. Such data are especially critical in time-series designs in which no other controls are available. Poor baseline data are characteristic of after-the-fact evaluations that are undertaken after a change in policy occurs.

Reliance on officially reported crime statistics to generate measures of the dependent variables is another problem. To the extent that the police or the public are highly sensitive to a policy change, they may have incentives to alter their reporting practices, either artificially inflating or deflating the crime rate. These artificially induced changes could then be misinterpreted as reflecting the presence or absence of deterrent effects. This problem is especially troublesome when the target offense involves no identifiable victim (*e.g.*, drunk driving) and so is unlikely to be reported. In this case, the recorded crime rates reflect the level of police activity directed against the offense more than the true incidence of the offense, and they are highly susceptible to artificial variations. One solution to this problem is to use other variables as indicators of the incidence of an offense. For example, in analyses of drunk driving, the rate of nighttime traffic fatalities is a proxy that is more reliable than arrests and is often used in place of drunk-driving arrests.

A number of features of deterrence research often limit the statistical "power"—the ability to detect small but meaningful changes in the dependent variable—of the statistical tools used. Variability in the reporting and recording of crimes contributes to a high variance in measured crime rates. Also, when comparing small jurisdictions (precincts or patrol beats), crimes are relatively rare and there are large chance variations in the measured rates. With such high-variance measures of the dependent variable, only sizable changes in the variables will be statistically significant; small but perhaps theoretically important changes are obscured by the variance in the measures. This problem of statistical power makes it particularly difficult to detect significant deterrent effects because the implemented changes in the independent sanction variables are often small and thus likely to be associated with only small changes in the dependent variables. The primary solutions to this problem involve observations over longer time periods or larger jurisdictions, although these solutions introduce additional aggregation problems of their own.

Other Limits on the Validity of the Evidence

In most deterrence research, particularly in quasi-experimental studies, the degree of control over the process being studied is quite limited. This enhances the claim of explanations other than deterrence for the observed results. For example, in the absence of appropriate control or comparison sites, the impact of other potential causal factors is an important competing explanation for any observed effects. Regression effects, resulting from specifically targeting changes in sanctioning behavior at the worst or best subgroups among offenders, must also be considered. In either event, the subsequent criminal behavior of the target population may reflect a regression back to the mean rather than a response to the experimental condition.

Another factor limiting the validity of results is the lack of replication of experimental studies. Instead, there is a proliferation of unique studies examining a wide variety of intervention strategies. Because most of the studies are not comparable, the results are generally limited to the specific crime types examined and the specific crime-control tactics invoked, and they are often restricted to the particular experimental locale. This inability to generalize from the results of specific studies is largely due to the lack of a general theory of deterrence that can incorporate and organize the individual experimental results. In this context, repeated replications of good research designs under slightly varied conditions are essential to the accumulation of knowledge.

RECOMMENDATIONS FOR RESEARCH

The current state of experimental and quasi-experimental research on deterrence, as reflected in the literature, is discouraging. However, most of the flaws encountered are remediable through the use of more careful research designs. Since most of the research opportunities in deterrence arise from legislatively or administratively imposed changes in sanctioning behavior, improved designs will usually require an increased awareness of changes before they are enacted. This will enable researchers to plan their research more carefully and perhaps influence the actual implementation of the changes.

To improve the quality of experimental and quasi-experimental research on deterrence, we recommend creating a panel with both operational and technical expertise to identify opportunities for such research and advise on the formulation and execution of study designs. The Panel recommends that the National Institute on Law Enforcement and Criminal Justice organize such a panel and support it with internal staff assistance.

The panel should seek out significant changes in policies or operations so it can act as a clearinghouse to promote evaluations of these natural experiments as the opportunities arise. Such opportunities are often not pursued now because researchers are not aware that they exist and because practitioners are neither sensitive to the research opportunities nor sufficiently experienced or technically skilled to undertake an evaluation without assistance. Examples of policy changes that might be profitably studied include the programs directed at finding "career offenders" and the attempts to decriminalize offenses legislatively or through changes in enforcement policy.

Controlled field experiments with alternative crime-control methods have been quite limited. It is extremely difficult to convince an agency involved in crime control to operate under experimental conditions and to design an experiment that does not violate ethical, due process, and operational constraints. Efforts should be intensified to seek out suitable opportunities, and especially to build on previous experiments, correcting those flaws that have been revealed in earlier studies.

There should be a major effort to organize a program of quasi-experimental studies. Knowledge will emerge from such studies when they are narrowly focused on homogeneous kinds of behavior and groups of offenders. While the findings from such studies will be difficult to integrate initially, they may in the long run contribute to a comprehensive general theory of threat and punishment. The appropriate way of integrating the findings will not become clear until the results from a number of such studies have been accumulated.

CAPITAL SANCTIONS

THE EVIDENCE ON THE DETERRENT EFFECT OF CAPITAL PUNISHMENT ON HOMICIDE

The question of whether capital punishment has any additional deterrent effect beyond that associated with imprisonment has been a subject of intense debate for generations.[53] Periodically, this debate emerges as a matter of major public concern. This has happened most recently in the series of U.S. Supreme Court decisions[54] regarding the constitutionality of capital punishment and in the Canadian Parliament's consideration of the abolition of capital punishment. In the most recent of the Supreme Court decisions, complex technical evidence on the deterrent effect of capital punishment was brought into the debate by the Solicitor General, who introduced an analysis by Ehrlich (1975a) in his *amicus curiae* brief.

The Ehrlich analysis showed a negative association over time between United States national homicide rates and the number of executions per homicide conviction, a proxy for the probability of execution. This association has been interpreted as demonstrating that capital punishment deters homicide and has been carried to the point of estimating the number of homicides averted per execution. Ehrlich's analysis contradicted earlier analyses that found no evidence that capital punishment deters homicide.

The earlier empirical efforts to test the deterrence hypothesis typically took three forms: (1) the comparison of the homicide rates in contiguous jurisdictions, some of which had abolished capital punishment (Campoin 1955, Sellin 1955, 1959); (2) the examination of time-

[53]Zeisel (1976) provides a useful review of the research on this question.

[54]Furman v. Georgia, 408 U.S. 238 (1972); Fowler v. North Carolina, 95 Sup. Ct. 223; Jerek v. Texas, 96 Sup. Ct. 2950; Woodson v. North Carolina; 96 Sup. Ct. 2978, Proffitt v. Florida; 96 Sup. Ct. 2976; and Gregg v. Georgia, 96 Sup. Ct. 2909.

series data on homicide rates within a jurisdiction during the years before and after the abolition of capital punishment (Sellin 1959, Walker 1969); and (3) the comparison of the murder rates in a jurisdiction just before and after the imposition of a death sentence or an execution (Dann 1935, Graves 1956, Savitz 1958).

While all the earlier studies failed to find evidence of a deterrent effect, they suffer from a number of methodological weaknesses.[55] The most serious flaw was the general failure to control adequately for the variety of demographic, cultural, and socioeconomic factors, other than the death penalty, that influence murder rates. Examining "similar" contiguous states or the same jurisdiction over short time periods represents some effort to hold these factors constant, but, when dealing with rare events like homicides and executions where the numbers are quite small, the crudeness of these controls could easily mask any effects that may exist. In addition, there were no controls for differences in noncapital sanctions, which could also influence homicide rates.

In some studies, different jurisdictions were compared on the basis of their statutes regarding capital punishment rather than by their practice, when the latter may be the more relevant factor affecting deterrence. Additionally, these analyses usually failed to separate the number of capital homicides (those homicides for which capital punishment was a legal sanction) from total homicides as the dependent variable, and variations in the larger number of noncapital homicides in the total could have masked a deterrent effect.[56]

More recently, Passell (1975) examined the differential deterrent effect of an execution over a prison sentence by explicitly including imprisonment variables (the rate of prison commitments per homicide and the mean or median time served in prison after a homicide conviction) in a cross-sectional analysis of state data in 1950 and 1960. He also considered the possibility that homicides and executions might be simultaneously related, with increases in the number of homicides increasing the demand for executions.

In a variety of nonsimultaneous and simultaneous formulations, Passell's estimates of the differential effect of executions per conviction

[55]Aside from the specific methodological flaws addressed, there is always a problem of interpretation in cases of a failure to observe a statistically significant effect. In these cases, it is difficult to decide whether the effect is indeed negligibly small or whether a real and substantial effect is masked by methodological problems or poor data. In a nonexperimental analysis of a complex social phenomenon, the statistical and data deficiencies are a particularly serious problem.

[56]These criticisms of the early capital punishment literature are expanded on in Bork *et al.* (1974), Peck (1976), Ehrlich (1975a), and Passell (1975).

are typically non-negative[57] and small.[58] It is possible, however, that Passell's failure to find an effect results from a number of problems in his analysis that could be masking a real effect. One problem is his failure to exclude the noncapital homicides. In addition, while Passell's simultaneous system is not described in sufficient detail for a careful review, his identification restrictions do not seem plausible, particularly those excluding socioeconomic variables, like unemployment and racial composition, from the crime function.[59] More fundamentally, the potential for finding a deterrent effect is inherently constrained by the difficulties in generating sufficient statistical power to discern any effect from the relatively infrequent homicide and execution rates.

Ehrlich (1975a), using time-series data for 1933-1969 in which homicides and executions were aggregated for the entire United States, reports a deterrent effect for executions. There have been a number of reanalyses of data equivalent to that used by Ehrlich.[60] All of these reanalyses have shown that Ehrlich's findings are sensitive to minor technical variations in the analysis. These variations include changes in the mathematical form of the relationship of homicide rates to their determinants (*e.g.*, a multiplicative form compared to a linear one) and the variables included as determinants of homicide (*e.g.*, including the aggregate crime index as a determinant). These reanalyses either reversed the direction of the presumed effect or greatly reduced its magnitude.

The most striking sensitivity of Ehrlich's findings is to the time period over which the analysis is conducted. No negative association is found for 1933-1961, so that the results are determined by the effect in 1962-1969. But during those eight years, *all* crime rates rose dramatically, and the frequency of executions declined (and had ceased by 1968). Thus, to conclude that a deterrent effect exists, one must assume that the steady rise in homicides over this eight-year period was caused at least in part by the decline in executions and that the trends in executions and in homicides were not generated either independently or by some common third cause, which might also account for the

[57]Ehrlich has also performed a cross-sectional analysis on state data. While the full study has not been made available to this Panel, Ehrlich (1975b) reports that he again finds evidence that capital punishment deters homicide. Without access to the Ehrlich paper, it was impossible to compare the Passell and Ehrlich analyses.

[58]The effects were less than twice their asymptotic standard errors (see footnote 34).

[59]The errors associated with the identification problem are discussed in greater detail in an earlier section, "Noncapital Sanctions: Analyses of Natural Variations," of this report and in Nagin (in this volume) and Fisher and Nagin (in this volume).

[60]These analyses include Passell and Taylor (1975) and Bowers and Pierce (1975). A further analysis by Klein *et al.* (in this volume) was prepared for the Panel.

rise in other crimes. If one makes these assumptions, statistical analyses contribute no further information to the test of the deterrence hypothesis. Moreover, the failure to discern any deterrent effect in the earlier 1933-1961 period, when there was more fluctuation in both homicide and execution rates, still remains unexplained.

In summary, the flaws in the null-effect results and the sensitivity of the Ehrlich results to minor variations in model specification and their serious temporal instability lead the Panel to conclude that the results of the analyses on capital punishment provide no useful evidence on the deterrent effect of capital punishment.

Our conclusion should not be interpreted as meaning that capital punishment does not have a deterrent effect, but rather that there is currently no evidence for determining whether it does have a deterrent effect. Furthermore, we are skeptical that the death penalty, so long as it is used relatively rarely, can ever be subjected to the kind of statistical analysis that would validly establish the presence or absence of a deterrent effect.

Our conclusion on the current evidence does not imply that capital punishment should or should not be imposed. The deterrent effect of capital punishment and its magnitude reflect only one aspect of the many considerations involved in the choice of the use of the death penalty. Those considerations include issues related to the value of human life, the moral justification of killing by government, and the appropriate form of public outrage at heinous crimes—all of which are likely to dominate policy decisions in comparison to inevitably crude estimates of the deterrent effects.

RECOMMENDATIONS FOR RESEARCH

The current evidence on the deterrent effect of capital punishment is inadequate for drawing any substantive conclusions. A major part of the problem is the highly aggregated nature of the data used. Future research requires much more intensive analysis of disaggregated data, which would proceed along the lines of separating different types of homicide (*e.g.*, separating capital and noncapital homicides), finding smaller and more homogeneous units of observation (preferably cities), and using time intervals shorter than a year in order to observe the short-term response to executions.

Opportunities for interrupted time-series studies of the effect of capital punishment on homicide are likely to appear if various states reinstitute execution in response to the recent Supreme Court decisions. If research on capital punishment is pursued, adequate baseline data establishing the recent trends in capital crimes should be collected and attempts should be made to discriminate among the various manifestations of the capital punishment threat, including the probability of execution given homicide, the rate of capital sentences or executions per year, and the media coverage of capital sentences or executions.

In undertaking research on the deterrent effect of capital punishment, however, it should be recognized that the strong value content associated with decisions regarding capital punishment and the high risk associated with errors of commission make it likely that any policy use of scientific evidence on capital punishment will require extremely severe standards of proof. The nonexperimental research to which the study of the deterrent effects of capital punishment is necessarily limited almost certainly will be unable to meet those standards of proof. Thus, the Panel considers that research on this topic is not likely to produce findings that will or should have much influence on policy makers.

Incapacitation

Incapacitation involves removing an offender from general society and thereby reducing crime by physically preventing the offender from committing crimes in that society.[61] The incapacitative effect of a sanction refers exclusively to that preventive effect and does not include any additional reduction in crime due to deterrence or rehabilitation.[62]

Decisions on whether or not to send individuals to prison are based on the offenses for which the individuals were convicted and their prior criminal records. Once imprisoned, they are prevented from committing further crimes in general society. Under sentencing policies more stringent than current ones, more convicted offenders might be sent to prison or they might be sentenced to longer average terms. Presumably, such policy changes will prevent some crimes; in order to assess this increment of crime reduction, some means for estimating the incapacitative effect of imprisonment is needed.

[61]A variety of existing institutional arrangements separate convicted offenders from the rest of society. They range from minimum security facilities like prison farms and work camps in remote areas to more secure institutions such as jails and prisons.

[62]The incapacitative effect refers only to crimes committed in society. Offenses committed while incarcerated, either against guards or fellow inmates, are explicitly not considered here. It should be noted, however, that these crimes committed or suffered inside institutions can represent an important factor in weighing the costs and benefits of alternative incapacitation policies.

ESTIMATES OF THE MAGNITUDE OF THE INCAPACITATIVE EFFECT

There are fewer problems in inferring the existence of effects from incapacitation than in establishing the deterrent effects of criminal sanctions. As long as the offenders who are imprisoned would have continued to commit crimes if they had remained free, there is a direct incapacitative effect: that is, the number of crimes at any time is reduced by the crimes avoided through the imprisonment of some criminals. The magnitude of that incapacitative effect is directly related to the rate at which an individual offender commits crime, λ crimes per year. If an individual would have remained criminally active in society during a period of incarceration of S years, the potential number of crimes averted by this offender's incapacitation is λS crimes.

There are factors that may operate to reduce the incapacitative effect to less than λS crimes. If a criminal would have reduced his rate of committing crimes or stopped committing crimes entirely during the period of imprisonment, then the number of crimes averted would be correspondingly less than λS. It is also possible that for some offenses, especially certain organized crimes involving vice or burglary managed by fences, the incarcerated offender would be replaced through an illegitimate labor market, and the incapacitative effect would be less than λS crimes.

A pattern of multiple offenders per crime, and especially gang activities, will similarly reduce the incapacitative effect if only one or a few of the participants are incarcerated and the collective criminal activity persists.[63] This phenomenon is likely to vary with age, being most common among juvenile offenders.[64] Unfortunately, there is very little empirical evidence about the magnitude of these diminishing ef-

[63]Using data from the National Crime Panel survey of criminal victimization, Reiss (1977b) indicates that such offenses by groups may be substantial. Victim reports indicate that 36 percent of all incidents where the number of offenders was known involved two or more offenders, and the offenders involved in these multioffender incidents accounted for 68 percent of all the known offender involvement.

[64]Some evidence of this was found by the Panel, using data from the National Crime Panel survey of victims (Reiss 1977a). Furthermore, that analysis revealed that patterns of multiple offenders vary considerably by crime type, particularly among crimes against the person. Robbery, for example, has much higher rates of multiple offenders than does burglary. The crimes averted by incapacitating an offender would thus depend on the mix of individual and group offenses in the individual's criminal activity.

fects. If these effects are large, ignoring them could result in an appreciable overestimate of the incapacitative effect.[65]

The net long-term benefits from incapacitation might also be affected by any possible rehabilitative or "criminogenic" effects of prison. To the extent that prisons rehabilitate criminals, resulting in lower individual crime rates or earlier terminations of criminal activity after release, there is an additional reduction in crime. If, on the other hand, prisons have a criminogenic effect, increasing an individual's propensity to commit crimes or extending the duration of criminal careers, the benefits in reduced crime from incapacitation may be offset by the additional crimes a criminal commits once released.

The available research[66] on the impact of various treatment strategies both in and out of prison seems to indicate that, after controlling for initial selection differences, there are generally no statistically significant differences between the subsequent recidivism of offenders, regardless of the form of "treatment." This suggests that neither rehabilitative nor criminogenic effects operate very strongly. Therefore, at an aggregate level, these confounding effects are probably safely ignored.

The literature on incapacitation contains a number of studies offering widely divergent estimates of the incapacitative effect of imprisonment. Some argue that these incapacitative effects are negligible, while others claim that a major impact on crime is possible through increases in the use of imprisonment. In reviewing these studies, the Panel has found that there is more consistency among the analyses than their opposite policy conclusions would suggest; they are in general agreement about basic assumptions, but differ in the particular parameter values used.[67] The principal disagreement is over the value of the individual crime rate, an issue that can only be resolved empirically. This is a task that should be given high priority.

All of the available models for estimating the incapacitative effect[68] rest on a number of important, but as yet untested, assumptions that

[65]Models of incapacitation could handle this effect by incorporating a probability, α, measuring the chance that an individual's crimes are indeed suppressed when the individual is imprisoned. In this event, the actual incapacitative effect would be more closely approximated by using the product $\alpha\lambda$ in place of λ in the model. Research into group structures would be necessary to estimate α for group offenders.

[66]For reviews of this research, see Robison and Smith (1971) and Lipton *et al.* (1975).

[67]See Cohen (in this volume) for a critical review of this literature.

[68]The principal contributors of these models are Avi-Itzhak and Shinnar (1973), Shinnar and Shinnar (1975), Greenberg (1975), Clarke (1974), and Marsh and Singer (1972). See Cohen (in this volume) for a critical review of these models.

characterize individual criminal careers. A criminal career is considered to begin at the first crime committed by an individual and to end at the last crime. During a career, an individual commits crimes, accumulates arrests and convictions for some crimes, and may be imprisoned for some time.

Most analysts model a criminal career as a stochastic process and incapacitation as a disruption to that process. In calculating the incapacitative effect, the models implicitly deal with offenders who operate alone and are not part of a larger criminal network. While free during a career, these criminals commit crimes at the rate of λ crimes per year. During a period of imprisonment of length S, the potential exists to prevent λS crimes.

Estimating the incapacitative effect of an imprisonment policy, however, also depends on the probability of being sentenced to prison if a crime is committed. This probability consists of the conditional probabilities of arrest given a crime, of conviction given arrest, and of a prison sentence given conviction. These probabilities are measures of criminal justice system performance, and they contribute directly to the level of incapacitation by determining the chance that a criminal is caught and convicted and so available for imprisonment.[69]

Estimates of the crimes averted by incapacitation should also be adjusted for the possibility that a career ends while an individual is imprisoned. Once a career ends, no further crimes are prevented and any time served after that does not contribute to the incapacitative effect. Characterizing this end of a criminal career requires information on the distribution of career lengths in the criminal population (*e.g.*, desistance probabilities by age).

The stochastic process models include a number of additional assumptions, which specify the dynamic features of the process and identify the mechanics for aggregating the behavior of individuals to obtain estimates of total effects. The principal assumptions that are questionable are those relating to the stability of the process over time, the relationships among the parameters, and the degree of similarity among

[69]The incapacitative effect can be estimated from the porportion of a career that a criminal spends in prison. Denoting the individual crime rate by λ, the probability of conviction upon committing a crime by q, the probability of imprisonment after conviction by J, the average time free between incarcerations is then $1/\lambda qJ$. If the average time served per incarceration (S) is short relative to the length of a criminal career, the proportion of time spent incarcerated is:

$$\frac{S}{\dfrac{1}{\lambda qJ} + S} = \frac{\lambda qJS}{1 + \lambda qJS}$$

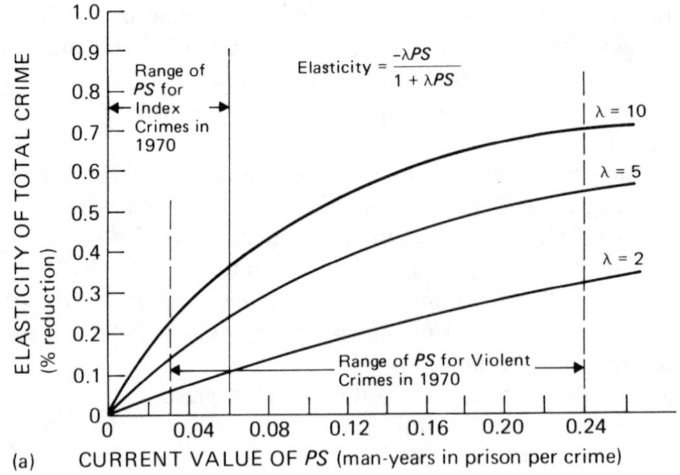

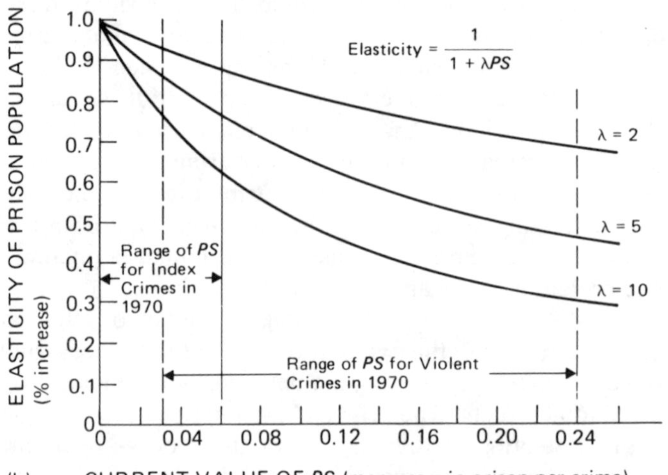

FIGURE 4 Elasticity of crime and imprisonment as a function of sanction leve. The elasticity measure indicates the percentage change in the dependent variable (total crimes or prison population) resulting from the incapacitative effect of a 1-percent change in sanction level (man-years in prison per crime).

individuals in the population. Typically, the model parameters are assumed constant over time and over all individuals, and they are assumed to be independent of one another. The assumption of homogeneous parameters over the entire criminal population is not particularly troublesome because the models can be generalized to incorporate distributions of the parameters. The assumption of independence among parameters is more fundamental, and, if it is not valid, important errors in estimates of the incapacitative effect can be introduced.

Two of the assumptions of independence are of particular concern: the assumption of independence between individual crime rates and the probability of arrest, and the assumption of independence between individual crime rates and individual career lengths. It may well be, for example, that individuals with high crime rates are more skilled at evading detection and therefore have lower apprehension rates. Because of their lower risk of detection and apprehension, they might also have longer careers. Alternatively, they might burn themselves out faster and have shorter careers. Whatever the nature of the relationship, the presence of strong dependencies among the parameters could bias the incapacitative effect that is estimated from the existing models.

The basic assumptions of the models have not yet been tested and only crude estimates of the parameters have been developed, typically from aggregate United States data. While these limitations are substantial, the models do facilitate exploration of the implications of various changes in the models' assumptions.[70] Furthermore, even in their currently primitive form, the models are quite useful for exploring the implications of various policy alternatives. For example, the models' prediction of the incapacitative effects of changes in imprisonment policy can be examined.[71]

Under the assumptions of the models, an additional man-year in prison (*e.g.*, one more individual serving one year in prison or two more individuals each serving six months) will prevent λ crimes, since λ is the number of crimes that each imprisoned individual would commit in a year if not imprisoned. However, the *relative* impact of λ crimes prevented per man-year in prison will vary with the crime rate and with the current prison population. Figure 4 illustrates these rela-

[70]Avi-Itzhak and Shinnar (1973), Shinnar and Shinnar (1975), and Shinnar (1977) have performed a number of sensitivity analyses; they have found that their model is reasonably "robust" in that its conclusions are not changed dramatically under different reasonable assumptions about the form of the distributions of individual criminal-career lengths and of individual crime rates over the population of criminals.

[71]See Cohen (in this volume) for the details of this analysis. The model used in this parametric analysis is the one developed in Avi-Itzhak and Shinnar (1973).

tive incapacitative effects of changes in imprisonment policy[72] through an analysis of the "elasticities"[73] of crime (Figure 4a) and of prison population (Figure 4b) with respect to changes in imprisonment parameters.

The principal imprisonment variables of concern are the probability of a prison sentence given a crime (P) and the average time served (S). The product of the two (PS) is the expected number of man-years in prison given the commission of a crime. Thus, PS is equivalent to the average number of man-years in prison per crime. Figure 4a shows that for a 1-percent increase in any of these variables (a 1-percent increase in P or S causes a 1-percent increase in PS), the percentage reduction in total crime through incapacitation is greatest when the current levels of the sanction variables (P, S, and hence PS) are high or when the individual crime rate (λ) is high. Conversely, the percentage reduction in crime due to incapacitation is smallest when the current sanction levels are low or when the individual crime rate is low.

Any increase in the imprisonment policy variables also results in an increase in the prison population, as measured by the resulting annual man-years of imprisonment.[74] As Figure 4b shows, the percentage increase in imprisonment resulting from a 1-percent increase in P, S, or PS is negatively related to the current values of the sanction levels and the individual crime rate. The larger the current level of these variables, the smaller the percentage increase in prison populations.

It would be useful to develop a measure of the costs of incapacitation in terms of greater prison use relative to the benefits in reduced crimes.

[72]Expanding the use of mandatory minimum sentences represents one such policy change. This would increase the probability of a prison term for those crimes for which the mandatory minimum is prescribed. If the mandatory minimum sentence is longer than the current time served, the model parameter representing time served would also increase.

[73]Elasticity is a measure of the responsiveness of the dependent variable to changes in an independent variable. Here it gives the percentage change in the dependent variable (total crimes or prison population) resulting from a 1-percent change in sanction level (man-years in prison per crime).

A formula for estimating the elasticity of crime reduction with respect to imprisonment (*i.e.*, the percentage reduction in crime per percentage increase in the imprisonment variables) is $-\lambda PS/(1+\lambda PS)$, where λ is the individual crime rate, P is the probability of imprisonment given a crime, and S is the mean time served. Similarly, the elasticity of the prison population with respect to the imprisonment variables is $1/(1+\lambda PS)$; see Cohen (in this volume) for the derivation of these expressions.

[74]This increase in the prison population does not take account of the possible long-term decreases in crime from any deterrent or rehabilitative effects associated with the increased use of imprisonment. The reported change in prison population reflects the equilibrium increase in population associated with a change in incapacitation policy, all else remaining unchanged.

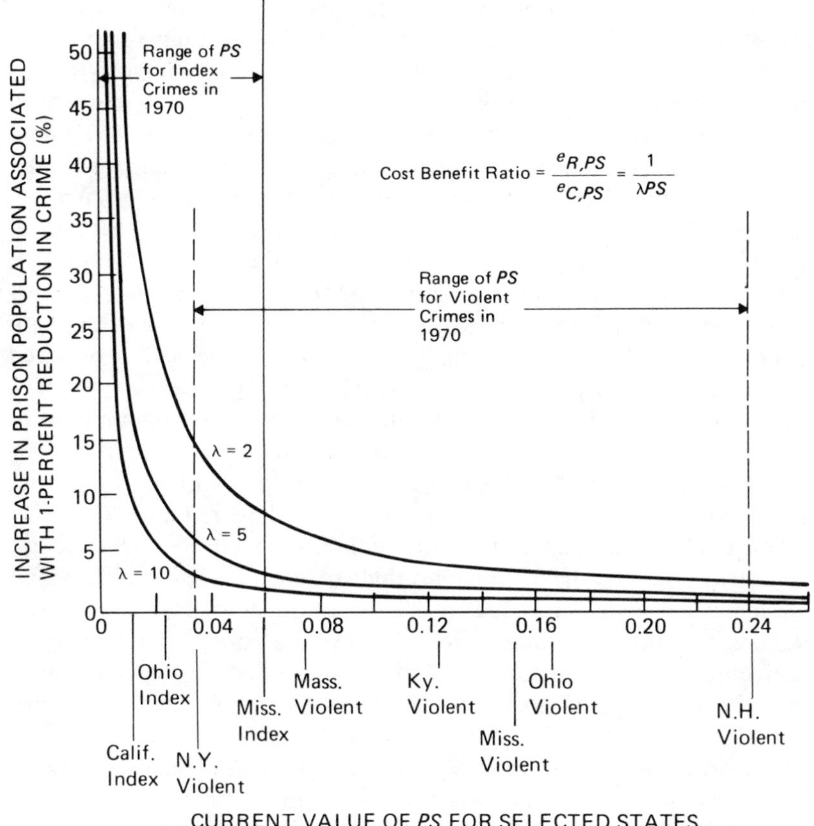

FIGURE 5 Cost-benefit ratio (percent increase in prison population required to achieve a 1-percent reduction in crime through incapacitation) as a function of the current values of the imprisonment parameters and the individual crime rate using the available models of incapacitation.

This can be accomplished by calculating the ratio of the elasticity of the prison population to the elasticity of crime reduction. This cost-benefit ratio, the percentage increase in the prison population required to achieve a 1-percent decrease in total crime from incapacitation alone, is shown in Figure 5. Also shown in Figure 5 are a range of the 1970 values of *PS* for violent crimes[75] and for index crimes in selected states.

[75]Violent crimes are the subset of the FBI index crimes including murder, forcible rape, robbery, and aggravated assault.

The cost-benefit ratio varies considerably with the value of *PS*. Figure 5 indicates that if sanction levels are already high (above 0.05 man-years in prison per crime), the additional cost in terms of the percentage increase in the prison population is only a few percent in order to achieve a 1-percent decrease in crime. For values of *PS* less than 0.05, on the other hand, the increases in the prison population associated with a 1-percent decrease in crime are much larger. With an assumed individual violent crime rate (λ) of five crimes per year and an expected time served per crime (*PS*) of 0.125 (the value in Kentucky), the population of offenders in prison increases only 1.6 percent for each 1-percent reduction in violent crimes. When current sanction levels are low, as they generally are for index crimes, the required increases in prison population are larger. For $\lambda = 5$ and $PS = 0.024$ (the value for index crimes in Ohio), the index prison population increases 8.3 percent for each 1-percent reduction in index crimes. For $\lambda = 5$ and $PS = 0.013$ (the value for index crimes in California), the increase in the index prison population is even larger, 15.7 percent.

These variations associated with different values of the sanction variables illustrate the distortions that arise when using aggregated parameter estimates, which conceal variations among different jurisdictions and different crime types. Because the policy objectives for a particular crime type in any jurisdiction will depend on the local conditions in that jurisdiction, disaggregated parameter estimates are needed.

We should also emphasize here that the numbers generated in this analysis should not be taken as exact. Too many uncertainties about the model and its parameters (*e.g.*, the effect of incapacitation on group crimes, the value of the individual crime rate) preclude such confidence in the numerical results. The relative magnitude and the direction of the relationships, however, are likely to be correct.

The sensitivity of the incapacitative effect to the particular values of the imprisonment variables has important implications in considering incapacitation policies to reduce crime. It has already been shown that the percentage reduction in crime from a given increase in incapacitation is least when the imprisonment sanction levels are already low.[76]

[76]Jurisdictions with low sanction levels may have the most to gain from deterrence by increasing their sanction levels. One might hypothesize that there are diminishing marginal returns from deterrence as sanction levels increase. At low sanction levels, the active criminal population would include many marginal criminals who would be easily deterred by even minimal increases in sanctions. At higher sanction levels, the active criminals are less easily deterred, and small increases in sanctions would not be likely to have much additional deterrent effect.

Jurisdictions with lower imprisonment probabilities and with lower expected times served in prison per crime also tend to be the ones with the highest crimes rates.[77] Thus, the high-crime-rate jurisdictions that are most likely to be looking to incapacitation as an important solution to their crime problem are likely to have to pay the highest price for it in terms of increased prison populations.

These effects are illustrated in Table 1, which presents the values of current sanction levels and the predicted costs, in terms of prison population, of crime reduction through incapacitation for selected states using an assumed value of the individual crime rate of five crimes per year. California and Massachusetts, for example, must increase their index prison populations by over 150 percent and 310 percent, respectively, in order to achieve a 10-percent reduction in index crimes through incapacitation;[78] for violent crimes, the prison-population increases are 23 percent and 27 percent, respectively.

As shown in Figure 5, the cost of an incapacitative strategy varies considerably with the crime types that are chosen as targets; the values of *PS* for all index crimes are generally much lower than the same values for violent crimes.[79] Thus, incapacitation is a more viable alternative when targeted at violent crimes. Under the assumptions of the available models, the figures presented in Table 1 indicate that such a strategy could reduce violent crimes with reasonable increases in the population of violent offenders in prison. This is in sharp contrast to

[77]For the 29 states for which data are available for 1970, the correlation between the index crime rate and the probability of imprisonment per crime is −0.64. (See Cohen, in this volume, for a description of the 1970 data.) The correlation between the index crime rate and the expected time served per crime (given by the product of the probability of imprisonment per crime and the average time served by those imprisoned) is −0.55. For violent crimes in the same 29 states, these correlations are −0.54 and −0.64, respectively.

[78]If additional deterrent effects on crime result from the increased use of imprisonment, this substantial increase in the prison population may be only temporary. If the amount of crime (and the number of criminals) decreases because of deterrence, the size of the prison population associated with the new imprisonment policy will also decrease.

[79]While the median time served for property crimes is somewhat smaller than for violent crimes, the major factor contributing to a smaller value of *PS* for all index crimes is the considerably smaller values of *P* (the probability of imprisonment given a crime) for property offenses. For the 29 states reporting adequate data in 1970 (Appendix C of Cohen, in this volume), the weighted aggregate values of *P* for the individual crime types were as follows: 0.3471 for murder; 0.0636 for rape; 0.0268 for robbery; 0.0144 for aggravated assault; 0.0059 for burglary; 0.0036 for larceny; and 0.0021 for auto theft. For all violent crimes, $P = 0.0295$, while for the property crimes, $P = 0.0043$.

TABLE 1 Variations in the "Cost" of Crime Reduction through Incapacitation for Selected States[a] (Using Available Models of Incapacitation)

State	1970 Index Crime Rate[b]	Estimated 1970 *PS* for Index Crimes[c]	1970 Violent Crime Rate[b]	Estimated 1970 *PS* for Violent Crimes[c]	Estimated 1970 Average Daily Prison Population for Index Crimes[d]	If $\lambda = 5$, Percentage Increase in Prison Population Needed for: 10-Percent Reduction Index Crime Rate	Reduction of 100 Crimes in Index Crime Rate	10-Percent Reduction Violent Crime Rate
California	4,307.0[H]	0.0127	474.8	0.0877	10,941[H]	157.2	36.1	22.8
New York	3,922.1	0.0076	676.0[H]	0.0351[L]	5,422	263.5	67.2	57.0
Massachusetts	3,004.0	0.0064[L]	202.9	0.0751	1,094	310.5	103.4	26.6
Ohio	2,376.6	0.0242	284.3	0.1663	6,126	82.5	34.7	12.0
Kentucky	1,924.5	0.0232	222.3	0.1247	1,437	86.1	44.8	16.0
New Hampshire	1,192.7	0.0170	56.0	0.2371[H]	150	118.0	98.9	8.4
Mississippi	863.4	0.0593[H]	179.3	0.1533	1,135	33.7	39.1	13.0
North Dakota	846.1[L]	0.0164	34.2[L]	0.1021	86[L]	122.0	144.2	19.6

[a] The states have been selected to include those with the most extreme values for the variables, along with some states in the middle of distribution.

[b] Crimes/100,000 population. SOURCE: U.S. Department of Justice, Federal Bureau of Investigation (1971) *Uniform Crime Reports: 1970* (Washington, D.C.: U.S. Government Printing Office).

[c] *PS* is the expected time served per crime in years and is estimated from the number of prison commitments per crime and the median time served in prison. SOURCE: U.S. Department of Justice, Bureau of Prisons (1971) *National Prisoner Statistics: State Prisoners Admissions and Releases, 1970* (Washington, D.C.: U.S. Government Printing Office).

[d] Under steady-state assumptions, the average daily prison population is estimated from the product of the expected time served per crime (*PS*) times the number of offenses known.

[H] and [L] indicate states with highest and lowest values, respectively, for the variables. California, for example, has the highest index crime rate and largest prison population, while North Dakota has the lowest index crime rate and the smallest prison population; Mississippi and Massachusetts, respectively, have the highest and lowest values of *PS* for index crimes, while New Hampshire and New York have the highest and lowest values of *PS* for violent crimes, respectively.

the much larger increases in the index prison populations required to achieve the same percentage reductions in the level of index crimes.[80]

Even though the percentage of crimes averted through incapacitation is not very large in high-crime-rate jurisdictions, the number of these crimes averted may be substantial. From a national perspective, there could well be an interest in the reduction of a given number of crimes, with little concern for where that reduction occurs. From that perspective, the high-crime-rate jurisdictions do look attractive.

As an example, the objective might be to reduce the index crime rate by 100 crimes per 100,000 population. Since crime rates vary among jurisdictions, 100 crimes in the index rate represents a different percentage reduction in different jurisdictions. For the 1970 values in Table 1, for example, a reduction of 100 in the index crime rate represents 19,766 fewer crimes in California (2.3 percent less) and 2,220 fewer crimes in Mississippi (an 11.6-percent decrease). While the percentage change in California is quite low when compared to Mississippi, the absolute number of crimes involved is considerably larger.

At a rate of five crimes prevented for each additional man-year in prison, the crime reduction in California will increase the prison population by 3,953, or 36.1 percent, while the reduction in Mississippi requires 444 additional prisoner years (a 39.1-percent increase). Thus, a uniform change in the absolute crime rate in each jurisdiction has a more homogeneous effect on the relative increase in prison populations in each state.

It must be reiterated, however, that these parametric analyses are presented for illustrative purposes only. Until the basic model is validated, the numerical results cannot be accepted, although the direction of the relationships will probably prevail. Nonetheless, the analyses do serve two useful purposes: first, as an example of the sort of analysis that will be possible with a well-defined model; and, second, as sources of predictions that can be used as a basis for testing the validity of the model.

PREDICTION OF INDIVIDUAL CRIMINALITY

There is a long tradition in sentencing of selectively imprisoning some individuals because of their prior criminal records. This is reflected in laws that prescribe mandatory sentences for habitual offenders. This differential treatment of convicted persons is typically justified by

[80]In this analysis, the same value of $\lambda = 5$ has been used for both violent and index crimes. If the values of λ were much lower for violent crimes, the differences between the two crime groups would be less than is shown. This issue cannot be resolved at this time because very little is known about the true value of λ for either group.

appeals to retributive rationales that encourage harsher penalties for persons who have clearly demonstrated their commitment to crime through repeated criminal activities. While selective imprisonment does not now involve explicit prediction of future criminality, a policy of selectively imprisoning the worst offenders (those who commit the more serious crimes and have a higher rate of committing crimes) has the potential of increasing the incapacitative effect.

If those persons whose individual crime rates are higher than the group average could be identified and selectively imprisoned, the incapacitative effect would be increased. Such a selective incapacitation policy, however, introduces both the technical problem of predicting individuals' future crime rates and the ethical and legal problems of explicitly imprisoning people to avoid crimes they may commit in the future.

The ethical questions derive from legal and philosophical positions on the appropriate functions of imprisonment.[81] One position is that the principal basis for determining sentence should be retribution. An extreme expression of this position is that prison sentences should be based only on "just deserts" for the current crime and that any utilitarian use of imprisonment, and especially selective incapacitation, is inherently unjust. On the other hand, most people believe imprisonment should have a more utilitarian purpose, with crime reduction as an appropriate function of imprisonment.

Selective incapacitation of offenders with higher crime rates as a means of enhancing the incapacitative effect inherently requires prediction of criminal propensity in order to identify such offenders. Use of such predictions, however, raises concern for the errors in them. Poor prediction not only undermines the utilitarian justification for selectively incapacitating some convicted offenders, but it also introduces concern for the injustice suffered by those who are imprisoned because their future crime propensity is erroneously predicted to be higher than it is.

The available research on predicting individual criminality is largely limited to attempts to distinguish between recidivists and nonrecidivists, where recidivism is variously defined as subsequent arrest, conviction, or imprisonment for specified crimes, often limited to violent offenses. These predictions attempt to discriminate among individuals on the basis of the average criminal propensities of the groups in which they fit (*e.g.,* based on attributes such as age, sex, marital

[81]For useful collections of articles representing a variety of views, see Acton (1969), Gerber and McAnany (1972), Murphy (1973), and Ezorsky (1972).

status, or military record). A review of various predictive studies of this sort reveals considerable variability in the estimated prediction error (Greenberg 1975, Monahan, in this volume, Monahan 1976, and Von Hirsch 1974).

A principal component of prediction error is the "false positive" problem, *i.e.*, imprisoning persons because of a prediction that they will commit crimes in the future when in fact they would not commit any. This problem is particularly severe when predicting behavior that has an inherently low probability; even good prediction procedures would suffer very high false-positive rates.[82]

The false-positive rate observed is sensitive to the threshold used for the criterion event. A review of the literature on prediction technology (Monahan, in this volume) reveals that estimates of "false positives" cover an extremely broad range of between 50 percent and 99 percent among the predicted positives. This range results largely from variations in the breadth of activities considered as "future criminality," the duration of the follow-up period in which a criminal act might be observed, and the level of proof required to conclude that a subsequent criminal act in fact occurred (*e.g.*, whether one relies on self-reports, arrests, or convictions).[83] Furthermore, many of those considered to be false positives may indeed be true positives who committed a criterion event, but who successfully evaded detection or conviction for that offense.

Estimating the individual crime rates (λ) of recidivists is even more difficult than predicting whether an individual will recidivate or not. In view of the considerable uncertainty about the accuracy of such estimation, it would be inappropriate at this point to consider using explicit predictions of individual crime rates as the basis for selectively incapacitating high-crime-rate offenders.

Nevertheless, certain schemes of differential sentencing of offenders may still be justified. The information to distinguish among offenders could be based on the individual's criminal record (including the current crime type and the number of previous convictions and incarcerations, also by crime type). The use of information other than prior criminal record in determining sentences may be unjust because of the discriminatory or capricious quality of such variables. Information on

[82]Von Hirsch (1974) illustrates the problem of false positives for rare events.

[83]If the criteria for subsequent criminality are stringent (*i.e.*, only the most serious offenses are considered, only conviction is considered, and the time of observation is short), then the incidence of such future criminality will indeed be low and the recorded false-positive rate would be very high. Conversely, if the criteria are less stringent and the event more common, then the false-positive rate would be lower.

hair color, for example, would be totally inappropriate to use in determining sentence, even if it were a good predictor. On the other hand, there is a long tradition that fully accepts taking account of the prior criminal record in determining a just sentence.

This practice could also achieve the benefits of selective incapacitation effects if persons with more extensive criminal records also have a higher propensity to commit future crimes. Some evidence is available indicating that an individual's prior criminal record is a reliable indicator of future criminality. In a four-year follow-up of the subsequent criminal activity of persons released from the federal criminal justice system in 1965, the FBI reports that the likelihood of a subsequent arrest for a new offense varied by the crime type of record in 1965, with reasonably high repeat rates for the predatory crimes of burglary, assault, and robbery (U.S. Department of Justice 1970, pp. 39-40). A study of recidivism in England and Wales reports that the likelihood of reconviction for a new offense increases with the number of prior convictions in a person's criminal record (reported in Wilkins 1969, p. 55). However, these results do not control for other factors that might be contributing to the observed difference, such as age and prior record in the United States data and type of disposition on the original charge in both the United States and English data.

RECOMMENDATIONS FOR RESEARCH

Model Development

Further theoretical development of incapacitation models is necessary to more accurately reflect variations in the patterns of individual criminal activity. To accomplish this, research should be directed at characterizing the patterns of individual criminal careers. The results of such research can form the basis for estimating model parameters and developing expanded or alternative incapacitation models.

Criminal careers should be examined for any significant relationships between different parameters, like individual crime rates, offenders' likelihood of being apprehended, and the length of the criminal career; the existing models ignore any such associations that might exist. Careers should also be examined for any shifts in the parameters that occur as the offender ages or accumulates a criminal record. If such shifts are found, they should be incorporated into incapacitation models.

It is also important to determine the extent to which offenders' criminal activity persists in the community even after the offenders are incapacitated. This may occur because of replacement of the imprisoned offenders from an illegitimate labor market or because of the continued activity of the groups of offenders from which they were removed. Where such patterns prevail, they significantly reduce the anticipated incapacitative effect. Thus, research should be pursued to examine offender networks, the process of recruitment into these networks, and the structure and persistence of groups of offenders. As information on these persistence phenomena is developed, it can provide estimates of additional parameters to be incorporated into incapacitation models.

All the current models are limited to a single homogeneous crime type. A richer model would reflect the fact that individual criminals engage in diverse criminal activities and should account for the fact that incarcerating a robber may also avert burglaries. Incorporating these considerations into a model will require a characterization of the sequence of crimes ("crime-switching") during a criminal career, including the degree to which individuals are "generalists" or specialize in certain crime types.

Parameter Estimation

All the models include parameters reflecting both the sanctioning behavior of the different components of the criminal justice system and the nature of individual criminal careers. While current estimates of the sanctioning parameters are easily obtained from criminal justice agency records, analysis of possible changes in incapacitation policy also requires knowledge of how the different parts of the criminal justice system respond to changes in their environments. First, operational constraints on the individual sanctions must be determined and the mechanisms by which those constraints are set must be identified (*e.g.*, through resource limitations, legislation, or agency policy). Second, the behavior of the criminal justice agencies must be studied to determine the kind and degree of adaptive response displayed in the face of changing policies or work loads.

It is necessary to know, for example, to what extent judges and prosecutors increase their use of dismissals when mandatory-sentence laws are passed and to what extent the decisions of parole boards reduce the actual time served in prison when prisons become overcrowded. Such information is important for assessing the degree to which anticipated gains in incapacitation from increased sanction levels in one part of the system are offset by compensating decreases elsewhere.

Empirical investigations should also be directed at estimating the parameters measuring the level of individual criminal activity, especially the individual crime rates (λ) and career lengths (T). Because the crimes an individual commits are not directly observable, the parameters are extremely difficult to measure. Furthermore, since estimates of the incapacitative effect are sensitive to variations in these parameters, these estimates should not be restricted to highly aggregated population averages. They should be disaggregated by crime type and demographic group and should reflect the statistical distribution of the parameters.

Data Needs

Two approaches to parameter estimation can be pursued: analysis of recorded arrest histories ("rap sheets") and offenders' self-reports. Each has its limitations; the self-reports have obvious problems of veracity, while analysis of rap sheets uses incomplete operational records and depends on as yet untested assumptions in order to project from observed arrests to unobserved crimes.

Improved self-report methods designed to elicit more truthful responses must be developed and tested. This will require increased efforts to develop validation techniques for self-report instruments. These efforts might include expansion of current work exploring the use of lengthy probing interviews with convicted offenders and the use of follow-up interviews and record checks to test the consistency of responses.

Arrest-record data bases must be improved for at least a sample of records to include dispositions, and especially to account for time served in jail and prison (when the person is not free to commit crimes or be arrested). A critical issue influencing the extrapolation from arrest rate to individual crime rate (λ) is the correlation between λ and the individual arrest probability; the magnitude of that correlation should be explored through self-report studies.

This research program will depend critically on securing rich data bases documenting individual criminal careers, including the crime types and dates of all arrests, convictions, and sentences. Longitudinal samples like the FBI's Careers in Crime file, appropriately augmented by juvenile data and better data on time served, should be developed. A survey of self-reported criminality for a subsample of such a sample should then be developed to provide the data needed on undetected crimes.

Organization and Management of the Research Program

COMMON DATA NEEDS

The need for rich sources of data is common to all empirical research, and research related to deterrent and incapacitative effects is no exception. Even though most research projects will meet their data needs primarily by *ad hoc* collection of data specifically for that project, there is a fundamental need for various standard data that can best be collected centrally. These will provide baseline observations and should stimulate a wide variety of research projects. Such common data bases would include two important classes of information: First, cross-sectional, time-series information on crimes and on the processing of suspects, defendants, and offenders by the criminal justice system; these data are important for studies of deterrence. Second, longitudinal information on criminal-career histories of individuals; these data are essential for estimation of incapacitation effects.

The cross-sectional data should include measures of criminal justice system performance that vary across jurisdictions—states, counties, cities, and Standard Metropolitan Statistical Areas. These measures should be consistently and comparably reported across jurisdictions and should include at least the following variables detailed at least annually by crime type category and, where appropriate, by demographic subgroups, including age, race, and sex:

- Number of reported crimes
- Number of arrests
- Number of persons charged in the court of general jurisdiction
- Number of convictions under the original charge and under a lesser charge
- Number of persons sent to each type of correctional institution
- Average time served by those released from each correctional mode.

These data can all be derived from combinations of existing agency statistics and offender-based tracking records like those used in the PROMIS system or the OBTS system. The critical need is for compatibility in the reporting structure across jurisdictions to facilitate the cross-sectional analysis.

In addition to the aggregate flow data and system statistics, a rich collection of data characterizing the development of individual criminal careers is needed, both to estimate how criminal careers would be interrupted by incapacitation and to estimate deterrent effects with individual-choice models. For these purposes, well-documented samples of offender records are needed, which include offenders' encounters with both the juvenile and adult criminal justice systems, their employment and educational histories, and their experience with various treatment and social-service programs. The individual criminal-career records should be collected for a sequence of age cohorts to assess changing behavior in the cohort and in the criminal justice system over time.

These data will be more detailed than is appropriate for operational use and too voluminous to be maintained for all offenders; therefore, it is important that such detailed records be maintained on a carefully drawn sample and that those records be updated regularly. Because of the sensitivity of such individual records, extensive precautions should be taken to ensure that the individuals whose records are maintained remain anonymous to all users of the records.

A variety of other basic data series should be maintained because cross-sectional data for only a single year are inadequate for deterrence analysis. A cross-sectional, time-series data base should be maintained on crimes, criminal justice system processing rates, and sanction levels imposed at the city level. This will require much more detailed information from court and correctional records at that jurisdictional level than is currently available.

For certain kinds of crimes, particularly index crimes, the data on the various crime types should be maintained at a much more disaggregated level in order to provide more homogeneous groupings.

To serve these data needs, a central depository of all research data collected by persons undertaking research on the criminal justice system should be maintained by the Law Enforcement Assistance Administration. (Such a depository is now being considered.) A condition of all federal research support might be that their data be submitted to that depository at a reasonable time after completion of the research projects.

ACCESSIBILITY OF DATA

A fundamental principle of science is the necessity for verification and replication of research findings. This insures against the perpetuation of spurious results arising from either the commission of technical errors (*e.g.*, measurement, recording, or computational errors) or from lack of knowledge of special conditions unique to a particular research design or setting. Such safeguards are especially important in nonexperimental research, in which the lack of systematic controls increases the possibility of erroneous conclusions.

In its evaluation of existing research on deterrence and incapacitation, the Panel found that efforts to duplicate reported results were often frustrated by restricted access to the supporting data. This situation is particularly objectionable when that research bears directly on public policy questions.

Once research findings are published, the principle of verification and replication requires open access to the details of the particular research designs used so that the necessary data can be reconstructed or collected anew. Under some conditions (*e.g.*, when the data are drawn entirely from previously published sources), it is reasonable to require that the actual data be made available. In all cases, published results should report or make accessible an "analytical file" containing an essential summary of the raw data from which the published results are derived.

The Panel supports the principle of open access to the data supporting published work. We recognize, however, that there are situations in which there are countervailing demands. Among these are a certain proprietary right of scholars to data whose collection involved a major investment of their effort. Thus, the requirement of disclosure is not without limits. In most cases, however, there is simply no excuse for restricting access to data supporting published results.

PEER REVIEW

The practice of peer review, which involves experts knowledgeable in both the theory and practice of a research topic, performs a valuable function of ensuring the quality of research supported by most funding agencies. To promote more successful research on crime and the effects of sanctions, the Panel recommends that the National Institute of Law Enforcement and Criminal Justice (Institute) establish a committee of methodological and substantive research experts to review proposals relating to deterrence and incapacitation. By virtue of their stature, the members of the review body would inevitably encourage research on deterrence and incapacitation and promote more careful work among their colleagues. Such a review committee would also serve the important purpose of screening out projects that are poorly designed or inherently infeasible by either rejecting projects or recommending improvements in their design.

ADVISORY BOARD

In research on topics such as deterrence and incapacitation, which is both important in its relationship to policy considerations and involves complex methodological issues, it would be desirable for the Institute to establish an advisory board to oversee developing research results. This board would consist of individuals conducting research on the topic, as well as methodological specialists expert in the relevant methodologies but not necessarily directly involved in the substantive topic. Such an advisory board would be responsible for reviewing results as they emerge in the research literature, for helping to provide objective assessment of the validity of the research findings for those looking for policy guidance, and for identifying the most fruitful next steps in the formulation of the research program.

In the operation of this Panel, a number of studies first became available after the primary work of the Panel was completed. These new studies should receive the same scrutiny as the material that was examined in the Panel's literature reviews; the process is inherently a continuing one that should be undertaken by a continuing body created by the Institute.

This advisory board should provide guidance to the research managers of the Institute on the most promising directions to pursue in further research and on basic data sources that should be created. It should stimulate as well as review research proposals submitted in deterrence and incapacitation.

References and Bibliography

Acton, H. B., ed. (1969) *The Philosophy of Punishment: A Collection of Papers*. London: Macmillan.

Andenaes, J. (1966) The general preventive effects of punishment. *University of Pennsylvania Law Review* 114(7):949-83.

Antunes, G., and Hunt, A. L. (1973) The deterrent impact of criminal sanctions: some implications for criminal justice policy. *Journal of Urban Law* 51(2):145-61.

Association of the Bar of New York (1975-1976) Drug Law Evaluation Project. Internal documents dated January 1975, September 1975, and February 1976.

Avi-Itzhak, B., and Shinnar, R. (1973) Quantitative models in crime control. *Journal of Criminal Justice* 1(3):185-217.

Avio, K., and Clarke, S. (1974) Property Crime in Canada: An Econometric Study. Prepared for the Ontario Economic Council.

Bailey, W. C. (1974) Murder and the death penalty. *Journal of Criminal Law and Criminology* 65(3):416-23.

Baldus, D., and Cole, J. W. (1975) A comparison of the work of Thorsten Sellin and Isaac Ehrlich on the deterrent effect of capital punishment. *Yale Law Journal* 85(2):170-86.

Bean, F., and Cushing, R. (1971) Criminal homicide, punishment and deterrence: methodological and substantive reconsiderations. *Social Science Quarterly* 52(2):277-89.

Beutel, F. K. (1957) *Some Potentialities of Experimental Jurisprudence as a New Branch of Social Science*. Lincoln, Neb.: University of Nebraska Press.

Blumstein, A., and Cohen, J. (1973) A theory of the stability of punishment. *Journal of Criminal Law and Criminology* 64(2):198-207.

Blumstein, A., and Larson, R. (1970) Models of a Total Criminal Justice System. Institute for Defense Analyses Report No. P-480. Arlington, Va.

Blumstein, A., and Nagin, D. (1977) The deterrent effect of legal sanctions on draft evasion. *Stanford Law Review* 28(2):241-75.

Blumstein, A., Cohen, J., and Nagin, D. (1976) The dynamics of a homeostatic punishment process. *Journal of Criminal Law and Criminology* 67(3):317-34.

Bork, R. H. (Solicitor General), *et al.* (1974) Fowler v. North Carolina, U.S. Supreme Court case no. 73-7031. Brief for U.S. as *amicus curiae:* 32-39.

Bowers, W. (1974) *Executions in America.* Lexington, Mass.: Lexington Books.

Bowers, W. J., and Pierce, G. L. (1975) The illusion of deterrence in Isaac Ehrlich's research on capital punishment. *Yale Law Journal* 85(2):187-208.

Boydstun, J. E. (1975) *San Diego Field Interrogation: Final Report.* Washington, D.C.: The Police Foundation.

California State Assembly Office for Research (1968) *Crime and Penalties in California.* Sacramento: State of California.

Campbell, B. A., and Church, R. M. (1969) *Punishment and Aversive Behavior.* New York: Appleton-Century-Crofts.

Campbell, D. T., and Ross, H. L. (1968) The Connecticut speed crackdown: time series data in quasi-experimental analysis. *Law and Society Review* 3(1):33-53.

Campion, D. R. (1955) Does the death penalty protect state police? Appendix F, Part I, Minutes of Proceedings and Evidence, No. 20, Joint Committee of the Senate and House of Commons on Capital Punishment and Corporal Punishment and Lotteries, Canadian Parliament. Reprinted in part in H. Bedau, ed., *The Death Penalty in America,* revised ed. Garden City, N.Y.: Anchor Books, 1967.

Carr-Hill, R. A., and Stern, H. H. (1973) An econometric model of the supply and control of recorded offenses in England and Wales. *Journal of Public Economics* 2(4):289-318.

Chaiken, J. M., Lawless, M., and Stevenson, K. (1974) *The Impact of Police Activity on Crime: Robberies in the New York City Subway System.* R-1424-NYC. Santa Monica: The Rand Corporation. Abbreviated version in *Urban Analysis* 3:173-205, 1975.

Chiricos, T. G., and Waldo, G. P. (1970) Punishment and crime: an examination of some empirical evidence. *Social Problems* 18:200-17.

Clarke, S. H. (1974) Getting 'em out of circulation: does incarceration of juvenile offenders reduce crime? *Journal of Criminal Law and Criminology* 65(4):528-35.

Cohen, M. R. (1971) Moral aspects of punishment. In Radzinowicz and Wolfgang, eds., *Vol. II: The Criminal in Society.* Crime and Justice. New York: Basic Books.

Cook, P. J. (1977) Punishment and crime: a critique of current findings concerning the preventive effect of criminal sanction. *Law and Contemporary Problems* (forthcoming).

Dann, R. (1935) The Deterrent Effect of Capital Punishment. Bulletin 29, Friends Social Service Series, Committee on Philanthropic Labor and Philadelphia Yearly Meeting of Friends.

Ehrlich, I. (1973) Participation in illegitimate activities: a theoretical and empirical investigation. *Journal of Political Economy* 81(3):521-65.

Ehrlich, I. (1975a) The deterrent effect of capital punishment: a question of life and death. *The American Economic Review* 65(3):397-417.

Ehrlich, I. (1975b) Deterrence: evidence and inference. *Yale Law Journal* 85(2):209-27.

Ezorsky, G., ed. (1972) *Philosophical Perspectives on Punishment.* Albany: State University of New York Press.

Feeley, M. (1975) The Effects of Heavy Caseloads. Paper presented at the 1975 Annual Meeting of the American Political Science Association, San Francisco, Calif.

Fisher, F. (1966) *The Identification Problem in Econometrics.* New York: McGraw Hill Book Company.

Forst, B. (1976) Participation in illegitimate activities: further empirical findings. *Policy Analysis* 2(3):477-92.

Gerber, R. J., and McAnany, P. D., eds. (1972) *Contemporary Punishment*. South Bend, Ind.: University of Notre Dame Press.

Gibbs, J. (1968) Crime, punishment and deterrence. *Southwestern Social Science Quarterly* 48(4):515-30.

Gibbs, J. (1975) *Crime, Punishment and Deterrence*. New York: Elsevier Scientific Publishing Co.

Glass, G. (1968) Analysis of data on the Connecticut speeding crackdown as a time-series quasi-experiment. *Law and Society Review* 3(1):55-76.

Graves, W. F. (1956) The deterrent effect of capital punishment in California. Reprinted in part in H. Bedau ed., *The Death Penalty in America*, revised ed. Garden City, N.Y.: Anchor Books, 1967.

Gray, L. N., and Martin, D. J. (1969) Punishment and deterrence: another analysis of Gibbs' data. *Social Science Quarterly* 50(2):389-95.

Green, E. (1961) *Judicial Attitudes in Sentencing: A Study of the Factors Underlying the Sentencing Practice of the Criminal Court of Philadelphia*. Cambridge Studies in Criminology, Vol. 15. London: St. Martins Press.

Greenberg, D. (1975) The incapacitative effect of imprisonment: some estimates. *Law and Society Review* 9(4):541-80.

Greenwood, M., and Wadycki, W. J. (1973) Crime rates and public expenditures for police protection: their interaction. *Review of Social Economy* 31(2):232-41.

Greenwood, P. W., Chaiken, J. M., Petersilia, J., and Prusoff, L. (1975) *Vol. III: Observations and Analysis*. The Criminal Investigation Process. R-1778-DOJ. Santa Monica: The Rand Corporation.

Hagan, J. (1974) Parameters of criminal prosecution: an application of path analysis to a problem of criminal justice. *Journal of Criminal Law and Criminology* 65(4):536-44.

Institute for Research in Public Safety (1971) *A Study of the Effects of Law Enforcement on Traffic Flow Behavior: Final Report*. Bloomington, Ind.: Indiana University.

Johnson, P., Levy, P., and Voas, R. (1976) A critique of the paper "Statistical Evaluation of the Effectiveness of Alcohol Safety Action Projects." *Accident Analysis and Prevention* 8(1):67-77.

Kelling, G., and Pate, A. (1974) *The Kansas City Preventive Patrol Experiment*. Washington, D.C.: The Police Foundation.

Kobrin, S., Hansen, E. W., Lubeck, S. G., and Yeaman, R. (1972) *The Deterrent Effectiveness of Criminal Justice Sanction Strategies: Summary Report*. Law Enforcement Assistance Administration, National Institute of Law Enforcement and Criminal Justice. Washington, D.C.: U.S. Government Printing Office.

Larson, R. (1975) What happened to patrol operations in Kansas City? A review of the Kansas City Preventive Patrol Experiment. *Journal of Criminal Justice* 3(4):267-97.

Levin, M. (1977) Delay in five criminal courts. Appendix D to Levin, *Urban Politics and the Criminal Courts*. Chicago: University of Chicago Press.

Lipton, D., Martinson, R., and Wilks, J. (1975) *The Effectiveness of Correctional Treatment: A Survey of Treatment Evaluation Studies*. New York: Praeger.

Logan, C. H. (1971) On "Punishment and Crime" (Chiricos and Waldo 1970): some methodological commentary. *Social Problems* 19(2):280-84.

Logan, C. H. (1972) General deterrent effects of imprisonment. *Social Forces* 51(1):64-73.

Logan, C. H. (1975) Arrest rates and deterrence. *Social Science Quarterly* 56(3):376-89.

Marsh, J., and Singer, M. (1972) Soft Statistics and Hard Questions. Discussion Paper HI-1712-DP, Hudson Institute, Quaker Ridge Road, Croton-on-Hudson, New York 10520.

McPheters, L., and Stronge, W. B. (1974) Law enforcement expenditures and urban crime. *National Tax Journal* 27(4):633-44.

Mitre Corporation (1976) *High Impact Anti-Crime Programs: National Level Evaluation.* Final Report. Eleanor Chelimsky, author. Vol. 1: Executive Summary. Vol. 2: Report. No. MTR-7148. Washington, D.C.: Law Enforcement Assistance Administration.

Monahan, J. (1976) The prevention of violence. Pages 13-35 in J. Monahan, ed., *Community Mental Health and the Criminal Justice System.* New York: Pergamon Press.

Munden (1966) An Experiment in Enforcing the 30 Mile/Hr. Speed Limit. Great Britain Department of Scientific and Industrial Research, Road Safety Laboratory Report No. 24.

Murphy, J. G., ed. (1973) *Punishment and Rehabilitation.* Belmont, Calif.: Wadsworth.

National Research Council (1976) *Surveying Crime.* Panel for the Evaluation of Crime Surveys. Washington, D.C.: National Academy of Sciences.

Orsagh, T. (1973) Crime, sanctions and scientific explanation. *Journal of Criminal Law and Criminology* 64(3):354-61.

Passell, P. (1975) The deterrent effect of the death penalty: a statistical test. *Stanford Law Review* 28(1):61-80.

Passell, P., and Taylor, J. B. (1975) The Deterrent Effect of Capital Punishment: Another View. Discussion Paper 74-7509, Columbia University, Department of Economics.

Peck, J. K. (1976) The deterrent effect of capital punishment: a comment. *Yale Law Journal* 85(3):359-67.

Phillips, L., and Votey, H., Jr. (1972) An economic analysis of the deterrent effect of law enforcement on criminal activities. *Journal of Criminal Law, Criminology, and Police Sciences* 63(3):336-42.

Pincoffs, E. L. (1966) *The Rationale of Legal Punishment.* New York: Humanities Press.

Pogue, T. F. (1975) Effect of police expenditures on crime rates: some evidence. *Public Finance Quarterly* 3(1):14-44.

Press, S. J. (1971) *Some Effects of an Increase in Police Manpower in the 20th Precinct of New York City.* R-704-NYC. Santa Monica: The Rand Corporation.

Reiss, A. (1977a) Patterns of Offending in Crime Incidents: Size of Offending Groups and Age of Offenders Involved in Major Crime Incidents Reported by Victims in the National Crime Survey. Data Report #1, Analytical Studies in Victimization by Crime, Department of Sociology, Yale University.

Reiss, A. (1977b) Understanding Changes in Crime Rates. Unpublished manuscript. Department of Sociology, Yale University.

Road Safety Laboratory (1963) Research on Road Safety. Great Britain Department of Scientific and Industrial Research.

Robertson, L. S., Rich, R. F., and Ross, H. L. (1973) Jail sentences for driving while intoxicated in Chicago: a judicial policy that failed. *Law and Society Review* 8(1):55-67.

Robison, J., and Smith, G. (1971) The effectiveness of correctional programs. *Crime and Delinquency* 17(1):67-80.

Ross, H. L. (1973) Law, science and accidents: The British Safety Act of 1967. *Journal of Legal Studies* 2(1):1-78.

Ross, H. L. (1975) The Scandinavian myth: the effectiveness of drinking-and-driving legislation in Sweden and Norway. *Journal of Legal Studies* 4(2):285-310.

Ross, H. L., Campbell, D. T., and Glass, G. V. (1970) Determining the social effects of a legal reform. *American Behavioral Scientist* 13(4):493-510.

Savitz, L. (1958) A study in capital punishment. *Journal of Criminal Law, Criminology and Police Science* 49(4):338-41.

Schwartz, R. D., and Orleans, F. (1967) On legal sanctions. *University of Chicago Law Review* 34(2):274-300.

Sellin, T. (1955) Death Penalty and Police Safety. Appendix F, Part I, Minutes of Proceedings and Evidence, No. 20, Joint Committee of Senate and House of Commons on Capital Punishment and Corporal Punishment and Lotteries, Canadian Parliament. Reprinted in part in H. Bedau, ed., *The Death Penalty in America,* revised ed. Garden City, N.Y.: Anchor Books, 1967.

Sellin, T. (1959) *The Death Penalty*. Philadelphia: American Law Institute.

Sellin, T., ed. (1967) *Capital Punishment*. New York: Harper.

Shinnar, R. (1977) The incapacitative function of prison internment: a quantitative approach. Special Issue of *Management Sciences* (forthcoming).

Shinnar, R., and Shinnar, S. (1975) The effects of the criminal justice system on the control of crime: a quantitative approach. *Law and Society Review* 9(4):581-611.

Shover, N., and Bankston, W. (1973) Some Behavioral Effects of New Legislation. Paper presented at Midwest Sociological Society meeting, Milwaukee, Wis.

Sjoquist, D. (1973) Property crime and economic behavior: some empirical results. *American Economic Review* 63(3):439-46.

Swimmer, E. (1974) Measurement of the effectiveness of urban law enforcement—a simultaneous approach. *Southern Economic Journal* 40(4).

Tittle, C. R. (1969) Crime rates and legal sanctions. *Social Problems* 16(4):409-23.

Tittle, C. R., and Rowe, A. R. (1974) Certainty of arrest and crime rates: a further test of the deterrence hypothesis. *Social Forces* 52(4):455-62.

U.S. Department of Justice (1970) *Uniform Crime Reports: 1969*. Federal Bureau of Investigation. Washington, D.C.: U.S. Department of Justice.

U.S. Department of Transportation (1972) *Alcohol Safety Action Projects*. DOT-HS-800-874. Washington, D.C.: U.S. Government Printing Office.

U.S. Department of Transportation (1974) *Alcohol Safety Action Projects: Evaluation of Operations*. DOT-HS-800. Washington, D.C.: U.S. Government Printing Office.

Vandaele, W. (1973) The economics of crime: an econometric investigation of auto theft in the United States. Pages 611-15 in *American Statistical Association, 1973 Proceedings of the Business and Economics Section*. Washington, D.C.: American Statistical Association.

von Hirsch, A. (1974) Prediction of criminal conduct and preventive confinement of convicted persons. *Buffalo Law Review* 21(3):717-58.

Walker, N. (1969) *Sentencing in a Rational Society*. London: Penguin Press.

Walker, N. (1971) Aims of punishment. In Radzinowicz and Wolfgang, eds., *Vol. II: The Criminal in Society*. Crime and Justice. New York: Basic Books.

Wilkins, L. T. (1969) *Evaluation of Penal Measures*. New York: Random House.

Wilkins, L. T., Kress, J. M., Gottfredson, D. M., Calpin, J. C., and Gelman, A. M. (1976) Sentencing Guidelines: Structuring Judicial Discretion. A report of the Criminal Justice Research Center, One Alton Road, Albany, New York 12203.

Wilson, J. Q. (1968) *Varieties of Police Behavior: The Management of Law and Order in Eight Communities*. New York: Atheneum.

Wilson, J. Q., and Boland, B. (1976) Crime. Chapter 4 in W. Gorham and N. Glaser, eds., *The Urban Predicament*. Washington, D.C.: The Urban Institute.

Witte, A. D. (1976) Testing the Economic Model of Crime on Individual Data. University of North Carolina, Chapel Hill, unpublished.

Wolpin, K. I. (1976) An Analysis of Crime in England and Wales: 1894-1967. Yale Law School, unpublished.

Zador, P. (1976) Statistical evaluation of the effectiveness of "Alcohol Safety Action Projects." *Accident Analysis and Prevention* 8(1):51-66.

Zeisel, H. (1976) The deterrent effect of the death penalty: facts v. faiths. In P. B. Kurland, ed., *The Supreme Court Review: 1976*. Chicago: University of Chicago Press.

Zimring, F. E. (1968) Bad Checks in Nebraska: A Study in Complex Threats. Center for Studies in Criminal Justice at the University of Chicago, unpublished.

Zimring, F. E. (1972) Of doctors, deterrence, and the dark figure of crime: a note on abortion in Hawaii. *University of Chicago Law Review* 39(4):699-721.

Zimring, F. E., and Hawkins, G. J. (1973) *Deterrence: The Legal Threat in Crime Control*. Chicago: University of Chicago Press.

COMMISSIONED PAPERS

The papers comprising the remainder of this volume were commissioned by the Panel to provide basic materials for its work. The papers by Nagin, Zimring, Cohen, and Monahan review the literature on specific aspects of deterrence and incapacitation; the papers by Klein *et al.* and by Vandaele involve reanalysis of data that has been reported in the deterrence literature; and the papers by Fisher and Nagin and by Manski explore some possible approaches for improving the estimates of deterrent effects.

Earlier drafts of these papers served as the basic materials for a conference convened by the Panel in Woods Hole, Massachusetts, on July 19–20, 1976 (see Appendix). The papers were discussed individually by identified discussants, as well as by Panel members and other conference participants. The authors were then given the opportunity to revise their papers for publication in this volume.

The Panel appreciates the contributions of the authors of these papers and the scholarship displayed in their work; their efforts were invaluable to the Panel in the preparation of its report. In many cases, the Panel agreed with the authors' conclusions; in a few cases, the Panel reached different conclusions. Thus, the report of the Panel may sometimes by at variance with the conclusions of these papers. The papers are presented for the significant contributions they make to the literature on deterrence and incapacitation.

General Deterrence: A Review of the Empirical Evidence

DANIEL NAGIN

I. INTRODUCTION

The hypothesis that the threat of punishment will deter crime is certainly not a new one. Bentham argued the deterrent efficacy of criminal sanctions in the 18th century. However, until 10 years ago, the deterrence hypothesis was considered largely on ethical or theoretical grounds, with little effort given to empirically testing the hypothesis. The dearth of empirical evidence has served to motivate a considerable number of empirical analyses of the hypothesis in recent years.

Deterrence is viewed as working in two principal fashions. One involves the effect of imposing criminal sanctions on the subsequent behavior of the individual actually punished. This deterrent effect, which has come to be known as "special deterrence," is generally studied in terms of recidivism behavior of the identified punished individual. On balance, recent evidence tends to suggest that special deterrence, which observationally is difficult to distinguish from other forms of "rehabilitation," is not operating. This tentative conclusion is suggested by the apparent invariance of recidivism to any type of spe-

---

Daniel Nagin is Assistant Professor of Policy Sciences, Institute of Policy Sciences and Public Affairs, Duke University.

NOTE: The research for this paper was partially supported by grant no. 75NI-99-0005 from the Law Enforcement Assistance Administration and by PHS grant no. RO1 MH 28437-01 from the National Institute of Mental Health, Center for Studies of Crime and Delinquency.

cial rehabilitative program (Lipton *et al.* 1975). The figures suggest that recidivism rates cannot be affected by varying the severity of punishment, at least within acceptable limits. The evidence, however, is still only preliminary.

The second type of deterrence is concerned with the symbolic effect that punishment may have on potential criminals. The imposition of sanctions on one person may demonstrate to the rest of the public the expected costs of a criminal act, and thereby discourage criminal behavior in the general population. This deterrent effect has come to be known as "general deterrence." The available empirical evidence on general deterrence is the subject of this review.

A series of empirical analyses in the 1960s (e.g., Gibbs 1968; Tittle 1969; Leibowitz 1965) showed a negative association between crime rates and two measures of criminal sanctions: the ratio of prison commitments to reported crimes (a measure of the certainty of imprisonment) and the time served in prison (a measure of the severity of punishment). These and a theoretical analysis by Becker (1967), emphasizing that crime (at least in part) may be a phenomenon arising from rational behavior, renewed an old debate over whether criminal sanctions deter crime. Subsequently, numerous analyses, generally econometric, have also attempted to investigate the deterrent effect of criminal sanctions. With one important exception (Forst 1976), inverse associations are found between crime rates and several sanction measures, primarily clearance rates,[1] imprisonment probability, and time served.

The empirically observed inverse associations can readily be construed as demonstrating the deterrent efficacy of criminal sanctions. Tullock (1974), in his review of this body of evidence, for example, concludes unequivocally that general deterrence is effective, and argues:

> We have an unpleasant method—deterrence—that works, and a pleasant method—rehabilitation—that (at least so far) never has worked. Under the circumstances, we have to opt either for the deterrence method or for a higher crime rate.

There are cogent reasons, however, for judging the evidence on the deterrence hypothesis as less than conclusive. Furthermore, the esti-

[1]Clearance rates give the proportion of reported crimes that are "solved." Crimes are generally "solved" by arresting a suspect. As such, clearance rates are used as measures of the probability of apprehension.

mates of the magnitude of the deterrent effect of each sanction for each crime type (the expected reduction in a particular crime resulting from a given increase in a particular sanction) are certainly not of sufficient accuracy for developing intelligent policy. The limitations in the available evidence follow from characteristics of the data used in the analyses and certain limitations in the models underlying the analysis. These shortcomings, which will be examined in detail, may be summarized as:

1. The processes underlying the generation of data on crime and sanctions offer alternative explanations for the observed inverse association between crime and sanctions. Variations either across jurisdictions or over time in police practices in the recording of offenses reported to them by the public or in the subsequent unfounding[2] of recorded offenses may, in themselves, be generating an inverse association between published crime rates and any sanction variable with published counts of crime in its denominator (e.g., clearance rate, prison commitments per crime). Jurisdictions that record fewer reported crimes and/or unfound more recorded crimes will tend to have lower crime rates and higher measures of such sanction rates.

Overt manipulation of clearances and crime reports will serve to generate an even larger negative association between crime rates and clearance rates. High clearance rates and low crime rates are used as indicators of an effective police department. Police departments may use their discretion not to record a reported offense or to unfound a recorded offense to manipulate reductions in published crime rates. Concurrently, the police, by offering suspects leniency if they admit to previously unsolved crimes, can also inflate clearance rates. The negative association between clearance rates and crime rates may simply reflect the varying intensity with which such practices occur across jurisdictions.

Similarly, the observed inverse association between prison commitments per crime and the crime rate may also be a reflection of the plea bargaining process. Plea bargaining will have the effect of understating in published statistics the actual number of prison commitments for more serious offenses because the commitments will be recorded for a less serious offense (e.g., assaults reduced to disorderly conduct). If

[2]An offense is said to be "unfounded" when: (a) circumstances following the report show that no crime actually occurred (e.g., a reported theft is in fact a case of misplaced property) or (b) there is good reason to believe that no crime occurred (e.g., it is suspected that an offense is reported merely to implicate another individual in wrongdoing).

plea bargaining is more prevalent in judicial systems that are overcrowded by increased crime, an inverse association between commitments per reported crime (a measure of probability of imprisonment) and crime rates will be induced that is not a reflection of deterrence.

2. Motivated by a belief that crimes and sanctions mutually affect one another, many recent analyses have postulated simultaneous systems where crime is presumed to affect sanctions as well as sanctions affecting crime. To separate empirically the mutual effects, *a priori* restrictions must be imposed on the behavior of the system. These restrictions have taken the form of selectively excluding significant exogenous variables from one equation in the system while including them in one or more of the other equations in the system. The restrictions are made on the assumption that a variable has a causal effect on the dependent variable in whose specification it is included, but has no causal effect on the dependent variable in whose specification it is excluded. If these exclusions are seriously in error, then the estimated coefficients are as unsuitable for inferring the effect of sanctions on crime as those estimated by non-simultaneous estimation procedures. The restrictions used to identify the crime-generating function are often implausible, consequently raising serious doubts about the interpretation of the estimated parameters.

3. The inverse association between crime and sanctions also reflects, at least in part, incapacitation effects rather than deterrent effects. In places where the probability of imprisonment is larger and/or time served is longer, a greater proportion of the criminal population will be incarcerated, *ceteris paribus*. The crime rate will thereby be reduced by physically constraining a greater proportion of the criminal element from committing crimes. It will be shown that the confounding of incapacitation and deterrent effects is perhaps substantial.

While it is the intention of this critique to show that the available evidence is not nearly as definitive as Tullock (1974) suggests and certainly not of sufficient accuracy or completeness for suggesting policy changes, it should not be construed to imply that deterrence is not operating, or that the evidence accumulated to date is without merit. Several of the analyses were obviously done with considerable care, and their results and models offer a departure point for further research. Nevertheless, a general conclusion that a deterrent effect of appreciable magnitude has been clearly established is premature.

In the next section, the available evidence will be summarized. The following three sections will address each of the three shortcomings.

II. PRIOR ANALYSES OF ASSOCIATIONS BETWEEN CRIMES AND SANCTIONS

General deterrence is inherently an aggregate phenomenon since it is reflected in the behavior of the entire population. Consequently, all analyses use aggregate data on crime-commission rates and examine the association of commission rates with various sanction measures. These are primarily: a) two measures of probability of apprehension (clearance rate and the ratio of arrests to reported offenses), b) a measure of probability of imprisonment (the ratio of prison commitments to reported crimes), and c) a measure of severity of punishment (mean or median time served). Table 1 summarizes key aspects of the evidence that will be reviewed here: the crime types and sanctions analyzed and the data and statistical techniques used.

While there are many analyses, the basic data sources used in these analyses are fewer, so that the number of "independent" observations is actually fewer than the number of analyses. The 1960 publication of National Prisoner Statistics (NPS) has been the primary source of sanction data for several analyses. Using statewide cross-sectional data, these analyses have examined the association between crime rates and two sanction variables: a) ratio of prison commitments in 1960 to reported crimes in 1959 or the average reported crimes for several years surrounding 1960, and b) mean or median time served. Gibbs (1968), Gray and Martin (1969), and Bean and Cushing (1971) analyzed these data for homicide only. Using regression models, zero-order correlations, or contingency tables, all find significant negative associations[3] between these sanction variables and the homicide rate.

Antunes and Hunt (1973) using regression analyses, Chiricos and Waldo (1970) using contingency tables, Tittle (1969) using rank-order statistics and contingency tables, and Logan (1971, 1972) using simple, partial, and part correlation analyze the association between each of

[3]When an association is referred to as "significant" here, a 0.05 level of significance for that hypothesis test is implied. The magnitudes of these associations are not addressed specifically here for several reasons. Many of the analyses do not give the prerequisite information necessary to estimate magnitudes via elasticities. When simultaneous systems are estimated, the equilibrium effect of changing a sanction cannot be directly computed from the crime-rate structural equation. The authors of the simultaneous analyses, with few exceptions, do not calculate the equilibrium effects. Finally, for reasons that will be elaborated, the magnitudes if determined are sufficiently inaccurate that they are of little real value for interpretation.

TABLE 1 Summary of Deterrence Analyses

Author(s)	Crime(s)	Sanction(s)[a]	Data Source(s) on Crimes and on Sanctions (Unit of Observation)[b]	Methodology[b]	Control Variable[a]	Variable to Identify Crime Function (Simultaneous Only)[a]
Gibbs (1968)	Homicide	P(I), T	1960 NPS 1959-1961 UCR (states)	Cont. Table	None	—
Gray and Martin (1969)	Homicide	P(I), T	1960 NPS 1959-1961 UCR (states)	OLS and Correlation	None	—
Bean and Cushing (1971)	Homicide	P(I), T	1960 NPS 1959-1961 UCR (states)	OLS	So or NW	—
Antunes and Hunt (1973)	Index Crimes	P_i (I), T_i	1960 NPS 1959-1960 UCR (states)	OLS	None	—
Chiricos and Waldo (1970)	Index Crimes	P_i(I), T_i	1950, 1960, and 1964 NPS, 1950-1951, 1960-1961, and 1963-1964 UCR (states)	Cont. Table	None	—
Tittle (1969)	Index Crimes	P_i(I), T_i	1960 NPS 1959-1963 UCR (states)	Cont. Table	?	—
Logan (1971, 1972)	Index Crimes	P(I), T	1960 NPS 1959-1963 UCR (states)	Correlation	None	—

Ehrlich (1973)	Index Crimes	$P_i(I)$, T_i	1960 NPS, 1959-1960 UCR 1940 and 1950 NPS and UCR (states)	OLS and Sim	Y, Pov, NW	$C_{i,t-1}$, Cop_{t-1} Un, Age, Urb, Sex, N, So, Edu
Forst (1976)	Index Crimes	$P_i(I)$, T_i	1972 U.S. Statistical Abstract and 1970 UCR (states)	Sim	Y, Pov, Un, Age, Sex, NW, Urb, Temp, Mig, NHW, PrExp	Cop, So
Vandaele (1973)	Auto Theft	P(A), P(I/A), T	UCR (annual data for entire U.S.) plus 1960 NPS and 1959-1960 UCR (states)	Sim	NW, Age, Un, Y, Pov, Price	Y, U_n, TC
Orsagh (1973)	Total Index Crimes	P(C)	*Crime in California* 1960 (Calif. cities and counties)	Sim	Age, Pov, Urb	Cop
Kobrin *et al.* (1972)	Total Index Crimes	P(A), P(J/A), P(C/J), T	Various sources of data (California counties 1968-1970)	Cont. Table and Correlation	N	—
Tittle and Rowe (1974)	Total Index Crimes	P(A)	1971 UCR "Crime in Florida" (municipalities and counties)	Correlation	Sex, Age, N, Un, Pov, Ed, NW	—
Sjoquist (1973)	Total Property Crime	P(A), P(C/A) T	1968 UCR, 1960 NPS and unpublished FBI data for 1968 (U.S. cities)	OLS	Y, N, NW, Ed, Den, Un, Pov.	—
Logan (1975)	Total Index Crimes	P(A)	1964-1968 unpublished data from UCR	Correlation	None	—

TABLE 1 *(Continued)*

Author(s)	Crime(s)	Sanction(s)[a]	Data Source(s) on Crimes and on Sanctions (Unit of Observation)[b]	Methodology[b]	Control Variable[a]	Variable to Identify Crime Function (Simultaneous Only)[a]
Wilson and Boland (1976)	Serious Robbery	P(A)	National Crime Panel Victimization Survey	OLS	Den, NW, Un	—
Phillips and Votey (1972)	Index Crimes	P(A)	1952-1968 UCR (annual data for the entire U.S.)	Sim	Un	Cop
McPheters and Stronge (1974)	Total Crimes	Cop	1970 UCR 1970-1971 *City Gov. Finances*	Sim	NW, Den, MuEx, Y, Pov, Un, Ed, Prop, Age	Tot. mun
Greenwood and Wadycki (1973)	Property Crimes and Person Crimes	Cop	1960 UCR 1962 *Census of Governments*	Sim	NW, Pov, Den, So, Prop.	Y, Tax
Swimmer (1974)	Index Crimes	Cop, T	1960 UCR 1962 *County, City Data Book*	Sim	NW, Y, N, Pov, So, Age, Un	Tax, City size
Carr-Hill, and Stern (1973)	Total Indictable Offenses	P(A), P(I)	Various published and unpublished sources (districts in England and Wales)	Sim	Prop, Urb	N, VC, MC,
Avio and Clarke (1974)	Canadian Property Crimes	$P_i(A)$ $P_i(C/A)$, T_i	Various published and unpublished Canadian Data Sources (Can. Prov.)	Sim	Un, Sex, NW, Rec.	Den, N, Cop, Car, VC.

Sellin (1959)	Homicide	Legal retention vs. abolition of capital punishment	UCR (annual data for several states)	Comparison of homicide rates in contiguous states	—	—
Ehrlich (1975)	Homicide	P(A), P(C/A) P(E/C)	UCR and NPS (Annual data for the entire U.S. 1933-1969)	Sim	Un, Y, Age, t	N, Cop, Gov, NW

*An "i" subscript on these sanction variables indicates that several crime types were analyzed and sanctions were estimated for each crime type i.

[a]*Key to Abbreviations for Sanction and Control Variables:*

P(A) = probability apprehension (e.g., clearance rate or arrests per crime)*
P(C) = probability of conviction (e.g., convictions per crime)*
P(J) = measure of probability of trial (e.g., trials per crime)*
P(I) = probability of imprisonment or other custodial treatment (e.g., prison commitments per crime)*
T = severity of punishment (e.g., time served in prison)*
P(E/C) = probability of execution given conviction
Cop = measure of intensity of police presences (e.g., police expenditures per capita or police per capita)
PrExp = prison expenditures per prisoner
C_i = crimes of type i per capita
TC = total crimes per capita
VC = proportion of crimes that are violent or crimes against persons
Y = median income
MC = proportion of population that is middle class
Pov = measures of poverty or income dispersion (e.g., percent of families with income below $3,000)
NW = measure of racial composition (e.g., percent non-white, percent American Indian)
Un = measure of employment opportunity (e.g., unemployment rate or labor participation rate)
Age = measure of age structure in population (e.g., percent of population between 25 and 35)
Sex = measure of sex structure in population (e.g., males per females)
N = total population

TABLE 1 *(Continued)*

Den = population density or housing density
Urb = measure of urbanization (e.g., percent of population living in Standard Metropolitan Statistical Areas [SMSAS])
So = southern regional variable
Ed = measure of educational levels (e.g., median years of schooling of population over 25 years old)
Prop = measure of property values (e.g., assessed property value per capita)
Mig = migration rate
NHW = Proportion of households that are not husband/wife households
Temp = average temperature
Rec = number of households with record players
Car = motor vehicle registrations per capita
Price = average price of new cars
MuEx = expenditures on recreation, education, etc.
Tot. mun = total municipal budget
Tax = per capita property taxes
t = time
Gov = government expenditures per capita
City size = geographical area of city (sq. miles)

[b]*Key to Abbreviations for Methodologies and Data Sources*

NPS = National Prisoner Statistics
UCR = Uniform Crime Reports
Cont. Table = Contingency Tables
OLS = regression (ordinary least squares or generalized least squares)
Sim = Simultaneous equation estimation procedures (e.g., two-stage least squares)

the index offenses[4] and the two imprisonment sanction measures. For homicide, their results are consistent with those cited above. For the remaining index crimes, only the ratio of commitments to crimes displays a negative and generally significant association with each of the index crime rates.[5] Chiricos and Waldo also partially replicate their analysis on similarly defined variables for 1950 and 1963. For both years, the probability of imprisonment (commitments/crimes) has an inverse association with each crime type although that association is generally not significant. They analyze the association between time served and crime rates only for 1963 and find no association for any crime type.

Only Bean and Cushing and Tittle, have attempted to control for differences in socioeconomic status (SES) and demographic characteristics across states. In their regression models, Bean and Cushing include either a southern regional variable or a percent-black variable. Since such factors as urbanization, age structure, poverty, etc., have also been suggested as contributing causes of crime, Bean and Cushing's very limited specification probably is not adequate. Tittle states that he has controlled for quite a few SES and demographic factors, but it is not clear how these variables are included in the analysis.

Ehrlich (1973) has done the most extensive analysis of the "1960 data." The analysis is done in a simultaneous framework, where crime rates, probability of imprisonment, and police expenditure per capita are mutually related. The estimated crime function for each crime type indicates a negative and statistically significant association between the probability of imprisonment and the crime rate. For each offense classification, he also finds a negative and generally significant association between time served and crime rate. Ehrlich includes measures of income distribution and racial composition in his specification of the crime function.

Using an identical specification of his crime function, but estimating it by regression in a nonsimultaneous framework, Ehrlich re-estimates his model for certain of the index offenses using data from 1950 and 1940. The estimated regression coefficients associated with both sanction measures are consistently negative but rarely significant. These

[4]It is not completely accurate to say that the index offenses are analyzed. Two of the crime categories analyzed, sex offenses and assault, are broader offense categories than the respective index offense categories, rape and aggravated assault. However, as shorthand, the term "index crimes" will be used here to denote this somewhat broader categorization.

[5]Logan found a negative and sometimes significant partial correlation of crime rate with time served holding imprisonment probability "constant." The simple correlation, however, was not significant.

results should be viewed with added caution because the FBI's reporting network was far less developed in those earlier years, and therefore the crime statistics are considerably less reliable than those used in the more recent analyses.

Using data for 1970, and a model similar to Ehrlich's, Forst (1976) examined the association of statewide index crime rates with probability of punishment and time served. His model has crime rates and probability of imprisonment simultaneously determined, whereas Ehrlich also includes police expenditures per capita among the simultaneously related variables. Forst finds *no* significant inverse associations between index crime rate and either sanction measures. This is the only study that finds no significant inverse associations between crime and sanctions. His results should be carefully weighed against the others, because it is one of the most thorough analyses. As can be seen in Table 1, Forst includes numerous SES and demographic variables in his specification that are not included in other specifications.

Vandaele (1973) couples an annual U.S. time-series of auto theft rates and sanctions for 1933 to 1969 with the 1960 statewide cross section of auto theft rates and sanctions and estimates a simultaneous model of the auto theft "industry." He finds a negative and significant association between auto theft rates and two sanctions, the clearance rate and the probability of conviction given an individual is charged. He finds no significant association between auto theft rates and time served.

There have been several analyses where data on crime rates and sanctions in California cities and counties serve as the basic units of observation. Using a 1960 cross section of cities and counties, Orsagh (1973) estimates a model that treats crime rates and probability of conviction (ratio of individuals convicted to reported crimes) as simultaneously related. Crime rates and conviction probabilities are computed over all index crimes. This estimated crime function indicates a negative and significant association between crime rates and the probability of conviction.

Using a time-series (1967-1970) cross section of California counties, Kobrin *et al.* (1972) correlate the reported major-felony crime rates[6] with: (a) the weighted number of arrests (no arrests = 0, arrest but dismissal at station = 1, reduction of charge = 2, etc.) per major felony, (b) the weighted number of charged felons held for trial at arraignment (dismissed = 0, charge reduced to misdemeanor = 1, felony charge sustained = 2) per felony charge, (c) the weighted

[6]The authors do not state what specific crimes are included among the "major felonies"; however, it appears that the classification is closely related to the index offenses.

number of defendants convicted (not convicted = 0, convicted of reduced charge = 1, convicted of original charge = 2) per defendant tried, and (d) the average weighted sentence (fine = 0, probation = 1, etc.).

The counties are partitioned on the basis of their total population into four subgroups. In three of the four, a negative and significant correlation is found between the weighted arrest rate and the felony crime rate. Although the other sanction variables have a negative correlation with the felony crime rate in each subgroup (with one exception), correlations are generally not significant at the .05 level.

Tittle and Rowe (1974) examined the association between the index crime rate and arrest probability where arrest probability is measured by index arrests per reported index crime. Their analysis is based upon two nonindependent data sets for 1971, where the units of observation are: (a) Florida counties and (b) municipalities in Florida with populations greater than 2,500. They find a negative and significant correlation between the index crime rate and arrest probability in both data sets. Further analyses indicated that the negative association was strongest in those observations where arrest probability was greater than .3. In observations where arrest probability was less than .3, no significant association was found. They interpret this result as an indication of a "threshold" effect where arrest probability is not effective as a deterrent below the threshold level of .3. They also examined the partial correlation between arrest probability and crime rate where the third variable being held "constant" was an SES or demographic measure and the negative association between crime rate and arrest probability persisted.

Wilson and Boland (1976) estimated the association between the serious robbery rate and arrest probability and found a negative significant association. The analysis is based on victimization data collected in 26 cities by the National Crime Panel.

Using data on a selected sample of U.S. cities for 1968, Sjoquist (1973) examined the association of the property-crime rates (the aggregate of burglary, larceny of $50 or more, and robbery rates) with several sanction measures: (a) the ratio of the total number of arrests in 1968 for property crimes to the total number of property crimes reported in 1968, (b) conviction rate for property crimes given arrest in 1968, and (c) the time served in 1960 for these crimes in the respective states where the cities are located. He specifies a model that, in addition to the sanction variables, includes numerous SES and demographic variables, and estimates it by regression. He finds a negative and statistically significant association between arrest probabilities and property crime rates. The association between probability of conviction given arrest and crime rate is sensitive to the inclusion of arrest probability. When the arrest probability is included in the specification, the association between probability of conviction and crime rate is negligible. When arrests are not included, the magnitude and significance of the association increases appreciably. In various of Sjoquist's specifications, the association of median sentence with property-crime rates is negative but generally not significant.

Logan (1975) also examined the association of the total index crime rate and each of the individual index crime rates with arrest probability. His unit of observation is the state, and the crime rate and arrest probabilities are calculated from time-aggregated crime and arrest statistics for 1964-1968. Except for homicide, he finds a negative and often significant association between crime rate and arrest probability. When he logarithmically transforms the variables, all the correlations still remain negative. He does not use any SES controls in the analysis.

Phillips and Votey (1972) estimate a model for the index crimes that treats clearance rates and crime rates as simultaneously determined. They find a negative and significant association between clearance rates and crime rates. The data used in their analyses appears to have been an annual time-series (1953-1968) for the United States.

There have been several studies that have examined the relationship of property crime to clearance rates alone or to police expenditures per capita alone. Police expenditures per capita is meant to be taken as a measure of the intensity of police presence, with a greater police presence hypothesized to be a deterrent to criminal activity. Using data on a 1970 cross section of the 43 largest U.S. cities, McPheters and Stronge (1974) estimate a simultaneous model of crime[7] and police expenditures. Swimmer (1974) also estimates such a simultaneous model using data for all cities with 100,000 or more residents in 1960. Both analyses find a negative and significant association between crime rates and police expenditures in the crime function. This result is not consistent with a similar analysis done by Greenwood and Wadycki (1973), using a 1960 cross section of U.S. SMSAs where they found a positive and significant association.

There have also been several analyses using data from countries other than the United States. Carr-Hill and Stern (1973) estimate a model where clearance rates, indictable offense rates,[8] and policemen

[7]The specific crimes entering this aggregate crime rate are not specified.

[8]Indictable offenses are "those offenses deemed serious enough to warrant the possibility of trial in front of a jury" (Carr-Hill and Stern, p. 7). They report that such offenses primarily include larceny, breaking and entering, and crimes against the person.

per capita are simultaneously determined. They use data on urban and rural districts in England and Wales for 1961 and 1966. They find a negative and significant association between the two sanction measures used in the analysis (clearance rates and the proportion of convicted defendants given custodial treatment) and the indictable offense rate.

Using data on a subset of the Canadian Provinces for 1970-1972, Avio and Clark (1974) estimate a model in which crime rates, clearance rates, and police expenditures per capita are simultaneously related. The model is estimated for robbery, breaking and entering, theft, and fraud. For each crime category, they find a negative and generally significant association between clearance rates and crime rates. The association of conviction probability is generally negative for each crime category, but often insignificant. A measure of sentence severity, however, has a positive and significant association with both the robbery and theft rates and no significant association with fraud and breaking and entering. Since so few observations were available for estimation (N = 24), statements about statistical significance should be interpreted with particular caution.

The 1972 U.S. Supreme Court decision *(Furman v. Georgia)* that held capital punishment, as it was being applied, to be unconstitutional rekindled interest in the question of whether the deterrent efficacy of capital punishment is greater than that offered by extended prison terms. There also have been two well-publicized analyses of the deterrent effect of capital punishment (Sellin 1959 and Ehrlich 1975). Their results, however, are conflicting. Sellin compared homicide rates in those states having capital punishment statutes with adjacent states not having capital punishment statutes. He finds that homicide rates are not less in the capital punishment states, and so he concludes that capital punishment is not operating as a deterrent. His results should not be regarded as definitive because he does not consider the frequency with which executions were carried out, he does not control for the level of other sanctions (such as probability of imprisonment or sentence length), and his use of adjacent states may not adequately control for differences in demographic and SES characteristics across states.

Ehrlich examined the association of national homicide rates and the frequency of executions over the period 1933-1969, controlling for the level of other sanctions and certain SES and demographic factors. He finds a substantial deterrent effect associated with capital punishment. Passell and Taylor (1975) have reanalyzed data nearly identical to that used by Ehrlich.[9] They find his results of an inverse association between probability of execution and homicide rate to be very sensitive to the time period used in the analysis and to minor changes in the specification of the model. They also find significant structural changes over the time period in the relationship between homicide rates and sanctions. These results cast serious doubts on the validity of Ehrlich's results.

In summary, then, analyses that have examined the association of clearance rates, arrest probabilities, or police expenditure per capita with crime rates find consistently negative and nearly always significant associations. These results have been observed across 9 different data sources (Kobrin *et al.* [1972], California cities and counties 1970-1972; McPheters and Stronge [1974] and Swimmer [1974], a 1970 cross section of U.S. cities; Sjoquist [1973], a 1968 cross section of U.S. cities; Avio and Clarke [1974], Canadian Provinces 1970-1972; Carr-Hill and Stern [1973], districts in England and Wales [1961 and 1966]; Vandaele [1973], a 1933-1969 U.S. time series and a 1960 cross section; Tittle and Rowe [1974], Florida counties and municipalities; Logan [1975], a 1964-1968 time series of states; Wilson and Boland [1976], 26 cities included in the NCP Victimization Survey).

The association between crime rates and two measures of probability of imprisonment (the ratio of prison commitments to reported crimes or prison commitments to persons charged)[10] has been examined in numerous analyses. Generally, a negative and significant association is found, although Forst's (1976) failure to find an association is an important exception. There are, however, far fewer independent data sets underlying the analyses than there are analyses. Seven of the analyses used the 1960 U.S. statewide cross section: Antunes and Hunt (1973), Bean and Cushing (1971), Chiricos and Waldo (1970), Ehrlich (1973), Gibbs (1968), Gray and Martin (1969), Tittle (1969), Logan (1971, 1972). Other analyses include: Forst (1976), 1970 statewide cross section; Kobrin *et al.* (1972), 1970-1972 California data; Vandaele (1973), 1933-1960 U.S. time-series and "1960 data"; Chiricos and Waldo (1970) and Ehrlich (1973), the 1950 U.S. cross section and respectively the 1964 and 1940 U.S. cross sections; Carr-Hill and Stern (1973), British data; Avio and Clarke (1974), Canadian data.

The evidence on the association between sentence severity, primarily measured by time served, and crime rates is much more equivocal.

[9]They report that the data are not precisely the same as Ehrlich's because Ehrlich is not altogether specific about how he computed certain variables.

[10]When this measure is used, clearance rates or arrest probabilities are included in the analysis.

Among the authors who use the 1960 NPS data on time served, all find negative and significant associations between sentence severity and homicide rates. Only Ehrlich (1973) and Logan (1971, 1972) find consistently negative and often significant associations between sentence severity and other index crime rates. Using the 1940 and 1950 NPS data on time served by crime type, Ehrlich also finds a negative but almost always insignificant association between time served and crime rates for a subset of the index crimes. Chiricos and Waldo (1970) find no negative and significant associations between time served and each of the index crimes (excepting sex offenses, which are not included in their analysis). Using 1970 NPS data on time served, Forst (1976) finds no association for any index crime types. Finally, Avio and Clarke (1974), using Canadian data, find a positive and often significant association between average sentence and both robbery and theft rates.

Taken as a whole, the evidence might be judged as providing reasonably definitive support of the deterrence hypothesis; Tullock (1974) judged it as such. However, the evidence is not as definitive as it might appear because of the difficulties that will be discussed in the following sections.

III. LIMITATIONS IN THE DATA ON CRIMES AND SANCTIONS

General deterrence is concerned not with the effect of punishment on the individual punished, but rather with its symbolic impact on the broad population. As such, general deterrence is an aggregate phenomenon involving the total population rather than an effect associated with identified individuals. Consequently, general deterrence can only be revealed in an inverse association between crime rates and the certainty and/or severity of sanctions imposed.[11] Typically, deterrence analyses have examined crime rates across locales with differing levels of sanctions, although a smaller number have examined crime rates in a single location over a period when sanctions have changed or have used both time-series and cross-sectional data. (See Table 1.)

In all these analyses, however, poor data on both crimes and sanctions has posed a chronic impediment to a definitive analysis of deter-

[11]Chambliss (1966) analyzed the deterrent effect of a "crack-down" on parking violations on a university campus with data drawn from a survey. In that survey the respondents were asked if the "crack-down" deterred them from parking illegally. A significant number said they were deterred. Aside from the question of whether such responses are valid, there are serious questions about the feasibility of a survey approach for the type of crimes, like the index category, that are of primary concern.

rence. The most widely acknowledged data problem is the non-reporting of crimes (Wolfgang 1963, U.S. President 1967, U.S. President 1969). In general, it is recognized that reported crime rates represent a significant understatement of actual crime rates. Victimization surveys conducted by the U.S. Bureau of the Census and the National Opinion Research Center have confirmed that there is a substantial under-reporting of crime. The Census Bureau's survey of eight large U.S. cities, for example, showed that about 50 percent of all robberies of individuals, 60 percent of all assaults, 50 percent of all household burglaries, and 70 percent of all household larcenies are not reported to the police.[12]

Inaccuracies in sanction measures have been less widely examined. Zimring and Hawkins (1973), however, are an important exception; they point out that statistics such as the ratio of arrests to reported crimes and the ratio of imprisonments to reported crimes are only very rough measures of the probability of apprehension and the probability of imprisonment, respectively.

In general, poor data have the effect of introducing added "noise" into an analysis, thereby making it more difficult to establish whether the phenomenon being investigated is actually operating. But certain sources of the inaccuracies in the data on crimes and sanctions could actually generate inverse associations between crime rates and sanctions that are not a reflection of an operative deterrence phenomenon. Such sources of inaccuracies are the subject of this section.

A. CLEARANCE RATES, ARRESTS PER CRIME, AND CRIME RATES

Clearance rates (the ratio of crimes "solved" to reported crimes) or the ratio of arrests to reported crimes are frequently used as measures of the probability of apprehension (e.g., Avio and Clark 1974, Carr-Hill and Stern 1973, Sjoquist 1973). Both of these measures are consistently found to have a negative and significant association with crime rates in general and with property crime rates in particular, an association that can be construed readily as an indication of the deterrent efficacy of the probability of apprehension.

Alternative explanations for the association, however, are also available. Excepting the population counts in the crime rate's denominator, crime rates, clearance rates, and the ratio of arrests to crimes are all generated solely from a single source—police records. Different practices, either across jurisdictions or over time in a given jurisdiction, in the recording of reported offenses, in the recording of

[12]Data from U.S. Department of Justice (1974), Table 4.

arrests, and in clearing crimes represent an important source of distortion in the data. These differences could, by themselves, be generating the observed inverse associations between crime rates and the two measures of the probability of apprehension.

The observed inverse association between measures of the probability of apprehension and crime rates could be explained by administrative differences across police departments in the extent to which discretion is allowed in the non-recording of offenses. Skolnick (1966), in a field study of two police departments in large U.S. cities, found a considerable difference in the latitude that each permitted in unfounding an offense. In the city in which considerable discretion was permitted, 20 percent of all reported offenses were not recorded in official crime statistics. Skolnick points out that this city would tend to have lower recorded crime rates and higher clearance rates than the other city, which permitted only very limited discretion in unfounding an offense. The higher clearance rate in the city that permits discretion results from removing the unrecorded offenses from the denominator of the clearance rate. This city will also tend to have a lower rate of recorded crimes, and so a negative association between crime rate and clearance rate will be displayed.[13]

Because high clearance rates (and arrests per crime) and low crime rates are often regarded as indicators of an effective police force, some departments will manipulate these statistics, and this will further distort their association. Clearance rates can be inflated by promising leniency or otherwise encouraging apprehended suspects to admit to unsolved crimes. Likewise, arrests can be increased because police have considerable discretion over whom they may arrest. Simultaneously, crime reports may be recorded as less serious than objective circumstance would dictate or simply judged as unfounded and not recorded at all.[14] A result of such simultaneous manipulations of crime reports, arrests, and/or clearances is that in some jurisdictions clearance rates and arrests per crime will be inflated and recorded crime rate deflated. If the intensity with which crime reports, clearances, and

[13]Skolnick does not address the effect that discretion in the nonrecording of offenses will have on arrests per crime. It is likely, however, that if discretion is allowed, arrests per crime will be increased because unfounded offenses for which no suspect can be arrested will not be included in the denominator of the ratio. Therefore, this same phenomenon of variations in discretion in the nonrecording of offenses will also generate an inverse association between recorded crime rates and arrests per crime.

[14]For example, a burglary could be recorded as a larceny or simply an unlawful entry. Likewise, an aggravated assault could be recorded as a simple assault or disorderly conduct or, as is often the case with assaults arising from domestic quarrels, not recorded at all.

arrests are manipulated varies either cross-sectionally or over time, then an inverse association will be generated between crime rates and both clearance rates and arrests per crime, even in the absence of any deterrent effects.[15]

The degree to which recorded crime rates and clearance rates, particularly for less serious crimes, are subject to intended or unintended distortions is graphically demonstrated in Table 2, which presents the number of crimes recorded, number of crimes cleared, and clearance rates in New York City before and after a 1965 change in police administration (and recording policies).[16] Recorded incidences of murder and non-negligent manslaughter remained relatively stable across the change in administration. Since homicide is perhaps the most serious of all crimes, it does not offer too much leeway for the exercise of discretion. However, for the less serious offenses, particularly the property-related crimes of burglary and robbery, there was a radical increase in recorded offenses that cannot be plausibly attributed only to increases in their incidence. Over the change in administration the absolute number of clearances remained stable for each crime type; in fact, for the three property crimes of larceny, burglary, and auto theft, total clearances actually decreased slightly.

The net result of what was apparently a vigorously instituted policy requiring the recording of reported crimes was a substantial increase in recorded crimes and a substantial reduction in clearance rates. The increase in the recorded crime rate was, of course, not a result of the decrease in the clearance rate. Rather, the opposite is the case—the decreased clearance rate was a result of the increased number of reported crimes that were recorded.

B. THE ASSOCIATION OF PRISON COMMITMENTS PER RECORDED CRIME WITH THE RECORDED CRIME RATE

Prison commitments per recorded crime have been used extensively as a measure of the probability of imprisonment (see Table 1). Like clearance rates and arrests per crime, the ratio of prison commitments to recorded crimes is consistently found to have a negative and generally significant association with crime rate (excepting Forst 1976). As with

[15]See the Technical Note for an analytical development of the effect of measurement error in crimes on the estimated association between crime rates and any sanction risk measure that includes crimes in its denominator. It is shown that such errors will force a negative association even in the absence of a deterrent effect.

[16]The example is drawn from Zimring and Hawkins (1973), who also use it to demonstrate the leeway police have to manipulate crime rates. The statistics on crimes cleared have been added.

TABLE 2 Reported Crimes and Crimes Cleared and Clearance Rate before and after a 1965 Change in Police Administration

Crime	Recorded Crimes[a]			Percent Change Between	Crimes Cleared[b]			Clearance Rates		
	1964	1965	1966	1965 & 1966	1965	1966	% Change	1965	1966	% Change
Murder and Non-Negligent Manslaughter	636	631	653	3	525	495	−6	83	76	−8
Forcible Rape	1,054	1,154	1,761	53	791	851	8	69	48	−30
Robbery	7,988	8,904	23,539	164	3,820	4,161	9	43	18	−58
Aggravated Assault	14,831	16,325	23,205	42	10,754	10,567	−2	66	46	−30
Burglary	45,693	51,072	120,903	137	14,824	13,865	−7	29	11	−62
Larceny $50	70,348	74,983	108,132	44	9,068	8,397	−7	12	8	−33
Auto Theft	32,856	34,726	44,914	29	7,875	5,504	−30	23	12	−39

[a]From *Uniform Crime Report*, 1964, 1965, and 1966.

[b]From unpublished statistics provided by the FBI; 1964 clearances were not available to us nor were statistics on arrests available for any of these years; thereby it was not possible to compute arrests per crime.

clearance rate and arrests per crime, the inverse association may be a reflection of distortions in the data on prison commitments and recorded crimes. The "New York" example clearly demonstrates the extent to which recorded crime rates are susceptible to intended or unintended distortions that limit their comparability over time and cross-sectionally. Data on commitments are less subject to large fluctuations that are artifactual. Therefore, even if the actual probability of imprisonment is identical in different locations, the ratio of commitments to recorded crimes may be substantially different because of differences in practices for recording reported crimes. The locations that record more reported crimes will tend to have higher crime rates and lower numbers of commitments per recorded crimes than the locations that record fewer of the reported crimes. Thereby an inverse association between crime rates and commitments per crime will be generated, even without any deterrent effects.

Plea bargaining, if motivated by high crime rates, perhaps because of overcrowding in courts, may also be contributing to the inverse association between commitments per recorded crimes and recorded crime rates. The plea bargaining process results in sanctioning an individual for a lesser crime than the crime type of the initial charge or indictment (i.e., a charge for assault might be reduced to disorderly conduct).

Since there are fewer charges for the relatively more serious offenses than for similar but less serious offenses (see Table 3), it is likely that the absolute number of charge reductions is inversely related to the seriousness of the crime (e.g., fewer aggravated assaults are transformed to simple assaults than simple assaults to disorderly conduct.) Thus, the flow into a crime type from more serious categories is likely to be less than the flow out to a less serious category. In this event, if an increase in crime rate generates an increase in plea bargaining, it will result in an understatement in the published statistics on the number of individuals committed to prison for each of the more serious crime types, and, in particular, for the index crimes.

TABLE 3[a] Persons Formally Charged by the Police, 1970 (3,025 cities; 1970 pop. 68,897,000)

Crime	Persons Charged	Crime	Persons Charged
Aggravated Assault	38,466	Robbery	23,320
Simple Assault	123,729	Burglary	97,282
Disorderly Conduct	217,237	Larceny	236,495

[a] *Uniform Crime Report*, 1970. Table 15.

As a result, the ratio of individuals committed to prison to the number of reported crimes will be relatively understated for serious crimes where plea bargaining is more prevalent. If, in fact, higher crime rates result in more plea bargaining, then an inverse association between this commonly employed ratio and crime rates will result.

The effect of the plea bargaining process on published statistics of time served by crime type is less clear. It is possible, however, that plea bargaining results in these statistics overstating the sentences imposed in individuals identified with a particular crime category. For example, if a robber is sentenced for the less serious charge of larceny, his sentence (which is recorded as a sanction for larceny) might well be greater than that typically given to an individual who committed only larceny. As such, the plea bargaining process, when motivated by increased crime rates, could have the effect of neutralizing any association that may exist between crime-specific rates and time served for that specific crime. The currently ambiguous evidence on the association of time served and crime rates is certainly consistent with this interpretation.

While it cannot be demonstrated conclusively that the observed associations between crime rates and sanctions are entirely spurious artifacts rather than deterrence, that possibility must be considered in any deterrence analysis. To establish that the observed associations are measuring primarily deterrent effects it is necessary to demonstrate that these alternative explanations have only a minor impact on the observed inverse associations. If, however, the impacts are found to be substantial, then it will be necessary to develop models that can separate the deterrent effects from the other effects. Since neither of these tasks is trivial and since neither is likely to be accomplished in the immediate future, considerations related to data inadequacies alone require that conclusions on the deterrent efficacy of criminal sanctions must still be viewed as less than definitive for index crimes.

IV. THE IDENTIFICATION OF SIMULTANEOUS SYSTEMS

Most recent deterrence analyses have analyzed the relationship between crime and sanctions in a "simultaneous" framework that presumes that crime and sanctions mutually affect one another. The deterrence hypothesis predicts that sanctions will affect crime rates. On the other hand, a basic postulate of economic theory, that resources display decreasing marginal productivity, suggests that increased crime rates may indeed reduce sanctions by "over-taxing" the resources of the criminal justice system. Additionally, sociologically motivated arguments (such as those in Blumstein and Cohen 1973 and Blumstein, Cohen, and Nagin 1976) can also be made for crime rates similarly affecting sanctions. Thus, if a negative association is observed between crime rates and sanction levels, it is not clear what is being measured—the deterrent effect of sanctions on crime, some negative effect of crime on sanctions, or both.

To separate the magnitudes of these two effects empirically, *a priori* assumptions about the behavior of the simultaneous relationship must be made. These assumptions are called "identification restrictions." In general, the restrictions are imposed by assuming that certain factors affect only crime rates but not sanctions, while other factors affect sanctions but not crime rates. Such restrictions must be imposed in order to separate empirically these two effects.

In a simultaneous system, the empirical information in the data alone is inherently insufficient for making consistent[17] estimates of the system's parameters. The identification restrictions are imposed to augment the empirical information in the data so that consistent estimates of the parameters can be made.

If, however, these assumptions are seriously incorrect, then an empirical analysis can be completely misleading[18] (i.e., the parameter estimates may remain seriously inconsistent). In particular, in the crime/sanction association, the simultaneous estimation attempts to partition an observed negative association between two factors that mutually affect one another. Thus, if the identification of the crime function is seriously incorrect, it is possible to conclude that sanctions deter crime when, in fact, there is no effect at all; or conversely that sanctions do not deter crime when, in fact, they do. Thus, identification is not a technical detail in estimation; a proper identification is a crucial aspect of estimation, and as such a model's identification requires very careful consideration.

This section summarizes the rationale for believing a simultaneous relationship exists between crime and sanctions, describes the relationship of identification to simultaneous estimation, and reviews the identification restrictions employed by authors using simultaneous equation estimation techniques.

While it is the intention of this section to call into question the results of several key analyses, it does not mean to imply that these analyses

[17] A parameter estimate is said to be consistent if its probability limit is the true parameter value. Intuitively, this is similar to saying that with a sufficiently large sample the parameter can be estimated with high probability with any desired precision. A parameter that is inconsistent will also generally be biased. The converse is often not the case.

[18] Fisher (1961) shows that the magnitude of the inconsistency in parameter estimates is directly related to the "correctness" of the identification restrictions.

using simultaneous models are without merit. If simultaneous processes are at work, simultaneous estimation is necessary. The intention is rather to point out the critical significance of identification, so that future research efforts might better deal with the identification problem.

Carr-Hill and Stern (1973), Ehrlich (1973), Forst (1976), and others have asserted that increased crime rates reduce clearance rates by "overtaxing" police resources. Since increased clearance rates also have been hypothesized to be crime-deterring, they assume that a simultaneous relationship exists between clearance rates and crime. Thus, any other sanction measure that is itself a function of clearance rate then also would have a simultaneous relationship with crime.

The hypothesis that crime rates inversely affect clearance rates follows from a postulate, often assumed in economic theory, that for a fixed level of resources (e.g., police officers, patrol cars) production functions display decreasing marginal productivity. The resources devoted to policing, and indeed to all functions of the criminal justice system (CJS), may also increase as crime rates increase, as is suggested by the McPheters and Strong (1974) and Swimmer (1974) analyses. This, however, does not alter the fact that crime rates and sanction levels are simultaneously related but only complicates the problem because the effect of crime rates on resource levels must be considered (see Cook 1977 for a further development of this issue). Although the police will clear more crimes in absolute terms when crime rates increase, the percentage cleared will decrease[19] (Figure 1).

A simultaneous relationship between crime rates and sentence lengths or conviction rates has also been conjectured, although there is disagreement about the nature of crime's effect on these two sanctions. Some have argued the plausibility of increased crime rates causing judges to get "tougher" and increase sentences. This hypothesis is raised, for example, by Forst.[20]

A contrary conjecture is that a general increase in crime will tend to reduce some sanctions. Blumstein and Cohen (1973) have hypothesized that society is willing to deliver only a limited amount of punishment. As crime rates increase, the standards defining criminal behavior and the severity of sanctions are made more lenient to deliver a relatively constant level of punishment. This might involve a general reduction in sanctions in response to an overall increase in crime, or a more selective response that is limited to specific crimes. Neither of

[19]It might seem odd to regard crime as an input to a production function, but crimes are a necessary "input" to a process whose "output" is *cleared* crimes.

[20]Brian Forst, personal communication.

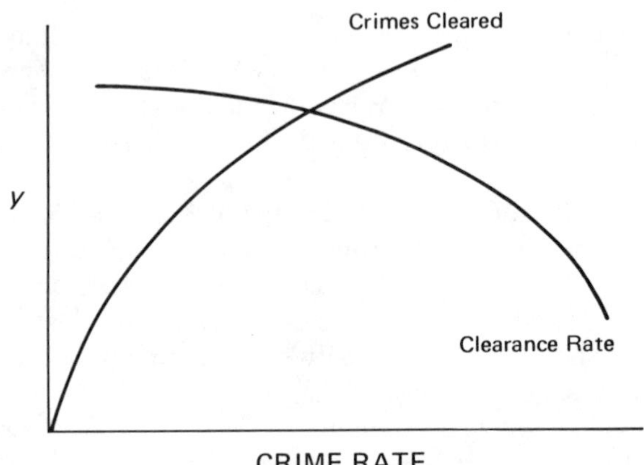

FIGURE 1 The relationship between numbers of crimes cleared and the clearance rate per crime for a fixed level of resources under the assumption of decreasing marginal productivity for police resources.

these hypotheses has yet been modeled formally and incorporated into a deterrence analysis, so further research along these lines is required.

The possibility of simultaneity between crime and sanctions raises serious obstacles to empirical analysis because simultaneous estimation requires that the simultaneous relationship be "identified." Identification is the keystone of simultaneous equation estimation, for the data alone are not sufficient for estimating the structural parameters of a simultaneous system "*no matter how extensive and complete those observations may be.*" (Fisher 1966, emphasis added).

Simultaneous estimation procedures were developed because classical regression techniques are inadequate for estimating the structural equations in a simultaneous system. In particular, when simultaneity exists, classical regression analysis will generate inconsistent coefficients. The inconsistency arises because the hypothesized structure of a system of equations with unobserved stochastic components necessarily (by the logic of the system) results in certain of the explanatory variables being correlated with the unobserved stochastic components. To see this, suppose two quantities x_t and y_t are determined by the expressions below:

$$y_t = a + bx_t + \epsilon_t \qquad (1a)$$

$$x_t = c + dy_t + u_t \qquad (1b)$$

With regard to the estimation of b and d, a necessary condition for generating a consistent estimate of b by classical regression is that x_t must be uncorrelated with ϵ_t. Similarly estimation of d by regression requires that y_t be uncorrelated with u_t.

Mathematically these conditions can be stated as:

$$E(x_t \epsilon_t) = 0 \tag{2a}$$

$$E(y_t u_t) = 0 \tag{2b}$$

If correlation does exist, then random fluctuations in the error will be attributed to the independent variable with which it is correlated, and thus bias the coefficient estimate.

However, from the structure of system (1), conditions (2) cannot be met logically, except in one very specific situation.[21] This can be shown by solving (1a) and (1b) for y_t and x_t, substituting the respective solutions into (2a) and (2b), and taking the expectations as follows:

$$\begin{aligned} E(x_t\epsilon_t) &= \frac{1}{1-bd}E[(c + da + d\epsilon_t + u_t)\epsilon_t] = \frac{1}{1-bd}[d\sigma^2_\epsilon + \sigma_{u\epsilon}] \\ E(y_t u_t) &= \frac{1}{1-bd}E[(a + bc + bu_t + \epsilon_t)u_t] = \frac{1}{1-bd}[b\sigma^2_u + \sigma_{u\epsilon}] \end{aligned} \tag{3}$$

where:

σ^2_ϵ = variance of ϵ_t
σ^2_ϵ = variance of u_t
$\sigma_{u\epsilon}$ = covariance of u and ϵ

Simultaneous estimation procedures generate consistent estimates of coefficients by developing estimates of the endogenous variables, y_t and x_t, called "instruments," which are purged of the error components (ϵ_t, u_t). Once purged of their stochastic component, the instrumental values of x_t and y_t are no longer correlated with the stochastic components. Consequently, the root cause of simultaneous bias is thereby finessed. The finesse, however, is not without a cost. Additional nonempirical information must be used to augment the data for estimation to be possible. That information comes in the form of "identification restrictions."

[21] If $d\sigma^2_\epsilon = b\sigma^2_\mu = \sigma_{\mu\epsilon}$, then parameter estimates will be consistent. However, there is no substantive basis for making this extremely strong assumption.

The correlation between a subset of the explanatory variables and the stochastic component inherently restricts the information that can be drawn from the empirically observed behavior of the system. As Fisher (1966) shows, the limits on the empirical information in a simultaneous system are such that the true parameters are indistinguishable from an infinite set of false parameters. The situation is completely analogous to the logical impossibility of finding a unique solution to a system of linear equations in N unknowns, when only $M < N$ independent equations are available. A unique solution can only be obtained if $N - M$ additional independent equations or restrictions are imposed.

Identification in simultaneous equation estimation requires the imposition of sufficient *a priori* restrictions on the behavior of the system so that the empirical information in the system is sufficiently augmented to allow the identification of the parameters driving the system. The $N - M$ augmental equations in the system of linear equations in N unknowns are as important in specifying a unique solution as the M original equations. Similarly, the identification restrictions are as important in the determination of the coefficients as the observational information. Consequently, if the identification restrictions are without foundation (that is, no plausible rationale can be provided for their imposition), then the coefficients that are estimated under the restrictions remain suspect of being inconsistent.

Typically, simultaneous systems are identified by including a certain exogenous[22] or predetermined variable in one or more equations in the system, while excluding it from at least one equation in the system. The exclusion must be justified on the grounds that the excluded variable does not directly affect the value of the endogenous variable from whose specification it is excluded. If a variable is excluded merely to facilitate estimation, then the coefficient estimates are likely to remain inconsistent and thus unsuitable for inference about the behavior of the system.

To illustrate the importance of identification, a simplified model of the simultaneous relationship between crime and clearance rates will be examined. Suppose, in system (1), y_t is the clearance rate in period t, and x_t is the crime rate in period t. Also suppose that unbeknownst to us, clearance rates do not in fact affect crime rate (i.e., $d = 0$), but increased crime rates do decrease clearance rates (i.e., $b < 0$). As they

[22]Exogenous variables are variables whose value is determined outside the specified system. Predetermined variables are values of endogenous variables determined in prior periods. Endogenous variables are those variables that are dependent variables in at least one of the equations in the system. [In system (1), x_t and y_t are endogenous.]

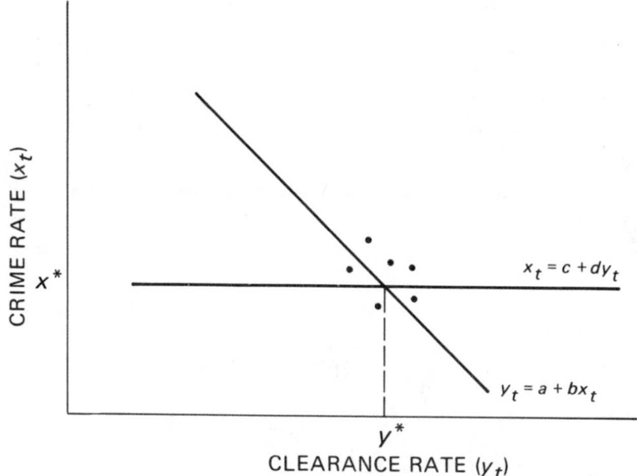

FIGURE 2 A simplified model of the relationship between crimes and sanctions in which sanctions do not affect crimes but crimes do affect sanctions.

stand, neither eqs. (1a) nor (1b) is identified because no identification restrictions have been imposed and thus the system is not estimable. The impossibility of estimation is reflected in Figure 2. The realizations of x and y for each period will be randomly scattered about the point (x^*, y^*), which is the unique solution of system (1) without the stochastic components (u_t, ϵ_t). Since neither function is "traced out" by the data, neither can be estimated.

Suppose, however, that (a) the average sentence in period t, T_t, does affect crime rates with longer sentences reducing the crime rate, and (b) that T_t is uncorrelated with ϵ_t and u_t [i.e., $E(T_t, \epsilon_t) = 0$ and $E(T_t, u_t) = 0$]. The presumed effect of T_t on x_t is illustrated in Figure 3. This additional information on T is incorporated into the model for x_t by reformulating (lb) as:

$$x_t = c + dy_t + fT_t + u_t \qquad \text{(lb')}$$

where:[23]

$$E(T_t, u_t) = 0$$
$$E(T_t, \epsilon_t) = 0$$

[23]The importance of these two assumptions to proper identification will be discussed.

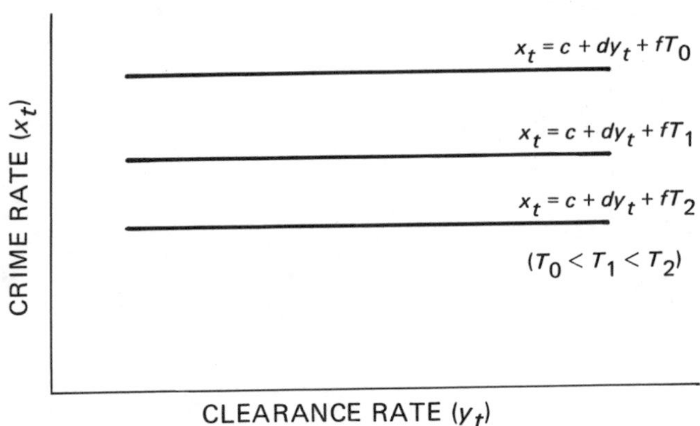

FIGURE 3 The crime rate as a function of the clearance rate and the average sentence (T_t) in a simplified model of the relationship between crimes and sanctions.

In Figure 4, the equation for the clearance rate, y_t, is superimposed on the crime functions in Figure 3. The intersections of these functions in Figure 4 indicate the expected equilibrium values of x_t and y_t that would be observed in each period.[24] Figure 4 also indicates that the equation for the crime rate, x_t, has "swept" along the equation for the clearance rate, y_t. If a line were drawn connecting the equilibrium values of x_t and y_t, then an approximation of the equation generating y_t would be estimated. This is precisely what a simultaneous estimation is meant to accomplish.

The crime function (lb′) is not estimable because it is not identified. The non-identifiability of the crime function is reflected by the absence of an equivalent "sweeping" of (lb′) by (la). The clearance-rate function, (la), is estimable only because of the *a priori* exclusion of T_t from this equation. The exclusion makes sense, however, because there is no reason to assume that sentences directly affect clearance rates.

If, however, it were arbitrarily (and, it so happens, erroneously) assumed that sentence, T_t, affected clearance rates and not crime rates, then the mechanics of simultaneous estimation would have allowed an equation for the crime rate to be estimated. That equation, however, would be essentially identical to the one obtained by drawing a line through the equilibrium values of x_t and y_t in Figure 4 and would be interpreted as evidence that sanctions deter crime. Thus, the estimated

[24]The actual equilibrium values will be different because ϵ_t and u_t will have different realizations in each period.

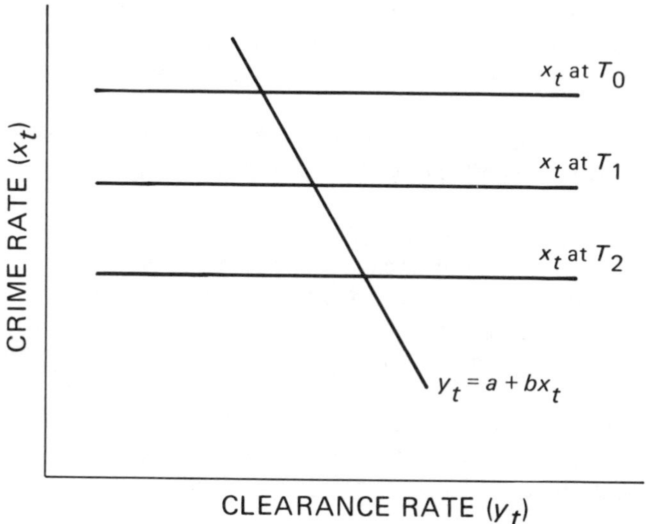

FIGURE 4 The identifying role of average sentence (T_t) in a simplified model of the relationship between crimes and sanctions.

relation would actually be the relationship describing the behavior of clearance rates and not crime rates, and so would be completely wrong.

Identification, thus, is not a minor technical point of estimation. If a system is not properly identified, one can draw completely erroneous conclusions from the estimated relationship. As this example demonstrates, one can in fact be estimating the clearance rate function and calling it the crime rate function. The results of this misidentification are particularly insidious because one can be misled into construing the actual negative effect of the crime rate on clearance rates as evidence of the reverse relationship, thereby erroneously supporting the deterrence hypothesis. Thus, with a sufficiently incorrect identification, one could conclude that the clearance rate deters crime, when in fact it has no effect on the crime rate.

In view of the importance of the identification problem, a review of some of the restrictions that have been used to identify the crime functions provides a useful perspective for making a judgment on whether these analyses have successfully separated the deterrent effect of sanction from the simultaneous relationship. When evaluating the validity of such restrictions, one should keep in mind that crime-function restrictions presume that the variables involved affect either sanctions, police expenditures per capita (a variable commonly hypothesized to be simultaneously related to crime), or other endogenous variables included in the model, but do not directly affect the crime rate itself.

Ehrlich (1973) identified his crime function by excluding from it (but including elsewhere in his model) the following variables:

1. The crime rate lagged one period
2. Police expenditures per capita lagged one period
3. Unemployment rate of civilian males aged 35-39
4. Percent of males aged 14-24
5. Percent of population living in SMSAS
6. Males per females
7. A southern regional variable
8. Mean years of schooling of population over age 25
9. Total population[25]

In Carr-Hill and Stern (1973), the crime function is identified by excluding:

1. Total population
2. Proportion of reported crimes that are violent
3. A measure of the proportion of the population that is middle class

In Avio and Clarke (1974), the crime function is identified by excluding:

1. Population density
2. The total population
3. Police expenditures lagged one period
4. Motor vehicle registration per capita lagged one period
5. Crimes against persons lagged one period

In Forst (1976), the crime function is identified by excluding:

[25]In his Ph.D. dissertation, Ehrlich (1970) estimates a crime function that includes the above unemployment, age, and education variables and found a negative and generally significant association between crime rate and sanctions. This crime function was identified in part by the exclusion of the remaining variables listed above, a different but still apparently arbitrary set of identification restrictions.

1. Police expenditure per capita in the current period (in this model police expenditures per capita is a function of the lagged crime rate)
2. A southern regional variable

In all these papers, identification of the crime function relies on exclusion from the crime function of socioeconomic variables (SES), demographic variables, regional variables, and lagged endogenous variables. It is difficult to imagine any plausible argument for the exclusion of the SES, demographic, and regional variables. Inter-correlation among these SES and demographic correlates of crime makes it difficult to determine which among them do have a causal association with crime, but it is simply not plausible to assume that such SES variables do not have a direct effect on crime, while also assuming that each does directly affect either sanctions or police expenditures per capita.[26]

Further, three of the analyses also use the exclusion of lagged endogenous variables (Ehrlich 1973, Carr-Hill and Stern 1973, and Avio and Clarke 1974) or a variable that is a function of a lagged endogenous variable (Forst 1976) to identify the crime function. For the estimation procedures employed, the use of such restrictions to identify rests crucially upon an assumption of no serial correlation in the stochastic disturbance terms in any of the equations including the crime rate equation, because these estimation procedures treat lagged endogenous variables and variables that are functions of them as uncorrelated with current disturbances.

The importance of this point can be seen in the context of the prior illustration on the use of excluded variables in identification. In that example, the exclusion of the exogenous variable, T_t, from eq. (1a) was a necessary condition for identification of that equation. For it to be sufficient, T_t additionally had to be uncorrelated with ϵ_t and u_t [i.e., $E(T_t, \epsilon_t) = 0$ and $E(T_t, u_t) = 0$]. If T_t is so correlated, then even simultaneous equation estimation methods will fail to generate consistent parameter estimates unless they account for the correlation. If, for example, $E(T_t, \epsilon_t) \neq 0$,[27] then it cannot be assumed that the expectation of eq. (1a) remains stable over different values of T_t. Thus, as the expectation of eq. (1b) shifts over the different values of T_t (see Figure

[26]Forst has provided me with the data set that he used in the analysis cited above. The crime function was re-estimated using the exclusion of the police expenditures variable as the sole identification restriction. The estimated effect of the sanction variables remained insignificant. However, for the reasons cited below, substantial questions remain as to whether even these estimates can be regarded as consistent.

[27]T_t may be correlated with ϵ_t either because T_t does in fact affect y_t and (since it is not included in the specification) is a component of ϵ_t, or because T_t is correlated with some other causal factor excluded from the specification.

4), the expectation of eq. (1a) will also shift. As a consequence, the equilibrium values of y_t and x_t over the different values of T_t cannot be taken as an approximate plot of eq. (1a) see (Figure 4).

When a lagged endogenous variable or a variable that is a function of such a variable is used in an identification, it too must be assumed uncorrelated with the disturbances. However, when the disturbances (or some subset) are serially correlated (e.g., $E(\epsilon_t \epsilon_{t-1}) \neq 0$) this assumption is logically impossible except possibly for specific parameter values (just as it was logically impossible to assume y_t and x_t to be respectively uncorrelated with ϵ_t and u_t except for specific parameter values).

Consequently, the validity of using a lagged endogenous variable or some variable that is a function of it as an identification restriction depends upon the absence of serial correlation in any of the disturbances. An assumption of serial independence reflects implicit assumptions about the real effects stemming from factors affecting the dependent variable but not explicitly included in the model, since the stochastic disturbance can be viewed as measuring their summed effect. For the assumption of serial independence to be tenable, the effects of these excluded factors must not be thought to be persistent over time, but instead must vary randomly from period to period. If they persist, then the stochastic disturbances will be correlated from period to period.

In the context of the crime function, eq. (1b′), these variables would include all SES, demographic, and environmental variables that affect crime. However, this is because of the simplistic nature of eq. (1b′) adopted for expositional purposes. As already remarked, if eq. (1b′) were to be estimated in practice, some such variables would be explicitly included. Nevertheless, some part of the stochastic disturbance, u_t, would still consist of these effects. It is impossible to include all the variables influencing crime either because we do not know all of them or because we cannot measure them. In addition, if the included variables affect crime in ways only approximated by the choice of functional form, then departures from that approximation also influence the disturbance term.

From this perspective on the factors generating u_t, it certainly appears unreasonable to assume no serial correlation in u_t. Many of the excluded variables, like SES and demographic variables, influencing u_t change only gradually over time. Thus, if the realized values of these variables are such that the disturbance is positive in period t, it is likely that their realized values in successive periods will result in disturbances that are positively correlated. One possible characterization of this relationship among the disturbances is the first-order autoregressive process in which $u_t = \phi u_{t-1} + \delta_t$ where δ_t is an independent and identically distributed disturbance.

When using data with a cross-sectional component, which are the most common type of data utilized in deterrence analyses, the likelihood of serial correlation is particularly high because there is likely to be particularly wide variation in the values of excluded variables across the sampling units (usually states). Put simply, locations with actual crime rates higher than those predicted by the regression equation in one year are likely to remain so in the next year.

The criticism made here should not be taken to mean that the analyses using simultaneous models are without merit. The insight that simultaneous processes are working between crime and sanctions and the attempts made to separate the magnitude of the separate effects represent significant steps forward in understanding the relationship of crimes to sanctions.

The possibility of simultaneous relationships between crime and sanctions, however, places added demands on a deterrence analysis and raises serious questions about our current capacity to identify and estimate the respective effects. At present, we understand very little about the processes in which crime is endogenous. Much more work is needed to determine more specifically just how crime may affect sanctions. It is hoped that such an effort will provide the new insights necessary for more appropriately identifying the reciprocal deterrent effect of sanctions on crime.

V. THE CONFOUNDING OF INCAPACITATION AND DETERRENT EFFECTS

During the period that an individual is incarcerated, he is physically constrained from committing crimes against the general community. As a consequence, his incarceration must have the effect of averting whatever crimes he might have committed if he were in the community. The aggregate incapacitation effect of imprisonment, the total number of crimes averted by physically confining a proportion of the total population, is an increasing function of both the probability of imprisonment and the time served. An increase in either of these sanctions will serve to reduce the potential criminal population at large, thereby reducing the crime rate.

However, the effectiveness of incapacitation may be seriously mitigated if the departure of the incarcerated criminals attracts new recruits as replacements or increases the criminal activity of the criminals remaining at large. For highly organized crimes like narcotics distribution, the incarceration of a distributor may well have no net effect on reducing distribution because he will be quickly replaced. However, for most index offenses, there is no such organization, the offense is more personal, and replacement is much less likely.

Since the incapacitation effect is an increasing function of the probability of imprisonment and time served, the observed inverse associations between these two sanction variables and crime rates must, in part, be measuring incapacitation effects. There have been, however, no empirical attempts to determine the magnitude of this confounding effect. Using the models for estimating incapacitation effects developed by Avi-Itzhak and Shinnar (1973) and by Shinnar and Shinnar (1975), it will be shown here that the confounding of incapacitation with deterrent effects in the estimated association may well be substantial.

Modeling incapacitation effects, even under an assumption of no deterrence, is very difficult. Such a model requires consideration of such factors as the probability of a person becoming a criminal, the length of a criminal career, crime commission rates during a criminal career, the probability of apprehension, and the length of incarceration. The model used to estimate the magnitude of incapacitation effects is based upon the following assumptions:

1. The number of crimes committed by an active criminal follows a Poisson process. The Poisson process is specified exactly by a parameter, λ, which is the expected number of crimes committed in a single time period.
2. The length of a criminal career is assumed to follow an exponential distribution. The exponential distribution is specified completely by a parameter, T, which is the mean length of a criminal career (the crime rate λ is independent of the career length).
3. There is a fixed probability, P, of being apprehended and imprisoned for each crime committed (P is independent of the number of crimes committed, λ). The average time served in prison is exponentially distributed with mean S.
4. Mean criminal career is long relative to mean sentence length, S.
5. The sanction parameters P and S do not affect λ or T. This assumption therefore ignores any effects of both special and general deterrence.

Under these assumptions a measure η, the ratio of actual crimes committed to the potential crimes that would have been committed in the absence of incapacitation, is derived. Potential crimes can also be viewed as the sum of actual crimes committed and the additional crimes avoided by incapacitation. Thus, η ranges between (0, 1), with smaller values of η reflecting a greater incapacitation effectiveness of incarceration. The measure η is shown to be (Shinnar and Shinnar 1975):

$$\eta = \frac{1}{1 + \lambda PS} \tag{4}$$

From eq. (4), η can be seen to be a monotonically decreasing function of λ, P, and S. Thus, by increasing the probability of imprisonment, P, and/or sentence length, S, the measure, η, will be decreased, reflecting the fact that criminals will be incapacitated for a greater proportion of their criminal career, thereby reducing the number of crimes actually committed.

To estimate the extent of confounding between incapacitation and deterrent effects, the elasticities of the crime rate with respect to either a change in the probability of incarceration or the time served will be derived from the Shinnar and Shinnar model of incapacitation above. Those elasticities will then be compared with the elasticities econometrically estimated in Ehrlich's "deterrence" model.

By definition, the elasticity (ϵ_x) of the actual crime rate, C_A, with respect to a change in a particular variable x (i.e, P or S) is:

$$\epsilon_x = \frac{dC_A}{dx} \cdot \frac{x}{C_A} \tag{5}$$

To derive ϵ_P and ϵ_S within the framework of the Shinnar and Shinnar model, it is first necessary to recognize that:

$$C_A = \eta C_p \tag{6}$$

where C_P = potential crime rate (actual crimes plus crimes avoided by incarceration).

Thus, combining (4) and (6) and differentiating:

$$\frac{dC_A}{dP} = \frac{-\lambda S}{(1+\lambda PS)^2} \cdot C_P \tag{7a}$$

or

$$\frac{dC_A}{dP} = -\lambda S \eta^2 C_P \tag{7a'}$$

and

$$\frac{dC_A}{dS} = \frac{-P\lambda}{(1+\lambda PS)^2} \cdot C_P \tag{7b}$$

or

$$\frac{dC_A}{dS} = -\lambda P \eta^2 C_P \tag{7b'}$$

Then, using the definition of elasticity (5) with the value of C_A given by (6), we find the same value for the two incapacitation elasticities:

$$\epsilon_P = \epsilon_S = -\lambda PS\eta \tag{8}$$

Eq. (8) can be used to estimate ϵ_P and ϵ_S, which can then be compared to their econometrically estimated counterparts, $\epsilon_P{}^*$ and $\epsilon_S{}^*$, which measure the combined incapacitation and deterrent effects. For the purposes of this comparison, we use Ehrlich's estimates of $\epsilon_P{}^*$ and $\epsilon_S{}^*$.

The comparison will be limited to a comparison of the elasticities for the aggregate crime index (rather than for the individual crime types), since the Shinnar and Shinnar model permits examining incapacitation effects for specific crime types only if criminals specialize. If switching between crime types is common, then incarcerating someone for one crime type will also result in a reduction in the other crime types in which he engages.

The available evidence on crime-switching behavior indicates that specialization is not common. The analysis of a juvenile cohort by Wolfgang *et al.* (1972) showed no evidence of specialization in juvenile offenders. Blumstein and Greene (1976) analyzed crime-switching behavior in a predominantly adult (over 18 years of age) population of offenders and found evidence of greater specialization but still observed considerable switching. Thus, consideration of incapacitative effects for the aggregate of the index crimes reduces the error incurred with a more narrowly defined crime type, but, of course it will not capture the incapacitation deriving from the incarceration of offenders sentenced for non-index offenses who also engage in index crimes.

To calculate ϵ ($=\epsilon_P=\epsilon_S$), estimates of P, S, and λ for index crimes in 1960 are necessary. (The Ehrlich estimates of $\epsilon_P{}^*$ and $\epsilon_S{}^*$ are made using 1960 data.) The probability of imprisonment given an index crime, P, for 1960 is estimated as the ratio of prison commitments for index offenses to total reported index crimes. In 1960, 50,479 prisoners were received in state prisons for index offenses[28] (not counting New Jersey and Alaska), and in fiscal 1961, 5,700 such prisoners were received in federal prisons, not counting Washington, D.C.[29] From Table 2 of the 1960 UCR, the number of index crimes in continental United States (excluding New Jersey, Alaska, and Washington, D.C., which were not included in the incarceration statistics) was 1,785,334. Thus, the 1960 value of P is estimated as 0.0315 for index crimes.

The variable S in the Shinnar model is defined as the average time served. No direct estimate of this variable is available for index offenses in 1960. It is estimated as the ratio of the average daily index-crime prison population in state prisons to receptions for index crimes in state institutions. Under a steady-state assumption, this ratio is equal to the mean time served for index offenses.[30] From Table P1 in the 1960 NPS, the year-end prison population for index offenses was 138,606 and from Table A1, the number of receptions for these offenses was 50,479. Thus, the 1960 value of S for index offenses is estimated as 2.72 years.

There are currently no well-documented empirical estimates of λ for 1960 or for any other year. Estimates range from about 2.5 to 10, and so for this analysis, ϵ_P and ϵ_S are estimated for $\lambda = 2.5$, 5, 7.5, and 10, to cover that range.

In Table 4, the incapacitation elasticities $\epsilon = \epsilon_P = \epsilon_S$, derived from eq. (6), are compared with two different values of $\epsilon_P{}^*$ and $\epsilon_S{}^*$ reported in Ehrlich (1973). One estimate is obtained using ordinary least squares and the other using a simultaneous-equation estimation technique. The ordinary least-square estimates of $\epsilon_P{}^*$ and $\epsilon_S{}^*$ are -0.523 and -0.584,

[28]This figure was calculated from Table A1 in the 1960 NPS and includes receptions for homicide, robbery, assault, burglary, larceny, auto theft and sex offense. As noted previously, these categories do not exactly coincide with the index crime definition.

[29]This figure was calculated from Table 206 in the 1961 *U.S. Statistical Abstract* and includes receptions for the same crime-type categories listed in footnote 28. Federal receptions for fiscal 1961 were used rather than 1960 in order to obtain crime-type categories consistent with the 1960 NPS. Also, calendar year 1960 of NPS overlaps half of fiscal year 1961, and federal reporting is only by fiscal year.

[30]A steady-state assumption is reasonable here because the state prison population remained relatively unchanged between 1960 and 1970. In 1960, the total state prison population was 189,739, and in 1970 it was 176,391 (*U.S. Statistical Abstract,* 1972, p. 160.)

TABLE 4 Comparison of Estimates for the Incapacitative Elasticity of Crime Due to Incapacitation and Deterrence Combined

		Econometrically Estimated Elasticities			
		Non-simultaneous		Simultaneous	
	Incapacitative Elasticity	$\epsilon_P^* = -0.523$	$\epsilon_S^* = -0.584$	$\epsilon_P^* = -0.991$	$\epsilon_S^* = -1.123$
λ	$\epsilon = \epsilon_S = \epsilon_P$	ϵ_P/ϵ_P^*	ϵ_S/ϵ_S^*	ϵ_P/ϵ_P^*	ϵ_S/ϵ_S^*
2.5	−0.179	0.34	0.31	0.18	0.16
5.0	−0.303	0.58	0.52	0.31	0.27
7.5	−0.395	0.76	0.68	0.40	0.35
10.0	−0.466	0.89	0.80	0.47	0.41

respectively. These are approximately half the magnitude of the estimates of $\epsilon_P^* = -0.991$ and $\epsilon_S^* = -1.123$ obtained from simultaneous estimation. The discussion in the previous section, which outlines the problems with the Ehrlich identification, makes it clear that there is no empirical basis for determining which are the "better" estimates. There is also considerable variation in the estimates of the incapacitation elasticities. As can be seen in Table 6, the magnitude of the incapacitation elasticity varies substantially over the range of λ, from -0.179 for $\lambda = 2.5$ to -0.466 for $\lambda = 10$.

The extent to which incapacitation effects account for the econometrically estimated elasticities is reflected by the ratios, ϵ_P/ϵ_P^* and ϵ_S/ϵ_S^*, which are shown in Table 6. If the econometric estimates in the denominator of these two ratios are taken as consistent estimates of the summed effect of both incapacitation and deterrent effects, then the ratios indicate the proportion of the econometrically observed association that can be attributed to incapacitation effects. The residuals of the ratios (i.e., $1 - \epsilon_P/\epsilon_P^*$ and $1 - \epsilon_S\epsilon_S^*$) are then the proportion due to deterrent effects alone.[31]

Because the "simultaneous" estimates of ϵ_P^* and ϵ_S^* are substantially larger than the ordinary least-square estimates, the ratios ϵ_P/ϵ_P^* and ϵ_S/ϵ_S^* are smaller for the simultaneous estimates. For the non-simultaneous estimates, ϵ_P/ϵ_P^* ranges from 0.34 to 0.89 and ϵ_S/ϵ_S^* from

[31] As has been discussed in prior sections, there is considerable question as to whether ϵ_P^* and ϵ_S^* are indeed consistent estimates. If the inconsistency has resulted in an overstatement of their values, then the proportion attributable to deterrence will be overstated. Likewise if they are understated, the proportion attributable to deterrence will also be understated. For the purpose of this discussion, the two estimates of ϵ_P^* and ϵ_S^* are taken separately as consistent estimates to provide some perspective on the degree to which the observed association is due to deterrence.

0.31 to 0.80, whereas for the simultaneous estimates, ϵ_P/ϵ_P^* ranges from 0.18 to 0.47 and ϵ_S/ϵ_S^* ranges from 0.16 to 0.41.

These ratios indicate that the proportion of the observed association that can be attributed to incapacitation alone depends strongly on the value of λ and on the estimated magnitude of the crime-sanctions relationship. If λ is high and the nonsimultaneous estimates of ϵ_P^* and ϵ_S^* are used, nearly all of the empirically observed association can be attributed to incapacitation. In contrast, if λ is low and the simultaneous estimates of ϵ_P^* and ϵ_S^* are used, then incapacitation explains only a small portion of the empirically derived estimates.

In conclusion, there is considerable uncertainty about the degree to which the observed negative association between the index crime rate and P or S in 1960 can be attributed to incapacitation rather than to deterrence. For the purpose of crime control, the distinction between incapacitative and deterrent effects may be viewed as largely academic, since both have crime-control effects that can be achieved similarly by increases in P or S or both. From this perspective, then, the extent of the deterrence/incapacitation confounding is unimportant. But from the scientific perspective of establishing the deterrent effect of sanctions, the contribution of incapacitation to the observed negative association must be accounted for. No analysis has yet been able to account adequately for this effect.

VI. CONCLUSION

A decade ago there were virtually no empirical analyses of the deterrence hypothesis for non-capital sanctions. Many people held strong positions for and against deterrence, but these opinions had virtually no scientific basis. The explicit empirical analyses of deterrence were almost exclusively limited to capital punishment, and these analyses suggested that capital punishment had no marginal deterrent effect beyond extended imprisonment.

The past decade has witnessed a burgeoning of analyses directed at testing the deterrence hypothesis for non-capital sanctions. In this critique over 20 published analyses are cited, and even this list is less than exhaustive. Yet, despite the intensity of the research effort, the empirical evidence is still not sufficient for providing a rigorous confirmation of the existence of a deterrent effect. Perhaps more important, the evidence is woefully inadequate for providing a good estimate of the magnitude of whatever effect may exist.

The development of public policy directed explicitly at crime control is dependent upon sound estimates of the magnitude of deterrent effects. Thus, policy suggestions, based upon the existing evidence, can only be made with a clear recognition of the inadequacy of the evidence. Accordingly, such suggestions must be very limited and posed with great caution.

This is in stark contrast to some of the presentations in public discussion that have unequivocally concluded that sanctions deter and that have made sweeping suggestions that sanctioning practices be changed to take advantage of the presumed deterrent effect. Certainly, most people will agree that increasing sanctions will deter crime somewhat, but the critical question is, By how much? There is still considerable uncertainty over whether that effect is trivial (even if statistically detectable) or profound. Any unequivocal policy conclusion is simply not supported by valid evidence.

Although more punitive sanctioning practices might legitimately be argued as a responsible ethical response to a truly significant crime problem, arguing such a policy on the basis of the empirical evidence is not yet justified because it offers a misleading impression of scientific validity. Policy makers in the criminal justice system are done a disservice if they are left with the impression that the empirical evidence, which they themselves are frequently unable to evaluate, strongly supports the deterrence hypothesis. Furthermore, such distortions ultimately undermine the credibility of scientific evidence as inputs to public policy choices. A more critical assessment of the evidence is needed if we are to see progress in the development of knowledge about deterrent effectiveness and its application to effective public policy.

TECHNICAL NOTE: AN ANALYTICAL TREATMENT OF MEASUREMENT ERROR

This section discusses an analytical treatment of the effect of measurement error in crimes on OLS parameter estimates of the deterrent effect of sanction risk. Ehrlich (1970) examined the inconsistency of such parameter estimates under the following assumptions:

$$\frac{C}{N} = \alpha_0 \left(\frac{S}{C}\right)^{\alpha} e_{\epsilon} \quad \text{(A1)}$$

$$\hat{C} = \pi C e^{\delta} \quad \text{(A2)}$$

where:

C = actual number of crimes
N = total population
S = number of people sanctioned (e.g., arrested, imprisoned, etc.)
$\hat{C}$ = measured number of crimes
ϵ, δ = independently and identically distributed random variables each with zero mean and finite variances

Ehrlich shows that if eq. (A1) is estimated by OLS with $\hat{C}$ substituted for C (since C is not observed), the probability limit of $\hat{\alpha}$ is:

$$\text{Plim } \hat{\alpha} = \alpha - (1 + \alpha) \cdot \frac{\sigma_\delta^2}{\sigma_P^2 + \sigma_\delta^2} \qquad \text{(A3)}$$

where:

σ_δ^2 = variance of δ
σ_P^2 = variance of $\ln \dfrac{S}{C}$

and the covariances $\sigma_{P,\epsilon}$, $\sigma_{P,\delta}$, and $\sigma_{\epsilon,\delta}$ are assumed equal to 0.

The effect of the inconsistency is more readily seen by making the substitution $\alpha = -1 + B$.

$$\text{Plim } \hat{\alpha} = (-1 + B) - B \cdot \frac{\sigma_\delta^2}{\sigma_P^2 + \sigma_\delta^2} \qquad \text{(A4)}$$

From eq. (A4), when there is any measurement error ($\sigma_\delta^2 \neq 0$) α will only be a consistent estimate of α if $B = 0$ (i.e., $\alpha = -1$). If $1 > B > 0$ (i.e., $0 > \alpha > -1$) then $\hat{\alpha}$ will tend to overestimate the magnitude of the deterrent effect ($\hat{\alpha} < \alpha$). If $B < 0$ (i.e., $\alpha < -1$), then $\hat{\alpha}$ will tend to underestimate the magnitude of the deterrent effect ($\hat{\alpha} > \alpha$). In general, measurement error drives the probability limit of $\hat{\alpha}$ to a negative value with the limit moving to a value of -1 as σ_δ^2 increases.

REFERENCES

Antunes, G., and Hunt, A. L. (1973) The deterrent impact of criminal sanctions: some implications for criminal justice policy. *Journal of Urban Law* 51(2):145-61.

Avi-Itzhak, B., and Shinnar, R. (1973) Quantitative models in crime control. *Journal of Criminal Justice* 1(3):185-217.

Avio, K., and Clarke, S. (1974) Property Crime in Canada: An Econometric Study. Prepared for the Ontario Economic Council.

Bean, F., and Cushing, R. (1971) Criminal homicide, punishment and deterrence: methodological and substantive reconsiderations. *Social Science Quarterly* 52(Sept.):277-89.

Becker, G. (1967) Crime and punishment: an economic approach. *Journal of Political Economy* 78(2):526-36.

Blumstein, A., and Cohen, J. (1973) A theory of the stability of punishment. *Journal of Criminal Law and Criminology* 64(2):198-207.

Blumstein, A., and Greene, M. A. (1976) Analysis of Crime-Type Switching in Recidivism. Unpublished paper, Carnegie-Mellon University, Pittsburgh, Pa.

Blumstein, A., Cohen, J., and Nagin, D. (1976) The dynamics of a homeostatic punishment process. *Journal of Criminal Law and Criminology* 67(3):317-34.

Carr-Hill, R. A., and Stern, H. H. (1973) An econometric model of the supply and control of recorded offenses in England and Wales. *Journal of Public Economics* 2(4):289-318.

Chambliss, W. (1966) The deterrent influence of punishment. *Journal of Crime and Delinquency* 12(Jan.):70-75.

Chiricos, T. G., and Waldo, G. P. (1970) Punishment and crime: an examination of some empirical evidence. *Social Problems* 18(Fall):200-17.

Cook, P. J. (1977) Punishment and crime: a critique of current findings concerning the preventive effect of criminal sanction. *Law and Contemporary Problems* 41(1).

Ehrlich, I. (1970) Participation in Illegitimate Activities: An Economic Analysis. Ph.D. dissertation, Columbia University.

Ehrlich, I. (1973) Participation in illegitimate activities: a theoretical and empirical investigation. *Journal of Political Economy* 81(3):521-65.

Ehrlich, I. (1975) The deterrent effect of capital punishment: a question of life and death. *American Economic Review* 65(3):397-417.

Fisher, F. (1961) On the cost of approximate specification in simultaneous equation estimation. *Econometrica* 29(2):139-70.

Fisher, F. (1966) *The Identification Problem in Econometrics*. New York: McGraw Hill.

Forst, B. (1976) Participation in illegitimate activities: further empirical findings. *Policy Analysis* 2(3):477-92.

Gibbs, J. B. (1968) Crime, punishment and deterrence. *Southwestern Social Science Quarterly* 48(4):515-30.

Gray, L. N., and Martin, D. J. (1969) Punishment and deterrence: another analysis of Gibbs' data. *Social Science Quarterly* 50(2):389-95.

Greenwood, M., and Wadycki, W. J. (1973) Crime rates and public expenditures for police protection: their interaction. *Review of Social Economy* 31(2):232-41.

Kobrin, S., Hansen, E. W., Lubeck, S. G., and Yeaman, R. (1972) *The Deterrent Effectiveness of Criminal Justice Sanction Strategies: Summary Report*. Law Enforcement Assistance Agency, National Institute of Law Enforcement and Criminal Justice. Washington, D.C.: U.S. Government Printing Office.

Leibowitz, A. (1965) Does Crime Pay? An Economic Analysis. M.A. Thesis, Columbia University.

Lipton, D., Martinson, R., and Wilks, J. (1975) *The Effectiveness of Correctional Treatment: A Survey of Treatment Evaluation Studies*. New York: Praeger.

Logan, C. H. (1971) On "Punishment and Crime" (Chiricos and Waldo 1970): some methodological commentary. *Social Problems* 19(2):280-84.

Logan, C. H. (1972) General deterrent effects of imprisonment. *Social Forces* 51(Sept.):64-73.

Logan, C. H. (1975) Arrest rates and deterrence. *Social Science Quarterly* 56(3):376-89.

McPheters, L., and Stronge, W. B. (1974) Law enforcement expenditures and urban crime. *National Tax Journal* 27(4):633-44.

Orsagh, T. (1973) Crime, sanctions and scientific explanation. *Journal of Criminal Law and Criminology* 64(3):354-61.

Passell, P., and Taylor, J. (1975) The Deterrent Effect of Capital Punishment: Another View. Discussion Paper 74-7509. Department of Economics, Columbia University.

Phillips, L., and Votey, H., Jr. (1972) An economic analysis of the deterrent effect of law enforcement on criminal activities. *Journal of Criminal Law, Criminology, and Police Science* 63(3):336-42.

Sellin, T. (1959) *The Death Penalty*. Philadelphia: American Law Institute.

Shinnar, R., and Shinnar, S. (1975) The effects of the criminal justice system on the control of crime: a quantitative approach. *Law and Society Review* 9(4):581-611.

Sjoquist, D. (1973) Property crime and economic behavior: some empirical results. *American Economic Review* 63(3):439-46.

Swimmer, E. (1974) Measurement of the effectiveness of urban law enforcement—a simultaneous approach. *Southern Economic Review* 40(4):618-30.

Tittle, C. (1969) Crime rates and legal sanctions. *Social Problems* 16(4):409-23.

Tittle, C. R., and Rowe, A. R. (1974) Certainty of arrest and crime rates: a further test of the deterrence hypothesis. *Social Forces* 52(4):455-62.

Tullock, G. (1974) Does punishment deter crime? *Public Interest* 36(Summer):103-11.

U.S. Department of Justice (1974) *Crime in Eight American Cities*. Information and Statistics Service. Washington, D.C.: U.S. Government Printing Office.

U.S. President (1967) *Crime and Its Impacts: An Assessment*. President's Commission on Law Enforcement and the Administration of Justice. Washington, D.C.: U.S. Government Printing Office.

U.S. President (1969) *Crimes of Violence: A Staff Report Submitted to the National Commission on the Causes and Prevention of Violence*. President's Commission on Violence. Washington, D.C.: U.S. Government Printing Office.

Vandaele, W. (1973) The economics of crime: an econometric investigation of auto theft in the United States. Pp. 611-15 in *American Statistical Association, 1973 Proceedings of the Business and Economics Section*. Washington, D.C.: American Statistical Association.

Wolfgang, M. (1963) Uniform Crime Reports: a critical appraisal. *University of Pennsylvania Law Review* 111(April):108-38.

Wolfgang, M., Figlio, R., and Sellin, T. (1972) *Delinquency in a Birth Cohort*. Chicago: University of Chicago Press.

Zimring, F., and Hawkins, G. (1973) *Deterrence: The Legal Threat in Crime Control*. Chicago: University of Chicago Press.

Policy Experiments in General Deterrence: 1970-1975

FRANKLIN E. ZIMRING

INTRODUCTION

The first years of the 1970s were a period of growing interest in the general deterrent impact of criminal sanctions both for social scientists and for those interested in crime as a problem of public policy. During this period, empirical studies of deterrence have come from two quite different research strategies, and they seem to suggest different policy conclusions about general deterrence.

One approach is to gather aggregate data on crime and other social indicators and to study the variations in crime that occur between jurisdictions or over time. The strategic concept is one of studying changes that occur naturally, attempting to control for all the other differences that occur in nature, either between areas or over time, to isolate the contribution of general deterrence to differences in noted

---

Franklin E. Zimring is Professor of Law and Director, Center for Studies in Criminal Justice, University of Chicago.

NOTE: I appreciate the helpful comments received from Joe Lewis, Police Foundation, James Q. Wilson, Harvard University, Anthony Japha, Drug Law Evaluation Project, Alfred Blumstein, Carnegie-Mellon University, and Richard Barnes, National Institute of Law Enforcement and Criminal Justice. Research support for the preparation of this report was provided by the Nancy G. and Raymond G. Feldman Fund at the University of Chicago Law School.

crime rates. Statistical tools, ranging from simple regression to complex simultaneous equations, are employed in the analysis of these data, and significant findings are frequently reported in the literature.[1]

The second approach attempts to assess the impact of changes in law enforcement on punishment policy by closely following what happens after particular policy shifts occur. Comparisons in reported crime rates are made before and after the policy change. In some studies, comparison or control areas are used to reduce the possibility that changes in the dependent variable (usually crime rates) are inaccurately attributed to the policy shift being examined. In general, the results reported in these "real change" studies have been less exciting than the estimates of deterrent effectiveness derived from some of the cross-sectional and time-series studies.[2]

This paper is a partial analysis of the products of the second approach over the period 1970-1975. Earlier studies are reported in previously published reviews (Zimring and Hawkins 1973). The period since 1970 is of special interest, because during that time, federal funds supported intervention research for the first time. A review of these 6 years is, thus, a "status report" on the investment of hundreds of millions of dollars in crime reduction programs that characterize general deterrence as a primary (though not exclusive) mechanism of crime prevention. The real-world context of these programs has produced numerous compromises in program design and research method calculated to drive the social science community at least half mad. Yet the travails of attempts to make changes in the real world are worthy of note, because any policy implications of general deterrence research depend on how policy is implemented in real-world settings. Equally important, the policy experiments I report have been the major investment in money and manpower devoted to deterrence issues over the past 6 years. For any scientific body to overlook this experience would be unthinkable.

This paper surveys the results of a series of initiatives designed to enhance general deterrent effects in particular settings. The first section of this paper analyzes four of the most important attempts to institute and measure the consequences of programs with general deterrent effects. The second section discusses some of the shortcomings of this type of research as a source of knowledge about general deterrence. The third section discusses the lessons of the studies under review for future research efforts and present policy planning. The final

[1]For a partial list of these studies, see Tullock (1974) and Tittle and Logan (1973).

[2]See for example Schwartz (1968), Ross (1973), and Zimring (1975). In Zimring (1975), there is a partial bibliography of intervention studies (note 5, p. 134).

section draws conclusions about method and substantive outcome, and the Appendix provides summaries of a number of other "legal impact" studies during the period in question. In the end, our recent experience with intervention efforts neither proves nor disproves any unitary theory of deterrence. Recent studies suggest, rather, that mixed results are an occupational hazard of policy interventions. It also appears that the political science of punishment policy, a generally neglected area, is of utmost importance in predicting the impact of policy initiatives. The final tone of this paper is equivocal—not an occasion for apology but a fact of life in research of this character; my hope is that the character of field research might soon be better understood.

I. FOUR CASE STUDIES

The assortment of policy evaluations reported here are my own nominees as the four most important of the period 1970-1975. None of these initiatives was undertaken with general deterrence as its only objective; it seems likely that no major allocation of resources will ever be devoted solely to general deterrence. One case study was a deliberate mix of public action money and private research (Kansas City). Two experiments were federally funded and evaluated by federally funded contractors—Alcohol Safety Action Programs (ASAP) and the High-Impact Anti-Crime Program. These two projects were the "big ticket" items during the decade. One intervention was initiated by then-Governor Rockefeller of New York and is being evaluated, after the fact, by a private group with federal funding. In no case can the evaluators be said to be totally disinterested in the evaluation outcome.

Each case study is meant to cover: (a) the background of the policy change, (b) methods of measurement for evaluation and (c) results of evaluation efforts to date. In each vignette, the richness of detail of the particular initiative has been sacrificed to the demands of brevity and common format.

A. TESTING PREVENTIVE PATROL: KANSAS CITY

The routine preventive patrol experiment was a product of private initiative and research funding and the cooperation of the Kansas City police department; as designed, the experiment was to test the effect on crime rates of: (a) lack of routine preventive patrol—i.e., "reactive" police beats, (b) normal routine preventive patrol levels, and (c) proactive routine patrol—i.e., preventive car patrol levels between two and three times normal level. The aim of the study was to test the efficacy of routine preventive car patrol (doubted by the designers) on crime levels and public perceptions. The research method was random assignment of police patrol areas. The assignments remained in place for 12 months after a 2-month "false start" period. Results were measured by police- and victim-reported crime rates as well as public service perceptions and some speculative inquiries about whether criminals had any perception of different area policies. Detailed records of differential clearance rates were not maintained—a potentially important uncounted deterrence variable. No significant difference in crime rate was noted, in accord with the original hypothesis.

The patrol experiment is one of few policy initiatives that have been analyzed in academic literature. Three issues emerging from the experiment of importance to this paper are the maintenance of experimental conditions, the power or sensitivity of the statistical tools, and the persuasiveness of the venture.

The "reactivity" issue has been extensively discussed in an exchange between Richard Larson and the Kansas City investigators.[3] Briefly stated, those police beats that were not subjected to "routine preventive patrol" still saw a number of police cars patrolling peripheral zones and responding to police calls. Thus, there is some doubt whether the police presence, which is the theoretical core of random preventive patrol, was sufficiently removed from the reactive beats to test the impact of withdrawal of police cars as cues for general deterrence. However, since the "proactive" segment of the study remained untainted, it appears that a doubling or trebling of routine preventive patrol from normal levels did not measurably affect crime rates.

The power issue is worthy of special mention in this context, because there is a substantial difference between stating that a policy had no measurable impact on crime rates and asserting that routine patrol intensities are unrelated to crime levels. At the theoretical level, this means simply that one cannot prove the null hypothesis in a controlled experiment. In Kansas City, the issue is more specific. Victim reports and official crime statistics were used as the dependent variables (Kelling and Pate 1974). The Kansas City results are credible, however, because the police and victim estimates are in agreement and because there are no consistent nonsignificant differences in crime rate that

[3]The dialogue on this issue between Richard Larson and the principal authors of the Kansas City Report appeared in the January 1976 issue of the *Journal of Criminal Justice*.

suggest deterrence masked by the insensitivity of the outcome measures.

Yet it is still far from true that the 1-year Kansas City experience is conclusive evidence of the lack of a preventive random patrol effect. What should have been a pilot effort, repeated in Kansas City and replicated in other settings, instead has been cited as a definitive work. And the experiment has not yet been reflected in police manpower allocations. Despite an endorsement of the experiment from the city's police chief, the "reactive" beats disappeared after the 1-year experiment. Kansas City planners have begun to search for more effective models of police patrol, but no police department has attempted to replicate or improve on the Kansas City experiment. It is almost as if the project had been relegated to the realm of intellectual history, as opposed to policy science.

B. "CRIME-ORIENTED PLANNING": THE HIGH-IMPACT ANTI-CRIME PROGRAM

A capsule description of this program is contained in the National Level Evaluation Report recently prepared by the Mitre Corporation (1976, pp. 403-404):

> The High-Impact Anti-Crime Program was inaugurated by the LEAA in January of 1972 after about 3 months of program planning. Eight American cities with serious crime problems (Atlanta, Baltimore, Cleveland, Dallas, Denver, Newark, Portland and St. Louis) had been chosen as the focus for the program whose announced goals were:
>
> - to reduce the incidence of five specific crimes (i.e., stranger-to-stranger person crime—murder, rape, assault and robbery—along with the property crime of burglary) by 5 percent in two years and by 20 percent in five years; and
> - to improve criminal justice capabilities via the demonstration of a comprehensive crime-oriented planning, implementation and evaluation process (the COPIE-cycle) . . .
>
> Under the program, $160 million (or approximately 20 million dollars per city) in LEAA discretionary funds were to be made available over a two-year period to the participating locales . . . within each Impact city, groups were either identified or created to administer the program at the local level.

The recipient cities were accorded considerable latitude in determining how to allocate the money and evaluate the consequences of elected program initiatives. The Mitre report continues (pp. 405-406):

The chief tool for the production of new knowledge was to be evaluation, a major focus of the program, intended to take place at three levels:

- at the project or city level . . .
- at the national level (examining program processes and results across the eight city programs); and
- at a global level (using LEAA/Bureau of the Census victimization surveys as a tool in the determination of overall program effects).

Somewhere between one-quarter and one-half of all High-Impact funds expended went to programs emphasizing policing strategies or increased case-prosecution efficiencies that might be expected to enhance the deterrent efficacy of the police and courts in relation to stranger-to-stranger crime.[4] A substantial proportion of High-Impact funds also went to diversion programs that might operate in the opposite direction.[5]

The evaluation of individual programs within the cities is described only in summary form in the Mitre final report. In general, these "project" evaluations were, according to the authors of the Mitre report, of poor quality. Many of the individual projects described as successful in the final report seem to be based on relatively crude evaluation strategies. Two examples may suffice (Mitre Corp. 1976, pp. 314 and 313):

1. the *Youth Recidivist Reduction project in Denver* induced a 65 percent drop in client Impact-crime re-arrests . . . compared to expected rates in the city of Denver. . . .
2. *Denver's Operation Identification* resulted in an average burglary rate for participants which was only 20 percent of the average rate experienced by non-participants.

In the first case, the claimed reductions seem to rely either on a before-and-after analysis (discounting high probabilities of regression) or on a comparison with a larger risk group whose characteristics are not described. The Operation Identification study, similarly, seems to ignore problems of noncomparability, self-selection, and regression. This seems particularly likely in view of other studies of Operation Identification that came to far less heartening conclusions.

[4]The principal investigator of the High-Impact Program National Level Evaluation estimates that slightly under half of all Impact grants went to programs that sought deterrence through greater police presence or improved police and court operations. The major share of this money was allocated to the police.

[5]Depending on one's definition of diversion, about a quarter of Impact-appropriated monies went to special service programs that could be loosely characterized as diversionary.

The Global Level Evaluation was to depend on National Crime Panel statistics on victimization; these statistics are not yet available. At present, we have only the National Level Evaluation report (Chapter 10), analyzing UCR-reported crime statistics for the eight cities. Its utility as deterrence research is constrained by a number of shortcomings in the data, although the report tells much about the process of criminal justice reform at the precinct level. No information is provided on conviction levels, sentencing patterns, arrest-to-crime ratios, or any other of the aggregated data that serve as independent variables in studies of general deterrence. The data presented on the supposed dependent variable, crime rates, does not address directly the offenses that were the target of the Impact deterrence effort: Stranger-to-stranger crime is not isolated and separately reported for any of the eight cities. Instead the aggregate crime categories of homicide, assault, rape, robbery, and burglary are reported. In addition, for all crimes other than burglary there is no evaluation strategy utilized in the presentation or analysis of the data. UCR numbers are presented graphically but no explicit method of time-series analysis or comparison is utilized. For all crimes other than burglary, there is no basis for drawing inferences about the relationship between Impact-city countermeasures and the crime rate.

For the crime of burglary, the Mitre report matched each Impact city with the mean rate experienced by six other cities that had similar trends in pre-1972 burglary patterns. It used the experience in those matched cities between 1972 and 1974 as a baseline against which to measure burglary performance in Impact cities. The published report from Mitre indicates that four of the Impact cities had levels of burglary in 1974 lower than those predicted for the six-city projection level (significance at < 0.01), while a fifth city, Denver, had a lower than expected burglary rate (significance at < 0.05). Atlanta, Portland, and St. Louis experienced no changes that were, in the aggregate, significantly different from those posited by the "sister cities" model.

The report itself indicates two important qualifications about the significance of these data. First, there are reasons to doubt that trends in UCR-reported rates of burglary reflect actual changes in crime rates (p. 366) and, second, it is questionable whether declines noted in the Impact cities can be causally attributed to the Impact programs (p. 365). In this connection, the report notes that Baltimore's sharp decline in reported burglaries was probably not attributable to the High-Impact program (p. 391).

Numerous additional questions can be raised about the validity and meaning of the burglary comparison. The Mitre final report did not list

TABLE 1 Composition of the Comparison Base for Each of the Impact Cities

ATLANTA	*DENVER*
Birmingham, Alabama	Columbus, Ohio
Long Beach, California	Memphis, Tennessee
Memphis, Tennessee	Minneapolis, Minnesota
Milwaukee, Wisconsin	Omaha, Nebraska
Richmond, Virginia	Phoenix, Arizona
Sacramento, California	Sacramento, California
BALTIMORE	*NEWARK*
Akron, Ohio	Akron, Ohio
Indianapolis, Indiana	Boston, Massachusetts
Pittsburgh, Pennsylvania	Columbus, Ohio
Richmond, Virginia	Miami, Florida
San Antonio, Texas	Minneapolis, Minnesota
Washington, D.C.	Pittsburgh, Pennsylvania
CLEVELAND	*PORTLAND*
Jacksonville, Florida	Birmingham, Alabama
Kansas City, Missouri	Indianapolis, Indiana
Louisville, Kentucky	Long Beach, California
Milwaukee, Wisconsin	Norfolk, Virginia
Pittsburgh, Pennsylvania	San Diego, California
San Diego, California	Tulsa, Oklahoma
DALLAS	*ST. LOUIS*
Indianapolis, Indiana	Indianapolis, Indiana
Long Beach, California	Kansas City, Missouri
Memphis, Tennessee	Miami, Florida
Minneapolis, Minnesota	Milwaukee, Wisconsin
Phoenix, Arizona	New Orleans, Louisiana
San Antonio, Texas	San Francisco, California

the group of matched sister cities or describe in detail the methods used to match Impact and sister cities. A background paper provided by Mitre[6] reports that each Impact city was linked to the six cities (out of 30 possibilities) that showed the most similar fluctuation in trends of monthly reported burglaries (p. 16):

> . . . (M)atches were to be based on the degree of association or correlation in the fluctuations in the monthly data over time rather than on absolute crime levels.

The sister cities are set forth in Table 1, reproduced from the background paper.

[6]Mitre Corporation, untitled draft manuscript on "Sister Cities" evaluation.

The list of cities raises some questions about the comparability of cities selected by a "black box" method that does not seek to control for absolute levels of crime.

These questions are compounded by the puzzling fact that in Baltimore, a city that experienced as sharp a decline as any other in the program, the evaluation report had doubts that the Impact city program produced the deviations from the sister city projections. If the program did not produce the deviations, what did?

The relative untrustworthiness of the UCR data proved a special problem for the Impact cities analysis. The Mitre report does not subdivide city-level crime reporting in ways that might explore the reason for variations in patterns of reported total burglary. In particular, city-wide commercial burglary levels are not separately analyzed in the cities (these are more likely to be reported to the police) and reporting practices in the Impact and control cities were not monitored and compared.

Furthermore, this multimillion-dollar evaluation of a $160-million program does not even attempt intercity comparisons using UCR data for any crime other than burglary. The report itself is silent on this topic, but its principal author produced two reasons that other crime comparisons were not attempted. First, since victim surveys were to be used as a principal tool of analysis, the collection and analysis of citywide, officially reported crime statistics were given a relatively low priority by the Mitre evaluation. Second, as a result of this low priority, sufficient resources for replicating the sister city projection were not available.[7]

One problem with this explanation is that the victim survey results cannot be used to replicate the type of sister city cross-sectional comparison because the "control" cities will not be represented in the victim survey results. Victimization surveys will provide some data on whether absolute levels of the five "target" crimes have increased or decreased, but they will operate without a basis for projection of what would have happened without the program. The irony is that the division of evaluation responsibility into "project," "national," and "global" evaluation produced a situation in which one cannot address impact on citywide crime levels. The High-Impact program evaluation cannot answer the question of whether the program had any impact at the city level!

In part, this omission is directly attributable to the unrealistic program goals that were present at the outset of the program design. If

[7]Conversation with Eleanor Chelimsky, June 1976.

there was any good reason to suppose that absolute levels of stranger-to-stranger crime would remain stable but for the program, victim survey data would provide an adequate test of the 20 percent reduction hypothesis at the end of 5 years.[8] Any less simplistic view of the determinants of city crime rates over time and the relationship between dollar investments in criminal justice and crime rates would alert the evaluators to the obvious need for other methods of measuring program impact.

C. ALCOHOL SAFETY ACTION PROGRAMS: THE LOST EXPERIMENT

In a 1968 report to Congress, the Department of Transportation (1968) nominated drinking drivers as causal agents in over half of all automobile crash fatalities in the United States. A federal initiative to demonstrate how such drivers can be controlled followed 2 years later. In 1970, eight sites—cities, counties, or states—were awarded Alcohol Safety Action Program (ASAP) grants to demonstrate how high-impact "target behavior" programs could reduce the social cost of drunk driving. The program was expanded through the early years of the 1970's, eventually to involve 35 different program sites.

The strategic ambitions of the ASAP program were more efficient apprehension of all drinking drivers and more effective differential treatment of the drivers apprehended. Drunk-driving arrests, the only measure of apprehension risk for this victimless crime, were to increase substantially.[9] Social drinkers were to be convicted and punished, either for driving under the influence of alcohol or for refusal to take breathalizer tests. Problem drinkers were to be arrested and channeled to treatment programs either though pretrial diversion or as a condition of probation after conviction. Each of the original eight sites was to have its own independent evaluation. In addition, a central evaluation group would set evaluation standards for the individual sites, determine what common measures all sites would report to the central authority, and provide a national-level evaluation (U.S. Department of Transportation 1974).

[8]As of this writing, the 1978 Victim Survey, originally designed to test this hypothesis, has apparently been cancelled.

[9]The appropriate measure for the risk of apprehension for drunk driving is the ratio of the number of arrests to the number of offenses committed. No good measures are available for the actual incidence of drunk driving offenses. However, as long as the base rate of offenses does not fluctuate substantially over the period of interest, the gross arrest rate is the best proxy measure of apprehension risk.

The ASAP program evaluation was not complete at the time of this writing. A final report was expected sometime late in 1976. But a series of interim reports by the Department of Transportation provides insight into the program, as well as data of value to students of general deterrence.[10]

The High-Impact initiative that followed within 2 years parallels the ASAP program extraordinarily. Both programs attempted to concentrate resources on specific target behaviors in a relatively small number of locations. In each case, eight sites were selected for the initial intervention and evaluation. ASAP evaluations, like High Impact, were divided into local and aggregate national efforts. ASAP site-selection strategy was, if anything, more obscure than that of the High-Impact program. The original grantees included four cities, one "twin city" site, two counties, and the state of Wisconsin. Neither project selected comparison or control areas at the time of site determination. In each case, a "before and after" comparison was to be the principal method of analysis. The coincidental emphasis and structure of ASAP and High Impact were just that—the earlier ASAP experience did not feed into the design or evaluation of the later LEAA program. Yet by the time the LEAA experiment was being designed, the Alcohol Safety Action Program was already experiencing difficulties related to initial site selection and a lack of comparison areas. With appropriate communication and comprehension between projects, LEAA's assault on stranger-to-stranger crime could have been significantly improved.

Ignorance of the Alcohol Safety Action Program is not confined to agencies of the federal government. While criticisms of and references to the ASAP project appear in the traffic safety literature, they are not found in the social science literature relating to general deterrence. This is regrettable because, unlike the High-Impact report, a large quantity of interesting data has been generated by the ASAP exercise. If properly audited and analyzed, these data are among the best available for assessing the impact of attempts to manipulate general deterrence variables. The special values of the ASAP data include: (a) relatively rich information on changes that occurred in the law enforcement and criminal justice system, (b) apparent, substantial changes in the risk of apprehension, and (c) the existence and use of outcome measures, such as variation in nighttime versus daytime fatal accidents, that provide accurate if insensitive indices of variations in drunk driving (independent of the vagaries of police offense reporting).

[10]The 1974 report (U.S. Department of Transportation 1974) is one of the most comprehensive of these interim reports. The earlier large report was published in 1972 as DOT-HS-800 874. The final evaluation report is due in the summer of 1976.

Table 2, from volume 3 of the 1974 report, summarizes data collected from the ASAP programs on arrests and criminal justice system outcomes in the 24 projects operating during 1972-1973.

These figures, and the raw data that lie behind them, provide more information on the impact of the program on arrests and court processing than is available in aggregate form from the entire national level evaluation of the High-Impact Anti-Crime Program. If the numbers can be validated, they show large variations in alcohol-related arrests and different patterns of adaptation to these arrest increases by the other constituent parts of the criminal justice system.

If these figures are accurate, there is a second special value to the ASAP data: large and differential increases in the risk of apprehension for driving under the influence of alcohol occur during the experiment. If the data are to be accepted at face value, alcohol-related arrests increased in all but one ASAP site, by as much as a factor of 44 and to a median value 2.5 times the number of arrests noted before the program began.

Fluctuations in the arrest rate are the best measure of apprehension risk available. With increases as large as those noted in the ASAP report over short periods of time, the arrest rate indicates the change in relative risk even though it does not provide an absolute level of risk for either the treatment or control period. We thus appear to have information on an experimental countermeasure that doubled or trebled the risk of being apprehended for a specific criminal offense—a nearly unique opportunity for the study of general deterrence outcome.

It is not surprising that these conditions occur for drunk driving, a victimless offense in which the degree of police emphasis and proactivity can produce more dramatic changes in arrest risk than in more serious crimes in which apprehension risks are higher and the role of police policy less significant. But apprehension policy is not the only reason an increase in alcohol-related arrests can occur: Changes in the way in which police choose to treat offenders may also have a significant impact on law enforcement statistics. For example, the 44-fold increase in alcohol-related arrests that occurred in Fairfax County, Virginia, is not only an extraordinary year-to-year change in its own right but also a significant deviation from the general ASAP pattern, which clusters between a doubling and a trebling of arrests. Does this mean that only 85 drinking drivers had been arrested in the year prior to the countermeasure or that a substantially greater number of drinking drivers were arrested for nonalcohol-related traffic charges? The latter interpretation must account for a substantial share of Fairfax County's unique performance. It is likely that a similar shift in strategy

TABLE 2 Evaluation of the Judicial and Legislative Countermeasure Activities: Summary of ASAP Impact, 1972-1973.

ASAP	Increase in Alcohol-related Arrests	Alcohol-related Arrests	Change Convictions	Change Reduced Charges	Court Processed	Change Dismissed	Change Acquitted	Receiving Presentence Investigation	Entering Rehabilitation	Processing Time Change	Change Backlog
	Percent	Number				Percent				Days	Percent
Albuquerque	242	3,686	7	−44	66	85	14	66	52	—	54
Charlotte	111	4,362	−23	−18	45	−25	−66	22	21	—	637
Denver	145	6,423	49	264	68	70	−53	32	22	−9	2
Vermont	152	1,213	38	−13	71	80	200	66	71	1	—
Baltimore	80	4,550	13	137	27	59	20	27	6	—	58
Boston	95	1,462	—	—	64	—	—	49	64	—	—
Cincinnati	692	3,642	48	15	50	11	56	50	30	—	124
Columbus, Ga.	136	3,460	−2	—	30	104	0	4	30	—	.27
Fairfax County, Va.	4,436	3,777	186	1,169	100	210	829	77	100	−16	120

Hennepin County, Minn.	117	7,393	29	165	91	−5	−27	91	42	0	100
Indianapolis	254	5,075	99	−34	40	29	10	40	31	15	127
Kansas City	125	5,547	−2	84	88	172	28	46	88	4	2
Lincoln	333	1,625	275	336	46	90	100	38	46	—	−37
Tampa	466	8,034	—	—	36	—	—	11	36	1	—
New Hampshire	173	7,703	61	—	12	95	137	12	7	−10	77
New Orleans	197	4,518	−9	102	24	−57	3	24	20	20	−17
Oklahoma City	0	4,887	138	24	32	338	226	32	31	10	50
Phoenix	32	8,871	−36	737	100	433	190	100	61	−4	2
Portland, Me.	71	2,377	−33	104	34	3	−57	24	34	—	151
Pulaski County, Ark.	519	5,963	4	29	93	0	58	93	18	−7	−90
Richland County, S.C.	95	2,634	−27	96	32	126	−58	32	29	2	21
San Antonio	348	5,061	32	100	34	14	0	20	34	0	−38
South Dakota	90	3,175	−13	80	63	77	−44	63	33	—	—
Wichita	135	1,412	—	—	43	—	—	43	42	—	−24

accounts for some of the noted increase in almost all the project areas. Thus, while the specific risk of apprehension for an alcohol-related offense may have increased dramatically, the aggregate traffic offense arrest risk facing the drinking driver probably increased less substantially. However, since an alcohol-related offense is more serious and the perceived risk of arrest for such an offense is a more specific communication about drunk driving, the ASAP arrest statistics are still among the more dramatic instances of deliberately induced change in apprehension risk that a student of intervention programs is likely to confront.

The third special value of the ASAP data is the existence of traffic fatality patterns as an independent measure of whether variations in traffic fatalities can be tied plausibly to changes in policy toward drinking drivers. Scientific knowledge about the relationship between alcohol and different patterns of accident behavior is more substantial than existing knowledge about the determinants of other crime rates. Those involved in fatal crashes have much higher concentrations of alcohol in the blood than do drivers not involved in such crashes. Nighttime fatal accident victims are far more likely to have high blood-alcohol counts than are daytime fatal-crash victims. Victims of fatal accidents involving collisions with fixed objects are more likely to have relatively high blood-alcohol concentrations. Because these findings were relatively well established in the scientific literature on drinking-and-driving, a variety of different measures of the impact of the ASAP program on drunk driving were theoretically available: Information about the time and circumstances of fatal crashes provides the ultimate "victim survey."

Of course, if reliable data on blood-alcohol concentration were available for all drivers involved in fatal crashes before and after ASAP, they would provide a specific and fairly sensitive test of the impact of the countermeasure on the highest risk form of drunk driving. Unfortunately, blood-alcohol concentration data are available for only a small and shifting sample of fatal-accident victims, and the Department of Transportation lacked both the time and the will to impose reliable baseline blood-alcohol concentration data as a precondition for award of an ASAP grant. Lacking data on blood-alcohol concentrations, the primary before-and-after standard by which program success was judged was a comparison of trends in nighttime versus daytime fatal accidents. The hypothesis was that any alcohol-specific countermeasure would have a more dramatic impact on nighttime than on daytime fatalities. The 1974 report dichotomizes accidents into night and day periods, and then attempts a before-and-after analysis at both the individual project and aggregate levels. The aggregated data show a general trend toward a lower proportion of total fatalities occurring at night, but this trend is statistically significant (< 0.05) only for the eight original ASAP projects, considered together, that had 2 years of program exposure (U.S. Department of Transportation 1974, Johnson *et al.* 1976). Critics of the report have asserted that the shift toward a smaller proportion of night fatalities was widespread and thus not plausibly attributable to ASAP (Zador 1976). A second criticism raised against the 1974 interim findings involved the lack of comparison areas to control for temporal changes in accident behavior. Using control areas selected after the fact, the critique of the 1974 report finds no significant decreases in total fatalities (Zador 1976); the reliability of that finding has been challenged by the authors of the 1974 report, principally because the tests used were insensitive (Johnson *et al.* 1976).

Whatever the ultimate verdict on the probable impact of ASAP on traffic fatalities, there are three intermediate lessons from the ASAP worth diligent attention. The first is the difficulty of measuring the magnitude of savings generated by general deterrence. Relatively small variations in the death rate attributable to drunk driving can have substantial social value. But the statistical problems associated with measuring those benefits are considerable, particularly when emphasis is placed on before-and-after analysis. This is true even in an area in which the scientific justification for using proxy data is more substantial than for other crimes.

A second lesson concerns the implications of ASAP as a "lost experiment," a program invisible to the social science community concerned with deterrence. Whatever social scientists could learn from ASAP about deterrence has not yet been learned. At the same time much data relevant to general deterrence has not yet been suitably analyzed. For example, Table 2 provides specific data on variations in alcohol-related arrests, convictions, and other outcomes for most of the operating ASAP projects. Despite the absence of comparable data from comparison areas, it is still possible to test some deterrence hypotheses by attempting to correlate, within the sample of projects, changes in a deterrence variable (such as arrest risk) with changes in the variables that are supposed to reflect variations in drunk driving. As a sample of this kind of approach, I chose to take percentage of change in alcohol-related arrests as an indicator of change in risk of apprehension for drunk driving and to take the percentage change in nighttime fatalities minus the percentage change in daytime fatalities as a measure of impact on drunk driving. The relationship between the two values when tested against the twenty-one "second phase" ASAP programs reported in Table 16 was a nonsignificant −.22.[11] It is quite possible that the regression of other risk variables against fatality results would yield stronger relationships. ASAP represents an important opportunity for the deterrence research community (drunk driving is one of the few offenses with a good measure of the independent variable), and the ASAP research could have been aided considerably by the contributions of that research community (e.g., in better formulation of the sanction measure, in establishing more rigorous controls). The failure of the research community to find ASAP, and of ASAP to find the research community, is a lamentable lacuna in a balanced agenda of research in deterrence.

One final lesson of the ASAP experience must be mentioned. The 1976 report on the ASAP program is going to have great difficulty teasing out the ASAP countermeasure effects for the periods after September 1973, because the energy crisis produced an unprecedented massive decline in traffic fatalities. This is important technically as a classic example of why comparison areas must be added to the temporal analyses.[12] For the policy scientist, there is an even more substantial lesson: strict enforcement of drinking-driving laws seems to have had far less impact on fatalities than the combination of high energy prices, the 55 mph speed limit, and federally required auto-safety engineering. The speed limit is a fairly well-documented lifesaver. There is little serious dispute that the national 55 mph limit saved lives where enforced, but there is some debate about the magnitude of the effect.[13]

[11]The measure for effectiveness that I used was to subtract fluctuations in daytime fatalities from fluctuations in nighttime fatalities for each of the projects on which relative arrest performance was available. If daytime fatalities decrease 15 percent and nighttime fatalities decrease 5 percent, the alcohol-specific value would be plus 10; if daytime fatalities increase 20 percent and nighttime fatalities only 10 percent, a negative 10 score would be achieved. Under this accounting scheme, an inverse correlation between percentage increase in arrests and the outcome variable is supportive of differential deterrence.

[12]Compare Zador (1976) with Johnson *et al.* (1976).

[13]See U.S. Department of Transportation (1975) and Campbell *et al.* (1976). Enforcing the speed limit deters because speeding is visible behavior. Potential speeders "learn" quickly in highway traffic from visible enforcement cues (police cars) and from the speed of other drivers. If the connection between alcohol and crash fatalities is as substantial as we now believe, lives may have been saved because drinking drivers were driving slower. Hard data on this precise topic are not yet available. It would be a fascinating study in comparative deterrence.

D. DETERRING HARD DRUG SALES: THE "ROCKEFELLER DRUG LAW" EVALUATION

Criminal sentencing was not a priority concern of the three policy initiatives previously discussed. By contrast, the package of legal changes introduced in New York in 1973 focused on stiff criminal sentences as the central mechanism to "deter the pusher and the violent addict and isolate for life those who will not be deterred."[14] The new legislation established three "A felony" offenses involving the sale or possession of narcotics and provided that each class-A felony would carry a maximum term of life, with minimum terms of 15 years (A-I), 6 years (A-II), and 1 year (A-III) in prison, to be followed by lifetime parole supervision after prison release. The legislation prohibited the reduction of any initial class-A felony charge below the A-III level, thus creating a mandatory sentence of from 1 year to life for convicted class-A felons.

A study group, proposed by The Association of the Bar of the City of New York and funded by the federal government, is in the process of evaluating the impact of the new laws on the criminal justice system, narcotics usage, and crime. Preliminary data from the project, while far from definitive in tracing the impact of the law, provides some insight into the difficulty of instituting change and of evaluating the consequences of that change in urban court systems and big city streets.

The heroin issue is an emotionally charged symbol of America's war on crime. Not all participants would agree that the need to evaluate the 1973 drug laws is apparent. On September 7, 1973, 6 days after the law went into effect, Governor Nelson Rockefeller was quoted as saying, "Heroin seems to be disappearing, drying up in the city."[15] Data developed by the bar association study group render that conclusion premature. The study group divided its efforts to assess the impact of the 1973 laws between New York City and the rest of the state, and it is using both before-and-after and intercity comparison data in its preliminary work. Efforts were made to assess the impact on the criminal justice system, on drug abuse, and on other major crimes.

With respect to the criminal justice system, the study has documented an increased number of prosecutions for serious drug felonies

[14]Governor Nelson Rockefeller, quoted in the *New York Times,* January 26, 1973, p. 1, col. 4.

[15]Governor Nelson Rockefeller, quoted in the *New York Times,* September 8, 1973, p. 17, col. 5.

in New York state outside New York City.[16] Drug arrests stayed stable in New York City, but there was an increased backlog in case dispositions, principally class-A drug felonies. The significance of the backlog is a matter of debate. For those who believe that criminal sentences after conviction must swiftly follow arrest, the noted delays can be seen as anti-deterrent. However, accused class-A felons might disagree, depending on whether they are awaiting trial in jail or on the street. Other than showing increased delay, the impact of the 1973 laws on the criminal justice system is a study in apparent irony. The laws were intended to increase rates of imprisonment and the length of prison sentences given to class-A defendants. Imprisonment rates for drug charges within the city of New York have not increased, if only because the backlog of cases has postponed class-A felony commitments to the adult correctional system past the period of available documentation. The rate of jail incarceration has, most probably, increased. And what about sentence severity? The effect of the provision that allows class-A felonies to be bargained down to the A-III level but no further is to postpone for years any decision about the impact of the laws on severity of sentences actually served. If the A-III felony becomes a primary mechanism for disposition in New York City's criminal courts, it will result in the class-A felony defendants being given a sentence that amounts to an indeterminate term from 1 year to life and makes the actual length of sentence dependent on the performance of the parole board.[17] The final irony, although politically appropriate, is that outside New York City, where the problem is less substantial, the response of the justice system has been more immediate and much more in the predicted direction. Disposition times are not increasing, sentencing is tougher, and the problem is more appropriately addressed (in terms of the legislation) precisely where the problem is less substantial.

Quite apart from the issues of certainty and severity of sanctions, which will not be successfully addressed for years, the bar association study has been examining some indicators of drug abuse, again independent of criminal justice system statistics, that might reflect on the

[16]The principal documentation available in July 1976 on the Drug Law Evaluation Project are internal documents dated January 1975, September 1975, and February 1976. Complete annual data were available only through the end of 1974 on the basis of these documents.

[17]One year is the shortest minimum sentence that a judge can give for an A-III felony. Preliminary data from the project suggest that it is also the modal sentence given in approximately two in every three A-III convictions in New York City in 1974. Project staff indicate that preliminary data confirm that the majority of class-A convictions documented to date are for the A-III offense. (The 1973 laws were amended in mid-1976 to allow further plea bargaining for A felonies.)

immediate general deterrent impact of the announced "get tough" policy. Admissions to methadone maintenance programs and the "youth share" of methadone maintenance admissions decreased in the period just before the effective date of the new law and increased modestly for one quarter after the law went into effect. The soft soundings available on heroin prices in New York City and other comparison markets suggests fluctuations independent of the impact of the law. Reported morphine overdose deaths, a theoretically promising but practically imprecise indicator, show a continuing decline that began in 1972.[18]

The inclusion of comparison sites, no matter how rough the comparison, is a vital element of the drug law evaluation. While this phase of the project is still in its infancy, Washington, D.C., has emerged as the principal drug abuse control city. To date, the two cities seem to have experienced similar patterns in methadone program enrollment and narcotic prices. A narcotic death comparison is forthcoming. Whether the 1973 legal changes will have any eventual effect, due to incarceration, special deterrence, or general deterrent impact, is unknown. Quick and measurable impact in New York City, the main arena of hard drug abuse in the United States, appears not to have been achieved.

If the search for impact on drug abuse has proved elusive, the analysis of general crime patterns promised by the initial evaluation will be even more of a problem. New York City and the rest of the state have experienced significant changes in criminality over the period since the effective date of the new laws, but the substantial changes experienced in the city and state have been paralleled throughout the country. The impact of the drug legislation or predicate felony provisions of the 1973 laws, while possibly present, has been overwhelmed by the larger forces that condition crime rates in the city, state, and nation. There will be no firm conclusion to reach other than that patterns in nondrug-felony crime cannot confidently be attributed to the 1973 legislation.

One may question the educational value of an exercise that in its early stages is so inconclusive, yet there are lessons here worth serious attention. First, in the context of the New York City criminal courts, the study of the 1973 Rockefeller legislation shows the resiliency of city criminal courts under the most sustained and sophisticated attack on business-as-usual in the last two decades. The drug legislation was a clear mandate for change—and some change occurred. But the net effect of court delay and other adaptive responses was to postpone, if not nullify, the basic thrust of the 1973 legislation.

[18]September 1975 staff report (see note 16).

Second, the legislation stands as an example of the "failure guarantee" in public policy toward crime. No matter what the eventual effects of the legislation, no politically possible penal regime is going to dry up the supply of drugs in New York City in a 6-day period. To expect or advertise a policy on such grounds is unwise as long as anybody is keeping score. A corollary proposition is that if no one is keeping score, it is always possible for political actors to declare the war won and withdraw the troops. In the case of the Rockefeller plan, the war is not won, the troops have not been withdrawn, but the law has been amended to allow greater flexibility in plea bargaining. Whether the legislation will have measurable policy consequences on crime rates and narcotics abuse is a question on which the jury is still out.

The jury did not expect to be out so long. The federally funded evaluation of the Rockefeller plan initiative is now entering the second of two scheduled phases of federal funding. It will be years before the impact of the 1973 legislation on sentence severity within New York City is known with any precision. I have the impression that more forthright results were expected much earlier in this particular episode of federally sponsored evaluation of changes in state penal policy. It takes at least 5 years of experience with a serious change in legal policy to evaluate the consequences of that change. In the present state of action research, one wonders whether any agency of government is ready to accommodate that kind of 5-year plan.

II. LIMITS TO KNOWLEDGE FROM INTERVENTION EXPERIMENTS

No study of intervention in crime control can reproduce the elegance or reliability of an easily replicated random assignment experiment. This section discusses some limits of the studies under examination, beginning with a number of problems chronic to field studies in crime control and proceeding, in the second half, to a catalogue of avoidable errors observed in the four vignettes in Section I and in other notable field efforts during the period.

A. INHERENT PROBLEMS

The major inherent limitations of the field study in crime control organize around the headings of measurability, sensitivity, absence of theory, specificity of findings, and the marginal nature of politically possible shifts in independent variables. A final constraint, the ethical problem of experiments in punishment policy, is separately discussed because, whatever its potential moral significance, it was of no practical importance during the period under study.

1. Problems of Measurement

Field studies that use crime rates as a dependent variable must depend on crime reported to and by the police and on victimization studies, or both, to estimate actual levels of victimization before and after a countermeasure is introduced or between test and comparison areas. The fallibility of official crime statistics has been recited often and need not be spelled out in this paper in any great detail. Particularly worthy of note, however, is the fact that policy experiments that give the police an incentive to change officially reported levels of crime may constitute a special problem of measurement. This is one possible explanation of the reduction of burglary noted in five of the eight High-Impact cities—a reduction that cannot, in the case of Baltimore, plausibly be associated with the Impact initiatives. On the other hand, a review of the High-Impact cities' performance with respect to robbery and of the three "deviant case" cities in burglary performance suggests that whatever theoretical incentive existed for the police to achieve crime control success by judicious use of the eraser was neither widespread nor apparent in the High-Impact study. In Kansas City, where the official hypothesis (though perhaps not police sympathies) moves in the direction of no significant change between the proactive, reactive, and controlled sites, there is no evidence of any major change in the relationship of crimes reported by the police. Some variation in police reporting is noted in the ASAP report, but in that study, the choice of measures (such as fatal crashes) that are independent of police discretion neutralizes this threat to experimental validity.

In theory, victim surveys represent the ideal answer to the notable imperfections in police-reported criminality. In practice, however, the victim survey device is also imperfect. Victim survey reports of certain crimes—aggravated assault is the principal example—seem to be inferior to police reports of the same episodes. For other crime categories, such as commercial burglary, victim survey estimates are accurate, but there is usually little reason to doubt the accuracy of parallel police statistics. Some crime categories, such as robbery among adults, present situations in which the victim survey statistics may be superior to those reported by the police.

Victimization surveys also present problems not encountered with police statistics. To begin with, as shown in Kansas City, any random assignment experiment that depends on victimization surveys will depend on relatively small samples in which relatively large fluctuations of crime rate cannot statistically be attributed to the countermeasure or confidently dismissed as chance variation. In the Kansas City patrol experiment, the fact that victimization and official crime statistics tended in the same direction and that among the nonsignificant findings there were no trends divergent from the hypothesis that animated the study provides some comfort to the researchers. But the sample-size problem is a substantial one. The High-Impact program, with huge victim sample groups, illustrates a second and related problem. In such a case, the victim survey is so expensive that while it can be performed in a test city, the natural tendency is not to perform parallel efforts in control or quasi-control areas. While there is no theoretical obstacle to test- and control-area victim surveys before and after an intervention, the considerable cost that large-scale surveys entail will diminish the importance of this tool in practice.

Finally, with respect to victim surveys, a common basis of interpretation is necessary because of the "pyramid phenomenon": the tendency for the largest number of reported acts in any crime category to cluster toward the low end of the seriousness scale. This problem is the undoing of victimization surveys of aggravated assault.[19] The problem is acute in all victim survey studies of index crimes.

2. *The Problem of Statistical Power*

The problem of power is closely associated with the sample-size problems encountered in victim surveys and with the high degree of variability and unpredictability of police statistics. The macrophenomena that determine crime in American cities are not well understood but produce considerable variance. In the natural course of events, crime statistics will vary widely between areas and over time. In victim surveys, these phenomena and the considerable estimation errors that are produced by relatively small samples of crime victims interact to produce circumstances in which it is difficult to confidently predict that apparent variations in crime rates over time are not statistical artifacts.

[19]The correlation between victim survey and police-reported aggravated assault has been noted in the Urban Institute study as being significant but negative. In the pilot victimization survey, victimization rates for whites are reported as exceeding those for blacks; this is particularly the case for younger age-groups, for whom official statistics on aggravated assault, shootings, and homicides all point sharply in a different direction. Part of the problem may be sample selection. But the threshold for criminal victimization is an important issue when one person's fist-fight is another's aggravated assault.

The practical problem is best captured in a metaphor that envisions the crime rate much like a set of unpredictable tidal motions. Natural forces related to demography, unemployment, temporal change, police reporting, fluctuations in the national economy, or some combination of all these features, are constantly occurring. Punishment policy changes are a small part of the tidal system. Given the substantial problems of measurement mentioned above, it is very difficult over time or between areas to isolate and measure the effects of punishment policy. Perhaps the best recent example of this phenomenon is H. Lawrence Ross's attempt to isolate what is peculiarly Scandinavian about drinking-driver policies and to discern by interrupted time-series study whether particular and partial discrete changes in Swedish criminal justice policy toward the drinking driver measurably reduced the rate of traffic fatalities (Ross 1975). There is little reason to question Ross's basic conclusion: No single policy observed produced a statistically significant measurable decrease in fatalities. Yet the peculiar set of circumstances that led to Sweden's drunk-driving policies did not occur in any single discrete period. The observer is left wondering whether Ross has not studied a series of small increments and whether the negative conclusion of Ross's research is more attributable to the marginal nature of the changes he studied, compounded by the problems of measurement we are now discussing, rather than to any conspicuous failure of social policy.

3. *The Marginality of Change*

The Ross study, as well as the vignettes discussed earlier, highlight the relationship between problems of measuring the significance of changes in crime as a dependent variable and the marginality of the shifts in detection and punishment policy that field experiments can produce. In Kansas City, relatively small areas were subjected to relatively important differences in patrol policy; the serious problem is one of the power of the experiment thus designed. In citywide or national deterrence programs, the problem of inference from experiments occurs because changes in the independent variable at the community level are relatively marginal. One faces a choice between dramatic fluctuations in the independent variable in settings in which the dependent variable may not be easily measured and widespread changes in the apprehension or punishment policy that may not be great enough to produce substantial changes. Even in Kansas City, it is an open question whether the potential criminals who were the target group of preventive patrol were aware that a change was in progress. For the eight Impact cities, even though increments in law enforcement expenditures between one-quarter and one-half of total 1970 criminal justice budgets were introduced in some cities, it is by no means clear that the changes induced were all that palpable once the system had digested them and reallocated manpower and budget.

Barring major change, and with the exception of relatively small-scale experiments, the scholar's ability to influence the deployment of criminal justice system resources is limited. Given these limits, changes in field conditions will tend to be small relative to the total pattern of law enforcement and adjudication. Given the problems of measurement mentioned above, results will be difficult to discern.

4. The Theory Gap

From subatomic physics through social psychology, the capacity of any experimental science to generalize from experimental experience to broader propositions depends on the amount and quality of general knowledge into which a particular experimental finding can be set. For deterrence research, this is particularly bad news. Unless one accepts the analogies of positive economics or the easy insights of armchair theory, our present knowledge of deterrence is singularly bereft of a general theoretical structure with which to incorporate and organize particular experimental findings. While the range of analogies to problems of deterrence is both wide and inviting, the number of established crime-specific theoretical propositions is discouragingly small. Whatever we learn about preventive car patrol in Kansas City does not fit neatly into a grid of other findings that lead to easy generalization. Kansas City may be different from other cities. Car patrol may be different from foot patrol. The relationship between car patrol variations and what other social scientists call the perceived certainty of punishment is obscure. The essential lesson of what I choose to call the theory gap is that knowledge about the efficacy of particular deterrent countermeasures will come in relatively small packages. This is not an argument against experimentation, particularly field experimentation. Rather, the conditions that lead to the necessity for such experimentation also limit our capacity to generalize from particular experimental findings to global theory. This condition is shared with much of social science. It is no less discouraging, or no less worthy of note, because of its own generality.

5. *The Morality of Experiment*

One problem not encountered in the 6 years of policy experimentation reviewed in this paper is the morality of experimental upward shifts in punishment policy. Most policy experiments are aimed at increasing apprehension risks or otherwise preventing criminal activities. Many of these—notably the High-Impact and Alcohol Safety Action programs—seek to balance increases in detection rates with diversionary programs designed to reduce the number of accused defenders subject to the full brunt of criminal sanction after conviction. The 1973 drug laws in New York are a notable exception. Yet there are few ethical problems in evaluating the 1973 changes, if only because the evaluators had little impact on fashioning the policy.

If rhetoric is any reflection of reality, we may be entering a new era, one in which the deterrence scholar becomes an advocate for more rigorous penal policy. When academics involve themselves in advocacy for "testing up" in penal sanctions, there are ethical problems to consider. To the extent that the magnitude of deterrent effects remains unknown, any argument for upward shifts in penal sanctions based on deterrence principles runs substantial ethical risk. The academic's role in creating such changes, rather than the changes themselves, are the focus of the discussion. The advocate of "getting tough to see what happens" is in much a similar position to the "radical noninterventionist": He is testing his theories in an environment where discernible social harm may outweigh the gains obtained.

The ethical problems with academic advocacy are compounded by what I consider to be the rather thin data base that exists in general deterrence arguments. While it is possible to argue to policy conclusions from existing macro-statistical studies, it appears that the exercise requires a fair measure of faith to accompany the present array of empirical evidence. The less reliable the data base, the greater the ethical risk through academic interventionism. In the operation of this panel, as in other interfaces between government and science, there are ethical as well as technical considerations of significance.

B. AVOIDABLE MISTAKES IN POLICY EXPERIMENTATION

There are a number of inherent limitations to the power of policy experiments in field settings. Very few of the efforts reviewed in this paper test those limits. In the majority of studies, avoidable mistakes outnumber and outweigh the unavoidable problems that confront experimentation in real-world situations.

First on any list of avoidable mistakes must be the poor site selection and evaluation design that have particularly characterized federally funded initiatives. The ASAP and High-Impact programs selected test sites using methods that can most charitably be characterized as unprincipled. Each initiative began with the assumption that before-and-after analysis without quasi-control site selection would be an adequate evaluation tool. In each case, that assumption was indefensible at the outset and quickly proved untrue. By the time the need for comparison areas became apparent, it was too late for such areas to be selected economically or by methods consistent with retaining confidence in the integrity of the evaluation. Comparison areas should be selected at the same time that test areas are chosen.

Equally widespread and equally lamentable is the crudeness, or in some cases absence, of reliable baseline data measurements. In three of the four principal studies reviewed here, the collection of baseline data occurred after the experiment had begun. It was thus too late to improve the quality of those data. For studies like ASAP and High Impact that depend on temporal comparison, the absence of meaningful "before" information is difficult to defend.

Also apparent was the lack of explicit theoretical models upon which major deterrence initiatives were based. The High-Impact program was based on the principle of "crime-specific planning." This is essentially an hypothesis about what will occur in a given city, but the program planners had no specific hypotheses about how the hypothesized change would occur. Crime rates were to be reduced by 20 percent, never mind how. Deterrence and diversion would be married into a model of optimal crime prevention; nobody ever bothered to design the model. The 1973 New York drug laws were designed to deter the pusher, but designed in a way that provided the same minimum penalty for the plea-bargaining pusher of large quantities of narcotics and for the semi-casual user. Immediate deterrence was the goal of the 1973 legislation; the principal vehicle for that deterrence was indeterminate sentences, neither fashionable at the time nor necessarily the best hope of a general deterrence policy built around sentence severity. The Kansas City experiment was designed around a theoretical hypothesis—the null hypothesis. Thus, while many of the econometric studies of the period may be faulted for being overly and unrealistically theoretically motivated, the absence of theory in field experimentation is equally discouraging.

It also appears that the major initiatives of the past 6 years compensated for their lack of theory with too much action. The ASAP had expanded to 35 sites at a cost of $78 million before the original eight projects had been evaluated. High Impact made huge investments in each of the eight cities when it was not obvious that the multiplicity of sites served any important scientific purpose. Indeed, multiple sites seem to have been used as an alternative to replication, guaranteeing that the lessons of earlier efforts could not be applied in later attempts.

If the policy experiments have been generous with money and experimental sites, they have been stingy with time, particularly time for evaluation. The Kansas City preventive patrol experiment disappeared at the stroke of 12 months. The ultimate test of the High-Impact program was to be a victim survey conducted in 1978—now canceled. One has to believe that time constraints are one principal reason no intercity comparisons were available for four of the five "stranger-to-stranger crimes," which were the major concern to the persons designing High Impact. The national-level evaluation had to be completed before the first post-program victimization surveys were available for preliminary analysis. The ASAPs have made a career of interim reports, each prepared under a hectic deadline.

In part, the governmental attitude that time is of the essence may reflect naive conceptions of the impact of legal threats on crime rates. If all one needs to reduce hard-core drug traffic in New York is to advertise, the research schedule for the bar association study was appropriate. If real changes in sentencing policy are the mechanism of change, the evaluation exercise must be as long and as slow as the schedule of expected effects.

Short time allocation for evaluation is not peculiar to general deterrence research. In the newer, action-oriented agencies of the federal government, research is an enterprise that is measured in fiscal years. When serious scholars confront the governmental consumers of evaluative research, the scholars give way, one of the more lamentable examples of consumer sovereignty in the last third of this century. Many academics refuse to get involved, an example of Gresham's Law that also does not bode well for the quality of federal evaluation exercises.

Unrealistic time dimensions are but one example of the manifold costs of the absence of truly independent evaluation of major policy countermeasures. By the time the government has spent so many millions of dollars in eight sites investing in "cost-effective" results and has let a contract to a research group to establish these results, truly independent evaluation is difficult. If the program was not a success under one set of measures, other measures should be tried. If the program was unsuccessful, what about the "concept"? (See for example Murray and Krug 1975.)

Consider the career of the Insurance Institute for Highway Safety, which has found failure in every driver-centered penalty-oriented traffic safety countermeasure it has evaluated.[20] Perhaps biases will be canceled out in the free marketplace of ideas that will characterize deterrence research in the latter half of this decade. It is hard to believe that such pre-investment will not prove a costly constraint on rigorous theory-building.

Of equal concern is the fact that policy experiments seem to be run in the style of single-elimination sports tournaments. Be it eight sites or one, the operating rule seems to be "one strike and you're out." The deliberate experiment in Kansas City has not been continued in that city or replicated anywhere else. The High-Impact concept seems to have joined the Smith Brothers and Tony the Tiger in the Advertising Hall of Fame, along with such LEAA temporary favorites as the Year-of-the-Victim. At this point, it is unclear how long the Drug Law Evaluation will continue under federal funding. A tradition of nonreplication, like the unrealistic time constraints placed on research, represents a gap between popular expectations and the requirements of social science. The popular and governmental expectation is that a policy either works or it does not, with the litmus test applicable relatively early in the policy change. Social science is slower and more qualified. In an important sense, it is not relevant to the demands of policymakers or policy consumers.

A number of subsidiary deficiencies are associated with the structure and assumptions of the policy experiments. One recurrent theme of the research vignettes in Section I is the failure of evaluators to measure data that would be considered critical by students of general deterrence. The High-Impact Anti-Crime Program did not even attempt to assess the sentencing behavior of criminal courts for stranger-to-stranger crime, probably a symptom of the weak involvement of most of these policy initiatives with the court systems that dispense punishment policy on a retail basis. Clearance and arrest rates were also notably absent from the High-Impact and Kansas City evaluations.

[20]The Institute sponsored in house the Zador (1976) research and the Robertson *et al.* paper reported on in the appendix. Both studies translate the lack of a statistically significant total fatality effect into conclusions that the policy was a failure. The Ross studies reported in the appendix, funded in part by the Institute, take a different approach, particularly in "Law, Science and Accidents" and the conclusion of "The Scandinavian Myth" (which partially backs off from the title). It is interesting to compare the methodology used by Robertson *et al.* and Zador (total fatalities) with that used by Williams *et al.* (see Appendix) in assessing the impact of changes in the minimun drinking age (proportion of drivers under 21 in nighttime fatal crashes).

Much of this data was presented in the ASAP interim reports, but it was not appropriately analyzed.

Lack of measurement should not be viewed as a sequence of isolated episodes but rather as a chronic pattern. There is a tendency for goal-oriented policy research to measure only the dependent variable while ignoring or downplaying the importance of measuring independent and mediating variables that may be crucial to the general deterrent impact of the reform.[21]

At a broader level, we face a communication gap of substantial proportions between interested parties in academia and government. The academic community by and large does not read governmentally sponsored research. When such reports are read, it is with the belief that the research is shoddy and such efforts have little to teach the academic empiricist. The government proceeds on its own course, occasionally co-opting academics on advisory committees but rarely taking the advice of social scientists with any degree of seriousness. Beyond their different interests and constituencies, it is fair to say that the parties are speaking different languages in the 1970s; it is not totally supercilious to suggest that translators will have to be retained for the first searching interchange between scholars and policy initiators on the subject of general deterrence.

In large part, the credibility gap that exists between academics and policy initiators as well as many flaws in program and research design stem from unrealistic program goals. When the government announces that it will reduce predatory crime by 20 percent, academic skepticism is justified and inevitable; when evaluation plans are built around unduly optimistic goals, it is likely that they will lack the capacity to measure more equivocal and more likely consequences.

Yet academic standards for policy research in deterrence are occasionally just as unrealistic. Fairly serious efforts, such as that in Kansas City, are sometimes dismissed because they are not perfect. Inherent problems of policy experimentation are used as an easy excuse to dismiss whatever lessons the policy experiments might teach and to endorse complex statistical methods of studying natural variation, which make some policy experiments seem rigorous by comparison. Issues of style, culture, and even social status play a role in the current low esteem of policy evaluations. Because these one-shot interventions cannot live up to their own unrealistic goals, many people are ready to assume that they can prove nothing. Because the experiments can

[21]The important exception to this pattern is the ASAP evaluation, in which a number of mediating variables were measured with some care at many of the ASAP sites.

prove nothing, many academic students of deterrence are willing to assume quite a different proposition: that we can learn nothing from them. It is with that in mind that we turn to some of the lessons that recent experimental policy initiatives provide for general deterrence theory and research in the coming years.

III. SOME LESSONS

Implicit in the mission of this panel is the question of whether present data on general deterrence can be translated into policy prescriptions. It is foolish to address this question without some knowledge of how models of policy change are implemented in real-world settings. And it is difficult to translate social science findings on the effects of variables—such as "certainty of apprehension"—without some indication of what system factors influence these variables and whether changes in law enforcement can produce increases in these aggregate measures. Our short list of policy experiments provides insights on the nature and measurement of induced changes in real-world settings. Some of the limits of policy experiments discussed earlier are also lessons of value for predicting the relationship of theory and practice. They tell us much about

1. The occupational hazards of implementing policy change
2. The need for a common set of operational principles in the investigation of deterrent effects
3. The credibility gap between social scientists and policymakers.

A. THE OCCUPATIONAL HAZARDS OF IMPLEMENTING POLICY CHANGE

The deterrence programs of the 1970-1975 years were diverse in subject matter and policy content. Nevertheless, the policy implementation process was similar in a number of respects. First, it is a safe generalization that no program was implemented in total conformity to its planned model. That is inevitable, unless one adopts the "High-Impact" strategy of refusing to specify in advance what changes in a criminal justice system are desired. The inevitable slippage between planning and practice is to be expected, particularly in criminal justice system programs, and it is a virtual certainty for programs that seek to modify the behavior of metropolitan court systems. To project costs and benefits without accounting for such processes (and learning more about their determinants) is foolhardy policy science.

A second lesson is that even relatively large programs have relatively marginal impact on the operation of criminal justice systems. In part, this reflects the sheer size of criminal justice systems in large American cities. But an equally important explanation is the capacity of criminal justice agencies to absorb additional funds and to adapt to program initiatives without making major changes in the way they do business. The resiliency of courts and police when policy changes are induced by outside money investments is formidable.

The relatively small changes we can make in criminal justice are a natural boundary on the extent of general deterrent payoffs that come from policy experiments. Such changes will occur against a background of larger shifts in crime rate that are unrelated to criminal justice policy. This not only complicates the problem of measuring deterrence but also makes a statement about the relatively humble role of punishment policy that must be better understood.

B. OPERATIONALIZING DETERRENCE VARIABLES

The social scientist who studies aggregate data may define "certainty" as the ratio of prison commitments or arrests to total crimes in an area under study. Findings from studies of this type, together with assumptions that law enforcement budgets are spent with a view toward optimal crime control, led one observer (Ehrlich 1974, p. 110) to assert:

> . . . an increase in the expenditure of police and courts in 1965 by $32 million could have reduced the loss from felonies by about $83 million.

As the intervention studies make clear, "certainty of apprehension" is not a unitary concept that flows naturally from the allocation of marginal police resources. An additional dollar spent on preventive patrol seems to have little impact on crime. More important, the design and the evaluation of field studies illustrate the need to disaggregate conceptions like "certainty of apprehension" into more operational units that policy shifts can achieve. The field experiment must test the impact of intermediate variables—foot patrol, car patrol, crime analysis teams, prosecutor screening units, and so forth. It is only at this level that general deterrence analysis has policy significance. Yet the macroscopic deterrence analyses of social science begin by assuming all that the policy experiments have yet to establish—the relation, in field settings, between what we can change and the aggregate difference those changes can make in crime control policy.

My call for a common language in deterrence research is thus informed by a bias toward the specific. Until we can operationalize the broad concepts now debated in the academic literature, it will not be possible to measure the extent to which deterrence is a cause rather than a consequence of variations in these mega-variables, or to determine how much is practically achievable in marginal deterrent benefits.

C. THE CREDIBILITY GAP

Much of this paper is based on the dubious assumption that scholars and evaluators have an important impact on crime control policy. To date, the opposite is probably closer to the truth. The policy recommendations of scholars are often used in political debates on crime control, but more as intellectual ballast than as the rudder or sail of public policy.

In short, policy makers do not trust social scientists. I am unprepared, on the record of the past few years, either to assert that they should trust them or to nominate one of several warring camps that they should endorse. But if deterrence research is to become a policy science of any significance, this credibility gap is a high-priority item.

IV. CONCLUSION

Two themes deserve special attention in concluding this survey. First, students of deterrence at all levels need to pay more attention to the political science of punishment policy. The policy experiments of the early 1970s show many of the ways in which the institutions of criminal justice affect deterrence initiatives. The macro-statistical studies of deterrence document wide variation in criminal justice policy but tell us little about how those variations happen, or why. Detailed analysis of how policies evolve can help explain the crime-punishment relationship as it illuminates some of the policy implications of research findings.

Second, there is a pervasive need for middle-range theory in deterrence studies. Concepts of "crime," "certainty of apprehension," "severity of sanctions," and "criminals" are too broad and too vague to serve as the foundation for policy research in real-world settings. Unpacking generalities into crime-specific theoretical propositions is perhaps the most important task confronting social science investigation of general deterrence.

REFERENCES

Campbell, K., Scott, R., and Tolkin, S. (1976) *Highway Safety: Effects of the Energy Crisis on U.S. Toll Roads.* DOT-HS-801 933. Washington, D.C.: U.S. Government Printing Office.

Ehrlich, I. (1974) Participation in illegitimate activities: an economic analysis. In G. S. Becker and W. M. Landes, eds., *Essays in the Economics of Crime and Punishment.* Reprinted with corrections from (1973) *Journal of Political Economy* 81(3):521-67 and with appendices from (1970) "Participation in Illegitimate Activities: An Economic Analysis," doctoral dissertation, Columbia University. New York: National Bureau of Economic Research (distributed by Columbia University Press).

Johnson, P., Levy, P., and Voas, R. (1976) A critique of the paper "Statistical Evaluation of the Effectiveness of Alcohol Safety Action Projects." *Accident Analysis and Prevention* 8(1):67-68.

Kelling, G., and Pate, A. (1974) *The Kansas City Preventive Patrol Experiment.* Washington, D.C.: The Police Foundation.

Mitre Corp. (1976) *High Impact Anti-Crime Programs: National Level Evaluation. Final Report.* Eleanor Chelimsky, author. Vol. 1: Executive Summary. Vol. 2: Report. No. MTR-7148. Washington, D.C.: Law Enforcement Assistance Administration.

Murray, C., and Krug, R. (1975) *The National Evaluation of the Pilot Cities Program.* Washington, D.C.: Law Enforcement Assistance Administration.

Ross, H. L. (1973) Law, science and accidents: the British Safety Act of 1967. *Journal of Legal Studies* 2(1):1-78.

Ross, H. L. (1975) The Scandinavian myth: the effectiveness of drinking-and-driving legislation in Sweden and Norway. *Journal of Legal Studies* 4(2):285.

Schwartz, B. (1968) The effect in Philadelphia of Pennsylvania's increased penalties for rape and attempted rape. *Journal of Criminal Law and Criminology* 59(4):509-15.

Tittle, C. R., and Logan C. H. (1973) Sanctions and deviance: evidence and remaining questions. *Law and Society Review* 7(3):371-92.

Tullock, G. (1974) Does punishment deter crime? *Public Interest* 36(1):103-11.

U.S. Department of Transportation (1968) *1968 Alcohol and Highway Safety Report.* Committee Print. Committee on Public Works, U.S. House. Washington, D.C.: U.S. Government Printing Office.

U.S. Department of Transportation (1974) *Alcohol Safety Action Project—Evaluation of Operations.* DOT-HS-800. Washington, D.C.: U.S. Government Printing Office.

U.S. Department of Transportation (1975) *The Effect of the Fuel Shortage on Travel and Highway Safety.* DOT-HS-801 715. Washington, D.C.: U.S. Government Printing Office.

Zador, P. (1976) Statistical evaluation of the effectiveness of Alcohol Safety Action Projects. *Accident Analysis and Prevention* 8(1):51-66.

Zimring, F. (1975) Firearms and federal law: the gun control act of 1968. *Journal of Legal Studies* 4(1):133.

Zimring, F. and Hawkins, G. (1973) *Deterrence: The Legal Threat in Crime Control.* Chicago: University of Chicago Press.

APPENDIX: AN ANNOTATED BIBLIOGRAPHY OF DETERRENCE EVALUATIONS, 1970-1975

FRANCES GALLAGHER
Center for Studies in Criminal Justice,
University of Chicago

SAN DIEGO FIELD INTERROGATION: FINAL REPORT[22]

This article is an analysis of field interrogation (FI) in San Diego. FI is the stopping, questioning, and sometimes frisking of a subject who has aroused a police officer's suspicion. The study was requested by the San Diego Police Department and financed by the Police Foundation in reaction to the frequent criticism that FI is an abuse of subjects' rights and a waste of police time.

The three areas chosen for examination were similar in terms of their demographic and socioeconomic compositions and in their prior reported crime histories. In each area a different policy was implemented. In one area, the police department temporarily suspended FI's altogether. In another area, police officers were deployed who had been specially trained in legal procedures and human relations by techniques that utilized videotape and role-playing and that provided the officers with more opportunity to develop self-awareness and a sensitivity to the subjects during actual field interrogations. The third area was patrolled by police receiving traditional training in the handling of FI's.

The researchers evaluated each of the three policies by its measurable effect on three factors: (a) reported crimes considered to be suppressible by the San Diego Police Department, (b) total arrest rates, and (c) police–community relations. The study was divided into a 7-month pre-experimental period, a 5-month post-experimental period, and a 9-month experimental period. The data were analyzed to determine the significant changes that occurred within each area during each period.

Boydstun drew five conclusions. First, some level of FI activity, when juxtaposed with no activity, contributed to a decrease in those classes of crimes that can be significantly affected by police patrol activities. This conclusion was partly supported by the finding that in

---

Frances Gallagher is Research Assistant, Center for Studies in Criminal Justice, University of Chicago.

[22]Boydstun, J. E. (1975) San Diego Field Interrogation: Final Report. Washington, D.C.: Police Foundation.

the no-FI area there was a significant increase in the monthly frequency of the selected classes of crimes. Moreover, when FIs were finally resumed in this area, there was a significant decrease in the monthly frequencies of these crimes.

Second, since most arrests did not result from FIs and since most FIs did not result in arrest, the authors concluded that it was the visibility of the process, rather than the results, that provided the deterrent threat to potential offenders.

Third, the frequency of arrest was not directly influenced by FIs. However, arrests were indirectly affected by FIs since the majority of officers found FI records helpful in clearing other cases.

Fourth, because a common criticism is that FIs are used to harass minority groups, the authors were particularly interested in the ethnicity of the subjects arrested and in the reasonableness of the arrests. They found that arrested whites and blacks were about equally likely to be held to answer. They also concluded that arrested Mexican-Americans were the least likely group to have been hassled by unjustified arrests, since more than 60 percent were held to answer by authorities. Additionally, the specially trained officers had the highest-quality arrests with the highest percentage of arrested subjects held to answer.

Finally, the regularly trained and the specially trained officers were both favorably regarded by the citizenry. However, in the area with specially trained police, where a greater amount of time was spent on FI, many of the minority respondents felt the police were spending too much time on interrogation. This finding led the authors to conclude that police-community relations would deteriorate if the low level of FI activity were increased. Although the community perceived no distinction between the conduct of those who were specially trained and those who received regular training, the subjects who were actually interrogated reacted much less favorably to the latter group. This finding provided some additional support to the author's conclusion that much of the special training was worth its cost.

THE IMPACT OF POLICE ACTIVITY ON CRIME: ROBBERIES ON THE NEW YORK CITY SUBWAY SYSTEM[23]

In 1965, to respond to the rapidly growing crime rate, the New York Transit Authority introduced special patrols in the subways from 8

[23]Chaiken, J. M., Lawless, M. W. and Stevenson, K. A. (1974) The Impact of Police Activity on Crime: Robberies on the New York Subway System. R-1424-NYC. Santa Monica, Cal.: Rand Corp.

p.m. to 4 a.m. This article is an examination of the deterrent effect of this manpower increase on crime.

In 1971 the researchers assessed the general effects on crime rates by first examining available summaries of crime statistics between 1963 and 1971. They then took a closer look at one of the more common crimes, robbery, in order to make suggestions regarding efficient methods of redeployment of the police. They ascertained the dates, locations, and times of robberies during specified periods of time and obtained information on some arrested robbers' characteristics.

After examining the overall crime statistics, the authors concluded that the increased manpower caused a "phantom effect" that for 8 months decreased serious crime rates at times and places where no actual increases in patrol occurred. This decrease suggests that uncertainty as to the deployment of police has a deterrent effect on potential offenders. Over the long run, however, the overall crime rate in the subway system continued to increase. Only during the hours of actual increased patrols did the reported crime rate drop substantially for a sustained period of time. "Six years later, reported rates for nearly all crime types between 8 p.m. and 4 a.m. had not returned to their 1964 and early 1965 levels."[24]

From the robbery statistics, the researchers conclude that most subway crimes occur in a small number of stations and in the portions of train routes that run between those stations. The high-crime locations are easily identified and tend to be where surface crime rates are also high. In addition, there appears to be an interrelationship between bus and subway robbery, with a crackdown in one system resulting in a robbery increase in the other system.

The authors divide robbery into two types, passenger robbery and token-booth robbery. Concurrent participation in both types was not common and, in fact, there were major differences between the two groups. The passenger robbers tended to be schoolchildren, who were often violent but who seldom used guns. Token-booth robbers were usually older, used guns, and were narcotics users, but seldom used

[24]After this evaluation was completed, evidence of data corruption by the transit police surfaced. In particular, it was charged that transit police officers were encouraged to record crimes occurring between the high intensity patrol hours (8 p.m. to 4 a.m.) as occurring at other times of the day or to downgrade the seriousness of offenses recorded during the peak patrol hours. The authors have since re-examined the data in light of these charges and conclude that despite the falsification, evidence of a deterrent effect still remains, although the magnitude of the effect was undoubtedly amplified by the corrupt recording practices. (See Chaiken, J. M. 1976. What's Known About Deterrent Effects of Police Activities. The Rand Paper Series, Rand Corporation, Santa Monica, California.)

violence. Token-booth robbers could not commit these lucrative robberies regularly for a long period of time without being apprehended. Successful apprehension, however, did not appear to act as a successful deterrent.

Finally, the Transit Authority detectives seem to have been as successful as the above-ground city police detectives in solving robberies. The transit detectives are more successful in arresting token-booth robbers because they employ a specialized force that devotes more time and manpower to the solution of these crimes.

Based on these conclusions, the authors suggest some deployment strategies that will reduce daytime crime. Although the transit police wish to increase their manpower so that the trains and the stations can be patrolled to the same extent during the day as at night, the authors believe that this approach would be too costly. They are most intrigued by their observation of the "phantom effect" and suggest that the transit police capitalize on the potential offenders' uncertainty regarding the actual dispersal of police by making temporary redeployments. In other words, the periods of the highest concentrations of manpower would be ever-changing. This experiment would be accompanied by careful tabulation of crime and arrest data to plan manpower schedules in target areas and, also, to determine whether the desired effects are being achieved.

They also suggest that, since the only major specialized unit within the Transit Authority Detective Division that has larger groups of patrolmen available for stakeout duty is assigned to Transit Authority robberies, a disproportionate amount of time and manpower is being devoted to preventing and solving crimes against the Transit Authority while inadequate resources are being allocated to the solution of crimes against the people who use the system.

SOME EFFECTS OF AN INCREASE IN POLICE MANPOWER IN THE 20TH PRECINCT OF NEW YORK CITY[25]

This study was occasioned by a 40-percent increase in police manpower in the 20th Precinct of New York City. The researchers limit themselves to two problems. The first is whether or not reported crimes in the 20th Precinct decreased and whether the change could be attributed to the manpower increase. The second is whether decreases

[25]Press, S. J. (1971) Some Effects of an Increase in Police Manpower in the 20th Precinct of New York City. R-704-NYC. Santa Monica, Cal.: Rand Corp.

in reported crime in this precinct were accompanied by increases in neighboring precincts.

Press utilized the daily police data on reported crime and on arrests for reported crime collected from January 1, 1963, to December 31, 1967. In order to determine whether a change in reported crime might have occurred even without a change in police manpower, he chose similar distant precincts as controls for the 20th Precinct. To test for displacement effects, three adjoining precincts, each with its own control precinct, were examined. The difference in average weekly crimes before and after the manpower increase was compared with the average difference in the control precincts. This difference was considered to be the net effect associated with the increase in manpower in the 20th Precinct. Moreover, he determined whether the net changes were attributable merely to sampling variation by testing the hypothesis of zero net change statistically. He also computed 95 percent confidence intervals for the true net change. Two of the three adjoining precincts were examined in the same fashion, while the third precinct and its control were treated somewhat differently because of certain peculiarities.

The author found that increased numbers of police decreased the precinct's reported rates in many outdoor crimes. Inside crimes were affected less, except for robbery and grand larceny, which showed the spectacular decreases of 21 percent and 49 percent, respectively.

Two of the three adjoining precincts showed no significant displacement effects. The third precinct showed an increase in crime, but it could not necessarily be attributed to displacement. This third case was complicated by a decrease in police manpower and by the author's inability to calculate confidence intervals.

Although Press reports that increased patrols decreased this area's reported crime without having any significant displacement effects, these results are highly qualified. The author concludes with suggestions for further study. The general applicability of his results, the extent of displacement effects, and the effects of changes on true rather than reported crimes are some of the problems to be addressed.

AN INSTANCE OF EFFECTIVE LEGAL REGULATION: MOTORCYCLIST HELMET AND DAYTIME HEADLAMP LAWS[26]

The author took advantage of the passage of laws requiring the use of motorcycle helmets and daytime headlamps in several states in order to

[26]Robertson, L. S. (1976) An instance of effective legal regulation: motorcyclist helmet and daytime headlamp laws. *Law and Society Review* 10(3).

study the impact of the new legislation on both the motorcycle fatality rate and individual compliance with the law.

In order to measure obedience to the law, observers in four cities sat beside heavily traveled freeways recording the total number of riders, those who used helmets, and those who used daytime lamps. In one city, the laws for both helmet and headlamp use were in effect; in another, neither law was in effect; the remaining two cities had either one or the other law in effect. The researchers discovered that in areas in which the laws had been enacted, a far greater proportion of the riders used helmets or headlamps than in places in which no law was in effect.

In order to estimate the relationship between helmet use laws and fatality rates, the researchers first obtained data on fatal crashes from police departments, motor vehicle administrations, or highway departments. They then calculated rates of motorcycle fatal crash involvement per 10,000 registered motorcycles per year for each state during a period extending from a year before the law's passage to a year after its passage. They made similar calculations in control states that had no such law.

To examine the effect of headlamp use laws on fatalities, they employed a different method. The number of reported motorcycle fatalities in states with laws for daytime headlamp use was divided by the sum of the fatalities in that state, together with the fatalities of the control state, for each year of the period studied. They then determined whether shifts in fatalities coincided with the passage of this law.

The author concluded that significant decreases in motorcycle fatalities occurred in states that put helmet use laws into effect. Because of the possible incomparability between the states with laws in effect and the control states, he was more guarded in his conclusion concerning headlamp use laws. He asserts—with reservations—that states, after enacting daytime headlamp use laws, had significant reductions in motorcycle fatalities.

Finally, Robertson suggests alternative methods of examining the impact of new legislation and policy changes. One is the use of the interrupted time-series model, a design particularly useful when the effects of a change are relatively small and a long time-series of data is available. When long time-series are not available but comparable control areas are, the conventional analysis of variance may be used. When both long time-series and comparison groups are present, one may use the author's approach in analyzing the headlamp use laws, a model sensitive to small effects of change as well as to the incomparability of the control groups.

THE EFFECT OF NEW-CAR SAFETY REGULATIONS ON FATALITY RATES[27]

This study was occasioned by changes in state and federal automobile safety regulations and was sponsored by the Insurance Institute for Highway Safety. The paper attempts to evaluate the effects of the different regulations on auto fatalities.

The author divided autos into three groups: (1) the pre-1964 cars are those manufactured before seat belts were made standard equipment in all cars sold in the United States; (2) the 1964-1967 class was characterized by the installation of seat belts and certain other safety devices installed in anticipation of the change in General Services Administration standards, which were to become effective in 1967; and (3) the post-1967 models met the even higher standards of the National Traffic and Motor Vehicle Safety Act.

Robertson carried out the study during the period 1972-1975 in Maryland, where he calculated the fatality rates for each auto group per 100,000 registered cars of that group for each year of the study. He obtained the data on fatal crashes from the state police and the numbers and years of registered vehicles from state registration data.

He concluded that the pre-1964 models had an average yearly occupant fatality rate of 44 per 100,000 registered cars. The 1964-1967 models averaged 35 occupant deaths per 100,000 registered cars, 20 percent less than the first group. The post-1967 cars had an average yearly occupant fatality rate of 27 per 100,000 registered cars, 23 percent less than the 1964-1967 class and 39 percent less than the pre-1964 group. In all three categories, rates of pedestrian fatalities were similar.

The author contends that the differences in the three groups' fatality rates could not be attributed to differences in the type of owner or the age of the cars. The pre-1964 autos had as high an occupant fatality rate when they were new as they did during 1972-1975, the period of the study.

JAIL SENTENCES FOR DRIVING WHILE INTOXICATED IN CHICAGO: A JUDICIAL POLICY THAT FAILED[28]

This article re-evaluates Chicago's supposedly successful police crackdown on drinking drivers in 1970-1971. The severity of the sentence for persons convicted of DWI (driving while intoxicated) was

[27]Robertson, L. S. (1976) The effect of new-car safety regulations on fatality rates. *Best's Review* 77(3):22–24.

[28]Robertson, L. S., Rich, R. F., and Ross, H. L. (1973) Jail sentences for driving while intoxicated in Chicago: a judicial policy that failed. *Law and Society Review* 8.

increased to 7 days, but there was no accompanying effort to increase the certainty of apprehension by altering methods of enforcement. The crackdown was based on the questionable assumption that most fatalities involving alcohol were caused not by problem drinkers, but by social drinkers who could be deterred by jail sentences.

The authors use Milwaukee as a control city and use the interrupted time-series model to interpret their data. They can use this model to test for a change in the upward or downward slopes of the curve as well as for changes in its general level. They can then determine whether changes in the time-series are attributable to chance.

Although there was a significant drop in the level of pedestrian fatalities, this downward trend had begun 2 years before the crackdown and had also occurred in Milwaukee. The changes in nonpedestrian fatalities were within the bounds of chance variation. Moreover, there was no change in the number of arrests for DWI, little change in the percentage of arrestees tested for blood-alcohol concentrations, and no significant change in the proportion of those convicted. In other words, the crackdown was accompanied by no significant transformations, a conclusion contrary to the assertions of the Chicago police.

The authors also suggest reasons for the failure of the crackdown. One is that the classification of convicted DWIs in Chicago into 20 percent alcoholics and 80 percent social drinkers is an oversimplification and an overestimation of the percentage of social drinkers in the population. There are many categories of DWIs, each of which must be dealt with differently. Strictly punitive measures would provide a sufficient deterrent threat to only a few of these. The general pattern of stress deviancy and the multiple convictions in the backgrounds of DWIs suggest that an increase in the probability of apprehension and the cooperation of police, courts, and social agencies will be required to deter the problem DWIs.

LAW, SCIENCE, AND ACCIDENTS[29]

This study was performed to determine the impact of the British Road Safety Act of 1967. The author examines the Act's effectiveness in reducing the casualty rate connected with drinking and driving and explores the attitudes of the public, the police, and the courts to determine the social factors that limited the Act's success.

The research was carried out in 1971-1972, and most of the data was analyzed on the basis of the interrupted time-series model. The author finds that the Act's deterrent effect was initially quite substantial. The

[29]Ross, H. L. (1973) Law, science, and accidents. *Journal of Legal Studies* 2.

government's publicity campaign, the scientific nature of the test, and the discretion given to police to test anyone suspected of having alcohol in his body or of having committed a moving traffic violation led the public to overestimate the certainty of apprehension. Consequently, after the passage of the Act, there was a sharp and immediate decrease in deaths and injuries. Random surveys showed that, although people did not reduce their alcohol consumption, they were less likely to drive after drinking.

However, police and judicial ambivalence toward enforcement of the Act ultimately diluted its provisions in practice. The populace eventually learned that they had overestimated the Act's effect, and its deterrent threat began to diminish.

Fearing a public relations problem, the police had reduced the Act's potential effectiveness by being very selective about administering the test and by making no changes in the amount of resources devoted to the apprehension of drinking drivers.

The courts, hostile to the infringement on judicial discretion, had also mitigated the Act's potential effect. Although there was a great increase in the number of charges of drinking and driving offenses after 1967 that resulted in convictions, the courts were quite receptive to those defendants who took advantage of loopholes in the law. Defendants succeeded even though they were driving with more than permitted blood-alcohol concentrations.

Ross concludes that the Act's initial deterrent effect has dwindled to almost nothing. "The significant change in the slope of the casualty rate curves—diminishing and (for fatalities) even reversing the prior decline—suggests that the savings achieved ought to be regarded as temporary." He suggests that a revival of the Act's deterrent effect depends on overcoming the organizational problems of police enforcement rather than on amending the Act itself.

THE SCANDINAVIAN MYTH[30]

This study attempts to determine the deterrent effect of the per se drinking and driving laws in Norway and Sweden. There was no policy change that occasioned this research, although the growing skepticism in Norway and Sweden regarding the efficacy of these laws was undoubtedly a factor inducing the study.

The author uses interrupted time-series analysis to analyze the results of the Swedish and Norwegian per se rules in 1941 and 1936. He

[30]Ross, H. L. (1975) The Scandinavian myth. *Journal of Legal Studies* 4.

then compares them to the more classical laws of Denmark and Finland.

Ross finds no significant difference in deterrent effects among the countries studied. Neither the certainty of punishment in Norway and Sweden, nor the particularism of the Danish punishment, nor the severity of sanctions in Finland produced any significant changes in the rate of accidents.

Since Ross is dealing with a long period of time in which statistics were often sparse and little information is available on other factors that might have influenced the crime rate, he does not regard these results as conclusively negative. Because of the problems in his analysis, he suggests that there is not much more evidence "one way or the other to be gleaned from further study of the origins of the present laws in Norway and Sweden." As an alternative, he encourages researchers to take advantage of projected changes in policy in order to study the effects of new laws.

SOME BEHAVIORAL EFFECTS OF NEW LEGISLATION[31]

The paper attempts to study the impact of legislation enacted in Tennessee in May 1971, providing for "mandatory jail sentences of at least 48 hours for anyone convicted of driving while intoxicated." The legislation also lowered the blood-alcohol concentration required for presumptive evidence of intoxication. The government sponsored no publicity campaign in connection with this legislation, and the researchers find no evidence of any significant change in enforcement in the handling of drinking drivers after arrest.

The authors, who conducted the study 2 years after the enactment of the legislation, first addressed the law's effect on fatalities. They computed monthly highway traffic fatalities for Tennessee as well as an average fatality rate for eight control states that border Tennessee for the period January 1965 through April 1972. The authors found no statistically significant reduction in either the level or the slope of the time-series. A similar picture exists in the control states.

The authors also conducted a statewide telephone survey of licensed drivers currently residing in Tennessee in order to determine the population's knowledge of the changes in legislation and their perception of their change in behavior in reaction to the legislation. The researchers found that only 41 percent knew of the change in the law. Of these, 44.6 percent were unable to mention a single provision of the law, while

[31]Shover, N., and Bankston, W. (1973) Some Behavioral Effects of New Legislation. Unpublished, University of Tennessee.

only 12.5 percent mentioned the mandatory jail sentence. Only four out of 56 felt that they had changed their drinking–driving behavior.

All these figures are significantly lower than the study done in conjunction with the British Road Safety Act, which was accompanied by changes in enforcement, a government-sponsored publicity campaign, and significant decreases in fatalities. After comparing the two studies, the authors conclude that an increase in the severity of the punishment without public awareness of the legislation and without an increased certainty of arrest does not affect deterrence and creates no perceived benefits.

THE LEGAL MINIMUM DRINKING AGE AND FATAL MOTOR VEHICLE CRASHES[32]

This article studies the connection between the reduction of the legal minimum drinking age and the number of fatal highway crashes. The authors had the opportunity to study this relationship when Michigan, Wisconsin, and Ontario lowered the legal minimum drinking age from 21 to 18 in 1971 and 1972. They examine these three areas and compare them to the nearby states of Indiana, Illinois, and Minnesota, where the legal minimum age remained 21.

The authors first analyze data on fatal crashes occurring in the 3 years preceding and in the year following the reduction in the legal drinking age. The test is whether change-states and comparison-states had comparable year-to-year fluctuations in proportions of drivers involved in fatal crashes prior to the law change and whether there was a systematic departure from that comparability after the law had changed.

After this first analysis, the authors conclude that the changes in the proportions of drivers involved in all fatal crashes after the 18-year-old minimum drinking age went into effect are statistically insignificant.

Because involvement in all fatal crashes is not the most sensitive indicator of alcohol involvement, the authors use alternative sets of data. Since nighttime fatal crashes and single-vehicle fatal crashes have often been shown to be reliable indicators of alcohol involvement, the authors also analyze these two types of data. They find inconsistent year-to-year increases and decreases before the law change but a consistent sharp increase in the changed states after the change, a dis-

[32]Williams, A. F., Rich, R. F., Zador, P. L., and Robertson, L. S. (1975) The legal minimum drinking age and fatal motor vehicle crashes. *Journal of Legal Studies* 4.

covery that enables them to conclude that the consistent increase in the proportion of drivers under 21 in nighttime fatal crashes and in single-vehicle fatal crashes probably resulted from the reduction in the legal minimum drinking age.

The authors also analyze the border areas of the states to determine the effect that the law change had on persons under 21 crossing state lines to obtain alcoholic beverages legally. The results were not statistically significant.

The article's estimates of excess involvement of 15- to 20-year-old drivers in fatal crashes range from 2.6 to 3.3 per 100,000 15- to 20-year-old population in the first year after the change in the legal minimum drinking age. The authors acknowledge that a shortcoming of their analysis is that there is no way to determine if the initial increase in losses will continue in subsequent years.

OF DOCTORS, DETERRENCE, AND THE DARK FIGURE OF CRIME: A NOTE OF ABORTION IN HAWAII[33]

In 1970, Hawaii decriminalized abortion and permitted in-hospital abortions for state residents during the first several months of pregnancy. The change in law presented the opportunity to study the deterrent effect of the criminal abortion law. The author used the relatively reliable Hawaii records to learn the characteristics of abortions performed during the first year of the new law. He also used the overall changes in birth rate as well as the birth rates of certain subgroups in order to estimate the number of abortions that were performed on Hawaiian citizens before the change. From these results, he determined whether those who requested abortions after the change in the law are similar to those who requested them before the change. He also estimates the number of women who were deterred by the prohibition prior to 1970. After concluding that abortion in Hawaii was relatively undeterred, the author suggests some of the factors necessary for deterrence, which were not present in Hawaii before 1970.

The author first examined the overall birth rate and found 2,866 more abortions but only 290 fewer births in the year after the change. If one assumes a stable birth rate (which one cannot) then 2,500 of these abortions would have been performed before the change. If one assumes a 9.6 percent increase in births, which is extremely high but represents Hawaii's increase in the previous year, then one finds that

[33]Zimring, F. E. (1972) Of doctors, deterrence, and the dark figure of crime: a note on abortion in Hawaii. *University of Chicago Law Review* 39.

1,000 of these abortions would have been performed regardless of their illegality. The conclusion is that the abortion law was ineffective, since the pre-change abortion rate is between one-half to two-thirds the rate of abortions after the change. Tabulations of the birth rates of the various ethnic groups also illustrate the law's weakness. Since the births to more abortion-prone groups are not rising by less or dropping by more than the rate of births to members of other groups, women who were highly abortion-prone after the change were abortion-prone before the change.

Since more than one-half the potential demands for abortion had been satisfied before the legalization, the author proposes several reasons for the ineffectiveness of the law. Because the number of requests was small in comparison with many other areas, and because those who requested illegal abortions were the highly motivated nondeterrable single women, the author suggests that in Hawaii there were additional moral and social barriers that prevented all but the highly motivated from requesting abortion before and after the legal change. Once these women had passed these greater barriers, they were rather insensitive to legal barriers. Also, even if abortion laws do not present a deterrent threat to the more motivated women, they can have a preventive effect by disrupting the referral process that links those who need abortions with those who will perform them. The Hawaiian law's weak threat for performing abortions encouraged the referral process and severely limited the law's preventive effect.

Finally, the author suggests that efforts should be made to determine whether, as time passes, the decriminalization of abortion undermines the feelings of guilt, which are the most important barrier to abortion.

The Incapacitative Effect of Imprisonment: A Critical Review of the Literature

JACQUELINE COHEN

I. INTRODUCTION

With continuing increases in crime, crime control policies—especially imprisonment—have been subjected to closer scrutiny to determine their present and potential effectiveness. As evidence of the general futility of various rehabilitation strategies in prisons accumulates[1] and the debate continues on the deterrent efficacy of prison sentences,[2] some have advocated abandoning prisons for new correctional strategies.[3] Yet a growing body of public officials and policy analysts have suggested that the benefits in reduced crime that come from simply incapacitating convicted offenders justifies the expanded use of prisons.[4]

Jacqueline Cohen is Research Assistant, School of Urban and Public Affairs, Carnegie-Mellon University.

NOTE: This study was sponsored in part by PHS Research Grant No. 1 RO1 MH 28437-01 from the National Institute of Mental Health, Center for Studies of Crime and Delinquency.

[1]Robison and Smith (1971), Martinson (1974), Lipton *et al.* (1975).

[2]Ehrlich (1974), Forst (1976), Nagin (in this volume).

[3]Martinson (1975).

[4]Wilson (1975a and 1975b), Ford, G. (1975), press release, "Remarks of the President at the Yale Sesquicentennial Convocation Dinner."

In recent years, several papers have appeared offering estimates of the reduction in crime due solely to incapacitation. These estimates, which do not account for the impact of deterrence, vary from a mere 5- to 10-percent increase in crime if current prison use were reduced or eliminated[5] to potential two- to fivefold decreases in crime if prison use were expanded through higher probabilities of prison for convicted offenders and/or longer times served for those imprisoned.[6] We, therefore, have apparently inconsistent estimates of the benefits of incapacitation. The purpose of this paper is to examine critically and compare the underlying assumptions and conclusions of these various estimates. It is hoped that this will clarify some of the issues in the debate over incapacitative effects and, thereby, over incapacitation policy.

A. SELECTIVE VERSUS COLLECTIVE INCAPACITATION

Before a brief summary is made of the incapacitation literature, a distinction must be made between what Greenberg (1975) calls "selective incapacitation" and "collective incapacitation." A policy of selective incapacitation involves the decision to imprison particular individuals because of the crimes they themselves would commit if they were allowed to go free. This is an analog to the preventive detention of arrested suspects, but it applies to convicted offenders. As such, it is subject to many of the same criticisms often leveled against preventive detention.

The most fundamental criticism deals with the injustice of imprisoning persons essentially for crimes they have not yet committed.[7] Since the deprivation of liberty associated with incapacitation constitutes a punishment, that punishment must be just, *i.e.,* befitting the crime. When the crime is not yet committed, however, what is a just punishment, especially if by the punishment you prevent the crime from ever occurring?

Even if one is prepared to accept the thesis that conviction of a crime confers on society the right to confine a person in order to prevent future crimes, the opponents of preventive detention and preventive confinement of convicted offenders go on to argue, with some merit, that convicted offenders are entitled to the same safeguards against unwarranted government interference and, in particular, the same standards of proof as accused offenders. Thus, preventive confinement

[5]Clarke (1974), Greenberg (1975), Ehrlich (1974).

[6]Marsh and Singer (1972), Shinnar and Shinnar (1975).

[7]See von Hirsch (1974).

can only be employed when there is no reasonable doubt about the future crimes.

To date, however, the various efforts to predict future crime have not been very successful.[8] If these predictions cannot be improved, there is no adequate justification for the selective incapacitation of some convicted offenders. Individual offenders may still be selectively confined in prison when convicted, but the imposition and degree of that punishment must be based on what they did, rather than on what they might do in the future.

Collective incapacitation refers to the benefits in reduced crime that accompany a sentencing policy without invoking any explicit predictions of the future criminality of particular individuals. Unlike selective incapacitation, individuals are sentenced to prison or not solely on the basis of their convicted offenses. On the average, however, these prison sentences may be imposed on more or fewer people and/or for different average terms. Such policy changes will have an impact on preventing crime. This can be estimated by considering the average consequences of the sentencing strategy and need not rely on estimates for the specific individuals involved.

To the extent that some predictive capability does exist for individuals, a policy of collective incapacitation based only on average considerations will not do as well in preventing crime as one that selectively identifies the worst offenders. The difference between the two is the price that is paid for considerations of equity. The subject of this paper is collective incapacitation, particularly estimates of the reduction in crime associated with different general sentencing policies.

II. SUMMARY OF INCAPACITATION LITERATURE

This section presents brief summaries of several papers that estimate the incapacitative effect of prison. The critical analysis of these estimates will be presented in a later section. Certain elements are common to all of the papers considered here. All refer to the individual crime rate and make implicit or explicit assumptions about the probability of arrest given a crime, the length of the criminal career, and the average sentence served. For the purpose of clarity, a single notation scheme will be used throughout. Where necessary the original notation in individual papers will be converted to the notation presented in Table 1.

[8]See Greenberg (1975), Monahan (1976) and von Hirsch (1974) for reviews of some of this literature on prediction.

TABLE 1 Notation Scheme[a]

Variable	Definition
λ	the individual crime rate while free (crimes/unit of time *free*)
λ^*	the individual "effective" crime rate (crimes/unit of *total* time)[b]
q	the probability of arrest and conviction given a crime
J	the probability of imprisonment given conviction
q_A	the probability of arrest given a crime
J_A	the probability of conviction and imprisonment given arrest[c]
S	average (or constant) prison sentence served
T	average (or constant) length of the criminal career
μ	the individual arrest rate while free ($\mu = \lambda q_A$)
μ^*	the individual "effective" arrest rate ($\mu^* = \lambda^* q_A$)

[a]Much of this notation is taken from Shinnar and Shinnar (1975).
[b]Total time includes both time free and time served in prison or jail.
[c]Note: $qJ = q_A J_A$.

A. CLARKE (1974)

Using data on a cohort of 9,945 Philadelphia boys (Wolfgang *et al.* 1972), Clarke estimates the proportion of FBI index crimes[9] averted by the incapacitation of juveniles (Clarke 1974). Clarke restricts his attention to the population P consisting of 381 "incarcerated offenders" (juveniles who were institutionalized at least once before age 18) and assumes age-specific, index "arrest"[10] rates, μ_i. Data are available on the number of juveniles institutionalized by age (I_i), but the length of stay is unavailable and is assumed to be 9 months. The number of index offenses attributed to these 381 boys (their "arrests") is also given by age (n_i). All the analyses are done separately by race (white and non-white).

The full-year equivalent of the number of boys at large at age i (N_i) is given by

$$N_i = P - I_i \times 0.75 \tag{1}$$

The individual "arrest" rate while free at age i is then

$$\mu_i = \frac{n_i}{N_i} \tag{2}$$

[9]The FBI index crimes include homicide and non-negligent manslaughter, rape, robbery, aggravated assault, burglary, larceny over $50, and auto theft.
[10]This refers to the juvenile equivalent of offenses resulting in arrest and includes all those offenses attributed to the juvenile by the police without formal arrest charges against the juvenile.

and the number of "arrests" averted by the incarceration of juveniles of age i (a_i) is

$$a_i = \mu_i \times 0.75I_i \tag{3}$$

Summing over all age-groups, the "arrests" averted represent 5 percent of the total index "arrests" for the white boys in the full cohort[11] and 15 percent of the total index "arrests" for the non-white boys in the full cohort. Assuming that the ratio of "arrests" to reported crimes is constant for all criminals and crime types and stationary over time (a single, constant q_A), these percentages can be applied to that portion of the total reported index crime that is committed by juveniles.

According to FBI data, juveniles represented 45 percent of total arrests for Part I offenses in 1972 (*Uniform Crime Reports: 1972,* Table 29). If adults and juveniles were arrested at the same rate per crime, then about 45 percent of reported offenses are committed by juveniles. Clarke, however, assumes that juveniles are *more likely* to be arrested than are adults, which would inflate their representation among arrests. Assuming that the juvenile arrest-to-offense ratio is 1.6 times the overall arrest-to-offense ratio, reported index offenses by juveniles are only 28 percent of the total reported index offenses.[12] Clarke then concludes that only 1 to 4 percent (0.5×0.28 and 0.15×0.28) of all known index crimes were avoided by the incapacitation of juveniles.

B. GREENBERG (1975)

While Greenberg addresses both selective and collective incapacitation, this summary will be limited to his estimates of the collective effect of current levels of incapacitation. The estimate rests on two basic elements: a) the rate at which non-virgins (persons previously arrested for some non-minor offense) commit index offenses, which is assumed a constant λ for all non-virgins, and b) the average sentence length, S. The number of index crimes averted by the incapacitation of N of these individuals is just $N\lambda S$.

The problem, however, is estimating the value of λ. For a constant probability of arrest for index offenses, λq_A is the annual index arrest

[11]The full cohort includes those boys who are never incarcerated as well as the incarcerated offenders.

[12]For A = the total number of arrests and C = the total number of offenses, this is derived as follows:

$$\text{assuming } \frac{0.45A}{pC} = 1.6\frac{A}{C}, \text{ then } p = \frac{0.45}{1.6} = 0.28$$

rate for non-virgins and $\lambda q_A T$ is the total expected number of non-virgin index arrests during an individual's career. With estimates of these quantities, bounds can be established on the possible values of λ.

Greenberg uses 1965 FBI data on criminal careers to estimate the annual index arrest rate for persons with at least one arrest as 0.5. He also relies on a paper by Blumstein and Larson (1969), in which they use a feedback model of the criminal justice system that accounts for recidivism, to estimate the total number of subsequent index arrests in a career (after a first arrest for an index offense) as between 2.2 and 2.9. Using these estimates of $\lambda q_A = 0.5$ and $\lambda q_A T = 2.5$, Greenberg concludes that $T = 5$ years and the lower bound on λ is 0.5 ($q_A \leq 1$).

The upper bound on λ is established less directly using relationships including the following variables:

λ = annual rate of committing index offenses for all persons previously arrested for some non-minor offense[13]
q_A = probability of arrest for an index offense
C = number of index offenses committed annually (reported and unreported)
V = annual number of virgin arrests[14] for non-minor offenses
V_I = annual number of virgin arrests for index offenses[15]
A = number of persons arrested annually for non-minor offenses
VT = number of non-virgin, active criminals in any year (under steady-state assumptions).

The basic relationship used by Greenberg is:

$$C > V_I + \lambda VT. \tag{4}$$

While Greenberg does not justify this relationship, it can be derived easily from the fact that the total arrests for index offenses in a year are

[13]Non-minor offenses include the index offenses of homicide, rape, robbery, aggravated assault, burglary, larceny over $50, and auto theft. Also included are: other larcenies; other assaults; arson; forgery; counterfeiting; fraud; embezzlement; possession of stolen property; weapons; narcotics; and gambling.

[14]A virgin arrest is a person's first arrest for a non-minor offense (including an index offense), even though such a person may have been previously arrested for a minor offense. Minor offenses include: vandalism, prostitution, sex offenses (except rape and prostitution), offenses against family and children, drunk driving, violation of liquor laws, drunkenness, disorderly conduct, vagrancy, suspicion, violation of curfew, loitering, running away, and all others except traffic violations.

[15]V_I is a subset of the virgin arrests for non-minor offenses, V, including only those first arrests for index offenses.

equal to the number of virgin arrests for index offenses plus all index arrests of non-virgins. Namely,

$$Cq_A = V_I + \lambda q_A VT \tag{5}$$

where

Cq_A = total number of arrests for index offenses in a year

V_I = annual number of virgin arrests for index offenses (including persons who may have been previously arrested for a minor offense)

$\lambda q_A VT$ = annual number of index arrests of non-virgins (persons previously arrested for some non-minor offense including some index offense).

Dividing all the terms of eq. (5) by q_A, we have

$$C = \frac{V_I}{q_A} + \lambda VT. \tag{6}$$

For $q_A < 1$, $V_I/q_A > V_I$. Thus, replacing V_I/q_A in eq. (6) by V_I we have eq. (4).

Greenberg then manipulates eq. (4) to obtain the inequality in terms of q_A and to include variables with empirical estimates.
First, V_I is subtracted from both sides and both sides are multiplied by q_A and divided by $C - V_I$; namely

$$\frac{(C-V_I)q_A}{C-V_I} > \frac{\lambda q_A VT}{C-V_I}$$

Then, multiplying the right-hand side by $(1/A)/(1/A) = 1$, the final relationship is

$$q_A > \frac{\lambda q_A T(\frac{V}{A})}{\frac{C}{A} - \frac{V_I}{A}}\,. \tag{7}$$

To estimate the lower bound on q_A, estimates of $\lambda q_A T$, C, A, V/A, and V_I/A are needed. Using Blumstein and Larson (1969), Greenberg has already estimated $\lambda q_A T$ as 2.5 arrests. The *Uniform Crime Report* for 1965 reports 2.78 million reported index crimes and 5.03 million total arrests for a reporting population of 135 million. To obtain C, the total number of index offenses actually committed in the United States, the 2.78 million reported crimes must be scaled up to account for the police agencies' not reporting to the FBI (covering about 59 million people) and for citizens' not reporting to the police. Using 3 as the ratio of total crime to crime reported to the FBI, Greenberg estimates C as 8.34 million index crimes. Similarly, scaling up the number of arrests to the total U.S. population of 194 million and taking 27 percent for the proportion of arrests for non-minor crimes among all arrests, A is 1.94 million arrests.

Good empirical estimates are not available for the fraction of virgin arrests among all arrests for non-minor crimes (V/A), or for the fraction of arrests for non minor crimes that are virgin arrests for index offenses (V_I/A). Nevertheless, some constraints can be placed on the values of these variables. The expected number of non-virgin, index arrests in a career ($\lambda q_A T$) is estimated as 2.5. Thus, the total number of index arrests in a career is no more than 3.5. Under steady-state assumptions, the total expected number of non-minor arrests in a career equals the reciprocal of the ratio of virgin arrests for non-minor offenses to total arrests for non-minor offenses in any year, $1/(V/A)$. Since index arrests are included among non minor arrests, the number of non-minor arrests exceeds the number of index arrests in a career. Thus, $A/V > 3.5$ and $V/A < 1/3.5 = 0.286$. Also, since $V_I < V$, $V_I/A < V/A$. Thus, with these constraints in mind, V/A and V_I/A are arbitrarily set at 0.25 and 0.20, respectively.

Substituting the numerical estimates of $\lambda q_A T = 2.5$, $C = 8.34$ million, $A = 1.94$ million, $V/A = 0.25$, and $V_I/A = 0.20$ into eq. (7), q_A must be greater than 0.15. For $\lambda q_A = 0.5$, then $\lambda < 3.33$ in 1965. By similar analysis using 1972 data, Greenberg calculates that the upper bound of λ for 1972 must be between 2.84 and 4.3.

To estimate the amount of crime avoided by current incapacitation policies, Greenberg uses the bounds $0.5 < \lambda < 3.33$. The number of additional index offenses that would be expected from lost incapacitation if the prison population were reduced is λ times the number of additional men freed. Reducing the present average daily prison population from about 200,000 to 100,000 (increasing the amount of time free by 100,000 man-years), the reduced incapacitative effect is from 50,000 to 333,000 additional index offenses for a 0.6- to 4.0-percent increase over the present estimated total of 8.34 million offenses. If prisons were eliminated entirely, there would only be a 1.2- to 8.0-percent increase in index crimes.

These results can also be interpreted in terms of the expected reductions in crime due to incapacitation if prison use were expanded. With current average prison terms of 2 years, *ceteris paribus,* an increase of 1 year in the average time served (a 50-percent increase) would result in a 0.6-percent to 4.0-percent decrease in crime from incapacitation alone.

Greenberg provides another estimate of individual crime rates using the rate of parolee returns to prison for new index offenses. Supplementing this with the clearance rate (which converts known offenses to arrests), the non-reporting rate, and the probability of return to prison given arrest for parolees, the number of index offenses committed per person can be estimated from data on returns to prison. After correcting for variations in the reporting rate and for the probable reduction in offenses due to custody, individuals are estimated to commit somewhat over two index offenses per year. This amounts to a 1- to 2-percent increase in index offenses nationally from lost incapacitation, if the prison population were reduced by 50 percent to 100,000.

In a footnote Greenberg provides another procedure for estimating the additional incapacitative benefits from increasing the time served. The basic model remains the same; all criminals are assumed to have the same individual crime rate, λ, and the same probability of apprehension given a crime, q_A. This alternative approach, however, does not require any explicit estimate of λ. Assuming that arrestees are a representative sample of all criminals, the percentage of crimes that would be averted by expanding prison terms by 1 year is given by the percentage of all arrestees in a year who were released from prison within the previous year.

For n_1 = the number of arrestees who were released from prison within the previous year and n_2 = all other arrestees, λn_1 gives the number of crimes committed by the arrestees released within the previous year and $\lambda(n_1 + n_2)$ gives the total number of crimes committed by all arrestees. If prison terms were expanded by 1 year, the crimes of those arrestees released within the previous year would be avoided. This percentage reduction in crimes is given by

$$\frac{\lambda n_1}{\lambda(n_1 + n_2)} = \frac{n_1}{n_1 + n_2} \quad . \tag{8}$$

Using data on a sample of arrestees in California in 1971, Greenberg estimates that the additional incapacitative effect for index offenses of a 1-year increase in sentences is 3-4 percent. This is consistent with his other estimate. He also notes that if recently released prisoners are more vulnerable to arrest than are other criminals (they have a higher q_A), then the average incapacitative effect based on the arrestee sample is overestimated using this approach.

C. SHINNAR AND SHINNAR (1975)

This paper presents a clearly specified model of the criminal career that explicitly deals with the difference between the individual crime rate while free and the effective rate or average rate given time served. All criminals are assumed to commit crimes at the same Poisson rate, λ.[16] Criminals are subject to arrest and conviction with probability q, and to imprisonment given conviction with probability J. The actual sentence served is exponentially distributed with mean S, and the length of criminal careers is exponentially distributed with mean T.

The basic relationship derived from the model is the ratio of the expected volume of crime under some criminal justice policy (as reflected in the values for q, J, and S) to the expected volume of crime if there were no imprisonment.[17] For any criminal, the expected number of crimes in a criminal career is just λT if there is no imprisonment. If, on the other hand, a criminal is arrested, convicted, and sent to prison during his career, his total number of crimes will be reduced by the same proportion that his time free is reduced. His effective crime rate, λ^*, will then be some fraction η of his rate while free (i.e., $\lambda^* = \eta\lambda$).

This fraction is

$$\eta = \frac{1}{1 + \lambda qJS} . \tag{9}$$

This is derived rigorously in Avi-Itzhak and Shinnar (1973), but an intuitive justification may be clearer. For comparatively long careers, T large with respect to S, the average time between prison commitments is just the reciprocal of the rate of prison commitments, $1/\lambda qJ$, and S is the average prison stay. The fraction of the total career that a criminal spends free is given by:

[16]This crime rate λ is constant throughout a career; it does not change as the offender ages or accumulates a criminal record. Under this assumption, the intervals between crimes are independently and identically exponentially distributed with parameter $1/\lambda$.

[17]This basic relationship and its bearing on incapacitation is just one outgrowth of several more general models of the criminal justice system that are developed in an earlier and technically more rigorous paper, Avi-Itzhak and Shinnar (1973).

$$\frac{\text{Average time between commitments}}{\text{Average time between commitments} + \text{average prison stay}} = \frac{\dfrac{1}{\lambda qJ}}{\dfrac{1}{\lambda qJ} + S} = \frac{1}{1 + \lambda qJS}$$

Applying this fraction to λT, the ratio of actual crime to potential crime in a career is also

$$\eta = \frac{\lambda T/(1+\lambda qJS)}{\lambda T} = \frac{1}{1+\lambda qJS}$$

The quantity $1-\eta$ [from eq. (9)] is the basis for estimating the incapacitative effect of various CJS policies. It gives the percentage reduction from the potential level of crime for an imprisonment policy. Using data for New York State, the authors compare the relative effectiveness of the CJS in 1940, 1960, and 1970. By making a steady-state assumption, the expected prison stay per crime committed, qJS, can be estimated from the average daily prison population divided by the number of crimes. In 1940, qJS was about 0.3-0.5. By 1960 qJS was down to 0.13, and in 1970 it was only 0.024. For $\lambda = 10$, this means that in 1940 the effective reduction from potential crime $(1 - \eta)$ was between 75 and 85 percent. By 1960, this was down to a 56 percent reduction, and by 1970 only a 20 percent reduction from potential crime.

Thus, by 1970, the incapacitative impact of imprisonment on crime was minimal. The authors emphasize, however, that the potential exists for a substantial incapacitative effect under different criminal justice system (CJS) policies. For example, with $J = 1.0$ (all convicted persons receive a prison sentence), an average sentence of 3 years, and an average time between conviction $(1/\lambda q)$ of one-half year, $\eta = 0.143$ instead of .800. However, this requires a 25-fold increase over the prevailing value of qJS in 1970 (0.600/0.024 for $\lambda = 10$). If the time between convictions is 1.5 years, crime is reduced to one-third the potential level, while qJS increases 8.3 times (0.200/0.024 for $\lambda = 10$). These comparisons illustrate the sensitivity of the incapacitative effect to the arbitrarily chosen values of the parameters. Significant reductions from the present level of crime require major increases in qJS.

Another interesting result of the model is the apparent multiplier effect of imprisonment. The authors present an example of an efficient CJS, one that reduces crime to only 25 percent of the potential. They then assume that the number of criminals increases 30 percent, but that the average daily prison population (man-years in prison per year) remains constant. The average portion of each individual's career spent in prison is also reduced by 30 percent ($0.7 \times 0.75 = 0.525$) and, thus, the effective crime rate, λ^*, for each criminal almost doubles from 0.25λ to 0.475λ. The total crime rate increases by $1.3 \times (0.475/0.25) = 2.5$. Thus, a 30-percent increase in criminals with no commensurate increase in the prison population results in a 150-percent increase in crime. The multiplier effect occurs because the reduction in the average prison stay increases the effective crime rate of the whole criminal population.

D. MARSH AND SINGER (1972)

Of the papers reviewed, Marsh and Singer are the only authors to consider a distribution of individual crime rates among criminals. Using hypothetical data, they analyzed robberies in New York City. First, they partitioned the population of robbers into six subpopulations, each with its own arbitrarily assigned robbery rate, λ_i. In the two illustrative examples presented, the assumed rates range from one robbery per year to 250 per year. Each subpopulation is also arbitrarily assigned a "conviction" rate per robbery committed (q_iJ_i).[18] The "conviction" rates may vary among the subpopulations or be a constant for all subpopulations. If they vary, the "conviction" rates are assumed to be lower for those groups with higher robbery rates.[19]

Using a very simple stochastic model, the probability that an individual is "convicted" during a year is just one minus the probability of no "convictions":

$$1 - (1 - q_iJ_i)^{\lambda_i} \tag{10}$$

The authors point out that as long as the "conviction" rates of the respective subpopulations do not decrease faster from group to group than the corresponding offense rates increase, higher offense groups will also have a higher probability of "conviction" in a year.

The total number of reported robberies in New York City in 1970

[18] In the later manipulations of the model it is clear that once convicted, a robber commits no more robberies that year. This strongly suggests that Marsh and Singer's "conviction" amounts to incarceration and therefore Marsh and Singer's probability of conviction given a crime is denoted by q_iJ_i, the probability of prison given a crime.

[19] This is a conservative assumption in the sense that if the correlation is the opposite, the results represent a lower bound on the true incapacitative effect.

was about 70,000. Based on non-reporting rates, the authors assume that the actual number of robberies is closer to 200,000. The total number of robbery "convictions" in a year is assumed to be between 2,000 and 5,000. Arbitrarily allocating the 200,000 robberies to the six assumed subpopulations of robbers, the authors can calculate the number of robbers in each group. The only constraint is that there should be fewer robbers in groups with higher offense rates.[20] Applying the "conviction" rate per year to the number of robbers yields the number of "convicted" robbers in each group.

For the total population of robbers, they then calculate three ratios: (a) robberies to all robbers, (b) robberies to "convicted" robbers, and (c) expected robberies to "convicted" robbers in the year after their release. The number of robberies to all robbers will be less than the weighted average robbery rate for the total population because "convicted" (and here incarcerated) robbers do not commit their full share of robberies. Also, in the examples, "convicted" robbers commit more robberies on the average than do all robbers and they can be expected to commit a sizable portion of the total robberies in the year after their release.

Thus, under the reasonable assumption that the "conviction" rates of the respective subpopulations of robbers do not decrease faster from group to group than their corresponding offense rates increase, those robbers who are detected by the system will have higher than average offense rates. Taking their expected number of robberies in the year after their release (which is discounted by possible "reconvictions" in that year) as an indicator, the possible reductions in robberies by imprisoning these "convicted" robbers for an extra year are significant. In the two examples presented by Marsh and Singer, their expected robberies represent from 35 percent to 48 percent of the total robberies in a year. The magnitude of this incapacitative effect is due to the assumption that robbers commit robberies at different rates and that those with higher offense rates are also more likely to be detected and thus imprisoned.

E. EHRLICH (1974)

Erhlich's principal concern is estimating the deterrent effect of imprisonment policies on the overall crime rate. Variations in these policies, however, also have an incapacitative effect associated with the re-

[20]This is a conservative assumption in the sense that if it is wrong, the results represent a lower bound on the true incapacitative effect.

moval of some criminals from free society. Both deterrence and incapacitation operate in the same direction, decreasing the crime rate by increasing the use of prison. Thus, at least some part of the deterrent effect estimated by Ehrlich can be attributed to incapacitation. Ehrlich acknowledges this fact and offers a technique for estimating that part of the total effect that can be attributed to incapacitation.

In a system with no deterrent effect, the total offense rate (crimes per population), C, is just the product of the individual crime rate while free (λ) and the number of offenders at large. For a steady-state system (no growth), this can be shown to be

$$C = \frac{\lambda N}{1+PS} \tag{11}$$

where N is the total number of offenders (in and out of prison), P is the probability that an offender is apprehended and imprisoned, and S is the average time served by those imprisoned. The elasticity (σ)[21] of C with respect to changes in P or S is the same, namely

$$\sigma_{CP} = \sigma_{CS} = \frac{-PS}{1+PS} \tag{12}$$

In the empirical analysis of cross-sectional data, Ehrlich reports that for the values of P and S observed, σ amounts to only about 10 percent of the magnitude of the estimated coefficients for the probability of a prison sentence given a crime and the time served in prison.[22] Based on the estimates reported in Ehrlich's Tables 4 and 5, a 50 percent reduction in the average time served would result in a 4.6 percent increase in index property offenses, a 2.5 percent increase in index persons offenses, and a 5.6 percent increase in all index offenses from lost incapacitation alone. These figures are consistent with the estimates provided by Clarke (1974) and Greenberg (1975).

[21]The elasticity is a measure of the responsiveness of the dependent variable to changes in an independent variable. It gives the percentage change in the dependent variable associated with a 1 percent change in the independent variable. For $Y = f(X)$, the elasticity of Y with respect to X is given by

$$\sigma_{YX} = \frac{dY}{dX} \cdot \frac{\overline{X}}{\overline{Y}}.$$

[22]Ehrlich (1974), p. 103, note 50.

III. CRITICAL ANALYSIS

Three of the papers discussed conclude that the potential increases in crime associated with a reduction in the present use of prison are minimal (Clarke 1974, Greenberg 1975, and Ehrlich 1974). The other two papers indicate that the potential gains in reduced crime from expanding the use of prison are sizable (Shinnar and Shinnar 1975 and Marsh and Singer 1972). The purpose of this critique is to examine the reasons for these different conclusions, to find some common ground if possible, and to explore the implications for new research directions.

In part, Clarke's and Greenberg's low estimates of the incapacitative effect of prison rest on their correspondingly low estimates of the individual crime rate. In each case, the potential increase in crime is given by the product of the number of additional man-years free and the individual crime rate while free (crimes committed per year, λ). For different reasons, both authors underestimate the individual crime rate while free.

Clarke (1974) uses data on the number of "arrests" at each age for juveniles in the sample of "ever incarcerated" offenders[23] and the number of juveniles institutionalized at each age. Using 9 months for the average time served, he estimates the full-year equivalents of the number of juveniles free at each age and attributes all "arrests" for that age to them. This procedure, however, ignores variations in the age of starting and ending a criminal career. For each age considered, *all* of the "ever incarcerated" juveniles who are not institutionalized during that year are assumed to be active in criminal careers. None have dropped out and none are still waiting to start their careers. Attributing the "arrests" to such "non-criminals" (juveniles whose crime rate is actually zero) will seriously deflate the estimate of individual "arrest" rates.

Table 2 compares Clarke's estimate for non-white boys with an alternative estimate that takes account of entry and dropping out from a career.[24] Data are available on the age of onset of detected criminal activities for the full delinquent cohort (Wolfgang *et al.*, 1972, Table 8.1). These data can be used to estimate the conditional probability of

[23]The sample of "ever incarcerated" offenders refers to those juveniles from the Philadelphia birth cohort who were institutionalized at least once before age 18 (n = 381).

[24]Both Clarke's estimates and the alternative estimates presented here assume that all the incarcerated boys would have remained criminally active during the year. Any within-year drop-out among these boys would reduce the number of crimes averted in both estimates.

TABLE 2 A Comparison of Clarke's Estimate of Individual "Arrest"[a] Rates and "Arrests" Averted[b] with an Estimate Allowing for Entry to and Drop-Out from the Criminal Career (Non-white boys)

Age 1	Number Incarcerated 2	Full-Year Equivalent of Number Incarcerated[c] 3	Conditional Probability of Onset by Age[d] 4	Total Active in Criminal Career[e] 5	Full-Year Equivalent of Number Free 6 = 5−3	Number of Index "Arrests" 7	"Arrest" Rate/ "Active" Boy at Large 8 = 7/6	Total "Arrests" Prevented by Incarceration 9 = 8 × 3	"Arrests" Prevented per Incarceration 10 = 9/2
7	(0)	(0)	0.0103	3.09 (300)	3.09 (300.0)	(3)	0.971 (.010)	0.000 (.000)	— (—)
8	(0)	(0)	0.0187	8.33 (300)	8.33 (300.0)	(13)	1.561 (0.043)	0.000 (.000)	— (—)
9	(3)	(2.25)	0.0495	21.92 (300)	19.67 (297.8)	(41)	2.084 (.138)	4.689 (.311)	1.563 (.104)
10	(7)	(5.25)	0.0737	40.14 (300)	34.89 (294.8)	(51)	1.462 (.173)	7.676 (.908)	1.097 (.130)
11	(15)	(11.25)	0.1028	62.50 (300)	51.25 (288.8)	(83)	1.620 (.287)	18.225 (3.229)	1.215 (.215)
12	(23)	(17.25)	0.1522	91.28 (300)	74.03 (282.8)	(129)	1.743 (.456)	30.067 (7.866)	1.307 (.342)
13	(40)	(30.00)	0.2112	123.36 (300)	93.36 (270.0)	(154)	1.650 (.570)	49.500 (17.100)	1.238 (.428)
14	(87)	(65.25)	0.2624	151.41 (300)	86.16 (234.8)	(164)	1.903 (.698)	124.171 (45.545)	1.427 (.524)
15	(103)	(77.25)	0.4138	183.25 (300)	106.00 (222.8)	(188)	1.774 (.844)	137.042 (65.199)	1.331 (.633)
16	(148)	(111.00)	0.6873	210.66 (300)	99.66 (189.0)	(249)	2.498 (1.317)	277.278 (146.187)	1.874 (.988)
17	(112)	(84.00)	1.0000	210.40 (300)	126.40 (216.0)	(156)	1.234 (.722)	103.656 (60.648)	.926 (.542)
TOTAL	(538)	(403.50)		1106.34 (3,300)	702.84 (2896.8)	(1231)	1.753 (.425)	752.304 (346.993)	1.398 (.645)

[a]This is the juvenile equivalent of offenses resulting in arrest. It includes all those offenses attributed to the juvenile by the police without formal arrest charges against the juvenile.

[b]Taken from Clarke (1974), Table 1. Clarke's figures appear in parentheses in this table. The totals sometimes differ from those in Clarke because age 6 has been excluded here.

[c]Assuming the average time served per incarceration is 9 months.

[d]The conditional probability of onset is the probability of beginning a criminal career (first "arrest") at age i given that one begins a career by age 17. They are calculated using data on age of onset for the full delinquent cohort available in Table 8.1 of Wolfgang, Figlio and Sellin (1972). The probabilities are calculated as the number of offenders whose first "arrest" is at age i divided by the number of eligible members remaining in the delinquent cohort (excluding those who already have an "arrest"). If the institutionalized cohort began their careers in the same way as the full delinquent cohort, these probabilities can be used to estimate the number entering careers at each age.

[e]Assuming exponentially distributed career length with mean of 10 years (a 10 percent drop-out rate per year) and different onset probabilities by age.

onset by age.[25] Applying these probabilities to the "ever incarcerated" cohort provides estimates of the number entering their careers at each age. In addition, assuming career lengths are distributed exponentially with a mean of 10 years, about one-tenth of the currently active criminals will end their careers each year.

Under these assumptions, the full-year equivalent of the number of criminally active boys who are free is reduced by more than one-fourth and the number of index offenses prevented by incarceration is more than doubled.[26] The estimates for white boys change even more. Thus, allowing for entry and dropping out from a career, the number of index "arrests" prevented now constitutes about 15 to 30 percent of all index "arrests" for the full cohort instead of 5 to 15 percent.

In going from index "arrests" for juveniles to total reported index offenses, Clarke makes an additional assumption that further underestimates the proportion of crimes prevented by incarceration. The proportion of all reported crimes committed by juveniles is unavailable. The FBI, however, does report the proportion of all arrests that are juveniles. In 1972, 45 percent of all persons arrested for Part I crimes were juveniles. Rather than apply the same proportion to reported crimes, Clarke assumes that juveniles are more likely to be arrested than adults. In fact, the juvenile arrest-to-offense ratio is assumed to be exactly 1.6 times the overall arrest-to-offense ratio. This is a strong assumption with no apparent empirical basis.

Using this assumption, Clarke concludes that 28 percent of all reported index offenses are committed by juveniles and thus only 1-4 percent (0.05×0.28 or 0.15×0.28) of all index crimes are averted by the incarceration of juveniles. If 45 percent of all index offenses are committed by juveniles (assuming no age bias in arrest), Clarke's fraction of crimes averted increases to 2-7 percent (0.05×0.45 or 0.15×0.45) of all index crimes. Using 45 percent as the proportion of offenses committed by juveniles together with consideration of entry and dropout from criminal careers, the index crimes averted become 7-14 percent (0.15×0.45 or 0.3×0.45) of all reported index crimes.

Greenberg (1975) makes a more fundamental error in his estimate of

[25]To the extent that individuals engage in crime without detection for some period of time, the conditional probability of onset is underestimated somewhat at early ages and correspondingly overestimated at later ages.

[26]With a longer mean career length ($T > 10$) and/or higher entry rates at younger ages, the increase in "arrests" averted will be less than that reported in Table 2; with a shorter career length ($T < 10$) and/or lower entry rates at younger ages the number of "arrests" averted will increase more than reported in Table 2.

individual crime rates. He fails to distinguish between the crime rate while free (λ) and the effective crime rate (λ^*) (i.e., the crime rate reduced by time served). To estimate the increase in crime associated with a decrease in the use of prison, the desired quantity is the crime rate while free (λ). The Greenberg estimates, however, are based on data reflecting the effective crime rate (λ^*).

The arrest rate for index crimes is taken from FBI data as 0.5 arrests per year, and the total number of non-virgin arrests for index offenses in a career, 2.5, is taken from estimates of a feedback model of the CJS. Both of these figures represent the number of arrests that result under a given CJS imprisonment policy. They are discounted from the rate while free by any time spent incapacitated.

Whatever the accuracy of Greenberg's estimates in other respects, his estimates are of the effective crime rate, λ^*. The magnitude of the error between the effective crime rate (λ^*) and the desired rate while free (λ) varies directly with the current incapacitative effect of prison. If the incapacitation effect is large, prison stays dramatically reduce realized crime and λ^* seriously underestimates λ. If, on the other hand, there is very little incapacitation effect, then the rate while free is not reduced very much by prison stays. In this case λ^* is quite close to λ and the estimated incapacitative effect is not seriously biased.

The use of λ^* in place of λ is not the only source of underestimation for λ. Greenberg uses an interesting approach to bound the possible values of the effective crime rate, λ^*. The lower bound on λ^* is derived by dividing the arrest rate of 0.5 arrests per year by the highest possible arrest probability, 1.0, resulting in a rate of $\lambda^* = 0.5$ crimes per year.

To specify the upper bound on λ^*, estimates of four variables are needed: (a) C—the number of index crimes committed in a year (reported and unreported), (b) A—the annual number of arrests for non-minor offenses, (c) V/A—the ratio of virgin arrests for non-minor offenses to all arrests for the same offenses, and (d) V_I/A—the ratio of virgin arrests for index offenses to all arrests for non-minor offenses. The annual number of arrests is not problematic. The available FBI data provides the basis for a reasonable estimate of 1.94 million non-minor arrests in 1965.[27] The total number of index crimes, however, is not directly available. This figure must be extrapolated from reported offenses and various estimates of the non-reporting rate.

Figure 1 shows the variations in the upper bound of λ^* that occur for different assumed reporting rates (holding A, V/A, and V_I/A constant).

[27]This number is extrapolated from the figure for the agencies reporting in 1965 to yield the estimated total for the United States as a whole.

For reporting rates below 50 percent, the upper bound of λ^* is very sensitive to minor changes in the reporting rate. In fact, within the most probable range of reporting rates of 25 to 50 percent,[28] the upper bound on λ^* varies between 4.4 and 2.1. The choice of a reporting rate is thus an important source of error in the final estimate of the effective crime rate, λ^*.

The ratios V/A and V_I/A are arbitrarily set by Greenberg at 0.25 and 0.20, respectively. The only constraints on these values are that $V/A < 1/3.5 = 0.286$ and $V_I/A < V/A$. Figure 2 shows the sensitivity of the resulting upper bound of λ^* to variations in these ratios. While the ratio V_I/A makes very little difference, the choice of V/A is an important factor. Marginally smaller values of V/A lead to larger values of λ^*. The combination of a lower reporting rate and a lower proportion of

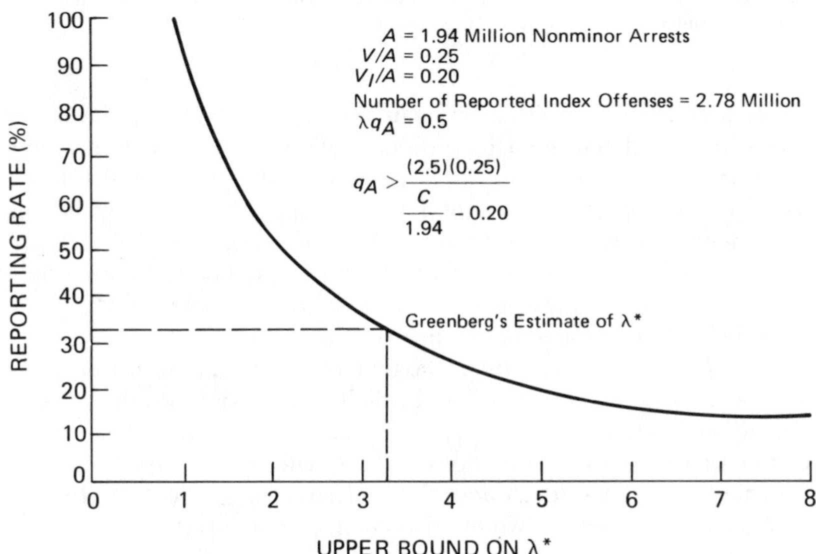

FIGURE 1 Greenberg's upper bound on the individual crime rate (λ^*) as a function of the reporting rate for index crimes–holding A, V/A, and V_I/A constant (Eq. 7).

[28]Victimization surveys in 18 U.S. cities (U.S. Department of Justice 1975, 1976) indicate relatively little variation in reporting rates among cities, with reporting rates of about 33 percent for all crimes in the personal sector, 45 percent for crimes of violence and 25 percent for crimes of theft.

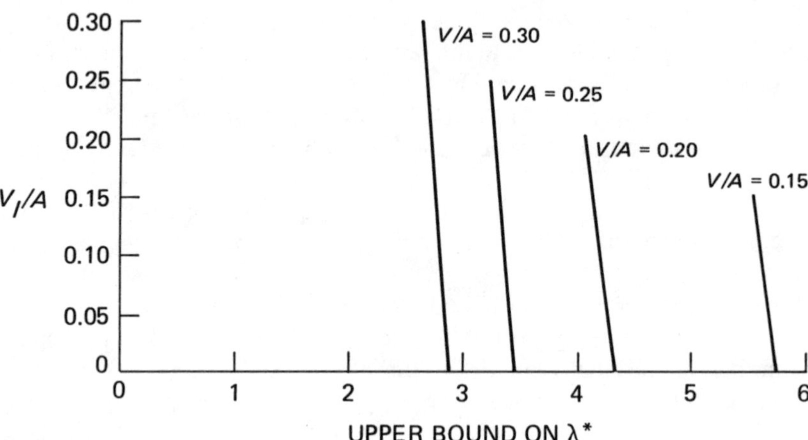

FIGURE 2 Greenberg's upper bound on individual crime rate (λ^*) as a function of the ratios V/A and V_I/A—holding A and C constant (Eq. 7).

virgin arrests among all arrests can significantly increase the upper bound for λ^*. If the reporting rate is taken as 30 percent rather than one-third and V/A is set at 0.15 rather than 0.25 ($V_I/A = 0.10$), the upper bound for λ^* is 6.25, not 3.33. The upper bound on λ^* is thus extremely sensitive to the values of the input variables. The fact that the values of these variables are often only poorly known considerably limits confidence in the validity of the resulting estimates of λ^*.

Ehrlich's low estimate of the incapacitative effect is also misleading. As with Clarke and Greenberg, the underestimate can be attributed to an unusually low estimate of λ. In Ehrlich's case, however, the value of λ in eq. (12) is a buried assumption that is only uncovered by a careful reconstruction of his assumptions and estimates.

In the theoretical development, the desired incapacitative effect is derived as a function of two imprisonment policy variables

P—the probability that an offender at large is apprehended and imprisoned (e.g., the number of prison commitments per offender at large)

S—the average time actually served in prison by an offender.

Both these variables are offender-based, that is, they reflect the costs in prison time incurred by an offender and not the costs associated with any single offense. The problem arises in the empirical estimates of these variables used by Ehrlich.

Both P and S are estimated using data from the *National Prisoner Statistics* for 1960. The estimate of S is straightforward, using the time served and inmate data for the appropriate state and crime type. P is estimated by the ratio of the number of prison commitments to the number of offenses committed. This is a measure of the probability of imprisonment associated with an offense, not the probability for an offender.

In Ehrlich's Appendix I, where the empirical estimates of the theoretical variables are documented, Ehrlich indicates that the ratio of the number of convicted offenders to total offenders is the appropriate estimate of the probability of conviction for an offender. He then argues that the desired ratio is the same as the number of offenses cleared by conviction divided by total offenses, if convicted offenders commit crime at the same rate as all other offenders. Namely,

$$\frac{C}{O} = \frac{\lambda C}{\lambda O} \tag{13}$$

for C = the number of convicted offenders, O = the total number of offenders at large, and λ = the constant individual crime rate while free. Presumably this same argument applies to the imprisonment ratios, thus justifying using the ratio of prison commitments to offenses as the estimate of P.

This argument, however, does not stand up when it is examined more closely. First, while the identity in eq. (13) is obvious, λC is not the number of offenses cleared by conviction. This would only be true if one assumed that all the offenses committed by an individual were cleared by his conviction. There is no doubt that some convicted offenders will be convicted for more than one offense, but this is far from assuming that all convicted offenders are convicted of, or even associated with, all the offenses they have committed. In fact, the number of offenses cleared by conviction and the number of offenders convicted differ by the number of multiple offenses for a single offender and/or the number of multiple offenders for a single convicted offense.

Likewise, for the probability of prison, λI (I = number of prison commitments) is not the number of offenses resulting in imprisonment. Except for cases of multiple offenders/offense or multiple offenses/offender, the number of prison commitments (I) in the numerator reflects the number of *offenders* committed to prison and not the number of *offenses* that result in a prison commitment. The variable actually used in Ehrlich's analysis is thus the probability of prison given an offense, $I/\lambda O$. To get the desired probability of prison for an offender, Ehrlich's $\hat{P}$ must be multiplied by some estimate of λ.

As it turns out, this confusion between an offender- and offense-based variable P has no effect on Ehrlich's estimated coefficients. Multiplying the variable P by a constant in the log-linear formulation will not change the coefficients. Ignoring the λ adjustment, however, does make a big difference in the estimate of the incapacitative effect.

The elasticity should be computed as:

$$\sigma = \frac{-PS}{1 + PS} = \frac{-\lambda\hat{P}S}{1 + \lambda\hat{P}S} \tag{14}$$

The evidence suggests that Ehrlich computed σ from

$$-\frac{\hat{P}S}{1 + \hat{P}S} \tag{15}$$

where $\hat{P}S$ is the expected prison stay for an offense. This amounts to assuming that $\lambda = 1$. In the United States as a whole in 1960, the estimate of $\hat{P}S$ for all index offenses was .105 (Shinnar and Shinnar 1975, Table 9). Substituting into eq. (15) the estimate of σ is 0.095 or about the 10 percent of the total elasticity of 0.991 (Ehrlich 1974, Table 5) attributed to incapacitation by Ehrlich.

Using eq. (14), Table 3 presents alternative estimates of the incapacitative effect for all index crimes for different assumed values of λ. For $\lambda = 10$, a 1-percent increase in P or S in 1960 results in a 0.512 percent decrease in crime. Thus, for values of λ, greater than unity, the incapacitative effect represents a considerably higher proportion of Ehrlich's coefficients than he acknowledges. Since Ehrlich's coefficients represent the total imprisonment effect combining deterrence and incapacitation, any increases in the incapacitative effect necessarily decrease the deterrent effect. This result calls into question Ehrlich's conclusions about a significant deterrent effect associated with prison stays.

In summary, then, it appears that Clarke, Greenberg, and Ehrlich have all underestimated the average crime rate. Such underestimation of λ will also result in an underestimate of the reduction from potential crime associated with present imprisonment policies. In turns out, however, that the magnitude of this underestimation of the incapacitative effect is not very large. Given the present low levels of incarceration, higher estimates of λ will not make the estimate of the incapacitative effect very much larger.

In the Clarke analysis, even with an average juvenile "arrest" rate as high as 5 index "arrests" per year (compared to Clarke's values of

TABLE 3 Estimates of the Elasticity (σ) of Crime in Response to Changes in the Probability of Prison for an Offender (P) or the Time Served in Prison (S) as a Function of the Individual Crime Rate while Free (λ) (For Index Crimes in the United States)

$$\sigma = \frac{-PS}{1+PS} = -\frac{\lambda\hat{P}S}{1+\lambda\hat{P}S}^{a}$$

	σ	
λ	1960 ($\hat{P}S$ = .105)[b] %	1970 ($\hat{P}S$ = .035)[b] %
1	−.095[c]	−.034
5	−.344	−.149
10	−.512	−.259
15	−.612	−.344
20	−.677	−.412

[a] σ gives the % change in the level of crime associated with a 1% change in $P = \lambda\hat{P}$ or S, where $\hat{P}$ is the probability of prison for an offense.

[b] Estimates of the expected prison stay per crime for index crimes in the United States as a whole reported in Table 9 of Shinnar and Shinnar (1975).

[c] The estimate of the incapacitative elasticity presented in Ehrlich (1974).

0.287 and 0.385), the number of "arrests" averted by institutionalization represents 64.3 percent of all index "arrests" for the Philadelphia cohort. Assuming, as Clarke does, that 28 percent of all reported index offenses are committed by juveniles, the crimes averted by incapacitation are 18 percent of all reported index crimes. Similarly in the Greenberg analysis, if the index crime rate while free is as high as 10 per year, increasing the total man-years free by 200,000 (eliminating prisons entirely) increases the number of index crimes by 2 million. The increase in crime from lost incapacitation is 24 percent over the present assumed level of 8.34 million. Applying the Ehrlich model to 1970 data, if λ is 10, a 100 percent reduction in average time served implies a 25.9 percent (100 × 0.259 percent) increase in crime from lost incapacitation. Even the Shinnar and Shinnar model, which explicitly considers the impact of time served on the crime rate and the possibility of drop-out while incarcerated, estimates that the incapacitative effect in 1970 in New York State was a 20 percent reduction from the potential level of crime with λ = 10. The crimes averted through incapacitation thus represented 25 percent of the realized crime (0.2/0.8).

All the authors considered would generally agree that the present incapacitative effect of prison is minimal. Their disagreement about the magnitude of that effect (4 percent or 8 percent or 20 percent) can be attributed almost entirely to their different estimates of the average crime rate while free. Naturally, the incapacitative effect is greater with higher individual crime rates. To illustrate the actual level of agreement among the models proposed by the different authors, the elasticity of crime in each model has been estimated using the same numerical estimates for the various model variables. The computation of these elasticities is available in Appendix A. The results are presented in Table 4.

To make the estimates comparable, the individual crime rates were increased for Ehrlich and Greenberg and the number of crimes committed was reduced to reported crimes for Greenberg. When a uniform 1 percent change in prison use is considered for all authors, the change in crime is almost the same for all models. Greenberg's model indicates a slightly greater response of crime to changes in the number of man-years served in prison. The difference, however, is due to the relationship between man-years served and the policy variables, λqJ and S. In Appendix A, it is demonstrated that the increases in λqJ or S must be greater than 1 percent in order to achieve a 1 percent increase in man-years served. The elasticities in Table 4 are, therefore, directly compatible.

There is another important source of bias that must be considered in all the models discussed so far. Shinnar has demonstrated[29] that when criminals have different individual crime rates, assuming a constant λ for all criminals will yield an underestimate of the incapacitative effect. To the extent that higher λ individuals are more likely to be incapacitated,[30] the actual number of crimes averted is greater than that estimated using an average value of λ. Because of this bias, estimates of the number of crimes averted by current incapacitative policies are particularly vulnerable to error. The actual number of crimes avoided will be larger (by some unknown amount) than estimated.

The more interesting policy question is: What can be expected from incapacitation if imprisonment policies are changed? The simple model used by Clarke and Greenberg, which just multiplies λ by the number of man-years of incarceration per year, is not very useful here. It can only be used to assess the impact of policies whose aggregate result is some specified change in the man-years served in prison. Without addi-

[29]Shinnar (1977).

[30]This will occur even if higher λ individuals have lower probabilities of imprisonment per crime, as long as in comparisons between individuals the ratio of the individual probabilities of prison is less than the reciprocal of the ratio of the individual crime rates (i.e., $q_iJ_i/q_jJ_j < \lambda_j/\lambda_i$ for $\lambda_i < \lambda_j$).

TABLE 4 Comparison of Elasticity[a] of Crime to Changes in Imprisonment Policies for Different Models Using the Same Numerical Estimates for All Models

Author	Variables[d]	Estimates of Variables	Expression for Total Crimes Committed	Elasticity Formulas[b]	Calculated Elasticity[c]
Greenberg (1975)	λ, I, C, N	$I \sim$ average daily prison pop. $C \sim$ number of reported index crimes	$C = \lambda(N - I)$	$\sigma_{CI} = \frac{-\lambda I}{C}$	−0.36
Shinnar and Shinnar (1975)	$\lambda, \lambda^*, q, J,$ S, C, N	qJS = expected prison stay/crime $\sim \frac{\text{average daily prison pop.}}{\text{number of crimes committed}}$	$C = \lambda^* N = \frac{\lambda N}{1 + \lambda qJS}$	$\sigma_{C,\lambda qJ} = \sigma_{C,S} = \frac{-\lambda qJS}{1 + \lambda qJS}$	−0.26
Ehrlich (1974)	λ, P, S, O, C	PS = expected prison stay/offender at large $\sim \lambda \cdot \frac{\text{average daily prison pop.}}{\text{number of crimes commited}}$	$C = \lambda O = \frac{\lambda N}{1 + PS}$	$\sigma_{CP} = \sigma_{CS} = \frac{-PS}{1 + PS}$	−0.26

[a] The elasticity is the percentage change in the dependent variable associated with a 1% change in an independent variable. For $Y = f(X)$ the elasticity of Y with respect to X, σ_{YX}, is given by $dY/dX \cdot \bar{X}/\bar{Y}$.

[b] See Appendix A for derivation of these elasticity formulas.

[c] Each elasticity is computed using the following values of the variables: $\lambda = 5$, average daily prison population = 200,000, and total index crimes committed = 2.78 million.

[d] Variable Definitions:

λ = individual index crime rate while free
λ^* = individual's effective index crime rate (discounted for any time served)
q = probability arrest and conviction for a crime
J = probability prison after conviction
P = probability prison for an offender at large = λqJ
S = average time served
C = total number of index crimes committed (reported only)
N = total number of offenders
O = number of offenders at large
I = number of man-years served in prison annually

tional assumptions, however, this simple model cannot directly translate changes in the arrest or imprisonment probabilities or increases in time served to the necessary changes in man-years served. The Shinnar and Shinnar model, on the other hand, explicitly considers the effects of the CJS parameters on the size of the prison population and the effective crime rate. Thus, using the expression $1 - \eta$, the effect of variations in the individual parameters (q, J, and S) can be evaluated.

Figure 3 presents $1 - \eta$ (the percentage reduction from the potential level of crime) as a function of qJS and λ. The reduction in crime is larger for larger values of qJS. Interestingly, the level of incapacitative effectiveness (percentage reduction in crime) varies most at the lowest levels of qJS, and tapers off as qJS increases. This larger variability at low values of qJS is more pronouned the higher the value of λ. As with qJS, the differences in impact on crime are greatest for the lower

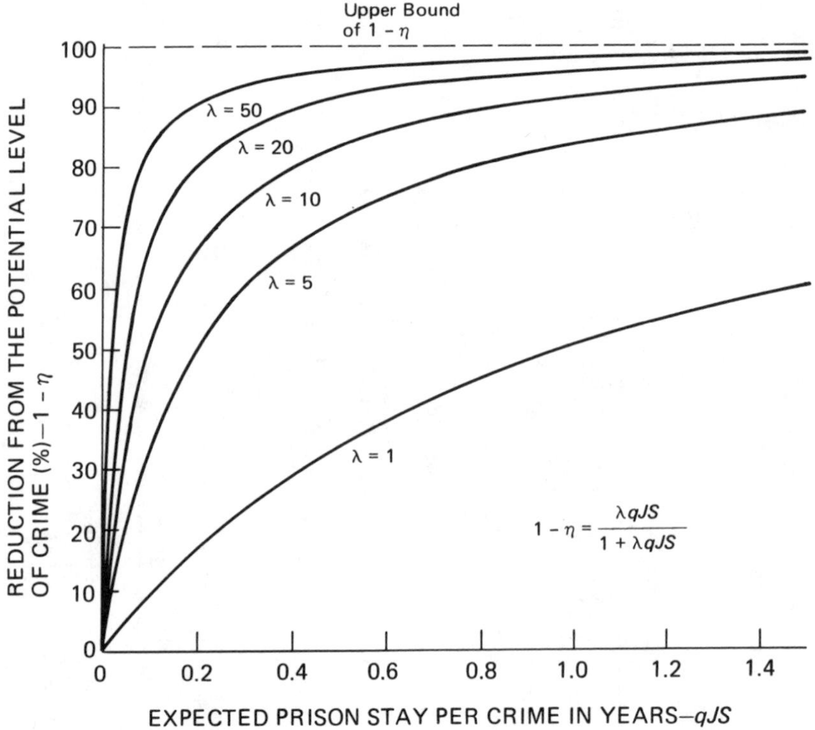

FIGURE 3 Percentage reduction from the potential level of crime (qJS=0) as a function of qJS and λ. The expression $1 - \eta = (\lambda qJS)/(1 + \lambda qJS)$ is from Shinnar and Shinnar (1975).

values of λ. Between $\lambda = 1$ and $\lambda = 5$, the incapacitative effect is quite sensitive to the particular value of λ chosen. Beyond $\lambda = 10$, the exact value of λ is less important to the level of crime reduction.

The simple stochastic model developed by Shinnar and Shinnar is quite robust. As the authors point out, it provides conservative (lower bound) estimates of the incapacitative effect of crime. Under different assumptions (e.g., λ distributed over the population of criminals, career length distributed other than exponentially) the incapacitative effect is equal to or greater than $1 - \eta$.

The potential for significantly larger reductions in crime when λ is not a constant, but rather a distributed random variable in the criminal population, is dramatized by the Marsh and Singer analysis. Their simple examples clearly illustrate that as long as qJ (the probability of apprehension, conviction, and imprisonment) does not decrease faster than λ increases within the population, those criminals actually imprisoned will always have a higher than average crime rate. Their imprisonment will thus avert more crimes than predicted using the average crime rate for the criminal population as a whole.

The Marsh and Singer formulation is certainly more satisfying, because it relaxes the restrictive assumption of a constant λ and instead allows λ to vary among criminals. This approach, however, introduces new problems when attempting to estimate empirically the λ_i. In addition to a λ_i, each subpopulation is also characterized by its own arrest, conviction, and imprisonment probabilities, q_i and J_i. Under optimal conditions, the data permit estimates of arrest rates, conviction rates, and imprisonment rates for individuals. If q_i is the probability of arrest given a crime, then the observed arrest rate within subpopulation i is given by $\mu_i = \lambda_i q_i$. Now, for any identified subpopulation, we have two unknown parameters to be estimated, λ_i and q_i, and only one data point, μ_i. Obtaining separate estimates for λ_i and q_i requires independent information or additional assumptions about one or both of these parameters.

One approach is to assume that the probability of arrest is constant for all subpopulations, $q_i = \overline{q}$. A single population $\overline{q}$ can then be estimated from the aggregate number of arrests and crimes.[31] The individual λ_i can then be estimated as $\mu_i/\overline{q}$. If q is, in fact, a constant in the population, the resulting λ_i will be satisfactory. There are also no problems if both λ and q are distributed within the criminal population, but the distributions are independent of one another. In this event, all

[31]Typically, only the number of reported crimes would be considered. However, reported crimes may be adjusted by some reporting rate to get an estimate of the total crimes committed (reported and unreported).

individuals within a subpopulation will have the same λ_i, but different q's. Since the q's within each subpopulation are likely to have the same distribution as that found in the total population, the expected value of q in each subpopulation will be equal to the expected value for the whole population. Thus, using the population mean does not bias the estimates of λ_i.

When λ and q are correlated, however, the estimates of λ_i using a constant $\overline{q}$ will be biased. For those subpopulations with a higher than average q_i, using $\overline{q}$ overestimates the true λ_i. Likewise, the true λ_i will be underestimated for subpopulations with a lower than average q_i. The nature of the bias will depend on the relationship between λ and q. In the case of λ and q positively related, the smaller λ_i's are underestimated, while larger λ_i's are overestimated. With λ and q negatively related, the smaller λ_i's are overestimated and larger λ_i's are underestimated.

If there is good reason to believe that λ and q are not independent, better estimates of λ_i and q_i can be obtained by specifying q_i as an explicit function of λ_i. In the absence of some independent data on the actual number of crimes committed by the members of a subpopulation, however, it is impossible to verify independently the assumed relationship. Thus, without independent knowledge of the q_i, estimating the distinct λ_i is a problem and the accuracy of these estimates rests entirely on the adequacy of the assumptions made about q.

The simpler Shinnar and Shinnar model avoids the above estimation problems. Nevertheless, some serious questions can be raised about the policy implications discussed by the authors. The first issue is the authors' claim of dramatic decreases in the effectiveness of the CJS in reducing crime over the past three decades. This claim is based on the changes in $1 - \eta$ (which dropped from 80 percent to 20 percent) that accompany changes in the estimates of *qJS while assuming a constant* λ. It is equally plausible to assume that at least some part of the dramatic increases in crime observed over the past 30 years is due to increasing criminality, reflected in a higher λ for individual offenders. In fact, if λ did increase over the period 1940 to 1970, the level of effectiveness of the CJS could have remained fairly constant despite the undeniable declines in qJS.

Figure 4 illustrates the trade-offs between changes in λ and qJS that are possible while maintaining a constant $1 - \eta$. Even if qJS were to drop from 0.2 to 0.1 while λ increases from 5 to 10, $1 - \eta$ would remain equal to 0.5, or a 50 percent reduction from the potential level of crime. It certainly seems plausible that at least some of the observed drop in qJS between 1940 and 1960 was accompanied by increases in λ. In this

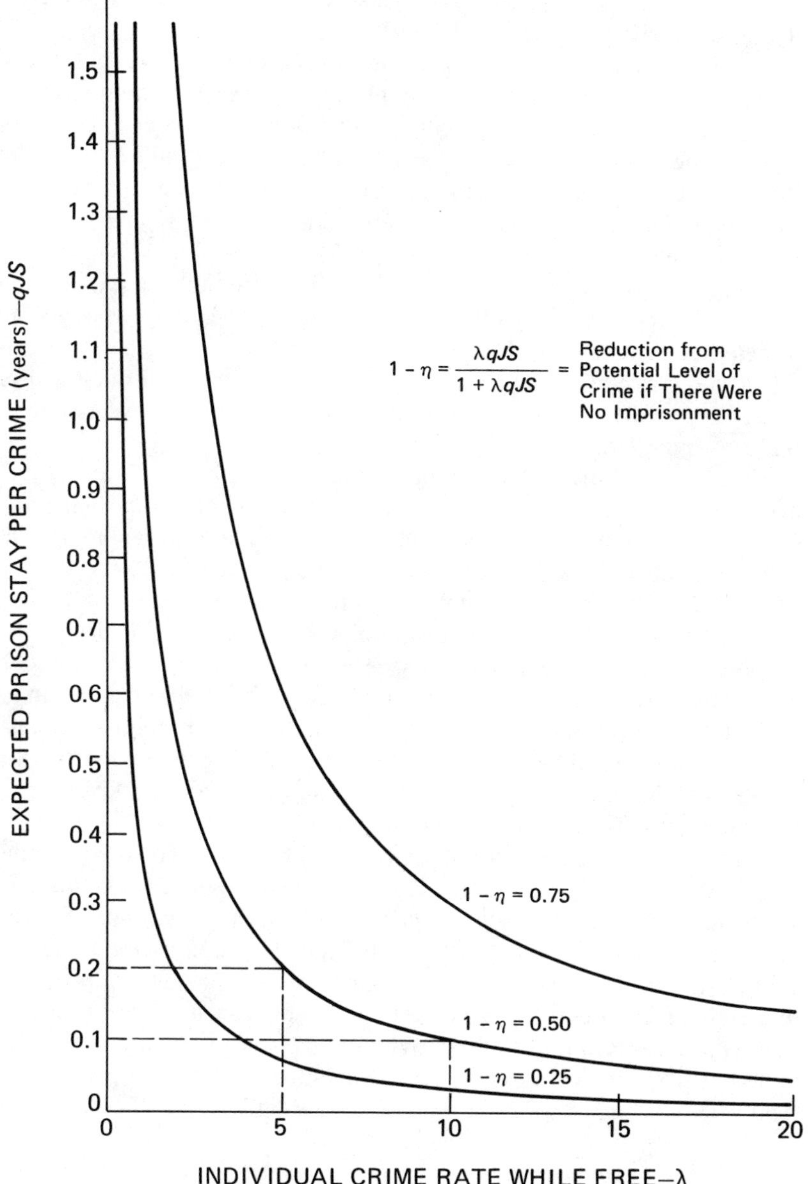

FIGURE 4 Trade-offs between CJS policy parameter (qJS) and individual crime rate (λ) while maintaining a constant effective reduction in crime ($1 - \eta$).

event, the CJS effectiveness (as measured by $1 - \eta$) need not have decreased nearly as much as the authors suggest.

This is just one example of the kind of problems that are introduced by the general assumption of constant parameters in the model. In the face of actual increases in criminality reflected by a higher λ, comparisons of the effeciveness of the system at different points in time are likely to be seriously misleading. Accurate estimates depend critically on having adequate estimates of the individual crime rate at different points in time.

Shinnar and Shinnar also argue that it is reasonable to expect that present CJS policies (as reflected by a low qJS) can be changed to increase qJS at least to historically achieved levels, 0.3 to 0.5. This would have a substantial impact on crime, reducing it to one-third or one-fifth its current level.[32] Several considerations, however, suggest that this overstates the real potential.

First, it is not clear that the individual parameters q, J, and S can accommodate anything more than minor adjustments from their present values. The three parameters include the probabilities of apprehension, conviction, and imprisonment and the average time served once in prison. Apprehension is a police function requiring the identification and arrest of a suspect. It is absolutely crucial because it brings the criminal into the CJS, where he can be incapacitated. There is no hope of significantly reducing crime through incapacitation if most criminals go undetected for long periods of time. The rate of apprehension, however, is not a very flexible parameter. In general, police departments do the best they can to identify and arrest suspects; present levels of q_A are not simply matters of policy that can be changed at will.

Conviction is a prosecutorial and judicial function. To some extent, conviction rates might be increased by improving police procedures in securing evidence to reduce the number of cases thrown out of court because of inadequate evidence or technical violations invoking the exclusionary rule. More convictions might also be achieved if prosecutors were able to devote more time to developing a case before trial. As with apprehension, however, conviction rates are typically not determined as a matter of policy. Given current caseloads and procedural requirements, prosecutors and judges are usually doing the best they can.

Furthermore, even if conviction rates in trials could be increased, perhaps through the relaxation of present due process constraints, the overall conviction rate might remain unchanged. Present conviction

[32]Assume $\lambda = 10$ and a present value of $qJS = 0.024$. Then $\eta_{0.3} = 0.25$, $\eta_{0.5} = 0.167$, $\eta_{0.024} = 0.806$ and $\eta_{0.3}/\eta_{0.024} = 0.31$, and $\eta_{0.5}/\eta_{0.024} = 0.21$.

rates, especially in urban areas, are the result of a combination of guilty pleas by defendants and convictions won in court. It is not clear how the current willingness to plead guilty might be affected by a more zealous effort to prosecute cases in court by prosecutors.

Both apprehension and conviction rates are the result of complicated processes involving such things as rules of evidence and a variety of procedural guidelines. They are not easily changed merely as a matter of policy. Imposing a prison sentence on a convicted offender and determining the length of time served are more amenable to policy manipulations. Operating within the constraints of what constitutes a just punishment, there is often a good bit of latitude on the exact sentence imposed after conviction. Undoubtedly many more people convicted of serious crimes (e.g., robbery) could be sentenced to prison than are now without overstepping the bounds of justice. Operating within currently legislated limits on maximum sentence, judges could also impose longer sentences and parole boards could delay releases on parole, thus increasing the time served. For a number of reasons, however, these otherwise possible measures may not be feasible.

For one thing, the probability of receiving a prison sentence once convicted and the probability of conviction are not entirely independent. In many urban courts, guilty pleas, which often result from some plea bargaining, constitute the bulk of all convictions. They are the lubricant that helps to keep heavily loaded courts functioning, and they are gained at the price of a lower chance of a prison sentence or shorter sentences upon conviction. If a sentencing policy of more and longer prison terms were enacted, it would no doubt have a profound effect on the conviction rate as the number of guilty pleas declined. The trial workload would also increase, potentially overloading the court system. Any gains in qJS made by increasing J and/or S could well be offset by the accompanying drop in q.

Aside from the constraints on the individual parameters already mentioned, the size of the prison population associated with any value of qJS is another potentially limiting factor. There is some strong evidence that there are limits on the amount of prison a society is willing to accept. Two papers on that subject (Blumstein and Cohen 1973 and Blumstein *et al.* 1976) argue that the level of punishment meted out by a society remains fairly stable over time. Data were presented in these papers on the imprisonment rates[33] in the United States, Norway, and Canada over time. Figure 5 presents the results for the United States, but it is illustrative of the general phenomenon. In each country, the

[33]Average daily prison population per 100,000 general population.

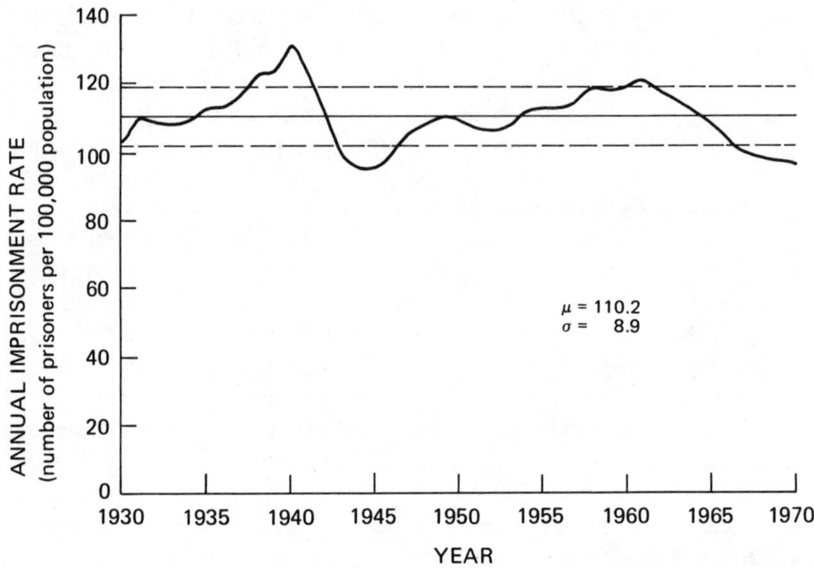

FIGURE 5 Annual imprisonment rate in the United States: 1930-1970. SOURCE: Blumstein and Cohen 1973, Figure 2.

rate was trendless, exhibiting a distinctive cyclic behavior about the mean with standard deviations that are only 10 to 20 percent of the mean. Periods of continuing increases in prison populations were followed by a downturn that moved the prison population back toward the mean. Likewise, periods of decreasing prison populations were followed by a sudden upturn.

Such a constraint on the use of imprisonment clearly sets limits on the possible increases in incapacitation rates. Shinnar and Shinnar (1975, p. 605) argue that increases of qJS of more than ten times present levels (from 0.024 to 0.3 for safety crimes) are possible. They go on to say that such a change would result in a fivefold decrease in crime and a "substantial but not extreme" (p. 606) increase in the prison population. In fact, they are talking about accomodating 40,000 to 60,000 prisoners in New York State for "safety" crimes (the violent index crimes and burglary) alone, compared with an average daily prison population in 1970 of only 9,000 for safety crimes and 12,500 for all felonies. The anticipated prison population for safety crimes in New York State would thus be about 25 percent of the total current prison population of the entire United States and represents an increase of 355 to 567 percent in the New York prison population. This is enormously greater than the 10- to 20-percent increase observed for the United States as a whole.[34]

While the current model and parameter estimates cannot be relied upon for exact numerical calculations of the incapacitative effects, they are useful for relative comparisons. In this spirit, a general parametric analysis of the model was performed. The results of this analysis reveal that the expected incapacitative effect on crime and prison populations of any change in imprisonment policy is sensitive to the current values of the individual crime rate and the imprisonment policy variables. For a criminal population of size N, the total number of crimes committed in a year (C) is given by the product of the individual effective crime rate (λ^*) and the number of criminals, namely:

$$C = \lambda^* N = \frac{\lambda N}{1+\lambda qJS} \tag{16}$$

Likewise, the total man-years of prison required annually (R) is obtained from the product of the expected prison stay per crime (qJS) times the number of crimes actually committed ($\lambda^* N$), or

$$R = \lambda^* NqJS = \frac{\lambda qJSN}{1+\lambda qJS} \tag{17}$$

The elasticity of C or R indicates the responsiveness of crime or prison population to changes in the imprisonment policy variables (q, J, S or their products). These are derived in Appendix B of this paper and presented for illustrative values of λ and qJS in Figure 6.

When an imprisonment parameter—the probability of a prison sentence given a crime (qJ), the average time served (S), or their product (qJS)—is increased by 1 percent, there is a greater percentage reduction in total crime through incapacitation when the current levels of these sanction variables are high and when the individual crime rate (λ) is high (Figure 6a). The percentage reduction in crime due to incapacitation is smaller when the current sanction levels and the individual crime rate are low.

Any increase in the imprisonment policy variables also results in an increase in the prison population, as measured by the resulting man-

[34]The average imprisonment rate in the United States between 1930 and 1970 was 110.2 prisoners per 100,000 general population, with a standard deviation of 8.9. Typically, the annual rate falls somewhere within ± one standard deviation from the mean. An increase between these limits (101.3 to 119.1) is only a 17.6-percent increase. (See Figure 5.)

Even in the recent period of more rapid growth, the national prison population only increased 37 percent over a 7-year period (from a rate of 96.7 in 1970 to 132.5 in 1976).

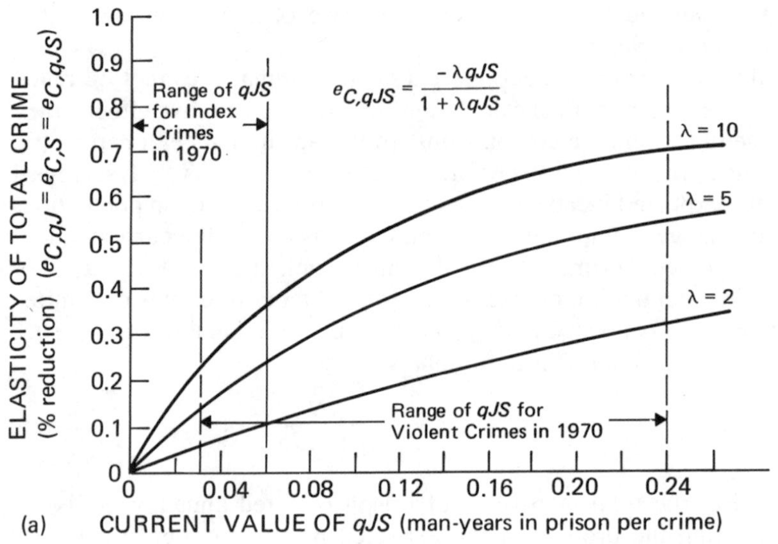

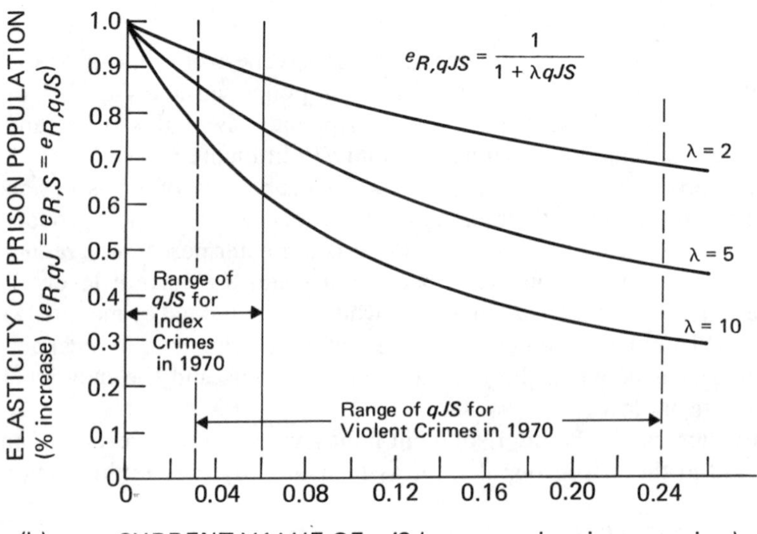

FIGURE 6 Elasticity of crime and imprisonment as a function of sanction level. The elasticity measure indicates the percentage change in the dependent variable (total crimes or prison population) resulting from the incapacitative effect of a 1-percent change in sanction level (man-years in prison per crime).

years of imprisonment annually (Figure 6b).[35] In this case, however, the magnitude of the percentage increase in prison use resulting from a 1 percent increase in qJ, S, or qJS is negatively related to the current values of the sanction levels and the individual crime rate. The larger the base level of these variables, the smaller the percentage increase in prison populations.

Combining the concepts reflected in Figures 6a and 6b provides a cost/benefit ratio for incapacitation under the assumptions of the model of incapacitation. This measure, the percent increase in the prison population required to achieve a 1-percent decrease in total crime from incapacitation alone varies considerably with the current value of qJS. Figure 7 indicates that if sanction levels are already high (say above .050 for different values of λ), the additional costs in terms of the percentage increase in the prison population required to achieve a 1 percent decrease in crime are not unreasonable. Below $qJS = .050$, on the other hand, the increases in the prison population associated with a 1-percent decrease in crime are much larger.

Consider, for example, violent crimes[36] in Kentucky. With an individual crime rate of 5 violent crimes per year and an expected time served per violent crime (qJS) of .125 years, the population of violent offenders in prison increases only 1.6 percent for each 1-percent reduction in violent crimes. When current sanction levels are low, as they generally are for index crimes, the required increase in prison population is larger. For $\lambda = 5$ and $qJS = .024$ (the value for index crimes in Ohio), the prison population increases 8.3 percent for each 1-percent reduction in index crimes. For $\lambda = 5$ and $qJS = .013$, as for index crimes in California, the increase in the prison population is even larger, 15.7 percent.

This difference in effect is due to the considerable differences in the base values for crime and prison population. At high values of qJS, the system is already operating very effectively and presumably already has a sizable proportion of the criminal population in prison and a fairly low crime rate. Any increase in qJS will only marginally increase the initially large prison population, while making a large fractional dent in an already low crime rate. At low values of qJS, the initial crime rate is

[35]This increase in the prison population does not take account of the possible long-term decreases in crime from any deterrent or rehabilitative effects associated with the increased use of prison. The reported change in prison population reflects only the equilibrium increase in prison population associated with a change in incapacitation policy, all else remaining unchanged.

[36]Violent crimes are the subset of the FBI index crimes including murder, rape, robbery and aggravated assault.

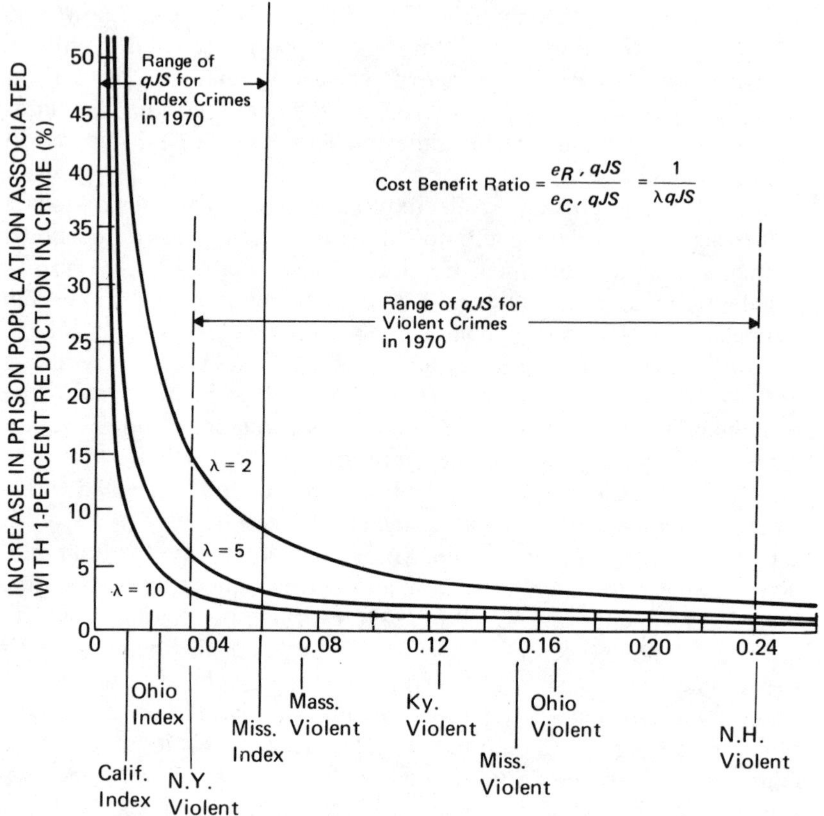

FIGURE 7 Cost-benefit ratio (percent increase in prison population required to achieve a 1-percent reduction in crime through incapacitation) as a function of the current values of the imprisonment parameters and the individual crime rate using the available models of incapacitation. NOTE: The 1970 values of *qJS* for selected states are indicated on the abscissa of the figure.

high and the prison population relatively small. In this situation, the changes that result from increasing *qJS* will have a greater proportional impact on the initially small prison population.

A similar parametric analysis was performed to examine the implications of the reduced incapacitative effects that result from a failure to adjust the imprisonment policy variables in the face of increases in criminality. Two possibilities were considered, one in which the average daily prison population (man-years in prison annually) is assumed to remain constant, and the other where the imprisonment policy variable, *qJS* (man-years in prison/crime), goes unchanged. The variable of interest is the net effect on crime of either an increase in the number of criminals (N) or an increase in the individual crime rate (λ).

The net effect on crime varies considerably with the factors considered. Two cases are particularly interesting because the net effect is different from the exogenously[37] induced change in crime (Figure 8).[38] When the size of the criminal population increases and the prison population remains constant, the increase in N is accompanied by a decrease in qJS. In this event, the increase in crime due to the change in N is compounded by reductions in the incapacitative effectiveness (Figure 8a). This compounding effect varies over λ and qJS, with those jurisdictions with the highest values of λ and qJS experiencing the greatest compounded increases in crime. With $\lambda = 10$ and $qJS = .30$, for example, a 1-percent increase in N is compounded yielding a total increase in crime of at least 4 percent.[39] For the lower values of qJS that prevail in most jurisdictions in the U.S. today, however, this compounding effect is less dramatic. For example, with $\lambda = 5$, the largest compounded increase for *index* crimes is 1.3 percent after a 1-percent increase in the size of criminal population. For *safety* crimes, the increase in crime is not more than 2.2 percent per 1-percent increase in N.

In contrast, when the individual crime rate (λ) increases and the imprisonment policy variable (qJS) remains constant, the increase in crime due to the change in λ is attenuated (Figure 8b). This reflects the greater incapacitative effectiveness associated with larger individual

[37]In the context of an incapacitation model, any changes in the level of crime that occur independently of the driving parameters of the model (q, J and S) are exogenously determined.

[38]In two instances, the prison population (R) constant while the individual crime rate (λ) increases 1 percent and the expected prison stay/crime (qJS) constant while the size of the criminal population (N) increases 1 percent, the total net increase in crime is just 1 percent and this effect is invariant over various values of λ and qJS.

[39]Because of the assumptions of the model (e.g., an invariant λ in the population), the amount of crime prevented through the current incapacitation policy is probably underestimated. Likewise, the estimates of the increase in crime associated with decreases in the use of imprisonment will also be underestimated. If the amount of bias in the estimates does not vary with the individual crime rate (λ) or the imprisonment policy variable, qJS (man-years in prison/crime), analysis of the model will provide useful insights into the relative effects on crime, even though the estimated magnitudes are themselves underestimated to some unknown extent.

Using the estimates of 4 percent for each 1-percent increase in criminals, a 30-percent increase in criminals would result in a 120-percent total increase in crime. This differs from the Shinnar and Shinnar estimate of a 150-percent increase in crime under similar circumstances. The difference is due to their assuming that a 30-percent increase in criminals will result in a 30-percent reduction in prison time. In fact, prison time is reduced to 1/1.3 of its original value, or a 23-percent reduction. With this correction , the two estimates of crime increase are the same.

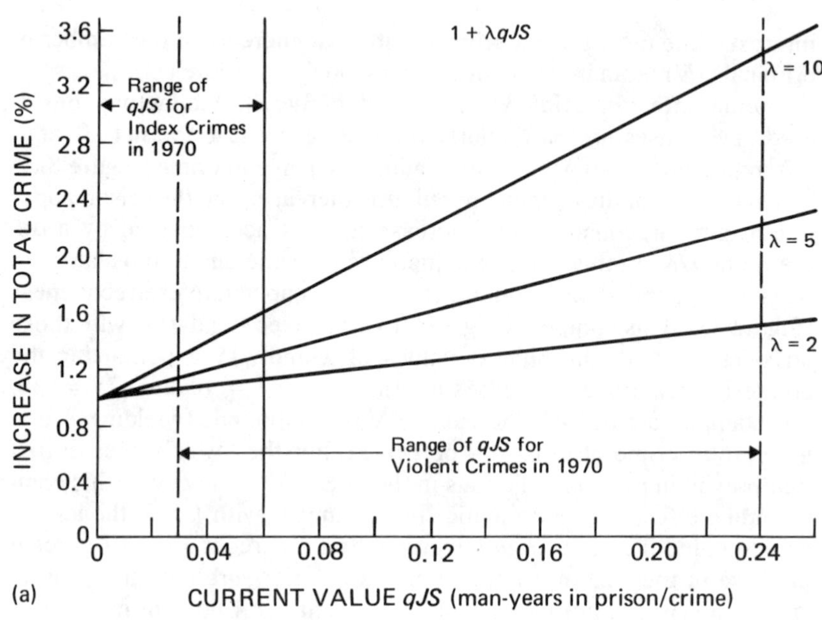

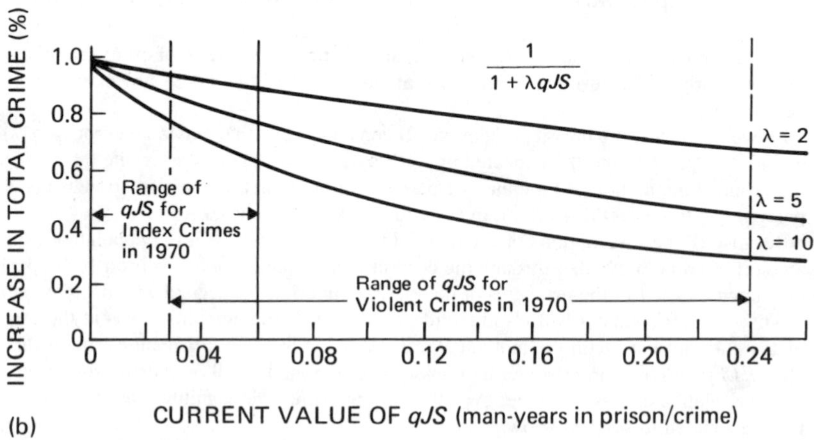

FIGURE 8 (a) Estimated percentage increase in total crime from reduced incapacitation associated with a 1-percent increase in the size of the criminal population–assuming a constant prison population. (b) Estimated percentage increase in total crime from reduced incapacitation associated with a 1-percent increase in the individual crime rate–assuming *qJS* remains constant.

crime rates; the larger λ, the more crimes that are averted during any period of incarceration. This effect varies over λ and qJS with high λ and high qJS jurisdictions experiencing the smallest increases in crime. Because of the more limited attenuation for low values of qJS, low sanction level jurisdictions have the most to lose in terms of increased crime by allowing the expected man-years in prison/crime (qJS) to remain constant in the face of an increasing λ. Nevertheless, the net increase in crime, regardless of λ and qJS, is smaller than might be expected from the increase in λ alone.

These variations in the policy implications associated with different values of the sanction variables illustrate the distortions in using aggregated parameter estimates that conceal variations among different jurisdictions and different crime types. Because the particular policy objectives appropriate for a particular crime type in any jurisdiction will depend on the local conditions in that jurisdiction, increased efforts are required to obtain disaggregated parameter estimates.

The sensitivity of the incapacitative effect to the particular values of the imprisonment variables has important implications for pursuing incapacitation policies to reduce crime. It has already been shown that the expected percentage increase in prison population to achieve a percentage reduction in crime is large when the imprisonment sanction levels are already low. There is some empirical evidence that jurisdictions with low imprisonment probabilities or low expected times served in prison per crime also tend to be the ones with the highest crime rates.[40] Thus, the high-crime rate jurisdictions that are most likely to be anxiously looking to incapacitation to relieve their crime problems can expect to have to pay the highest price for this relief.

In Table 5, which presents values for some illustrative states, California, New York and Massachusetts must increase their prison populations more than 150 percent in order to achieve a 10-percent reduction in index crimes through incapacitation.[41] The cost of an incapacitative strategy, however, varies considerably with the crime

[40]For the 29 states in 1970 for which data are available, the correlation between the index crime rate and the probability of imprisonment per crime is −.64. (See Appendix C for a description of the 1970 data.) The correlation between the index crime rate and the expected time served per crime (given by the product of the probability of imprisonment per crime and the average time served by those imprisoned) is −.55. For violent crimes in the same 29 states these correlations are −.54 and −.64, respectively.

[41]If additional deterrent effects on crime result from the increased use of imprisonment, this substantial increase in the prison population may be only temporary. If the amount of crime (and the number of criminals) decreases because of deterrence, the size of the prison population associated with the new imprisonment policy will also decrease. These effects are not considered here.

TABLE 5 Variations in the "Cost" of Crime Reduction through Incapacitation for Selected States[a] (Using Available Models of Incapacitation with $\lambda = 5$)

State	1970 Index Crime Rate[b]	Estimated 1970 *qJS* for Index Crimes[c]	1970 Violent Crime Rate[b]	Estimated 1970 *qJS* for Violent Crimes[c]	Estimated 1970 Average Daily Prison Population for Index Crimes[d]	% Increase in Prison Population to Achieve: 10% Reduction Index Crime Rate	Reduction of 100 Crimes in Index Crime Rate	10% Reduction Violent Crime Rate
California	4307.0[H][a]	.0127	474.8	.0877	10,941[H]	157.2	36.1	22.8
New York	3922.1	.0076	676.0[H]	.0351[L]	5,422	263.5	67.2	57.0
Massachusetts	3004.0	.0064[L]	202.9	.0751	1,094	310.5	103.4	26.6
Ohio	2376.6	.0242	284.3	.1663	6,126	82.5	34.7	12.0
Kentucky	1924.5	.0232	222.3	.1247	1,437	86.1	44.8	16.0
New Hampshire	1192.7	.0170	56.0	.2371[H]	150	118.0	98.9	8.4
Mississippi	863.4	.0593[H]	179.3	.1533	1,135	33.7	39.1	13.0
North Dakota	846.1[L]	.0164	34.2[L]	.1021	86[L]	122.0	144.2	19.6

[a]The states have been selected to include the states with the most extreme values for the variables (as indicated by an H for highest and L for lowest), along with some states in the middle of the distribution. California, for example, has the highest index crime rate and largest prison population, while North Dakota has the lowest index crime rate and the smallest prison population; Mississippi and Massachusetts respectively have the highest and lowest values of *qJS* for index crimes, while New Hampshire and New York have the highest and lowest values of *qJS* for violent crimes, respectively.

[b]Crimes/100,000 population. Source: U.S. Department of Justice, Federal Bureau of Investigation (1971) *Uniform Crime Reports: 1970*. Washington, D.C.: U.S. Government Printing Office.

[c]*qJS* is the expected time served/crime in years and is estimated from the number of prison commitments per crime and the median time served in prison. Source: U.S. Department of Justice, Bureau of Prisons (1970) *National Prisoner Statistics: State Prisoners Admissions and Releases*. Washington, D.C.: U.S. Government Printing Office.

[d]Under steady state assumptions, the average daily prison population is estimated from the product of the expected time served per crime times the number of offenses known.

types that are chosen as targets.[42] As indicated in Figure 6 and 7, the values of qJS for all index crimes are generally much lower than the same values for the subset of violent crimes.[43] Thus, incapacitation is a more viable alternative to reduce violent crimes.

Under the assumptions of the available models, the figures presented in Table 4 indicate that such a strategy could reduce violent crimes by as much as 10 percent with only minimal increases in the prison population (usually less than 30 percent). This is in sharp contrast to the much larger increases in prison population required to achieve the same reductions in the level of index crimes.

The possibility that there are constraints on prison use also raises the question of optimally allocating this scarce resource. The distribution of λ in the population is particularly relevant here. The Marsh and Singer paper illustrated the added power of incapacitation when λ is distributed. Under reasonable assumptions about the relationship between λ and the probability of imprisonment given a crime, individuals with higher crime rates are also more likely to be imprisoned, if only by chance alone. If improved techniques were available to identify the highest λ offenders, the potential would exist for even greater gains from incapacitation. In the face of constraints on prison use, the ability to discriminate between high- and low-λ offenders is particularly important for maximizing the incapacitative effect of the available resources.

In addition to considering variations in individual λ's, tradeoffs may also be required among different crime types. In the face of increasing public alarm about robberies, for example, more convicted robbers may be sent to prison. To accommodate the increase in robbers, however, the probability of a prison term or the length of sentences may have to be reduced for other, less serious crimes.

There are a number of distinctive features in estimating the incapacitative effect of a policy that incapacitates selectively by crime type. For one thing, the relative costs and benefits of incapacitation can be compared for different crime types. Those crime types for which λ is highest will bring the greatest gains in reduced numbers of

[42]This point was made by R. Shinnar in his review of a draft of this paper.

[43]While the median time served for property crimes is somewhat smaller than for violent crimes, the major factor contributing to a smaller value of qJS for all index crimes is the considerably smaller values of the probability of imprisonment for a crime (qJ) for property offenses. For the 29 states reporting adequate data in 1970 (see Appendix C of this paper), the overall values of qJ for the individual crime types were as follows: 0.3471 for murder, 0.0636 for rape, 0.0268 for robbery, 0.0144 for aggravated assault, 0.0059 for burglary, 0.0036 for larceny, and 0.0021 for auto theft. For all the violent crimes together, $qJ = 0.0295$, while for the property crimes $qJ = 0.0043$.

crime. However, they may not be the crime types of greatest concern. Suppose, for example, that the individual burglary rate is twice the individual robbery rate. In this event, trade-offs must be made between avoiding crimes that are more threatening to the public (robberies) at the cost of possibly avoiding far more burglaries with the same prison resource. The relative benefits of these competing alternatives must be weighed against one another in the final choice of a policy.

A more detailed characterization of individual criminal behavior is also required to estimate incapacitative effects by crime type. Individual crime rates must now be estimated by crime type. The pattern of individual crime-switching behavior is also important. At one extreme, crime-switching may be highly specialized, when the probability of repeating the same crime type is quite high. At the other extreme, crime-switching may be random with subsequent crime types completely independent of the prior crime types committed.

The particular mode of switching behavior has serious implications for the success of a strategy to incapacitate for the purpose of reducing selected crime types. If criminals tend to be specialized, then more robberies will be averted by imprisoning convicted robbers. But, if the next crime type is independent of previous crime types, then an individual with a prior record of robberies is no more likely to commit a subsequent robbery than is any other criminal. In this case, there is little to be gained in reduced robberies by a policy that selectively incapacitates convicted robbers.

IV. CONCLUSIONS

A number of issues have been raised in this critique in response to the existing body of research on incapacitation. There are, however, some central themes in this critique, which will be extracted and presented in a more concise fashion in this section. In many respects, the principal outcome of this effort is a set of guidelines for a research program designed to yield improved estimates of incapacitation through greater knowledge about individual crime-committing behavior.

A recurrent theme in this review has been the inadequacy of current estimates of the individual crime rate. The various papers discussed typically required only an average rate, yet either $\bar{\lambda}$ was underestimated or the authors avoided empirical estimates altogether. Marsh and Singer illustrated the additional power of an incapacitative strategy when λ is distributed in the population of criminals. However, to date there have been no empirical estimates of the distribution of λ.

Aside from the empirical weaknesses of present estimates, there are also some conceptual deficiencies. The discussion of a possible constraint on the prison population highlights the need to go beyond a concern for population averages. In particular, the ability to discriminate between different individuals' λ's and a characterization by crime type are important for possible allocation decisions. Clearly, the most pressing research requirement for estimating the incapacitative effect is to provide adequate estimates of the individual crime rate λ. The best estimates will account for

- variations in λ by crime type
- variations in λ across the criminal population
- variations in λ during an individual career.

Such estimates of λ will require better data on criminal careers than are presently available. For the level of detail outlined, self-reports by acknowledged criminals are probably the best source. However, these will have to be augmented by estimates from official arrest and crime statistics in order to deal with the inevitable response biases in the self-reports. Two main shortcomings in existing official statistics will also have to be overcome. First, they fail to document time served, so that the recorded arrests and convictions can be attributed only to the time an individual is at large. This is crucial to estimating individual arrest and/or conviction rates while free. Second, the statistical relationship between an individual's crime rate (λ) and his probability of apprehension (q_A) is unknown. The exact nature of this dependency is crucial to estimating unobserved crime rates from the observed arrest or conviction rates.

The time-served issue is probably the easiest to remedy. There is a growing body of data bases that follow the criminal careers of the persons sampled. If increased efforts are made to record commitment and release dates from any institutions, time served can be eliminated in estimating arrest rates. The relationship between λ and q is more problematic. There is no hope of resolving this issue using only official statistics. The two parameters λ and q cannot be adequately separated without some independent information about one or both parameters. Self-reports on crime, arrest, and conviction experiences as corroborated by official records for the same individuals may provide some useful insights into λ and q and their relationship.

Judging from the apparently conflicting stances of the authors, it appeared at first that there were nearly irreconcilable differences among the various estimates of the incapacitative effect of prison.

However, a closer examination of the estimates and their underlying assumptions reveals many points in common and few fundamental disagreements. For example, there is general agreement among the authors reviewed that the incapacitative effect of current CJS policies is not very large. The crimes averted do not account for a very significant portion of the crimes committed. The authors disagree only about the exact magnitude of the effect, and this disagreement is almost entirely due to their use of different estimates of λ.

To some extent, the low estimates of the incapacitative effect are due to the use of a single constant λ that reflects an average collective effect. This estimate is accurate only if λ is indeed homogeneous (constant) in the population or if it is heterogeneous with all offenders equally likely to be imprisoned. As Marsh and Singer point out, the average effect underestimates the true effect, if λ is heterogeneous and high λ individuals are more likely to be imprisoned. The magnitude of this underestimate cannot be determined without estimates of the joint distribution of λ and qJ in the population of criminals.

There are some differences of opinion about the potential gains in increased incapacitation if prison use were increased. Some acknowledge that crime can be decreased significantly through the expanded use of prison (Shinnar and Shinnar, Marsh and Singer, and Greenberg), while others foresee only limited gains (Clarke). The final position adopted, however, depends on the current values of q, J, and S and whether one allows for extreme or only marginal increases from present levels of incarceration.

The Shinnar *et al.* model represents the best approach to estimating the incapacitative effect available to date. Not only does it incorporate most of the assumptions of the other authors, but also it has the added advantage of providing a means of handling the discounting of crime rates by time served and the possibility of drop-out from the criminal career. The model, however, rests on a variety of simplifying assumptions and could be considerably improved by introducing richer complexity into the representation of criminal careers.

An alternative model would

- Incorporate heterogeneity in crime rates and the probabilities of arrest, conviction, and imprisonment, including variations over individuals and crime types.
- Explore alternative distributions for the different variables and attempt to validate them empirically
- Consider the implications of various dependent relationships among different aspects of a career (e.g., probability of apprehension

varying with crime rates, sentence lengths varying with prior convictions)

• Introduce non-stationarity into the process, particularly variations in crime rates over time and changes in the size of the criminal population

• Explicitly incorporate possible constraints on individual CJS parameters or the resulting prison population, thereby providing a means for assessing the effects of alternative strategies for allocating prison resources over individuals and/or crime types.

Future research should be directed at pursuing these issues.

REFERENCES

Avi-Itzhak, B., and Shinnar, R. (1973) Quantitative models in crime control. *Journal of Criminal Justice* 1(3):185-217.

Blumstein, A., and Cohen, J. (1973) A theory of the stability of punishment. *Journal of Criminal Law and Criminology* 64(2):198-207.

Blumstein, A., and Larson, R. (1969) Models of a total criminal justice system. *Operations Research* 17(2):199-232.

Blumstein, A., Cohen, J., and Nagin, D. (1976) The dynamics of a homeostatic punishment process. *Journal of Criminal Law and Criminology* 67(3):317-34.

Clarke, S. (1974) Getting 'em out of circulation: does incarceration of juvenile offenders reduce crime? *Journal of Criminal Law and Criminology* 65(4):528-35.

Ehrlich, I. (1974) Participation in illegitimate activities: an economic analysis. In G. S. Becker and W. M. Landes, eds., *Essays in the Economics of Crime and Punishment.* [Reprinted with corrections from (1973) *Journal of Political Economy* 81(3):521-67 and with appendices from (1970) "Participation in Illegitimate Activities: An Economic Analysis," doctoral dissertation, Columbia University.] New York: National Bureau of Economic Research (distributed by Columbia University Press).

Forst, B. (1976) Participation in illegitimate activities: further empirical findings. *Policy Analysis* 2(3):477-92.

Greenberg, D. (1975) The incapacitative effect of imprisonment: some estimates. *Law and Society Review* 9(4):541-80.

Lipton, D., Martinson, R., and Wilks, J. (1975) *The Effectiveness of Correctional Treatment: A Survey of Treatment Evaluation Studies.* New York: Praeger.

Marsh, J., and Singer, M. (1972) Soft Statistics and Hard Questions. Discussion paper HI-1712-DP. Hudson Institute, Quaker Ridge Road, Croton-on-Hudson, New York 10520.

Martinson, R. (1974) What works? questions and answers about prison reform. *The Public Interest* 35(Spring):22-54

Martinson, R. (1975) Testimony at Hearing on Parole Legislation of the Texas House of Representatives' Committee on Criminal Jurisprudence, November 1975. Copies available from the Center for Knowledge in Criminal Justice Planning, 38 E. 85th Street, New York, N.Y. 10028.

Monahan, J. (1976) The prevention of violence. Pgs. 13-35 in J. Monahan, ed., *Community Mental Health and the Criminal Justice System.* New York: Pergamon Press.

Robison, J., and Smith, G. (1971) The effectiveness of correctional programs. *Crime and Delinquency* 17(1):67-80.

Shinnar, R. (1977) The incapacitative function of prison internment: a quantitative approach. *Management Science* (forthcoming special issue).

Shinnar, R., and Shinnar, S. (1975) The effects of the criminal justice system on the control of crime: a quantitative approach. *Law and Society Review* 9(4):581-611.

U.S. Department of Justice (1975) *Criminal Victimization Surveys in 13 American Cities*. Law Enforcement Assistance Administration, National Criminal Justice Information and Statistics Service. Washington, D.C.: U.S. Government Printing Office.

U.S. Department of Justice (1976) *Criminal Victimization Surveys in Chicago, Detroit, Los Angeles, New York and Philadelphia: A Comparison of 1972 and 1974 Findings*. Law Enforcement Assistance Administration, National Criminal Justice Information and Statistics Service. Washington, D.C.: U.S. Government Printing Office.

von Hirsch, A. (1974) Prediction of criminal conduct and preventive confinement of convicted persons. *Buffalo Law Review* 21(3):717-58.

Wilson, J. Q. (1975a) Lock 'em up and other thoughts on crime. *New York Times Magazine* March 9, 1975.

Wilson, J. Q. (1975b) *Thinking about Crime*. New York: Basic Books.

Wolfgang, M., Figlio, R. M., and Sellin, T. (1972) *Delinquency in a Birth Cohort*. Chicago: University of Chicago Press.

APPENDIX A: COMPUTATION OF THE ELASTICITY OF INDEX CRIMES TO CHANGES IN IMPRISONMENT POLICIES

Both Clarke and Greenberg compute the total number of crimes averted as $\lambda \cdot I$, the individual crime rate (λ) times the total number of man-years served in prison annually (I). The number of crimes currently committed, C, is given by $\lambda(N - I)$, where N is the total number of offenders. The percentage increase in crime if prisons were abandoned entirely is then

$$\frac{\lambda \cdot I}{C}(100)$$

The elasticity of crime, or the percentage change in crime accompanying a 1 percent change in the man-years served in prison, is

$$\sigma_{CI} = \frac{dC}{dI} \cdot \frac{I}{C} = \frac{-\lambda I}{C}.$$

Clarke restricts his attention to the crimes averted by the incarceration of juveniles, using data for a cohort in Philadelphia. Since a number of restrictive assumptions are needed to generalize these results beyond Philadelphia and to all index crimes, the elasticity for

Clarke will not be considered. The total number of reported index crimes is 2.78 million and the total man-years served in prison is 200,000. Thus, for $\lambda = 5$, the total percentage increase in crime if prisons were abandoned is 36 percent and the elasticity of crime to a 1-percent change in the man-years served is −0.36 percent.

For Shinnar and Shinnar, the total number of crimes committed at any time is $\lambda^* N$, where λ^* is the effective crime rate and N is the size of the offender population (including offenders in and out of prison). Since

$$\lambda^* = \frac{\lambda}{1+\lambda qJS},$$

the total number of crimes is

$$C = \frac{\lambda N}{1+\lambda qJS}.$$

The elasticity of crime in response to a 1-percent change in λqJ is

$$\sigma_{C,\lambda qJ} = \frac{dC}{d(\lambda qJ)} \bullet \frac{\lambda qJ}{C} = \frac{-\lambda NS}{(1+\lambda qJS)^2} \bullet \frac{\lambda qJ}{\lambda N/(1+\lambda qJS)} = \frac{-\lambda qJS}{1+\lambda qJS}. \tag{A-1}$$

Likewise, the elasticity with respect to S is

$$\sigma_{C,S} = \frac{dC}{dS} \bullet \frac{S}{C} = \frac{-\lambda N(\lambda qJ)}{(1+\lambda qJS)^2} \bullet \frac{S}{\lambda N/(1+\lambda qJS)} = \frac{-\lambda qJS}{(1+\lambda qJS)}. \tag{A-2}$$

Interpreting λqJ as the probability of prison for an offender at large, P, we see that the expression for the elasticity in the Shinnar and Shinnar model is identical to the expression for the elasticity proposed by Ehrlich (1974).

To compute the elasticity for Shinnar and Shinnar or for Ehrlich, we need estimates of λ and qJS. The quantity qJS may be interpreted as the expected prison stay per crime. This may be estimated from the average prison population divided by the total number of crimes reported. Using $qJS = 200{,}000/2{,}780{,}000 = 0.072$. For $\lambda = 5$,

$$\sigma = \frac{-.36}{1.36} = .26\% .$$

The Greenberg elasticity is slightly larger than the Shinnar *et al.* or Ehrlich elasticity, even though the same numerical estimates of the variables were used here. This difference is due to the relationship between the total man-years served in prison annually and the policy variables λqJ and S. In a steady-state system, the total man-years served in prison annually can be estimated from the number of prison commitments in a year, and the average time served

$$I = N(\lambda^* qJ)S$$

where

N = total number of offenders
$\lambda^* qJ$ = expected number of prison commitments per offender under the present CJS imprisonment policy
S = average time served.

The average number of prison commitments per offender is discounted to reflect the reduction in crimes actually committed by incarceration. On the average each offender can only commit λ^* offenses. He is also subject to incarceration only for the crimes actually committed and not for all those crimes he might commit if he were always free. In the Shinnar and Shinnar model

$$\lambda^* = \frac{\lambda}{1+\lambda qJS} \quad .$$

Therefore,

$$I = \frac{N \cdot \lambda qJS}{1+\lambda qJS}$$

and the percentage change in I accompanying a 1-percent change in λqJ or S is

$$\sigma_{I,\lambda qJ} = \sigma_{I,S} = \frac{1}{1+\lambda qJS} \leq 1 \ . \qquad \text{(A-3)}$$

Thus, the number of man-years in prison changes slower than λqJ or S. Therefore, the 1-percent change in the prison population used to compute the Greenberg elasticity represents a *more than* 1-percent change in λqJ or S. The Greenberg estimate and the Shinnar and Shinnar or Ehrlich estimates are therefore directly compatible.

APPENDIX B: COMPUTATION OF THE ELASTICITY OF CRIME AND PRISON POPULATION IN THE SHINNAR AND SHINNAR MODEL

The basic relationship derived in the Shinnar and Shinnar model is

$$\eta = \frac{1}{1+\lambda qJS} \ ,$$

which gives proportional reduction in the individual crime rate as a result of any time served in prison. For λ, the individual crime rate while free, the effective crime rate λ^* is then

$$\lambda^* = \lambda\eta = \frac{\lambda}{1+\lambda qJS} \ .$$

The total number of crimes actually committed in a year is

$$C = \lambda^* N = \frac{\lambda N}{1+\lambda qJS} \qquad \text{(B-1)}$$

where N is the number of criminals.

The elasticity (σ) of crime in response to a 1-percent change in the expected prison stay per crime (qJS) is

$$\sigma_{C,qJS} = \frac{dC}{d(qJS)} \cdot \frac{qJS}{C} = \frac{-\lambda^2 N}{(1+\lambda qJS)^2} \cdot \frac{qJS}{\dfrac{\lambda N}{1+\lambda qJS}} = \frac{-\lambda qJS}{1+\lambda qJS} \ . \qquad \text{(B-2)}$$

Expression B-2 also gives the elasticity of crime with respect to qJ or S, namely:

$$\sigma_{C,qJ} = \frac{dC}{d(qJ)} \cdot \frac{qJ}{C} = \frac{-\lambda^2 NS}{(1+\lambda qJS)^2} \cdot \frac{qJ}{\dfrac{\lambda N}{1+\lambda qJS}} = \frac{-\lambda qJS}{1+\lambda qJS}$$

or

$$\sigma_{C,S} = \frac{dC}{dS} \cdot \frac{S}{C} = \frac{-\lambda^2 NqJ}{(1+\lambda qJS)^2} \cdot \frac{S}{\dfrac{\lambda N}{1+\lambda qJS}} = \frac{-\lambda qJS}{1+\lambda qJS} \ .$$

The average prison stay per criminal during a year is computed from the expected stay per crime and the individual's *effective* crime rate, namely:

$$\lambda^* qJS = \frac{\lambda}{1+\lambda qJS} \cdot qJS = \frac{\lambda qJS}{1+\lambda qJS} \quad .$$

The total number of man-years of prison required in a year (i.e., the annual prison population) is just the product of the average stay per criminal and the number of criminals, or

$$R = \frac{N\lambda qJS}{1+\lambda qJS} \quad . \tag{B-3}$$

The elasticity of the prison population with respect to a 1-percent change in the expected prison stay/crime is given by:

$$\sigma_{R,qJS} = \frac{dR}{d(qJS)} \cdot \frac{qJS}{R} = \frac{\lambda N(1+\lambda qJS)-N\lambda^2 qJS}{(1+\lambda qJS)^2} \cdot \frac{qJS}{N\lambda qJS/(1+\lambda qJS)}$$

$$= \frac{\lambda N}{(1+\lambda qJS)^2} \cdot \frac{qJS(1+\lambda qJS)}{N\lambda qJS} = \frac{1}{1+\lambda qJS} \, . \tag{B-4}$$

Likewise, the elasticity of the prison population with respect to qJ or S is also given by,

$$\sigma_{R,qJ} = \sigma_{R,S} = \frac{1}{1+\lambda qJS}$$

Expression (B-2) gives the effect of changes in the imprisonment policy variables on total crime. The amount of crime might also be affected by changes in the individual crime rate (λ), or in the size of the criminal population (N). Within the context of the Shinnar model these changes in criminal behavior are exogenously determined [i.e, they are not the result of changes in the driving parameters in the model (q, J or S)]. Expressions (B-1) and (B-3) will be used here to examine the net effect on crime of holding the expected prison stay per crime (qJS) or the annual prison population (R) constant in the face of exogenously determined increases in crime.

For total crimes expressed as in (B-1) the percentage increase in crime for a 1-percent increase in the size of the criminal population is given by:

$$\sigma_{C,N} = \frac{dC}{dN} \cdot \frac{N}{C} = \frac{\lambda}{1+\lambda qJS} \cdot \frac{N}{\lambda N/(1+\lambda qJS)} = 1 \ . \qquad \text{(B-5)}$$

Now holding the prison population (B-3) constant at some value, K, the imprisonment policy variable, qJS, can be expressed as

$$qJS = \frac{K}{\lambda N - \lambda K} \ . \qquad \text{(B-6)}$$

The elasticity of qJS with respect to N is then:

$$\sigma_{qJS,N} = \frac{dqJS}{dN} \cdot \frac{N}{qJS} = \frac{-\lambda K}{(\lambda N-\lambda K)^2} \cdot \frac{N}{K/(\lambda N-\lambda K)} = -\frac{\lambda N}{\lambda N-\lambda K} \ .$$

A 1-percent increase in N thus results in a $\lambda N/(\lambda N - \lambda K)$-percent decrease in qJS. This reduces the system's incapacitative effectiveness in controlling crime and so will lead to further increases in crime. From the elasticity of crime to changes in qJS (B-2), we know that a 1-percent decrease in qJS results in a $\lambda qJS/(1 + \lambda qJS)$-percent increase in crime. So the additional percentage increase from the $\lambda N/(\lambda N - \lambda K)$-percent decrease in qJS is approximately:

$$\frac{\lambda N}{\lambda N-\lambda K} \cdot \frac{\lambda qJS}{1+\lambda qJS} = \frac{\lambda N}{\lambda N-\lambda K} \cdot \frac{\lambda K/(\lambda N-\lambda K)}{1+[\lambda K/(\lambda N-\lambda K)]} = \frac{\lambda K}{\lambda N-\lambda K} = \lambda qJS$$

Thus, holding the prison population constant, the total increase in crime from a 1-percent increase in the size of the criminal population, N, is $(1+\lambda qJS)$ percent.

Again holding the annual prison population constant at K, the net effect of a 1-percent increase in the individual crime rate (λ) can be evaluated. From (B-1) the elasticity of crime to changes in λ is:

$$\sigma_{C,\lambda} = \frac{dC}{d\lambda} \cdot \frac{\lambda}{C} = \frac{N}{(1+\lambda qJS)^2} \cdot \frac{\lambda}{\lambda N/(1+\lambda qJS)} = \frac{1}{1+\lambda qJS} \ . \qquad \text{(B-7)}$$

With a constant prison population, however, the increase in λ will also affect the incapacitative effectiveness of the system. Using (B-6), the elasticity of qJS with respect to changes in λ can be computed as:

$$\sigma_{qJS,\lambda} = \frac{d(qJS)}{d\lambda} \cdot \frac{\lambda}{qJS} = \frac{-K}{(N-K)\lambda^2} \cdot \frac{\lambda}{K/[\lambda(N-K)]} = -1 \ .$$

This 1-percent decrease in qJS results in a $\lambda qJS/(1+\lambda qJS)$ percent increase in crime (B-2). Thus the total increase in crime from a 1-percent increase in λ with a constant prison population is just:

$$\frac{1}{1+\lambda qJS} + \frac{\lambda qJS}{1+\lambda qJS} = 1\% .$$

Using the same approach, the net effect of changes in N and λ can be evaluated for a constant qJS. In the case of exogenously determined increases in crime, qJS can only remain constant if appropriate increases in the prison population accompany the increases in crime. Furthermore, since qJS is assumed to remain constant, the total increase in crime is not affected by any further reductions in the incapacitative effectiveness of the system. Thus, for qJS constant and a 1-percent increase in the criminal population, N, the total increase in crime is given by (B-5) as 1 percent. Likewise, a 1-percent increase in individual crime rates (λ) yields a $1/(1+\lambda qJS)$-percent increase in crime (B-7).

APPENDIX C: DATA ON CRIME RATES AND PRISON USE FOR U.S. STATES IN 1970

Statistics are available on commitments to prison and time served by crime type in 1970.[44] These data are limited to court commitments with sentences of 1 year or longer and include reports for only 33 states.

To minimize the possible biases from using data for persons with sentences of 1 year or more, the total number of commitments to prison for these persons was compared with the total number of commitments reported with no restrictions on sentence length.[45] Four states[46] were eliminated because of discrepancies in excess of 20 percent of the total number of commitments reported without restrictions on sentence length. Of the 29 remaining states, there were no comparison figures

[44]U.S. Department of Justice, Bureau of Prisons. *National Prisoner Statistics—State Prisoners: Admissions and Releases, 1970*. Washington, D.C.: U.S. Department of Justice, Law Enforcement Assistance Administration.

[45]U.S. Department of Justice, Bureau of Prisons. 1972. *National Prisoner Statistics: Prisoners in State and Federal Institutions For Adult Felons, 1968, 1969, 1970*. Washington, D.C.: U.S. Government Printing Office.

[46]For Delaware, South Carolina, Vermont, and West Virginia, the number of commitments with sentences of 1 year or more underreported the total number of commitments reported elsewhere by 20 percent or more. In addition, discrepancies between 10 and 15 percent were found for Washington and New York.

for three states.[47] Because serious inconsistencies were relatively rare among the states actually compared, these states were not excluded from consideration.

The probability of imprisonment given a crime (qJ) was computed for index offenses by dividing the number of prison commitments for index offenses by the number of index offenses reported by the police.[48] Approximations were sometimes necessary because the crime types were not always compatible. In particular, all commitments for sex offenses were considered as commitments for rape, commitments for assault were treated as commitments for aggravated assault and commitments for larcenies other than auto theft were considered as commitments for the index offense of larceny (≥ $50). In each case the prison commitments category is broader than the index crime category. However, since it is unlikely that many persons are committed to prison for the less serious offenses included in these categories, this approximation should not be seriously in error.

Time served is only reported for intervals (e.g., under 6 months and 1 year to under 18 months). The median time served (S) for each offense was determined by choosing the midpoint of the median interval. The median time served for all index offenses combined or all violent offenses combined was then computed as the weighted average of the median times served for the individual offenses involved.

Under steady-state assumptions, the average daily prison population for index offenses or for violent offenses is estimated from the product of the expected time served per crime (qJS) times the number of offenses known. This figure is always less than the total average daily prison population reported elsewhere (U.S. Department of Justice 1972).

Table C-1 presents the resulting crime and prison data for states in 1970 along with the cost/benefit ratio indicating the percentage increase in the prison population required to achieve a 1-percent decrease in crime for $\lambda = 5$.[49]

[47]Maryland, Minnesota, and Nevada.

[48]U.S. Department of Justice, Federal Bureau of Investigation. 1971. *Uniform Crime Reports: 1970*. Washington, D.C.: U.S. Government Printing Office.

[49]For values of $\lambda<5$ the cost/benefit ratio will be larger than reported in the table and for values of $\lambda>5$ the ratio will be smaller than reported.

TABLE C-1 Crime Rates and Prison Use by State in 1970

State	A. Index Offenses						
	Average Daily Prison Population[a]	Index Crime Rate[b]	Estimated Probability of Prison/ Crime (qJ)[c]	Median Time Served (in years) (S)[c]	Estimated Time Served/ Crime (in years) (qJS)	Estimated Prison Population for Index Offenses	% Increase in Index Prison Population to Achieve 1% Reduct- ion in Crime $(\lambda = 5)$[d]
Arizona	1648	3445.2	.0067	2.515	.0169	1032	11.87
California	≈26000	4307.0	.0036	3.535	.0127	10914	15.72
Colorado	2110	3662.2	.0071	1.214	.0086	695	23.20
Connecticut	1730	2574.9	.0080	1.215	.0097	757	20.58
Georgia	5086	2206.7	.0207	1.960	.0406	4112	4.93
Hawaii	246	3396.2	.0023	2.665	.0061	160	32.63
Idaho	386	1785.1	.0091	1.628	.0148	188	13.50
Illinois	6819	2347.1	.0079	2.223	.0176	4591	11.39
Kansas	1816	2143.8	.0124	1.866	.0231	1114	8.64
Kentucky	2825	1924.5	.0209	1.112	.0232	1437	8.61
Maine	545	1141.6	.0205	1.376	.0282	320	7.09

Maryland	≈5100	3347.0	.0164	1.166	.0191	2508	10.46
Massachusetts	≈2000	3004.0	.0037	1.741	.0064	1094	31.05
Minnesota	1600	2103.4	.0021	8.467	.0178	1425	11.25
Mississippi	1715	863.4	.0282	2.104	.0593	1135	3.37
Missouri	3340	2765.0	.0106	1.543	.0164	2121	12.23
Montana	296	1636.8	.0138	1.154	.0159	181	12.56
Nevada	679	3996.2	.0075	2.663	.0200	391	10.02
New Hampshire	239	1192.7	.0140	1.211	.0170	150	11.80
New Mexico	828	2865.5	.0082	2.394	.0196	571	10.19
New York	≈12250	3922.1	.0039	1.946	.0076	5422	26.35
North Dakota	109	846.1	.0117	1.402	.0164	86	12.20
Ohio	9200	2376.6	.0113	2.145	.0242	6126	8.25
Oklahoma	3136	1950.9	.0262	1.480	.0388	1937	5.16
South Dakota	379	1152.1	.0185	1.648	.0305	234	6.56
Tennessee	3247	1888.3	.0171	1.964	.0336	2490	5.95
Utah	480	2372.8	.0056	2.305	.0129	324	15.49
Washington	2871	3156.6	.0070	1.856	.0130	1399	15.38
Wyoming	234	1745.1	.0133	1.703	.0227	132	8.83

[a] U.S. Department of Justice, Bureau of Prisons (1972). *National Prisoner Statistics: Prisoners in State and Federal Institutions For Adult Felons, 1968, 1969, 1970*. Washington, D.C.: U.S. Government Printing Office.

[b] U.S. Department of Justice, Federal Bureau of Investigation (1971) *Uniform Crime Reports: 1970*. Washington, D.C.: U.S. Government Printing Office.

[c] U.S. Department of Justice, Bureau of Prisons *National Prisoner Statistics—State Prisoners: Admissions and Releases, 1970*. Washington, D.C.: U.S. Department of Justice, Law Enforcement Assistance Administration.

[d] Using the expressions for the elasticities derived in Appendix B, the cost/benefit ratio is computed from the ratio of the elasticity of prison over the elasticity of crime and equals: $-1/(\lambda qJS)$.

TABLE C-1 *(Continued)*

	B. Violent Offenses					
State	Violent Crime Rate[b]	Estimated Probability of Prison/ Crime (qJ)[c]	Median Time Served (in years) (S)[c]	Estimated Time Served/ Crime (in years) (qJS)	Estimated Prison Population for Violent Offenses	% Increase in Violent Prison Population to Achieve 1% Reduction in Crime $(\lambda=5)$[d]
Arizona	370.3	.0282	3.322	.0937	615	2.13
California	474.8	.0206	4.256	.0877	8309	2.28
Colorado	356.7	.0320	1.847	.0591	465	3.38
Connecticut	170.4	.0654	1.354	.0886	458	2.26
Georgia	304.5	.0707	2.432	.1719	2402	1.16
Hawaii	121.8	.0416	3.242	.1349	127	1.48
Idaho	123.3	.0592	2.144	.1269	112	1.58
Illinois	467.9	.0231	2.750	.0635	3302	3.15
Kansas	202.8	.0509	2.405	.1224	558	1.63
Kentucky	222.3	.0687	1.815	.1247	892	1.60
Maine	82.8	.0936	2.460	.2302	189	.87

Maryland	624.9	.0504	1.342	.0676	1657	2.96
Massachusetts	202.9	.0377	1.993	.0751	867	2.66
Minnesota	152.0	.0147	9.596	.1411	816	1.42
Mississippi	179.3	.0546	2.808	.1533	609	1.30
Missouri	405.9	.0274	2.066	.0566	1075	3.53
Montana	111.4	.0633	1.794	.1136	88	1.76
Nevada	398.6	.0339	3.258	.1104	215	1.81
New Hampshire	56.0	.1574	1.507	.2371	98	.84
New Mexico	292.8	.0363	3.133	.1137	338	1.76
New York	676.0	.0173	2.032	.0351	4316	5.70
North Dakota	34.2	.0616	1.657	.1021	22	1.96
Ohio	284.3	.0402	4.138	.1663	5035	1.20
Oklahoma	197.8	.0729	2.134	.1556	787	1.29
South Dakota	92.5	.0666	2.500	.1665	103	1.20
Tennessee	274.9	.0450	2.762	.1243	1341	1.61
Utah	137.7	.0315	3.333	.1249	182	1.60
Washington	221.3	.0296	2.568	.0760	573	2.63
Wyoming	113.1	.0585	2.114	.1237	47	1.62

[a]U.S. Department of Justice, Bureau of Prisons (1972). *National Prisoner Statistics: Prisoners in State and Federal Institutions For Adult Felons, 1968, 1969, 1970.* Washington, D.C.: U.S. Government Printing Office.

[b]U.S. Department of Justice, Federal Bureau of Investigation (1971) *Uniform Crime Reports: 1970.* Washington, D.C.: U.S. Government Printing Office.

[c]U.S. Department of Justice, Bureau of Prisons *National Prisoner Statistics—State Prisoners: Admissions and Releases, 1970.* Washington, D.C.: U.S. Department of Justice, Law Enforcement Assistance Administration.

[d]Using the expressions for the elasticities derived in Appendix B, the cost/benefit ratio is computed from the ratio of the elasticity of prison over the elasticity of crime and equals: $-1/(\lambda qJS)$.

The Prediction of Violent Criminal Behavior: A Methodological Critique and Prospectus

JOHN MONAHAN

I. OVERVIEW

The identification of persons who reliably can be predicted to engage in dangerous behavior has been called "the greatest unresolved problem the criminal justice system faces" (Rector 1973) and "the paramount consideration in the law-mental health system" (Stone 1975). It is the purpose of this paper to suggest how the problem of predicting dangerous behavior might be clarified by improved methods of empirical research. Current public policies that rely upon the prediction of violence will be briefly reviewed, the empirical data to date will be summarized, and hypotheses will be offered to account for the obtained findings. Following this, five general recommendations for future research in violence prediction will be presented, each with a specific proposal for implementation.

John Monahan is Assistant Professor, Program in Social Ecology, University of California, Irvine.

NOTE: I would like to thank Alfred Blumstein, Gilbert Geis, Raymond Novaco, Paul Meehl, Andrew von Hirsch, James Q. Wilson, Henry Steadman, Carol Warren, and Thomas Halatyn for their insightful discussion of this paper.

II. CURRENT POLICY USES OF VIOLENCE PREDICTION

The task of identifying violence-prone individuals has been allocated to the criminal justice and mental health systems. In both systems, predictions of violence[1] are variables in decision-rules relating to who should be institutionalized and who should be released from an institution—the institution being a jail, prison, civil mental hospital, or hospital for the criminally insane.

In the criminal justice system, predictions of violence may be introduced in at least five stages of the judicial process (compare Shah 1976): (a) decisions whether or not to grant bail, and, if bail is to be granted, decisions on the level at which bail is set; (b) decisions whether certain offenders should be transferred from juvenile to adult court for trail; (c) sentencing decisions imposing probation or imprisonment or death[2], and, if imprisonment is imposed, decisions on the length of imprisonment; (d) parole decisions; and (e) decisions whether to invoke special statutes dealing with "dangerous sex offenders," "dangerous mentally ill offenders," or "habitual" criminals (Monahan and Hood 1976).

In the mental health system, predictions of violence are employed primarily in terms of decisions regarding civil commitment to a mental hospital and release from such commitment.

Two recent and contradictory trends in public policies involving the prediction of violence are clearly discernible. One is the increased reliance upon the "dangerousness standard" as the primary or sole justification for civil commitment in the mental health system; many states now follow California's 1969 lead in rewriting commitment laws to emphasize the role of violence prediction (*Harvard Law Review* 1974). The second trend is the decreased reliance upon predictions of violence in determining release from prison in the criminal justice system. Several state legislatures (e.g., California, Maine) have recently passed or are now considering bills to abolish indeterminate sentences

[1]A distinction between "violence," "violent behavior," "dangerousness," and "dangerous behavior" will not be attempted in this report, although arguments can be made in favor of using one term rather than another (Sarbin 1967, Megargee 1976).

[2]The United States Supreme Court recently held that it was not unconstitutional for a state to make the imposition of the death penalty on an offender convicted of certain categories of murder contingent upon a prediction that he or she would be violent in the future. "It is, of course, not easy to predict future behavior. The fact that such a determination is difficult, however, does not mean that it cannot be made" (Jurek v. Texas, 96 S.Ct. 2950 [1976]).

in which the prisoner's release date is determined by a parole board and based in part upon a prediction of his potential for future violence, in favor of sentences of a more definite length set by the judge (*cf.* Morris 1974; Twentieth Century Fund 1976; von Hirsch 1976).

III. SUMMARY OF VIOLENCE PREDICTION RESEARCH

The eight major research efforts attempting to validate predictions of violence are summarized in Table 1.[3]

Wenk *et al.* (1972) report three massive studies on the prediction of violence undertaken in the California Department of Corrections. In the first study, a violence prediction scale that included variables such as commitment offense, number of prior commitments, opiate use, and length of imprisonment was able to isolate a small group of offenders who were three times more likely to commit a violent act than parolees in general. However, 86 percent of those identified as violent did not, in fact, commit a violent act while on parole.

In the second study, over 7,000 parolees were assigned to various categories keyed to their potential aggressiveness on the basis of their case histories and psychiatric reports. One in five parolees was as-

TABLE 1[a] Research Studies on the Prediction of Violence

Study	% True Positives	% False Positives	N Predicted Violent	Follow-up Years
Wenk *et al.* (1972) Study 1	14.0	86.0	?	?
Wenk *et al.* (1972) Study 2	0.3	99.7	1630	1
Wenk *et al.* (1972) Study 3	6.2	93.8	104	1
Kozol *et al.* (1972)	34.7	65.3	49	5
State of Maryland (1973)	46.0	54.0	221	3
Steadman (1973)	20.0	80.0	967	4
Thornberry and Jacoby (1974)	14.0	86.0	438	4
Cocozza and Steadman (1976)	14.0	86.0	96	3

[a]Updated from Monahan (1976).

[3]This section draws heavily from Monahan (1975, 1976) and Monahan and Cummings (1976).

signed to a "potentially aggressive" category, and the rest to a "less aggressive" category. During a 1-year follow-up, however, the rate of crimes involving actual violence for the potentially aggressive group was only 3.1 per 1,000, compared with 2.8 per 1,000 among the less aggressive group. Thus, for every correct identification of a potentially aggressive individual, there were 326 incorrect ones.

The final study reported by Wenk *et al.* (1972) sampled over 4,000 California Youth Authority wards. Attention was directed to the record of violence in the youth's past and an extensive background investigation was conducted, including psychiatric diagnoses and a psychological test battery. Subjects were followed for 15 months after release, and data on 100 variables were analyzed retrospectively to see which items predicted a violent act of recidivism. The authors concluded that the parole decision maker who used a history of actual violence as his sole predictor of future violence would have 19 false positives in every 20 predictions, yet "there is no other form of simple classification available thus far that would enable him to improve on this level of efficiency" (p. 399). Several multivariate regression equations were developed from the data, but none was even hypothetically capable of doing better than attaining an 8-to-1 false-to-true positive ratio.

Kozol *et al.* (1972) have reported a 10-year study involving almost 600 offenders. Each offender was examined independently by at least two psychiatrists, two psychologists, and a social worker. A full psychological test battery was administered and a complete case history compiled. During a 5-year follow-up period in the community, 8 percent of those predicted not to be dangerous became recidivists by committing a serious assaultive act, and 34.7 percent of those predicted to be dangerous committed such an act. While the assessment of dangerousness by Kozol and his colleagues appears to have some validity, the problem of false positives stands out. Sixty-five percent of the individuals identified as dangerous did not, in fact, commit a dangerous act. Despite the extensive examining, testing, and data gathering they undertook, Kozol *et al.* were wrong in two out of every three predictions of dangerousness. (For an analysis of the methodological flaws of this study, see Monahan 1973b, and the rejoinder by Kozol *et al.* 1973.)

Data from an institution very similar to that used by Kozol *et al.* have recently been released by the Patuxent Institution (State of Maryland 1973). Four hundred and twenty-one patients, each of whom received at least three years of treatment at Patuxent, were considered. Of the 421 patients released by the court, the psychiatric staff opposed the release of 286 on the grounds that they were still dangerous and recommended the release of 135 as safe. The criterion measure was any new offense (not necessarily violent) appearing on FBI reports during the first 3 years after release. Of those patients released by the court against staff advice, the recidivism rate was 46 percent if the patients had been released directly from the hospital, and 39 percent if a "conditional release experience" had been imposed. Of those patients released on the staff's recommendation and continued for outpatient treatment on parole, 7 percent recidivated. Thus, after 3 years of observation and treatment, between 54 and 61 percent of the patients predicted by the psychiatric staff to be dangerous were not discovered to have committed a criminal act.

In 1966, the U.S. Supreme Court held that Johnnie Baxstrom had been denied equal protection of the law by being detained beyond his maximum sentence in an institution for the criminally insane without the benefit of a new hearing to determine his current dangerousness (*Baxstrom v. Herold*, 1966). The ruling resulted in the transfer of nearly 1,000 persons "reputed to be some of the most dangerous mental patients in the state [of New York]" (Steadman 1972) from hospitals for the criminally insane to civil mental hospitals. It also provided an excellent opportunity for naturalistic research on the validity of the psychiatric predictions of dangerousness upon which the extended detention was based.

There has been an extensive follow-up program on the Baxstrom patients (Steadman and Cocozza 1974). Researchers find that the level of violence experienced in the civil mental hospitals was much less than had been feared, that the civil hospitals adapted well to the massive transfer of patients, and that the Baxstrom patients were being treated the same as the civil patients. The precautions that the civil hospitals had undertaken in anticipation of the supposedly dangerous patients—the setting up of secure wards and provision of judo training to the staff—were largely for naught (Rappaport 1973). Only 20 percent of the Baxstrom patients were assaultive to persons in the civil hospital or the community at any time during the four years following their transfer. Furthermore, only 3 percent of Baxstrom patients were sufficiently dangerous to be returned to a hospital for the criminally insane during 4 years after the decision (Steadman and Halfon 1971). Steadman and Keveles (1972) followed 121 Baxstrom patients who had been released into the community (i.e., discharged from both the criminal and civil mental hospitals). During an average of 2½ years of freedom, only nine of the 121 patients (8 percent) were convicted of a crime and only one of those convictions was for a violent act. The researchers found that a Legal Dangerousness Scale (LDS) was most predictive of violent behavior. The scale was composed of four items: presence of juvenile record, number of previous arrests, presence of convictions for violent crimes, and severity of the original Baxstrom offense. In subsequent analyses, Cocozza and Steadman (1974) found that the only other variable highly related to subsequent criminal activity was age (under 50 years old). In one study, 17 of 20 Baxstrom patients who were arrested for a violent crime when released into the community were under 50 and had a score of 5 or above on the 15-point Legal Dangerousness Scale. Yet the authors conclude (pp. 1013-1014)

> For every one patient who was under 50 years old and who had an LDS score of 5 or more and who was dangerous, there were at least 2 who were not. Thus, using these variables we get a false positive ratio of 2 to 1. . . . Despite the significant relationship between the two variables of age and LDS score and dangerous behavior if we were to attempt to use this information for statistically predicting dangerous behavior our best strategy would still be to predict that none of the patients would be dangerous.

The Supreme Court's Baxstrom decision prompted a similar group of "mentally disordered offenders" in Pennsylvania to petition successfully for release in *Dixon v. Pennsylvania,* 1971. The results of the release of 438 patients have been reported by Thornberry and Jacoby (1974) and are remarkably similar to those reported by Steadman. Only 14 percent of the former patients were discovered to have engaged in behavior injurious to another person within 4 years after their release.

Finally, Cocozza and Steadman (1976) followed 257 indicted felony defendants found incompetent to stand trial in New York state in 1971 and 1972. All defendants were examined for a determination of dangerousness by two psychiatrists, with 60 percent being predicted to be dangerous and 40 percent not so. Subjects were followed in the hospital and in the community (if they were eventually released) during a three year follow-up. While those predicted to be dangerous were slightly but insignificantly more likely to be assaultive during their initial incompetency hospitalization than those predicted not to be dangerous (42 percent compared with 36 percent), this relationship was reversed for those rearrested for a crime after their release, with 49 percent of the dangerous group and 54 percent of the not-dangerous group rearrested. Predictive accuracy was poorest in the case of a rearrest for a violent crime, "perhaps the single most important indicator of the success of the psychiatric predictions." Only 14 percent of the dangerous group, compared with 16 percent of the not-dangerous group, were rearrested for violent offenses. While these data are susceptible to alternative interpretations (Monahan, in press[a]), the authors believe that they constitute "the most definitive evidence available on the lack of expertise and accuracy of psychiatric predictions of dangerousness" and indeed represent *"clear and convincing evidence* of the inability of psychiatrists or of anyone else to accurately predict dangerousness."

The conclusion to emerge most strikingly from these studies is the great degree to which violence is overpredicted. Of those predicted to be dangerous, between 54 and 99 percent are false positives—people who will not, in fact, be found to have committed a dangerous act. Violence, it would appear, is vastly overpredicted, whether simple behavioral indicators or sophisticated multivariate analyses are employed and whether psychological tests or thorough psychiatric examinations are performed.

Several factors have been suggested that might account for the great degree of overprediction found in the research (Monahan 1976).

1. *Lack of corrective feedback to the predictor.* The individual is usually incarcerated on the basis of the prediction and so it is impossible to know whether or not he actually would have been violent (Dershowitz 1970).

2. *Differential consequences to the predictor of overpredicting and underpredicting violence.* False negatives lead to much adverse publicity, while false positives have little effect on the predictor (Steadman 1972).

3. *Differential consequences to the individual whose behavior is being predicted.* A prediction of violence may be necessary to ensure involuntary treatment (Monahan and Cummings 1975).

4. *Illusory correlations between predictor variables and violent behavior.* The often cited correlation between violent behavior and mental illness, for example, appears to be illusory (Gulevich and Bourne 1970, Sweetland 1972).

5. *Unreliability of violence as a criterion event.* There is little consensus as to the definition of violence, and great unreliability in verifying its occurrence (Monahan and Geis 1976).

6. *Low base rates of violence.* The prediction of any low-base-rate event is extremely difficult (Rosen 1954).

7. *Low social status of those subjected to prediction efforts.* Overprediction may be tolerated in part because of class biases in the criminal justice and mental health systems (Geis and Monahan 1976, Monahan *et al.* in press).

IV. FUTURE RESEARCH DIRECTIONS IN THE PREDICTION OF VIOLENCE

The conclusion of Wenk and his colleagues (1972) that "there has been no successful attempt to identify, within . . . offender groups, a subclass whose members have a greater than even chance of engaging again in an assaultive act" is widely shared by researchers in the field (e.g., Stone 1975, Megargee 1976). There is no consensus, however, on the implications of this conclusion for future research. Some agree with Wilkins's (1972) assessment of a major California prediction study that "research along these lines does not seem worthwhile to press. Perhaps this study should be 'the last word' for some time in attempts to 'predict' violence potential for individuals." Others side with Halatyn (1975) that the empirical studies to date "reflect data and design limitations which should stimulate rather than stifle further research."

While the future may bear out Wilkins's pessimistic judgment, we shall proceed here in the spirit of Halatyn's remarks and assume that the last word on violence prediction has yet to be uttered. A series of research priorities shall be articulated that, if successfully implemented, might improve the ability to predict violence to a point at which it could provide useful information to policy decision makers. The ensuing discussion will consider the criterion variables that define violent or dangerous criminal behavior and the predictor variables that attempt to forecast it. In each of these categories, several recommendations will be made to improve the quality of research in the prediction of violence, and specific proposals for research projects will be offered.

Recommendation One: Research on violence prediction must employ multiple definitions of violence.

Proposal One: Violence should be defined in a hierarchy including (a) the four FBI *violent index crimes of murder, forcible rape, robbery, and aggravated assault, and (b) all assaultive acts against persons.*

The choice of a definition of violence for research purposes would be made more simple if there were a consensus among either the public or professional groups as to what behaviors should be counted as dangerous. Unfortunately, no such consensus exists (Monahan and Hood, in press). Given this fact, the appropriate research strategy would seem to lie in the direction of multiple definitions of violence. Research on violence prediction should use several hierarchical definitions of the criterion, each succeeding one being more inclusive than that before it.

This would have two substantial advantages over the current proliferation of studies employing a single arbitrary definition of violent or dangerous behavior:

1. It would allow a greater degree of comparability across studies. As things stand now, it is very difficult to compare the results of prediction research projects that use different criteria. Even projects as similar as Kozol *et al.* (1972) and state of Maryland (1973) did not use similar criteria. Kozol *et al.* defined their criterion as "serious assaultive acts," while at Patuxent, the definition was "any new offense, not necessarily violent."
2. It would facilitate policy implications being drawn from the research. Violence, as Skolnick (1969, p. 4) notes "is an ambiguous term whose meaning is established through political processes." If researchers could present policy makers with a series of plausible definitions of violence, each with attendant empirical data with regard to predictability, the final choice of definition could be left in the political arena (Heller and Monahan 1977).

In establishing multiple definitions of violence, it should be noted that the more inclusive the definition, the greater the predictive accuracy: Large targets are easier to hit than small ones. The data bear out this axiom. One attempt to predict "assaultive behavior" had 16 percent true positives when the criterion was defined as "homicide, all assaults, attempted murder, battery, forcible rape and attempt to rape"; 22.6 percent true positives when the criterion was expanded to include "other sex offenses and kidnapping"; and 53 percent true positives when assaultive behavior was construed still more loosely to encompass "all of the above plus robbery, all sex offenses, weapon offenses and disturbing the peace" (cited in Halatyn 1975). While predictive accuracy is indeed increased as definitions of violence expand, there comes a point at which it is arguable whether one is studying violence or simply any kind of lawbreaking. Including "disturbing the peace" as violent, for example, would seem to stretch the concept to its breaking point.

It would be reasonable to specify initially that at least two levels of the criterion must be identified in future research. One level should be violence in its most strict construction, and the other should be somewhat more inclusive in nature. The narrowest definition of violent crime in common use is that employed by the Federal Bureau of Investigation (e.g., Kelley 1976). Violent crime, according to the FBI, is restricted to (a) murder, (b) forcible rape, (c) robbery, and (d) aggravated assault. There would seem to be little disagreement that these four acts are indeed violent ones.

At the more inclusive level, the kinds of acts referred to by Cocozza and Steadman (1974) and Rubin (1972) as "assaultive behavior against persons," or more formally by Megargee (1976) as "acts characterized by the application or overt threat of force which is likely to result in injury to people" appear reasonably to be definable as violent. According to Megargee (p. 5):

> this use of the term [violent] includes, but is not restricted to, such criminal acts as homicide, mayhem, aggravated assault, forcible rape, battery, robbery, arson, and extortion. Criminal behavior not likely to result in injury to people, such as noncoercive thefts or vandalism, are excluded, as are business practices which, although injurious to people, do not involve the application of force.

It is not possible to list precisely all the crimes to be included in this second-level definition of violence, since the categorization of crimes differs from state to state and since many violent acts will result in civil commitment rather than arrest (Cocozza and Steadman 1974). Yet the thrust of defining violence in terms of "assaultive acts against persons" could be captured in future research studies and could add substantially to our ability to compare various prediction efforts and draw policy-relevant information from them.

In research on clinical predictions[4] of violence, it would also appear necessary to achieve a consistency between the "working definitions" of violent behavior employed by the individuals making the predictions and the definitions used in the follow-up research. If a psychiatrist considers "writing a bad check" to be a sufficiently dangerous behavior to justify institutionalization to prevent its occurrence (*Overholser v. Russell,* 1960), and if the validation researcher is limiting his or her definitions of dangerousness to the FBI violent index crimes and assaultive behavior against persons, it is not surprising that overprediction would be reported. Rather than overprediction, however, this would more properly be a case of unsynchronized definitions. Even if the predictions were perfectly accurate—if those predicted to write bad checks actually wrote them—the follow-up researcher using less inclusive definitions of violence would report them as false positives. The two ways in which this inconsistency could be resolved are to match the follow-up criteria to the working definitions used by the clinicians

[4]See the discussion of Recommendation 4 in Section IV for a discussion of clinical and actuarial prediction.

predicting violence, or to provide the clinicians with the definitions to be used in the follow-up and have them predict according to those definitions. Given the need for consistency across different prediction studies, as well as within each prediction study, the latter alternative would appear to be preferable.

Recommendation Two: Research on violence prediction must employ multiple time-periods for follow-up validation.

Proposal Two: Studies should report follow-up results at (a) 1 year, (b) 3 years, and (c) 5 years after release.

The empirical attempts to validate predictions of violence have used a follow-up period of from 1 to 5 years (Table 1). It is self-evident that the longer the follow-up period, the more likely one is to find high rates of true positives, due to the fact that each individual has more opportunity to commit a violent act. Given the difficulty of predicting low-base-rate events, lengthening the follow-up period will have the effect of increasing the base rate, and hence lowering the probability of false positives. The data bear this out. The two studies employing a 1-year follow-up had false positive rates of 99.7 and 93.8 percent, while the six studies using a 3- to 5-year follow-up had false positive rates of 86.0, 86.0, 86.0, 80.0, 65.3, and 54.0 percent.

As with the definition of the criterion, the specification of the follow-up period is not a case of choosing the "best" way to do research. Multiple follow-up periods would serve the same function as multiple definitions: They would increase comparability between studies and facilitate the generation of policy-oriented knowledge. As an attempt at this needed "standardization" of research studies, the reporting of follow-up results at 1-year, 3-year, and 5-year intervals would appear to be both reasonable and feasible.

In the case of predictions by mental health professionals, it would seem that a specification of the duration of the follow-up periods should be made at the time of the original predictions. It would then be possible for different predictions to be made for each of the follow-up periods. For example, a psychiatrist could predict that a given offender or patient had a 30-percent probability of committing a violent act within 1 year after release, a 60-percent probability within 3 years, and an 80-percent probability within 5 years.

Recommendation Three: Research on violence prediction must employ multiple methods of verifying the occurrence of violent behavior.

Proposal Three: Verification methods should be employed in a hierarchy including (a) conviction rates; (b) conviction rates and arrest rates; (c) conviction rates, arrest rates, and rates of civil commitment to mental hospitals; and (d) all of the above plus self-report.

In the prediction studies to date, police arrest rates have been the primary means of verifying whether or not a violent act has occurred during the follow-up period. For at least two reasons, however, arrest rates are inadequate methods of verification: Most violent behavior is never reported to the police, and the violent behavior that is reported often does not lead to the recording of an arrest.

On the first point, a recent victimization study in eight major American cities found that only 40 to 50 percent of all violent crime was reported to the police. The reporting rate for simple assault ranged from 27 to 39 percent (U.S. Department of Justice 1974). While the reasons for not reporting a crime are varied (e.g., embarrassment, fear of retaliation, low opinion of police effectiveness), the result of underreporting is surely to reduce the usefulness of arrest records as a means of verifying the occurrence of violent behavior (Halatyn 1975).

Added to this is the fact that the "clearance rate" of reported crime (i.e., the percentage of reported crime that results in an alleged offender being charged and taken into custody) is far from perfect. While the clearance rate for murder is reasonably high (79 percent), the clearance rates for forcible rape (51 percent), aggravated assault (63 percent), and robbery (27 percent) are such that a large portion of the violent crime that is reported never finds its way into police statistics (Kelley 1976).

In addition to the standard reasons given to account for the low clearance rates for violent crime (e.g., unidentified offenders, lack of evidence, unwillingness of the victim to press charges, etc.), one factor especially relevant to validation studies of the prediction of violence is that mental hospitalization is often used by the police as an alternative to arrest. As Cocozza and Steadman (1974, p. 1013) noted in their follow-up of the "criminally insane" Baxstrom patients, "some of the patients were rehospitalized for behavior very similar to that displayed by other patients who were arrested for violent crimes." One Los Angeles study found that 33 percent of police referrals to a medical center psychiatric unit had as their primary precipitating incident "some degree of aggressive behavior." In none of these cases was an arrest made (Jacobson *et al.* 1973).

When these limitations on the use of official crime statistics are taken in concert, they suggest that many persons classified as false positives in prediction research actually may be leading active careers in violent crime but simply have not yet been apprehended and charged or, if they have been apprehended, they have been diagnosed as "dangerous to others" and processed through the mental health rather than the criminal justice system.

If it is violent behavior, rather than arrests for reported violent crime, that prediction researchers are really interested in, they would do well to broaden their procedures for verifying its occurrence. Criminal justice statistics are estimates of the amount of violent behavior occurring in a given group predicted to be violent. As such, they should be used along with other indicators of violent behavior to arrive at the most reliable estimate possible.

Each estimate of violent behavior will have its own error costs. Reliance solely upon conviction rates for violent crime to verify the occurrence of violent behavior would tend to avoid the erroneous recording of events as violent, but at an enormous cost in the nonrecording of violent events that do occur.[5] Arrest records likewise will underestimate crime to the extent that it is unreported or uncleared, but against this underestimation there must be a consideration of those innocent persons who are arrested and later acquitted or have the charges dropped. This is even more true with data on civil commitments to mental hospitals, in which discretion as to the definition of violence and the procedures for certifying its occurrence is great (Monahan 1973a, 1973b, 1977a, 1977b).

Additional validation procedures are needed that do not rely upon the official statistics that so underrecord violent behavior. One such procedure is self-report. Self-report methodologies have been used extensively in the study of delinquency (Hirschi 1969) and might be applied fruitfully to the study of adult violence. In this regard, Toch (1969) has developed a "peer interview" technique whereby parolee research assistants interview other parolees regarding instances of violent behavior. With appropriate guarantees of confidentiality, such methods may provide an extremely valuable addition to the use of official statistics to validate predictive judgments. A representative sample of a cohort of ex-prisoners or ex-patients whose potential for violence is being assessed could be interviewed by other ex-prisoners or ex-patients at 1-, 3-, and 5-year intervals to obtain data on actually committed, but not recorded, violent behavior.

As with the definition of violence and the duration of the validation period, multiple methods for verifying the occurrence of violent behav-

[5]It should be clear that the use of estimates of criminality other than conviction is for research purposes only, since due process considerations preclude their use in the disposition of individual cases.

ior would appear appropriate in future research. A hierarchy of validation procedures beginning with convictions then sequentially adding arrests, mental hospital commitments,[6] and self-reports might be a viable approach. Such a tack, as earlier, should increase comparability across prediction studies and facilitate the derivation of policy implications from the data.

Recommendation Four: Research on violence prediction should stress actuarial rather than clinical methods.

Proposal Four: Actuarial models of the clinical decision-making process should be constructed.

The two generic methods by which violent behavior (or any other kind of event) may be anticipated are known as clinical and actuarial prediction. In clinical prediction, a psychologist, psychiatrist, parole board member, or other person acting as a "clinician" considers what he or she believes to be the relevant factors predictive of violence and renders an opinion accordingly. This was the method used in the Kozol, Steadman, Thornberry and Jacoby, and Patuxent studies reviewed earlier. The clinician may rely in part upon actuarial data in forming the prediction, but the final product is the result of an intuitive weighting of the data in the form of a professional judgment. Actuarial (or statistical) prediction refers to the establishment of statistical relationships between given predictor variables (e.g., age, number of prior offenses) and the criterion of violent behavior. This method was used in the Wenk *et al.* series of studies. The prediction variables may include clinical diagnoses or scores on psychological tests, but these are statistically weighted in a prediction formula.

One of the "great debates" in the field of psychology has revolved around the relative superiority of clinical versus actuarial methods. It is one of the few such debates to emerge with a clear-cut victor. With the publication of Paul Meehl's classic work in 1954 and its many subsequent confirmations (Sawyer 1966), actuarial methods have come to be recognized as the generally superior way of predicting behavior.

At first glance, the research reviewed above on the prediction of violence would appear to constitute an exception to this rule. The five clinical studies have reported substantially better predictions than the three actuarial ones. While several confounding factors make this

[6]By commitment here is meant commitment to a mental hospital through the police power rather than the *parens patriae* power of the state (Kittrie 1971, Shah 1977). Thus, in California, a civil commitment as "dangerous to others" should be counted in validation studies, while commitment as "gravely disabled" (which is defined as an inability to feed, clothe, or house oneself) should not.

comparison problematic (e.g., the base-rate for violent behavior was higher, and the follow-up period longer for the clinical than for the actuarial studies), it would at least be fair to conclude that the actuarial method has not shown the same superiority over the clinical method in the case of violence as it has with the prediction of other behaviors.

Two conflicting interpretations might be drawn from a comparison of the clinical and actuarial studies. One is that clinical prediction methods really do constitute the best way to predict violent behavior, and that future research should focus on improving the predictive accuracy of clinicians. The other is that actuarial methods have not yet lived up to their potential, judging from their performance in other areas, and that a priority for future research should be the development of more sophisticated actuarial models. We shall argue for the latter interpretation.

While it is undoubtedly true that much can be done to improve the accuracy of clinical predictions of violence—including the multiple definitions, validation periods, and methods of verification mentioned earlier and the inclusion of situational variables, to be discussed below—the impression persists that clinicians have taken their best shot at predicting violence and that future improvements will not drastically alter the two-to-one false positive ratio reported so consistently. The Kozol and Patuxent studies, for example, both involved extensive multidisciplinary examinations over a lengthy period of observation in nationally recognized institutions. The base rates for violence in their populations were high, the follow-up periods long, and the criteria generous. Still, a majority of the predictions were erroneous in both cases.

Actuarial studies, on the other hand, have often been based on "general purpose variables" (Wenk and Emrich 1972) rather than on theoretically derived predictors and have been employed with short follow-up periods on populations with very low base-rates of violent behavior. There have been few actuarial studies of any sort, and all have relied on data from a single source (the California Department of Corrections). It would seem that actuarial methods need to be pursued with more vigor before an exception is declared to the general superiority of actuarial over clinical prediction.

But perhaps too much has been made in the past of distinguishing actuarial and clinical methods, and not enough of how each might contribute to the other. Clinical predictions, as was noted, may take into account actuarial tables, and actuarial prediction may incorporate clinical judgments. Two possible strategies for cross-fertilization, therefore, suggest themselves. One is to provide clinicians with as much actuarial information as possible, to see if this affects their predictions. The other is to construct actuarial models based upon the variables used in the clinical decision-making process.

On the first point, Hoffman *et al.* (1974) presented actuarial prediction tables to parole board members reviewing the files of adult male inmates for parole consideration. The board members were then asked for their own clinical predictions and for a decision on whether the inmates should be paroled or kept in prison. They found that the correlation between statistical risk estimates based on the actuarial tables and the board's clinical risk estimates was 0.74 when the actuarial tables were presented to board members before they made their clinical judgments, and 0.53 when the tables were not provided. The correlation between risk estimates and the outcome of the parole decision was 0.30 when the actuarial tables were provided and 0.18 when they were not. The provision of actuarial data, therefore, affected both the clinical judgments of the parole board and its parole decisions in the predicted direction.

The difficulty with this strategy is that it is, in effect, matching clinical judgments to actuarial ones. This will result in improved predictive accuracy only to the extent that the actuarial predictions are, in fact, better than clinical ones would be. In the prediction of violence, however, actuarial predictors have not yet shown their superiority. Based on the results reviewed earlier, influencing clinical predictions to look more like actuarial ones could result in lowered predictive accuracy in the case of violent behavior. This is especially true in light of the fact that Hoffman *et al.* (1974) found that actuarial data were more likely to result in increasing clinical predictions of unfavorable parole outcome (when the actuarial data suggested such an unfavorable outcome) than they were to result in decreased predictions of unfavorable outcome (when the actuarial data were in the favorable direction). This would mean even more false positives if such a strategy were applied to the prediction of violence.

The other possible rapprochement between clinical and actuarial prediction lies in the construction of actuarial models of clinical decision making. Along these lines, Gottfredson *et al.* (1975), relying upon a study that found that the primary variables influencing parole decision making were severity of offense, "parole prognosis," and institutional behavior, developed systematic decision-making guidelines to be fed back to the parole board members from whom the factors were originally derived. They operationalized severity of offense on a 6-point scale and parole prognosis on an 11-point "salient factor" actuarial table, and they developed guidelines concerning the mean sentence served for each severity/risk level. These guidelines were presented to the parole decision makers, as they were reviewing cases, who were asked to record their reasons if their recommended sentence in a given case was outside the range provided (poor performance in the institution, for example, could be one reason for exceeding the guidelines). While no comparison groups were used in this study, the researchers found that 63 percent of the parole recommendations were within the guidelines presented.

Creating actuarial models of the clinical decision-making process in the prediction of violent behavior could have two advantageous effects. First, it would make explicit the variables used in clinical decision making. These variables could then be incorporated on their own account into actuarial models so that their predictive accuracy could be independently assessed. Second, it could increase consistency both between and within individual decision makers, and this increased consistency or reliability could itself lead to improved predictions. As Goldberg (1970) has stated, "linear regression models of clinical judges can be more accurate diagnostic predictors than the humans who are modeled." He goes on to note that a clinician can incorporate and evaluate a great deal of information but that he or she lacks the reliability of a computer always to respond to similar information in similar ways (p. 423):

> [The clinician] "has his days": Boredom, fatigue, illness, situational and interpersonal distractions all plague him, with the result that his repeated judgments of the exact same stimulus configuration are not identical. He is subject to all those human frailties which lower the reliability of his judgments below unity. And, if the judge's reliability is less than unity, there must be error in his judgments—error which can serve no other purpose than to attenuate his accuracy.

Goldberg took a subsample of psychologists' judgments on predicting psychosis from psychological tests and derived a statistical model of their decision-rules. He then had the clinicians and the statistical model of the clinicians compete in predicting psychosis (defined independently) for the rest of the sample. The model won, since it was not subject to the same random errors as were the clinicians from whom it was derived.

It is important to separate the reliability of predictions from their accuracy or validity. Creating statistical models of the clinical prediction process may increase the reliability of the process substantially, but it will increase predictive accuracy or validity only to the extent that some random error is eliminated. Deriving an actuarial model of a clinical prediction process that has low reliability and low validity will result only in a model with high reliability and almost-as-low validity. The model, in other words, will not be much better than the clinical judgments on which it is based. It may, however, be much quicker and cheaper than human predictions.

Since clinicians do appear to have some (albeit meager) ability to predict violent behavior, a priority for future research should be to create statistical models of the clinical prediction process. The factors obtained could themselves be used in a prediction model (as in Goldberg 1970), or they could be fed back to the clinical decision makers in a systematic fashion to see if they would make more consistent judgments when presented with, in effect, their own preferred data base (as in Gottfredson *et al.* 1975).

Recommendation Five: Research on violence prediction should include situational as well as dispositional predictor variables.

Proposal Five: Situational variables should be derived from conceptions of human environments in terms of (a) personal characteristics of the environment's inhabitants, (b) reinforcement properties of the environment, and (c) the psychosocial climate of the environment.

After one has defined the criteria, specified the validation periods, selected the methods of verification, and decided upon a clinical or an actuarial prediction format, it remains to choose the variables upon which one will base the prediction effort. Ideally, these predictor variables should be related to the criterion variables by virtue of their causal implication in some theory of violent behavior. Yet unlike theories of aggression (e.g., Bandura 1973), theories of human violence have not generated a great deal of scholarly interest (Megargee 1969). This has left the person who would predict violence with only his or her own implicit theory of violence to guide in the selection of predictor variables.

As it happens, since many of the individuals involved in violence prediction efforts have been mental health professionals or others who have adopted a "mental health ideology," almost all of the variables that have been investigated as predictors of violence have been dispositional variables. That is, they have referred to fixed or relatively enduring attributes or traits of the person under study, such as age, sex, race, prior criminal record, or psychiatric history and diagnosis. This reliance upon dispositional variables or personal traits has characterized not only the prediction of violence but the prediction of all types of behavior. The result has been the same in each case: low correlations between predictor and criterion variables (Mischel 1968; *cf.* Bem and Allen 1974). In this regard, Arthur (1971), reviewing studies of the prediction of military performance, has stated that a prediction "sound barrier" exists, since "no matter how much information about the individual one adds to the predictive equation, one cannot bring the correlation coefficient between individual characteristics and prediction criteria much above about .40" (p. 544). This "sound barrier" remains unbroken by research on the prediction of violence.

An alternative to the dispositional or trait perspective in the mental health fields has arisen that offers a possible source of previously overlooked variables to include in prediction research. While the roots of the ecological perspective on human behavior have been planted for some time (e.g., Park 1925), it is only recently that this approach has been taken seriously in psychology (Kelly 1966, Moos and Insel 1974, Stokols 1977).

The ecological or environmental perspective on human behavior derives in part from a new appreciation of Kurt Lewin's (Lewin *et al.* 1939) dictum that behavior is a joint function of characteristics of the person and characteristics of the environment with which he or she interacts. Until recently, psychological and psychiatric research had focused almost solely on dispositional or person variables. The ecological approach attempts to right this imbalance by an emphasis upon situational or environmental variables, as they interact with personal characteristics. While environmental research of relevance to the topic of violent behavior has been initiated (Newman 1972, Monahan and Catalano 1976), there has as yet been no empirical attempt to apply the ecological or environmental perspective to the problem of prediction. This is despite the fact that there is coming to be widespread agreement with Moos's statement (1975a) that "to adequately predict individual aggressive behavior, one must know something about the environment in which the individual is functioning" (p. 13).

The use of environmental or situational variables in prediction differs from the use of personal or dispositional variables in at least one major way. In the case of dispositional variables, one has only to establish a relationship between the predictors and the criterion. Since the dispositional variables refer to fixed or relatively enduring characteristics of the person, one knows immediately whether any obtained relationship can be applied to a given case: An individual subject will not change from white to black, from male to female, or from 45 to 25 years old over the duration of the follow-up. In the case of situational predictors, however, one must establish both a statistical relationship between a given situation and violent behavior and the probability that the individual will in fact encounter that situation. One might, for example, predict with a high degree of accuracy that a given class of offenders will resort to violent behavior when confronted with a situation they interpret as a challenge to their masculinity. To predict the actual occurrence of violent behavior, however, one would then have to perform a separate prediction concerning whether they will encounter such situations during the period under investigation.

It can be argued that the inclusion of situational variables is the most pressing current need in the field of violence prediction research. The principal factor inhibiting the development of situational predictors of violence is the lack of comprehensive ecological theories relating to the occurrence of violent behavior.

Moos (1973) has identified six different ways of conceptualizing human environments that have been used in previous research:

1. *Ecological dimensions,* including meteorological, geographic, and architectural variables;
2. *Dimensions of organization structure,* including staffing ratios and organization size;
3. *Personal characteristics of milieu inhabitants,* implying that the character of an environment depends upon the characteristics (e.g., age, sex, abilities) of those who inhabit it;
4. *Behavior settings,* defined by Barker (1968) as units with both behavioral and environmental components (e.g., a basketball game);
5. *Functional or reinforcement properties of environments,* suggesting that people vary their behavior from one setting to another principally as a function of the reinforcement consequences in the different environments; and
6. *Psychosocial characteristics and organizational climate,* in which the characteristics of an environment, as perceived by its members, are measured on various psychosocial scales.

Of these six extant conceptualizations of human environments, two (ecological dimensions and dimensions of organizational structure) appear not to be relevant to the prediction of individual violence, and another (behavior settings) is in an insufficient state of development to allow for its current application to the topic of prediction. The remaining three all provide guidance for the formation of environmental predictors of violence.

Conceptualizing environments in terms of the personal characteristics of milieu inhabitants might lead a researcher to inquire of the about-to-be-released prisoner or mental patient who he or she would be living, working, and recreating with in the post-release environment. The pooled base-rate probabilities of violence for these individuals (given their age, sex, and prior history of violence, for example) should, according to this approach, relate significantly to the probability of violent behavior being committed by the ex-prisoner or ex-patient who enters the environment.

Emphasizing the functional or reinforcement properties of environments would lead the researcher to a behavioral analysis of the reward contingencies operating in the environments in which the predicted individual would be functioning. If, in a given environment, desired rewards (e.g., material goods, peer approval, self-esteem) can be obtained only by committing violent behavior, then the probability of violence in this environment would be high, according to reinforcement theory.

Finally, environments may be conceptualized for the purpose of prediction according to their psychosocial characteristics and organizational climate. According to Moos, this "social climate" perspective "assumes that environments have unique 'personalities' just like people. Personality tests assess personality traits or needs and provide information about the characteristic ways in which people behave. Social environments can be similarly portrayed with a great deal of accuracy and detail" (1975a, p. 4). He has devised a series of scales to measure the perceived social climates of prisons, hospital wards, community-based treatment programs, classrooms, military units, and families (1975a, 1975b). Common to all these scales are three basic dimensions of the environment: (a) relationship dimensions, such as the degree to which the environment is supportive and involving; (b) personal development dimensions, such as the degree of autonomy the environment provides; and (c) system maintenance and system change dimensions, including the degree to which the environment emphasizes order, organization, and control.

Drawing from Moos's extensive body of research, scales might be derived to describe the psychosocial environment in which a prisoner or mental patient is likely to return when released from an institution. For example, the relationship dimension could be operationalized in terms of items such as, "Is the individual likely to be returning to a parent or spouse, or will he or she be living alone? If the individual will be living with someone else, how likely is that other person to be supportive of a nonviolent lifestyle?" The personal development dimension might involve items concerning how likely the individual will be to attain a satisfying life-style (e.g., as the leader of a peer group) without resort to violence. System maintenance and dimensions of system change might be operationalized by estimates that the individual will be employed in a satisfying job (Cook 1975, Witte 1976, Monahan and Monahan 1977).

It should be clear that these three methods of describing environments overlap greatly and that some situational predictor items would fit equally well under any of the three rubrics. It should also be clear that situational variables are being proposed for use in addition to, rather than instead of, dispositional variables in actuarial or clinical prediction schemes. It is the interaction of dispositional and situational variables that holds the greatest promise for improved predictive accuracy. Ideally, it eventually might be possible to make differential predictions of the sort that an individual with dispositional characteristics of type *N* would have *X* probability of violent behavior if he resided in environment type *A*, and *Y* probability if he resided in environment type *B*. But in order to reach this nirvana of prediction, it will be necessary for researchers to begin the arduous task of compiling and verifying a catalog of situations that relate to the future occurrence of violent behavior. The three nonexclusive approaches to conceptualizing human environments reviewed above could provide a framework for deriving specific predictor items that could then be applied to a cohort of prisoners or mental patients about to be released from institutions and validated during follow-up periods by the multiple methods specified previously.

V. CONCLUSION

We have examined the research to date on the prediction of violent criminal behavior and suggested several ways in which research in the future might improve upon it. The prediction of violence is an area of intrinsic scientific interest and policy importance as well.[7] In the latter regard, it is well to keep in mind that improvements in prediction technology can inform but not determine public policy. The risks must be borne by the false positives who languish in institutions and the victims of false negatives who lie in the streets. It is a rare prisoner who will accept with equanimity the explanation that he must be denied parole because the odds are one-in-three that he will be violent upon release. It is an even rarer victim of violent crime who will care to listen

[7]The policy implications of prediction research have been addressed in von Hirsch (1972), Dershowitz (1973, 1974), Wilkins (1975), Shah (1976, 1977), Wexler (1976), Fagin (1976), Dix (1976), and Monahan (in press [b]) in addition to the references cited previously.

to a treatise on the difficulty of predicting low-base-rate events. The task of research is to provide the most accurate estimates possible of the relative risks to the individual and to society of various procedures for predicting violence. Their weighting remains, as it must, in the political process.

REFERENCES

Arthur, R. (1971) Success is predictable. *Military Medicine* 136:539-45.

Bandura, A. (1973) *Aggression: A Social Learning Analysis*. Englewood Cliffs, N.J.: Prentice-Hall.

Baker, R. (1968) *Ecological Psychology: Concepts and Methods for Studying the Environment of Human Behavior*. Palo Alto: Stanford University Press.

Bem, D., and Allen, A. (1974) On predicting some of the people some of the time: the search for cross-situational consistencies in behavior. *Psychological Review* 81:506-20.

Cocozza, J., and Steadman, H. (1974) Some refinements in the measurement and prediction of dangerous behavior. *American Journal of Psychiatry* 131:1012, 1020.

Cocozza, J., and Steadman, H. (1976) The failure of psychiatric predictions of dangerousness: clear and convincting evidence. *Rutgers Law Review* 29:1084-1101.

Cook, P. (1975) The correctional carrot: better jobs for parolees. *Policy Analysis* 1:11-54.

Dershowitz, A. (1970) Imprisonment by judicial hunch: the case against pretrial preventive detention. *The Prison Journal* 50:12-22.

Dershowitz, A. (1973) Preventive confinement: a suggested framework for constitutional analysis. *Texas Law Review* 51:1277-1324.

Dershowitz, A. (1974) Indeterminate confinement: letting the therapy fit the harm. *University of Pennsylvania Law Review* 123:297-339.

Dix, G. (1976) "Civil" commitment of the mentally ill and the need for data on the prediction of dangerousness. *Americal Behavioral Scientist* 19:318-34.

Fagin, A. (1976) The policy implications of predictive decision-making: "likelihood" and "dangerousness" in civil commitment proceedings. *Public Policy* 24:491-528.

Geis, G., and Monahan, J. (1976) The social ecology of violence. Pages 342-56 in T. Lickona, ed., *Morality: Theory, Research and Social Issues*. New York: Holt, Rinehart, & Winston.

Goldberg, L. (1970) Man versus model of man: a rationale, plus some evidence, for a method of improving on clinical inferences. *Psychological Bulletin* 73:422-32.

Gottfredson, D., Hoffman, P., Sigler, M., and Wilkins, L. (1975) Making paroling policy explicit. *Crime and Delinquency* 21:34-44.

Gulevich, G., and Bourne, P. (1970) Mental illness and violence. Pages 309-26 in D. Daniels, M. Gilula, and F. Ochberg, eds., *Violence and the Struggle for Existence*. Boston: Little, Brown.

Halatyn, T. (1975) Violence Prediction Using Actuarial Methods: A Review and Prospectus. Unpublished manuscript. National Council on Crime and Delinquency, Research Center, Davis, California.

Harvard Law Review (1974) Developments in the law: civil commitment of the mentally ill. note. 87:1190-1406.

Heller, K., and Monahan, J. (1977) *Psychology and Community Change*. Homewood, Ill.: Dorsey Press.

Hirschi, T. (1969) *Causes of Delinquency*. Berkeley: University of California Press.

Hoffman, P., Gottfredson, D., Wilkins, L., and Pasela, G. (1974) The operational use of an experience table. *Criminology* 12:214-28.

Jacobson, D., Craven, W., and Kushner, S. (1973) A study of police referral of allegedly mentally-ill persons to a psychiatric unit. Pages 533-51 in J. Snibbe, and H. Snibbe, eds., *The Urban Policeman in Transition*. Springfield, Ill. Charles Thomas, 1973, 533-51.

Kelley, C. (1976) *Crime in the United States*. Washington, D.C.: U.S. Government Printing Office.

Kelly, J. (1966) Ecological constraints on mental health services. *American Psychologist* 21:535-39.

Kittrie, N. (1971) *The Right to Be Different*. Baltimore: Johns Hopkins University Press.

Kozol, H., Boucher, R., and Garolfalo, R. (1972) The diagnosis and treatment of dangerousness. *Crime and Delinquency* 18:371-92.

Kozol, H., Boucher, R., and Garofalo, R. (1973) Dangerousness. *Crime and Delinquency* 19:554-55.

Lewin, K., Lippett, R., and White, R. (1939) Patterns of aggressive behavior in experimentally created 'social climates.' *Journal of Social Psychology* 10:271-99.

Meehl, P. (1954) *Clinical versus Statistical Prediction*. Minneapolis: University of Minnesota Press.

Megargee, E. (1969) A critical review of theories of violence. Pages 1037-1115 in D. Mulvihill and M. Tumin, eds., *Crimes of Violence*. Vol. 13. Washington, D.C.: U.S. Government Printing Office.

Megargee, E. (1976) The prediction of dangerous behavior. *Criminal Justice and Behavior* 3:3-22.

Mischel, W. (1968) *Personality and Assessment*. New York: Wiley.

Monahan, J. (1973a) The psychiatrization of criminal behavior. *Hospital and Community Psychiatry* 24:105-107.

Monahan, J. (1973b) Abolish the insanity defense? Not yet. *Rutgers Law Review* 26:719-40.

Monahan, J. (1975) The prediction of violence. Pages 15-35 in D. Chappell and J. Monahan, eds., *Violence and Criminal Justice*. Lexington, Mass: Lexington Books.

Monahan, J. (1976) The prevention of violence. Pages 13-35 in J. Monahan, ed., *Community Mental Health and the Criminal Justice System*. New York: Pergamon Press.

Monahan, J. (1977a) Social accountability: preface to an integrated theory of criminal and mental health sanctions. Pages 241-55 in B. Sales, ed., *Perspectives in Law and Psychology: The Criminal Justice System*. New York: Plenum Press.

Monahan, J. (1977b) Empirical analyses of civil commitment: critique and context. *Law and Society Review* 11:619-28.

Monahan, J. (in press [a]) Prediction research and the emergency commitment of dangerous mentally ill persons: a reconsideration. *American Journal of Psychiatry*.

Monahan, J. (in press [b]) Strategies for an empirical analysis of the prediction of violence in emergency civil commitment. *Law and Human Behavior*.

Monahan, J., and Catalano, R. (1976) Toward the safe society: police agencies and environmental planning. *Journal of Criminal Justice* 4:1-7.

Monahan, J., and Cummings, L. (1975) The prediction of dangerousness as a function of its perceived consequences. *Journal of Criminal Justice* 2:239-42.

Monahan, J., and Cummings, L. (1976) Social policy implications of the inability to predict violence. *Journal of Social Issues* 31:153-64.

Monahan, J., and Geis, G. (1976) Controlling "dangerous" people" *Annals of the American Academy of Political and Social Science* 423:142-51.

Monahan, J., and Hood, G. (1976) Psychologically disordered and criminal offenders: perceptions of their volition and responsibility. *Criminal Justice and Behavior* 3:123-34.

Monahan, J., and Hood, G. (in press) Ascriptions of dangerousness: The eye (and age, sex, education, location, and politics) of the beholder. In R. Simon, ed., *Research in Law and Sociology*. Greenwich, Conn.: Johnson.

Monahan, J., and Monahan, L. (1977) Prediction research and the role of psychologists in correctional institutions. *San Diego Law Review* 14:1028-38.

Monahan, J., Novaco, R., and Geis, G. (in press) Corporate violence: research strategies for community psychology. In T. Sarbin, ed., *Community Psychology and Criminal Justice*. New York: Human Sciences Press.

Moos, R. (1973) Conceptualizations of human environments. *American Psychologist* 28:652-65.

Moos, R. (1975a) *Evaluating Correctional and Community Settings*. New York: Wiley.

Moos, R. (1975b) *Evaluating Treatment Settings*. New York: Wiley.

Moos, R., and Insel, P., eds. (1974) *Issues in Social Ecology*. Palo Alto: National Press.

Morris, N. (1974) *The Future of Imprisonment*. Chicago: University of Chicago Press.

Newman, O. (1972) *Defensible Space*. New York: Macmillan.

Park, R. (1925) *The City*. Chicago: University of Chicago Press.

Rappaport, J. (1973) A response to "Implications from the Baxstrom Experience." *Bulletin of the American Academy of Psychiatry and the Law* 1:197-98.

Rector, M. (1973) Who are the dangerous? *Bulletin of the American Academy of Psychiatry and the Law* 1:186-88.

Rosen, A. (1954) Detection of suicidal patients: an example of some limitations of the prediction of infrequent events. *Journal of Consulting Psychology* 18:397-403.

Rubin, B. (1972) Prediction of dangerousness in mentally ill criminals. *Archives of General Psychiatry* 27:397-407.

Sarbin, T. (1967) The dangerous individual: an outcome of social identity transformations. *British Journal of Criminology* 7:285-95.

Sawyer, J. (1966) Measurement and prediction, clinical and statistical. *Psychological Bulletin* 66:178-200.

Shah, S. (1976) Dangerousness: A Paradigm for Exploring Some Issues in Law and Psychology. Presented as the David Levine Invited Address at the meeting of the American Psychological Association, Washington, D.C.

Shah, S. (1977) Dangerousness: Some definitional, conceptual, and public policy issues. Pages 91-119 in B. Sales, ed., *Perspectives in Law and Psychology*. New York: Plenum Press.

Skolnick, J. (1969) *The Politics of Protest*. New York: Simon and Schuster.

State of Maryland (1973) Maryland's Defective Delinquency Statute—A Progress Report. Department of Public Safety and Correctional Services. Unpublished manuscript.

Steadman, H. (1972) The psychiatrist as a conservative agent of social control. *Social Problems* 20:263-71.

Steadman, H., and Cocozza, J. (1974) *Careers of the Criminally Insane*. Lexington, Mass: Lexington Books.

Steadman, H., and Halfon, A. (1971) The Baxstrom patients: backgrounds and outcome. *Seminars in Psychiatry* 3:376-86.

Steadman, H., and Keveles, G. (1972) The community adjustment and criminal activity of the Baxstrom patients: 1966-1970. *American Journal of Psychiatry* 129:304-10.

Stokols, D., ed. (1977) *Psychological Perspectives on Environment and Behavior: Conceptual and Empirical Trends.* New York: Plenum Press.

Stone, A. (1975) *Mental Health and Law: A System in Transition.* Washington, D.C.: U.S. Government Printing Office.

Sweetland, J. (1972) "Illustory Correlation" and the Estimation of "Dangerous" Behavior. Doctoral dissertation, Indiana University.

Thornberry, T., and Jacoby, J. (1974) The Uses of Discretion in a Maximum Security Mental Hospital: The Dixon Case. Paper presented at the annual meeting of the American Society of Criminology, Chicago, Illinois.

Toch, H. (1969) *Violent Men.* Chicago: Aldine.

Twentieth Century Fund (1976) *Fair and Certain Punishment.* New York: McGraw-Hill.

U.S. Department of Justice (1974) *Crime in Eight American Cities.* Washington D.C.: U.S. Government Printing Office.

von Hirsch, A. (1972) Prediction of criminal conduct and preventive confinement of convicted persons. *Buffalo Law Review* 21(3):717-58.

von Hirsch, A. (1976) *Doing Justice: The Choice of Punishments.* New York: Hill & Wang.

Wenk, E., and Emrich, R. (1972) Assaultive youth: an exploratory study of the assaultive experience and assaultive potential of California Youth Authority wards. *Journal of Research in Crime and Delinquency* 9:171-96.

Wenk, E., Robinson, J., and Smith, G. (1972) Can violence be predicted? *Crime and Delinquency* 18:393-402.

Wexler, D. (1976) *Criminal Commitments and Dangerous Mental Patients: Legal Issues of Confinement, Treatment and Release.* Washington, D.C.: U.S. Government Printing Office.

Wilkins, L. (1975) Cited in E. Wenk and R. Emrich, Assaultive youth: An exploratory study of the assaultive experience and assaultive potential of California Youth Authority wards. *Journal of Research in Crime and Delinquency* 9:171-96.

Wilkins, L. (1975) Putting "treatment" on trial. *The Hastings Center Report* 5:35-48.

Witte, A. (1976) Testing the Economic Model of Crime on Individual Data. Unpublished manuscript, Department of Economics, University of North Carolina.

Participation in Illegitimate Activities: Ehrlich Revisited

WALTER VANDAELE

I. INTRODUCTION

Since the publication of Ehrlich's work on the economics of crime (see Ehrlich 1970, 1973, 1975b), there has been a surge of interest in the economics of crime and punishment in general and in the validity of Ehrlich's empirical results in particular.

In this paper we will re-analyze the cross-section data used by Ehrlich in his 1973 article, "Participation in Illegitimate Activites: A Theoretical and Empirical Investigation." The objective of this study is to re-examine the data to judge, within the context of the theoretical model developed by Ehrlich, whether the deterrent effects of punishment are real or an artifact of a particular model specification.

Walter Vandaele is Assistant Professor, Graduate School of Business Administration, Harvard University.

NOTE: This paper was prepared while on leave at the University of California, Los Angeles, Department of Economics. Funds for this research were made available through the Associates of the Graduate School of Business Administration under the Division of Research, Harvard University; the National Science Foundation under grants nr-76-08863 A01 and SOC 76-15546; and the National Bureau of Economic Research. A. Blumstein, J. Chaikin, F. Fisher, B. Forst, Z. Griliches, W. Landes, C. Manski, D. Nagin, A. Reiss, and F. Zimring provided helpful comments for which I am grateful. I. Ehrlich, G. Eyssen, J. Pratt, and R. Shapiro read the draft and offered many valuable suggestions.

Any conclusions reached in this paper are valid only within the context of Ehrlich's theoretical model and for the data set on hand, and they should not be casually carried over to data sets for a different time period or a different country. In addition, they do not preclude the possibility that alternative ways of looking at the criminal process might result in models that could lead to a different conclusion.

The paper is divided into five parts. In Section II, the data are briefly discussed. In Section III we have reproduced Ehrlich's model specification and subsequently corrected for apparent estimation mistakes. Section IV contains the results of different model specifications and the effects of omitting certain states from the analysis. The conclusions are contained in Section V. The appendixes give graphs of some variables as well as a list of the actual data used.

II. DATA SET

The data available[1] for the present investigation are for crimes in 1960 in 47 states of the United States (New Jersey,[2] Alaska, and Hawaii were excluded). For each state, the reported crime rate (Q_i/N) was studied for each of the seven FBI index crimes[3] with i referring to the types of crime: murder, rape, assault, larceny, robbery, burglary, and auto theft—in addition to two sanction variables: P_i, the probability of prison commitment (the probability of imprisonment), and T_i, the average time served in prison when sentenced for a particular crime (the severity of punishment). Of these crimes, murder, rape, and assault will be referred to as violent crimes (crimes against the person) whereas the remaining four, robbery, burglary, larceny, and auto theft, are considered property crimes. Eleven variables of socioeconomic status have also been used: family income (W), income distribution (X), unemployment rate for urban males in the age group[4] 14-24 (U) and in the age group 35-39 (U_{35-39}), labor force participation rate (LF), educational level (Ed), percentage young males (Age) and percentage nonwhites (NW) in the population, percentage of the population in Standard Metropolitan Statistical Areas ($SMSA$), sex ratio ($Males$), and place of occurrence (a Dummy variable for the north and south of the United States, with south $=1$, *Dummy*). In addition, per capita police

[1]We are indebted to I. Ehrlich for making the 1960 cross-section data available.

[2]The state of New Jersey was omitted because there were no data available on the number of commitments to state prisons.

[3]For a definition of these index crimes, see Appendix A.

[4]The unsubscripted variables U, LF, and Age refer only to the age-group 14-24.

expenditure in each state for 1960 (Exp) and for 1959 (Exp_{59}) have been used to describe the resources available to combat crime.

An extensive literature exists on the inadequacies of the available crime data and the possible effects of these on the values of the estimated coefficients (see, e.g., Ehrlich 1973 [Appendix]; Nagin [in this volume]; Vandaele 1975 [Ch. 4 and Appendix 4]; Bowers and Pierce 1975). The major difficulties result from the failure to report crimes and from the inaccuracies in the sanction measures.

III. EHRLICH REVISITED

Since the early 1960's, there have been a number of empirical analyses investigating the effects of punishment on the crime rate. (For a review of the literature see, e.g., Nagin [in this volume]; Vandaele 1975 [Ch. 1 and 3].) A negative association between the level of punishment and the crime rate was found by all studies except that of Forst (1976), which used 1970 cross-sectional data for the United States. The elasticity of the crime rate to changes in the probability of imprisonment[5] has generally been larger in absolute value than the time-served elasticity.

We first re-analyzed Ehrlich's (1973) model in order to clarify the specifications used in the published results. In Appendix C, Tables 1 to 5 contain the empirical results as published (Ehrlich 1973, 1974; Tables 2 to 6), whereas Tables 6 to 10 report our results. Comparing[6] the two sets of tables we observe:

1. The point estimates obtained by OLS of the coefficients in the All Offenses equation are different (see Tables 1 and 6).

2. The coefficients of determination, R^2, are different in the two sets of tables. These differences cannot be explained by the mere fact that the coefficients of determination in Tables 1 to 5 are adjusted for degrees of freedom but those in Tables 6, 7, and 8 are not. In the latter tables, the R^2 is the simple correlation coefficient between the observed weighted dependent variable and the forecasted weighted dependent variable.

3. The Seemingly Unrelated Regression estimates (SUR) as reported by Ehrlich, Tables 3 and 4, could not be reproduced.

[5]The x-elasticity of y, or the elasticity of y with respect to x, is defined as the percentage change in y divided by the percentage change in x. Mathematically this is equal to $(dy/y)/(dx/x)$ or equivalently $d\ln y/d\ln x$.

[6]In Tables 3, 4, and 5 the ratio of the point estimate to its standard error is given in parentheses, whereas in the recalculated tables the standard error itself is reported.

4. We observed the presence of several typographical errors in Table 3 and, in particular, Table 5. The reported results in Table 5 have been extended to include the estimates of all the coefficients rather than just those for unemployment rate (U), labor force participation rate (LF), and *Age* (Tables 8, 9, and 10).

5. In calculating the weighted ordinary least-squares estimates (columns 4, 5, and 6 of Table 5), Ehrlich incorrectly used $N^{1/4}$ instead of $\sqrt{N}$ as weights in the model. In addition, there was an error in the labor force participation data, and therefore this part of the table is not reproduced.

6. Unlike the results published in Ehrlich (see Table 7), the weighted 2SLS results[7] reported in Table 5 show the unemployment rate elasticity in the larceny equation to be positive. After introducing the unemployment rate (U), the labor force participation rate (LF), and the age distribution (*Age*) variables (see Tables 7 and 10), we found that the weighted 2SLS estimates of the elasticities of the probability of imprisonment (P_i) and of the time served (T_i) were essentially unchanged despite the introduction of these additional variables.

In the course of the recalculation of Ehrlich's tables, we discovered several additional inaccuracies in the data or the model specification.

7. In the calculation of the 2SLS weighted estimates, we discovered that in the first stage (the reduced form stage), the *Dummy*, being one of the reduced form variables, had not been weighted with $\sqrt{N}$, the square root of the state population size. This problem was brought to Ehrlich's attention, and the coefficients of production function of law enforcement activities, equation (4.5) in Ehrlich (1973), were corrected in the 1974 reprint. Unfortunately, no corrections had been made in the other equations.

8. As mentioned above, there was an error in the labor force participation rate data. Figure 1 shows that the labor force participation rate in Rhode Island amounted to 266 percent, whereas the correct labor force participation rate in that state was 53.1 percent. The corrected data is plotted in Figure 2. As a result, all the estimates in Table 5 and the new Tables 8, 9, and 10 must be recalculated.

[7] In reporting the 2SLS results we have put a "hat" over the endogenous variable on the right-hand side to indicate that in the second stage of the estimation procedure we have used the predicted value of the endogenous variable based on the reduced form, a regression of that variable on all the exogenous variables in the model.

Tables 11 to 15 give the results after correcting both for the *Dummy* weighting and the Rhode Island labor force participation rate. The 2SLS weighted estimates (see Tables 7 and 11) show smaller deterrence elasticities in absolute magnitude than previously reported, except for auto theft and the probability of imprisonment elasticity in the murder equation. Comparing the unweighted 2SLS results, Tables 9 and 14, the point estimates of the coefficients of unemployment rate, labor force participation rate, and age distribution are substantially changed, on occasion even in algebraic sign. However, within the model specification analyzed, the effect of these variables remains inconclusive because of the large confidence intervals.

The weighted 2SLS point estimates, as reported in Table 15, were again different from those of Ehrlich's tables, and from our recalculated results in Table 10. After correcting the labor force participation for Rhode Island and using a proper weighting scheme, the effect of *LF* is no longer consistently negative and significantly different from zero for specific crimes against the person. Indeed, for rape the effect of *LF* is positive, although with very broad confidence intervals. For all offense categories, except murder, the introduction of *U, LF,* and *Age* had virtually no effect on the probability of imprisonment and the severity of punishment elasticities.

9. It can also be seen in Figure 3 that there are states with none[8] of their population living in Standard Metropolitan Statistical Areas (SMSAS). These states are Georgia, Idaho, Vermont, and Wyoming. We are surprised that Georgia is among these states, as its capital (Atlanta) is an SMSA.

IV. MODEL SPECIFICATIONS

This section forms the core of this paper and contains the results of introducing several changes in the model specification. Before embarking on making changes, the need for using a weighted regression estimation procedure was evaluated. The estimated residuals in different equations estimated by OLS or 2SLS showed a negative correlation between the absolute value of the estimated residuals and the population size. A similar finding was reported by Ehrlich. Therefore, it was decided to evaluate the different model specifications only after weighting all the variables with the square root of the population size.

[8]Because the model specification used by Ehrlich required that logarithms be taken from this variable, the value zero was replaced by .10 before taking the logarithms.

A. EFFECT OF URBAN-RURAL AND NORTH-SOUTH VARIABLES

Several authors have suggested that such variables as percentage of the population living in SMSAS and the southern state Dummy variable *(Dummy)* be included in the crime rate function (see, e.g., Nagin [in this volume], Forst 1976). Ehrlich was aware that this was a possible model specification (see Ehrlich 1973, pp. 548 and 563).

Table 16 contains the OLS results of including either the *Dummy* or the *SMSA*. To focus attention on the deterrence issue, only the elasticities for imprisonment and time served, in addition to the coefficient of either the *Dummy* or the *SMSA*, are reported. Comparing Table 16 with Table 6, we see that there were really no major differences either in the point estimates or in the standard error of the estimates, although there is a tendency for the point estimate of the coefficient of time served to be smaller in absolute value. We therefore concluded that the inclusion of these variables in the model specification would not alter the basic conclusions of Ehrlich's paper.

B. CHANGES IN THE REDUCED FORM SPECIFICATION

The Identification Issue

In the most recent deterrence analyses, simultaneous equation models (SEM) have been built to analyze the economics of crime. (See Phillips and Votey 1972; Ehrlich 1973; Greenwood and Wadycki 1973; McPheters and Stronge 1974; Vandaele 1975; Forst 1976.) The deterrence hypothesis states that sanction variables such as the probability of imprisonment, P, and the time served in prison, T, will be negatively related to the crime rates. In general, both P and T are determined by the public's allocation of resources to law enforcement activities. These, in turn, are likely to be affected by the crime rate itself[9] and the resulting social losses. It is specifically in order to analyze these interactions that a simultaneous equation model is used.

A common problem in a simultaneous equation model is the identification of the parameters. This problem has been discussed extensively in the econometric literature (see, e.g., Fisher 1966; Johnston 1972, Chapter 12). Usually, identification of a particular equation is guaranteed by imposing *a priori* restrictions on the model specification, such

[9]Some authors have argued that since budgets are established prior to the start of the year, it seems plausible to model the expenditure on law enforcement equation as a function of last year's crime rate. However, given that the focus of this paper is on the deterrence effects, this last equation has not been re-analyzed.

as the restriction that certain variables present in some equations of the model are not part of that particular equation. This is justified if variables excluded from this equation do not directly affect the dependent variable.[10] Therefore, if the estimates differ depending upon the variables in the equation, the model builder should justify carefully the choice of included and excluded variables.

In examining the identification problem of the crime function within the context of Ehrlich's model, several routes are possible. We could delete from the model some variables not included in the crime function, or we could include in the crime function additional variables that are already part of the model. The first identification analysis, therefore, involves making changes in the reduced form of the model and no changes in the crime equation itself, whereas the second type of analysis results in no changes in the reduced form, but an increase in the number of variables that are part of the crime function.

Properly defined, identification can only be addressed within the context of a theoretical model. The aim of this section, however, is to determine whether or not different types of identification lead to significantly different parameter estimates. If so, we should not attempt to draw the conclusion that one identification specification is better than another, but that there is a serious need for re-examination of the model specification. If, on the contrary, the data do not produce different estimates, then we can conclude that the analysis of the data is not sensitive to a particular model specification and, as a result, there is some flexibility in the structure of the theoretical model.

Table 17 contains the results of introducing changes in the reduced form of the model. In order to concentrate on the deterrence issue, only the imprisonment and time-served-in-prison elasticities are reported. The first two columns in Table 17, called Reduced Form 1, correspond to results previously reported in Table 11 and make use of the reduced form of the results reported by Ehrlich. Reduced Form 2 was obtained by deleting three variables from the model: lagged police expenditure (Exp_{59}), unemployment rate for adults (U_{35-39}), and sex ratio (Males). In Reduced Form 3, three other variables were deleted: urbanization (SMSA), education (Ed), and population size (N). Table 17 shows that the effect of these changes on the point estimates and standard error of the estimates is minimal. However, the point estimates of the deterrence elasticities tend to be larger in absolute value.

[10]Using the terminology of a simultaneous equation model, the variables are mainly grouped into two categories, endogenous and exogenous variables. Basically, endogenous variables are those variables that are determined by the equations of the model, whereas exogenous variables affect the model but are not in turn affected by it.

The second identification analysis is reported in the first two columns of Table 21. Recall that Ehrlich excluded the following variables from the crime equation: Exp_{59} (per capita police expenditures in 1959), $(Q_i/N)_{59}$ (reported crime rate in 1959), N (the state population size), U_{35-39} (unemployment rate for urban males 35-39 years of age), *Age* (percentage of young males), *SMSA* (percentage of population in SMSA), *Males* (sex ratio), *dummy* (location dummy), and *Ed* (educational level). For all but the first two variables, the exclusion of these variables from the crime equation seems somewhat arbitrary.

Underlying Ehrlich's model specification is the assumption that the last seven variables have a causal relationship with any of the other two endogenous variables in the model, the probability of imprisonment or the per capita police expenditure, but not with the endogenous crime rate itself. Our proposition, therefore, is to re-estimate an enlarged model in which the crime equation includes these seven exogenous variables. As a result, the only exogenous variables that are part of the SEM model, but are not in the crime equation, are Exp_{59} and $(Q_i/N)_{59}$. In other words, the excluded variables from the crime equation are Exp_{59} and $(Q_i/N)_{59}$. We define this equation to be identified with the variables Exp_{59} and $(Q_i/N)_{59}$.

Comparing these estimates with the results obtained when these exogenous variables were not part of the equation (Table 11) or with an intermediate specification in which unemployment rate, labor force participation rate, and age distribution were included (Table 15), we observe in Table 21 that for all crime types the imprisonment elasticity is larger in absolute value. The changes in the elasticity of the time served are not always in the same direction: some point estimates show an increase, others show a decrease in absolute value. The elasticity of the time served for murder became positive, although with a broad confidence interval.

In a third modification in the model specification, we make no changes in the crime function itself, but identify the equation only with the variable Exp_{59}. We claim that there is only one additional exogenous variable in the SEM besides the ones already in the crime function; therefore, the reduced form of this specification contains the following variables: constant, $\ln T_i$, $\ln W$, $\ln X$, $\ln NW$, and $\ln Exp_{59}$. The results of this analysis are reported in the first two columns of Table 22. As compared to the basic model (Table 11), we immediately observe that almost all point estimates of the deterrence elasticities are larger in absolute value. This is in contrast with results reported in Table R-15 of Ehrlich (1970). In the latter table, Ehrlich used the basic model as was used in Table 11, but excluded $(Q_i/N)_{59}$ from the reduced form equation and found that the deterrence elasticities were smaller in absolute value.

C. OMITTING CERTAIN STATES

Careful examination of the data brought to light several apparent inconsistencies in the probability of imprisonment. Recall that P_i is computed as the ratio of the number of persons committed in a given year to state (and, in the case of auto theft, also federal) prisons to the number of offenses known to have occurred in that same year. Not all those convicted are committed to prisons; some (especially young offenders) are sent to correctional institutions or released on probation. Also, the year of commitment to prisons is not necessarily the year in which the crime was committed. Therefore, the data on the probability of imprisonment serve only as an approximate measure of the objective probability of imprisonment.[11] In Figures 4 to 8 we have plotted the data for several probabilities of imprisonment. Notice that several of these so-called probabilities are larger than one, notably for the following offenses and states:[12]

Figure 4:	Vermont	P (assault):	156%
Figure 5:	Utah	P (murder):	111%
	Vermont	P (murder):	100%
Figure 6:	Vermont	P (rape):	222%
	Wisconsin	P (rape):	129%
Figure 7:	Vermont	P (murder and rape):	210%
	Wisconsin	P (murder and rape):	104%
Figure 8:	Vermont	P (person):	175%

Therefore, although there are no mistakes in the data, the way the data are reported poses serious questions as to the validity of this data series as a proxy for the objective probability of imprisonment.

As a result, we propose to delete the states with these data abnormalities. If the results of the analysis are a trustworthy representation of the underlying processes, the values of the estimated coefficients should not be influenced by the specific states chosen for the analysis. Thus, serious doubt would be cast on the validity of the empirical results if deletion of the observations for some states substantially

[11]Also, the theoretically relevant variable in Ehrlich's model is the average offender's subjective probability that he will be apprehended and punished by imprisonment for his engagement in a specific crime in a given year. It is assumed that the objective probability of imprisonment, as suggested by the available data, is a good proxy (see Ehrlich 1974, p. 124).

[12]The data on imprisonment for rape really refer to the category Sex Offenses.

affected the values of the coefficients associated with the measures of deterrence.[13]

The results of a recalculation of Ehrlich's basic model after omitting the state of Vermont are reported in Table 18. We initially omitted only this state because most of its probabilities of imprisonment for crimes against the person were larger than 100 percent. Comparing Table 18 with Table 11, the results show that all coefficients retain the same algebraic sign and the same magnitude of the standard error. The maximum change in the point estimate, 13 percent, occurred for the coefficient of the probability of imprisonment in the burglary equation.

D. IDENTIFICATION AND STATE EFFECT

Because changing the identification (see Section B) and deleting Vermont (Section C) produced some, but in general minor, changes in the basic empirical results obtained by Ehrlich, we undertook a more extensive analysis in which the identification was altered and the states with a probability of imprisonment larger than 100 percent were deleted. The results are reported in Tables 19 to 24.

Let us first concentrate on the property crimes. Since the probability of imprisonment for property crimes was nowhere larger than 100 percent, we expected no major differences between results of analyses in which all states were included, in which Vermont was omitted, and in which Utah, Vermont, and Wisconsin were omitted. The results confirm this expectation. When the crime equation was only identified with ln Exp_{59}, there were few differences from the previous analyses (see Tables 22, 23, and 24), whereas when this equation was identified both with ln Exp_{59} and ln $(Q_i/N)_{59}$, there are some larger differences, but only for burglary and larceny (see Tables 19, 20, and 21).

Because of the outlying observations in the probabilities of imprisonment for some of the crimes against the person (see Figures 4 to 8), differences were expected after the deletion of the states Utah, Vermont, and Wisconsin. In the initial evaluation of these outliers by omitting only Vermont with no changes in the identification, the differences appeared to be minor (see Table 18). However, as soon as the crime equation was identified differently, either with ln Exp_{59} or ln Exp_{59} and ln $(Q_i/N)_{59}$, differences were observed (see Tables 19 to 24). When the crime equation was only identified with lagged police ex-

[13]It can be argued that the whole analysis should have been done by leaving out some randomly selected states and building the model based on the remaining states. Then, to validate the model, the crime rates in the omitted states could have been predicted.

penditure, ln Exp_{59}, the results for murder and assault became unstable, possibly due to multicollinearity. In the murder equation, the point estimates for the coefficients of the deterrence variables change in algebraic sign, although with broad confidence intervals. For other crimes against the person, the differences due to the change in the identification restrictions and the omission of states are minor. When the equations for crime against the person were identified by the exclusion of both lagged police expenditure (ln Exp_{59}) and lagged crime rate [ln $(Q_i/N)_{59}$], the apparent instability disappeared, although there were still substantial differences in the results for the murder equation. Here the point estimate of time-served-in-prison elasticity became positive, and the imprisonment elasticity almost doubled in magnitude.

Based on this analysis, we have to conclude that with the exception of the instability in both the murder and assault crime equation, the results obtained within the framework of Ehrlich's model are not sensitive to modifications in the identification or the states included in the analysis.

E. LOG-LINEAR SPECIFICATIONS

Economic theory is capable of indicating which variables should be included in a model. However, the theory does not define the exact functional form to be used in an empirical analysis. Ehrlich used a log-log relationship in order to verify the negative relationship between the deterrence variables and the crime rate. Table 25 reports the results of a study of the following log-linear model

$$\ln(Q_i/N) = \alpha_0 + \alpha_1 P_i + \alpha_2 T_i + \alpha_3 W + \alpha_4 X + \alpha_5 NW.$$

In order to facilitate the comparison with the 2SLS results reported in Table 11, the elasticities calculated at the mean value of the right-side variables are reported. Larger elasticities were generally found when the model was estimated in the log-linear functional form. There were exceptions. For assault and auto theft, the elasticity of the time served decreased drastically, although the point estimates had large confidence intervals.

To facilitate the choice of whether the log-log or log-linear form of the model was preferable, the coefficient of determination was calculated using OLS. Little difference was observed, although the R^2 was slightly larger for the log-log form.

V. CONCLUSION

In this paper we have re-analyzed the 1960 cross-sectional data for crimes across different states used in Ehrlich's (1973) paper. The re-examination of the data indicated inaccuracies in the data as well as in the reported results. Section III contains a re-analysis of Ehrlich's model to correct for the data inaccuracies.

The results of the analyses of different model specifications, reported in Section IV, in general indicated negative point estimates for the elasticities of the probability of imprisonment and the time served. The magnitudes of these elasticities were similar across the different specifications.

The only large changes in the point estimates occurred in the murder and assault equation when these equations were only identified with lagged police expenditures and the lagged crime rate and certain states were omitted. However, in this situation the estimates were very unstable, possibly due to excessive multicollinearity. It appears, therefore, that with the available data and within the present model, the negative relationship between the crime rate and the probability of imprisonment and between the crime rate and the time served is not spurious.

REFERENCES

Bowers, W. J., and Pierce, G. L. (1975) The illusion of deterrence in Isaac Ehrlich's research on capital punishment. *The Yale Law Journal* 85(2):187-208.

Ehrlich, I. (1970) Participation in Illegitimate Activities: An Economic Analysis. Unpublished Ph.D. dissertation, Columbia University.

Ehrlich, I. (1973) Participation in illegitimate activities: a theoretical and empirical investigation. *Journal of Political Economy* 81(3):521-65.

Ehrlich, I. (1974) Participation in illegitimate activities: an economic analysis. Pages 69-134 in G. S. Becker and W. M. Landes, eds., *Essays in the Economics of Crime and Punishment*. (Reprinted with corrections from [1973] *Journal of Political Economy* 81(3):521-65 and with appendixes from [1970] "Participation in Illegitimate Activities: An Economic Analysis," Ph.D. dissertation, Columbia University.) New York: National Bureau of Economic Research (distributed by Columbia University Press).

Ehrlich, I. (1975a) On the relation between education and crime. Pages 313-37 in F. T. Juster, ed., *Education, Income, and Human Behavior*. New York: McGraw-Hill Book Company.

Ehrlich, I. (1975b) The deterrent effect of capital punishment: a question of life and death. *The American Economic Review* 65(3):397-417.

Fisher, F. M. (1966) *The Identification Problem in Econometrics*. New York: McGraw-Hill Book Company.

Forst, B. E. (1976) Participation in illegitimate activities: further empirical findings. *Policy Analysis* 2(3):477-92.

Greenwood, M., and Wadycki, W. J. (1973) Crime rates and public expenditures for police protection: their interaction. *Review of Social Economy* 31(2):232-41.

Johnston, J. (1972) *Econometric Methods*. 2nd ed. New York: McGraw-Hill Book Company.

McPheters, L., and Stronge, W. B. (1974) Law enforcement expenditures and urban crime. *National Tax Journal* 27(4):633-44.

Phillips, L., and Votey, H. L., Jr. (1972) An economic analysis of the deterrent effect of law enforcement on criminal activities. *Journal of Criminal Law, Criminology, and Police Science* 63(3):336-42.

Vandaele, W. (1975) The Economics of Crime: An Econometric Investigation of Auto Theft in the United States. Unpublished Ph.D. dissertation, University of Chicago.

APPENDIX A: CLASSIFICATION OF CRIME INDEX OFFENSES

Definitions[14] of crime classifications used are

1. *Murder* (Criminal homicide): Murder and non-negligent manslaughter: all willful felonious homicides as distinguished from deaths caused by negligence. Excludes attempts to kill, assaults to kill, suicides, accidental deaths, and justifiable homicides. Justifiable homicides are limited to: (a) the killing of a person by a peace officer in line of duty; and (b) the killing by a private citizen of a person in the act of committing a felony.
2. *Rape* (Forcible rape): Rape by force, assault to rape, and attempted rape. Excludes statutory offenses (no force used—victim under age of consent).
3. *Robbery* Stealing or taking anything of value from the care, custody, or control of a person by force or violence or by putting that person in fear, such as strong-arm robbery, stickups, armed robbery, assault to rob, and attempts to rob.
4. *Assault* (Aggravated assault): Assault with intent to kill or for the purpose of inflicting severe bodily injury by shooting, cutting, stabbing, maiming, poisoning, scalding, or by the use of acids, explosives, or other means. Excludes simple assault, assault and battery, fighting, etc.
5. *Burglary* (Breaking or entering): Burglary, housebreaking, safecracking, or any breaking or unlawful entry of a structure with the intent to commit a felony or a theft. Includes attempts.

[14]U.S. Department of Justice, Federal Bureau of Investigation. *Crime in the United States: Uniform Crime Report 1970*, p. 61.

6. *Larceny* Theft (except auto theft): Fifty dollars and over in value; thefts of bicycles, automobile accessories, shop lifting, pocket-picking, or any stealing of property or article of value that is not taken by force and violence or by fraud. Excludes embezzlement, "con" games, forgery, worthless checks, etc.
7. *Auto Theft* Stealing or driving away and abandoning a motor vehicle. Excludes taking for temporary or unauthorized use by those having lawful access to the vehicle.

APPENDIX B: SYMBOLS AND SOURCES OF THE VARIABLES[15]

Age Age distribution: the percentage of males aged 14-24 in the total state population.

Dummy Dummy variable distinguishing place of occurrence of the crime (south = 1). The southern states are: Alabama, Arkansas, Delaware, Florida, Georgia, Kentucky, Louisiana, Maryland, Mississippi, North Carolina, Oklahoma, South Carolina, Tennessee, Texas, Virginia, and West Virginia.

Ed Educational level: the mean number of years of schooling of the population, 25 years old and over.

Exp Police expenditure: the per capita expenditure on police protection by state and local government in 1960. Also available is the per capital expenditure in 1959: Exp_{59}. Sources used are *Governmental Finances in 1960* and *Governmental Finances in 1959,* published by the U.S. Bureau of the Census.

LF Labor force participation rate of civilian urban males in the age-group 14-24.

Males The number of males per 100 females.

N State population size in 1960 in hundred thousands.

NW Nonwhites: the percentage nonwhites in the population.

[15]All the data relate to calendar year 1960 except when explicitly stated otherwise.

P_i The probability of imprisonment: the ratio of the number of commitments to state (and, in the case of auto theft, also federal) prisons in a given year to the number of offenses[16] known to have occurred in that same year. The data on the number of commitments are obtained from the *National Prisoner Statistics* bulletins of the Federal Bureau of Prisons and refer to prisoners received from court by state institutions for adult felony offenders during calendar year 1960. Also, the data on rape relates to sex offenses in general.

(Q_i/N) The crime rate: the number of offenses known to the police per 100,000 population in 1960. Also available is $(Q_i/N)_{59}$, the crime rate in 1959. The source is the *Uniform Crime Report* of the Federal Bureau of Investigation.

SMSA The percentage of the state population living in Standard Metropolitan Statistical Areas.

T_i Time served: the average time served in months by offenders in state prisons before their first release.

U Unemployment rate of urban males in the age-group 14-24, as measured by census estimate.

U_{35-39} Unemployment rate of urban males in the age-group 35-39.

W Wealth as measured by the median value of transferable goods and assets or family income.

X Income inequality: the percentage of families earning below one-half of the median income.

[16]The subscript i refers to a specific crime.

APPENDIX C: TABLES

TABLE 1 OLS (Weighted) Regression Estimates of Coefficients Associated with Selected Variables in 1960, 1950, and 1940: Crimes against the Person and All Offenses (Dependent Variables Are Specific Crime Rates)[a]

	Estimated Coefficients Associated with Selected Variables						
Offense and Year	a Intercept	b_1 with $\ln P_i$	b_2 with $\ln T_i$	c_1 with $\ln W$	c_2 with $\ln X$	e_1 with $\ln NW$	Adj. R^2
Murder							
1960	−0.6644[a]	−0.3407	−0.1396[a]	0.4165[a]	1.3637[a]	0.5532	.8687
1950[b]	−0.7682[a]	−0.5903	−0.2878	0.6095[a]	1.9386	0.4759	.8155
Rape							
1960[b]	−7.3802[a]	−0.5783	−0.1880[a]	1.2220	0.8942[a]	0.1544	.6858
Assault							
1960	−13.2994	−0.2750	−0.1797[a]	2.0940	1.4697	0.6771	.8282
1950	−0.7139[a]	−0.4791	−0.3839	0.5641[a]	0.9136[a]	0.5526	.8566
1940	−0.2891	−0.4239	−0.6036	0.7274[a]	0.5484[a]	0.7298	.8381
Murder and Rape							
1960[b]	−1.8117	−0.5787	−0.2867	0.6773[a]	0.9456	0.3277	.6948
Murder and Assault							
1950[b]	1.0951[a]	−0.7614	−0.3856	0.3982[a]	1.1689[a]	0.4281	.8783
Crimes against Persons							
1960[b]	−4.1571[a]	−0.5498	−0.3487	1.0458	0.9145	0.4897	.8758
All Offenses							
1960	−7.1657	−0.5255	−0.5854	2.0651	1.8013	0.2071	.6950
1950	−1.5081[a]	−0.5664	−0.4740	1.3456	1.9399	0.1051	.6592
1940	−5.2711	−0.6530	−0.2892	0.5986	2.2658	0.1386	.6650

NOTE: The absolute values of all regression coefficients in Tables 1 and 2, except those marked [a], are at least twice those of their standard errors; [b] indicates regressions in which the absolute difference ($\hat{b}_1 - \hat{b}_2$) is at least twice the value of the relevant standard error $S(\hat{b}_1 - \hat{b}_2)$.

[a]Reprinted with permission from I. Ehrlich, Participation in illegitimate activities: a theoretical and empirical investigation, *Journal of Political Economy* 81(3):525-65, 1973 (University of Chicago Press).

TABLE 2 OLS (Weighted) Regression Estimates of Coefficients Associated with Selected Variables in 1960, 1950, and 1940: Property Crimes (Dependent Variables Are Specific Crime Rates)[a]

Offense and Year	Estimated Coefficients Associated with Selected Variables						
	a Intercept	b_1 with $\ln P_1$	b_2 with $\ln T_1$	c_1 with $\ln W$	c_2 with $\ln X$	e_1 with $\ln NW$	Adj. R^2
Robbery							
1960[b]	−20.1910	−0.8534	−0.2233[a]	2.9086	1.8409	0.3764	.8014
1950[b]	−10.2794	−0.9389	−0.5610	1.7278	0.4798	0.3282	.7839
1940	−10.2943	−0.9473	−0.1912[a]	1.6608	0.7222	0.3408	.8219
Burglary							
1960[b]	−5.5700[a]	−0.5339	−0.9001	1.7973	2.0452	0.2269	.6713
1950	−1.0519[a]	−0.4102	−0.4689	1.1891	1.8697	0.1358	.4933
1940	−0.6531[a]	−0.4607	−0.2698	0.8327[a]	1.6939	0.1147	.3963
Larceny							
1960	−14.9431	−0.1331	−0.2630	2.6893	1.6207	0.1315	.5222
1950	−4.2857[a]	−0.3477	−0.4301	1.9784	3.3134	−0.0342[a]	.5819
1940	−10.6198	−0.4131	−0.1680[a]	0.6186	3.7371	0.0499[a]	.6953
Auto Theft							
1960	−17.3057	−0.2474	−0.1743[a]	2.8931	1.8981	0.1152	.6948
Burglary and Robbery							
1960	−9.2683	−0.6243	−0.6883	2.1598	2.1156	0.2565	.7336
1950	−3.0355[a]	−0.5493	−0.4879	1.3624	1.6066	0.1854	.5590
Larceny and Auto Theft							
1960	−14.1543	−0.2572	−0.3339	2.6648	1.8263	0.1423	.6826
1950	−3.9481[a]	−0.3134	−0.4509	1.9286	2.9961	−0.0290[a]	.5894
Property Crimes							
1960	−10.1288	−0.5075	−0.6206	2.3345	2.0547	0.2118	.7487
1950	−2.8056	−0.5407	−0.4792	1.5836	2.2548	0.0755	.6253

NOTE: Same references as in Table 1.

[a]Reprinted with permission from I. Ehrlich, Participation in illegitimate activities: a theoretical and empirical investigation, *Journal of Political Economy* 81(3):525-65, 1973 (University of Chicago Press).

TABLE 3 2SLS and SUR (Weighted) Regression Estimates of Coefficients Associated with Selected Variables in 1960: Crimes against the Person and Total Offenses[a]

Offense	Coefficient (β) Associated with Selected Variables					
	a Intercept	b_1 with $\ln \hat{P}_i$	b_2 with $\ln T_i$	c_1 with $\ln W$	c_2 with $\ln X$	e_1 with $\ln NW$
	A. 2SLS Estimates					
Murder						
$\hat{\beta}$	0.316	−0.852	−0.087	0.175	1.109	0.534
$\hat{\beta}/S\hat{\beta}$	(0.085)	(−2.492)	(−0.645)	(0.334)	(1.984)	(8.356)
Rape						
$\hat{\beta}$	−0.599	−0.896	−0.399	0.409	0.459	0.072
$\hat{\beta}/S\hat{\beta}$	(−0.120)	(−6.080)	(−2.005)	(0.605)	(0.743)	(0.922)
Murder and Rape						
$\hat{\beta}$	2.703	−0.828	−0.350	0.086	0.556	0.280
$\hat{\beta}/S\hat{\beta}$	(0.732)	(−6.689)	(−3.164)	(0.172)	(1.188)	(5.504)
Assault						
$\hat{\beta}$	−7.567	−0.724	−0.979	1.650	1.707	0.465
$\hat{\beta}/S\hat{\beta}$	(−1.280)	(−3.701)	(−2.301)	(2.018)	(2.111)	(3.655)
Crimes against the Person						
$\hat{\beta}$	1.635	−0.803	−0.495	0.328	0.587	0.376
$\hat{\beta}/S\hat{\beta}$	(0.380)	(−6.603)	(−3.407)	(0.570)	(1.098)	(4.833)
All Offenses						
$\hat{\beta}$	−1.388	−0.991	−1.123	1.292	1.775	0.265
$\hat{\beta}/S\hat{\beta}$	(−0.368)	(−5.898)	(−4.483)	(2.609)	(4.183)	(5.069)
	B. SUR Estimates					
Murder						
$\hat{\beta}$	−1.198	−0.913	−0.018	0.186	1.152	0.542
$\hat{\beta}/S\hat{\beta}$	(−0.033)	(−3.062)	(−1.710)	(0.361)	(2.102)	(8.650)
Rape						
$\hat{\beta}$	0.093	−0.930	−0.436	0.333	0.425	0.065
$\hat{\beta}/S\hat{\beta}$	(0.019)	(−6.640)	(−2.318)	(0.502)	(0.692)	(8.841)
Assault						
$\hat{\beta}$	−6.431	−0.718	−0.780	1.404	1.494	0.460
$\hat{\beta}/S\hat{\beta}$	(−1.103)	(−4.046)	(−2.036)	(1.751)	(1.871)	(3.801)

NOTE: The underlying regression equation is

$$\ln\left(\frac{Q}{N}\right) = a + b_{1i} \ln \hat{P}_i + b_{2i} \ln T_i + c_{1i} \ln W + c_{2i} \ln X + e_{1i} \ln NW + \mu_i.$$

[a]Reprinted with permission from I. Ehrlich. Participation in illegitimate activities: a theoretical and empirical investigation. *Journal of Political Economy* 81(3):525-65. 1973 (University of Chicago Press).

TABLE 4 2SLS and SUR (Weighted) Regression Estimates of Coefficients Associated with Selected Variables in 1960: Property Crimes[a]

Offense	Coefficient (β) Associated with Selected Variables					
	a Intercept	b_1 with $\ln \hat{P}_i$	b_2 with $\ln T_i$	c_1 with $\ln W$	c_2 with $\ln X$	e_1 with $\ln NW$
	A. 2SLS Estimates					
Robbery						
$\hat{\beta}$	−11.030	−1.303	−0.372	1.689	1.279	0.334
$\hat{\beta}/S\hat{\beta}$	(−1.804)	(−7.011)	(−1.395)	(1.969)	(1.660)	(4.024)
Burglary:						
$\hat{\beta}$	−2.121	−0.724	−1.127	1.384	2.000	0.250
$\hat{\beta}/S\hat{\beta}$	(−0.582)	(−6.003)	(−4.799)	(2.839)	(4.689)	(4.579)
Larceny						
$\hat{\beta}$	−10.660	−0.371	−0.602	2.229	1.792	0.142
$\hat{\beta}/S\hat{\beta}$	(−2.195)	(−2.482)	(−1.937)	(3.465)	(2.992)	(2.019)
Auto Theft						
$\hat{\beta}$	−14.960	−0.407	−0.246	2.608	2.057	0.102
$\hat{\beta}/S\hat{\beta}$	(−4.162)	(−4.173)	(−1.682)	(5.194)	(4.268)	(1.842)
Larceny and Auto						
$\hat{\beta}$	−10.090	−0.546	−0.626	2.226	2.166	0.155
$\hat{\beta}/S\hat{\beta}$	(−2.585)	(−4.248)	(−2.851)	(4.183)	(4.165)	(2.603)
Property Crimes						
$\hat{\beta}$	−6.279	−0.796	−0.915	1.883	2.132	0.243
$\hat{\beta}/S\hat{\beta}$	(−1.937)	(−6.140)	(4.297)	(4.246)	(5.356)	(4.805)
	B. SUR Estimates					
Robbery						
$\hat{\beta}$	−14.800	−1.112	−0.286	2.120	1.409	0.346
$\hat{\beta}/S\hat{\beta}$	(−2.500)	(−6.532)	(−0.750)	(2.548)	(1.853)	(4.191)
Burglary						
$\hat{\beta}$	−3.961	−0.624	−0.996	1.581	2.032	0.230
$\hat{\beta}/S\hat{\beta}$	(−1.114)	(−5.576)	(−4.260)	(3.313)	(4.766)	(4.274)
Larceny						
$\hat{\beta}$	−10.870	−0.358	−0.654	2.241	1.785	0.139
$\hat{\beta}/S\hat{\beta}$	(−2.52)	(−2.445)	(−1.912)	(3.502)	(2.983)	(1.980)
Auto Theft						
$\hat{\beta}$	−14.860	−0.409	−0.233	2.590	2.054	0.101
$\hat{\beta}/S\hat{\beta}$	(−4.212)	(−4.674)	(−1.747)	(5.253)	(4.283)	(1.832)

NOTE: Same reference as in Table 3.

[a]Reprinted with permission from I. Ehrlich. Participation in illegitimate activities: a theoretical and empirical investigation. *Journal of Political Economy* 81(3):525-65. 1973 (University of Chicago Press).

TABLE 5 Alternative Estimates of Elasticities of Offenses with Respect to Unemployment and Labor-Force Participation of Young Age Groups in 1960 (Dependent Variables Are Specific Crime Rates)[a]

	Ordinary Least-Squares (OLS)						Two-Stage Least-Squares (2SLS)					
	Unweighted			Weighted			Unweighted			Weighted		
Crime Category	d_1	d_2	e_2	d_1	d_2	e_2	d_1	d_2	e_2	d_1	d_2	e_2
Robbery												
$\hat{\beta}$	0.148	−0.346	—	−0.297	−0.431	—	−0.634	−0.793	—	−0.749	−0.920	—
$\hat{\beta}/S\hat{\beta}$	(−0.383)	(−1.145)	—	(−0.838)	(−1.208)	—	(−1.281)	(−2.006)	—	(−1.968)	(−1.754)	—
Burglary												
$\hat{\beta}$	−0.078	0.059	0.909	−0.084	0.216	—	−0.306	−0.136	—	−0.033	0.334	—
$\hat{\beta}/S\hat{\beta}$	(−0.333)	(0.301)	(1.415)	(−0.380)	(0.944)	—	(−1.115)	(−0.559)	—	(−0.154)	(1.107)	—
Larceny												
$\hat{\beta}$	0.186	0.573	—	0.091	0.430	—	0.214	0.487	—	−0.103	−0.033	—
$\hat{\beta}/S\hat{\beta}$	(0.955)	(2.056)	—	(0.326)	(1.395)	—	(0.711)	(1.188)	—	(−0.306)	(−0.067)	—

Auto theft												
$\hat{\beta}$	0.147	0.435	1.062	−0.137	0.373	—	0.516	0.401	—	−0.315	0.174	—
$\hat{\beta}/S\hat{\beta}$	(0.534)	(1.984)	(1.328)	(−0.553)	(1.360)	—	(0.188)	(1.396)	—	(−0.365)	(0.519)	—
Murder												
$\hat{\beta}$	−0.132	−0.656	1.803	−0.178	−0.602	1.622	−0.151	−1.510	2.072	−0.324	−0.822	1.293
$\hat{\beta}/S\hat{\beta}$	(−0.388)	(−2.264)	(1.875)	(−0.636)	(−2.018)	(2.043)	(−0.268)	(−2.456)	(1.298)	(−0.227)	(−1.966)	(1.698)
Rape												
$\hat{\beta}$	0.238	−0.728	1.339	0.222	−0.654	1.605	0.286	−0.851	1.430	0.209	−0.576	2.043
$\hat{\beta}/S\hat{\beta}$	(0.853)	(−3.232)	(1.660)	(0.828)	(−2.363)	(2.080)	(0.428)	(−3.366)	(1.603)	(0.774)	(−1.902)	(2.583)
Assault												
$\hat{\beta}$	−0.073	−0.325	2.792	−0.083	−0.314	2.164	−0.132	−0.162	3.403	−0.389	−0.168	1.345
$\hat{\beta}/S\hat{\beta}$	(−0.219)	(−1.044)	(2.885)	(−0.268)	(−0.903)	(2.431)	(−0.283)	(−1.370)	(2.492)	(−0.938)	(−1.272)	(1.938)
All Offenses												
$\hat{\beta}$	0.037	0.159	1.044	0.049	0.275	1.157	−0.129	−0.481	1.386	−0.169	0.004	—
$\hat{\beta}/S\hat{\beta}$	(0.172)	(0.768)	(1.709)	(0.262)	(1.264)	(2.051)	(−0.421)	(−1.288)	(1.606)	(−0.806)	(0.012)	—

NOTE: d_1: coefficient of ln U; d_2: coefficient of ln LF; e_2: coefficient of ln Age.

[a]Reprinted with permission from I. Ehrlich, Participation in illegitimate activities: a theoretical and empirical investigation, *Journal of Political Economy* 81(3):525–65, 1973 (University of Chicago Press).

TABLE 6 OLS (Weighted)[a] Estimates[b]

Crime Category	Intercept	$\ln P_i$	$\ln T_i$	$\ln W$	$\ln X$	$\ln NW$	R^2
Murder	−0.666	−0.341	−0.140	0.417	1.364	0.553	0.940
	(3.192)	(0.138)	(0.105)	(0.436)	(0.466)	(0.054)	
Rape	−7.381	−0.578	−0.188	1.222	0.894	0.154	0.947
	(4.078)	(0.099)	(0.169)	(0.561)	(0.540)	(0.066)	
Assault	−13.300	−0.275	−0.180	2.094	1.469	0.677	0.982
	(4.160)	(0.079)	(0.230)	(0.598)	(0.600)	(0.075)	
Murder and Rape	−1.814	−0.579	−0.287	0.678	0.946	0.328	0.975
	(3.197)	(0.094)	(0.101)	(0.438)	(0.420)	(0.050)	
Robbery	−20.194	−0.853	−0.223	2.909	1.841	0.376	0.976
	(4.811)	(0.120)	(0.227)	(0.682)	(0.652)	(0.071)	
Burglary	−5.570	−0.534	−0.900	1.797	2.045	0.227	0.994
	(3.289)	(0.096)	(0.211)	(0.445)	(0.407)	(0.052)	
Larceny	−14.942	−0.133	−0.263	2.689	1.620	0.132	0.989
	(3.776)	(0.069)	(0.222)	(0.523)	(0.521)	(0.062)	
Auto Theft	−17.307	−0.247	−0.174	2.893	1.898	0.115	0.991
	(3.228)	(0.066)	(0.134)	(0.455)	(0.446)	(0.051)	
Burglary and Robbery	−9.269	−0.624	−0.688	2.160	2.115	0.257	0.995
	(2.977)	(0.099)	(0.178)	(0.421)	(0.388)	(0.049)	
Larceny and Auto Theft	−14.155	−0.257	−0.334	2.665	1.826	0.142	0.994
	(3.029)	(0.068)	(0.162)	(0.424)	(0.421)	(0.049)	
Crimes against the Person	−4.158	−0.550	−0.349	1.046	0.915	0.490	0.989
	(3.609)	(0.088)	(0.127)	(0.489)	(0.454)	(0.064)	
Property Crimes	−10.129	−0.508	−0.621	2.335	2.054	0.212	0.996
	(2.707)	(0.088)	(0.173)	(0.377)	(0.354)	(0.044)	
All Offenses	−7.674	−0.552	−0.640	2.020	1.806	0.232	0.997
	(2.783)	(0.099)	(0.177)	(0.375)	(0.349)	(0.042)	

[a] In order to induce homoscedasticity, all variables in the regression, including the constant, are multiplied with $\sqrt{N}$, with N the state population size in 1960.

[b] Between parentheses is the standard error of the estimate. Degrees of freedom: 41.

TABLE 7 2SLS[a] (Weighted)[b] Estimates[c] (Incorrect Weighting Scheme)

Crime Category	Intercept	$\ln \hat{P}_i$	$\ln T_i$	$\ln W$	$\ln X$	$\ln NW$
Murder	0.317	−0.852	−0.087	0.175	1.109	0.534
	(3.736)	(0.342)	(0.125)	(0.524)	(0.559)	(0.064)
Rape	−0.597	−0.896	−0.399	0.408	0.459	0.072
	(5.005)	(0.147)	(0.199)	(0.675)	(0.618)	(0.078)
Murder and Rape	2.704	−0.828	−0.350	0.086	0.556	0.280
	(3.693)	(0.124)	(0.111)	(0.503)	(0.468)	(0.055)
Assault	−7.568	−0.724	−0.979	1.650	1.707	0.465
	(5.957)	(0.196)	(0.425)	(0.818)	(0.809)	(0.127)
Robbery	−11.025	−1.303	−0.372	1.689	1.278	0.334
	(6.110)	(0.186)	(0.266)	(0.858)	(0.770)	(0.083)
Burglary	−2.121	−0.724	−1.127	1.384	2.000	0.250
	(3.647)	(0.121)	−(0.235)	(0.487)	(0.427)	(0.055)
Larceny	−10.664	−0.371	−0.602	2.229	1.792	0.142
	(4.859)	(0.150)	(0.311)	(0.643)	(0.599)	(0.070)
Auto Theft	−14.959	−0.407	−0.246	2.608	2.057	0.102
	(3.594)	(0.097)	(0.146)	(0.502)	(0.482)	(0.055)
Larceny and Auto Theft	−10.093	−0.547	−0.626	2.226	2.166	0.155
	(3.904)	(0.129)	(0.220)	(0.532)	(0.520)	(0.060)
Crimes against the Person	1.636	−0.803	−0.496	0.328	0.559	0.376
	(4.306)	(0.122)	(0.145)	(0.576)	(0.509)	(0.078)
Property Crimes	−6.278	−0.797	−0.915	1.883	2.132	0.243
	(3.241)	(0.130)	(0.213)	(0.444)	(0.398)	(0.051)
All Offenses	−1.388	−0.991	−1.123	1.292	1.775	0.265
	(3.773)	(0.168)	(0.251)	(0.495)	(0.424)	(0.052)

[a]The reduced form variables are: constant, ln *Age*, *Dummy*, ln *Ed*, ln Exp_{59}, ln X, $\ln(Q_i/N)_{59}$, ln *Males*, ln *NW*, ln N_t, ln *SMSA*, ln T_i, ln W, ln U_{35-39}. The equations are identified with the following variables: ln *Age*, *Dummy*, ln *Ed*, ln Exp_{59}, $\ln(Q_i/N)_{59}$, ln *Males*, ln N, ln *SMSA*, ln U_{35-39}.

[b]In order to induce homoscedasticity, all variables in the regression, including the constant, are multiplied with $\sqrt{\mu N}$, with N the state population size in 1960.

[c]Between parentheses is the standard error of the estimate. Degrees of freedom: 41.

TABLE 8 OLS—(Unweighted) Estimates[a] Including Unemployment and Labor Force Participation of Young Age Groups in 1960 (Labor Force Participation Variable in Error)

Crime Category	Intercept	$\ln P_i$	$\ln T_i$	$\ln W$	$\ln X$	$\ln NW$	$\ln U$	$\ln LF$	$\ln Age$	R^2
Murder	− 6.230	−0.562	−0.434	0.399	0.231	0.431	−0.132	−0.656	1.803	0.848
	(6.435)	(0.192)	(0.170)	(0.659)	(0.679)	(0.075)	(0.340)	(0.290)	(0.961)	
Rape	− 9.366	−0.472	0.138	0.715	−0.352	0.103	0.237	−0.728	1.338	0.693
	(5.337)	(0.099)	(0.125)	(0.580)	(0.585)	(0.058)	(0.278)	(0.225)	(0.806)	
Assault	−20.534	−0.331	−0.135	1.909	0.770	0.485	−0.073	−0.325	2.797	0.858
	(6.122)	(0.100)	(0.234)	(0.653)	(0.702)	(0.079)	(0.334)	(0.311)	(0.970)	
Robbery	−19.649	−0.740	−0.008	2.614	1.273	0.350	−0.147	−0.346	—	0.789
	(5.167)	(0.147)	(0.221)	(0.747)	(0.775)	(0.070)	(0.385)	(0.302)		
Burglary	− 8.350	−0.401	−0.599	1.581	1.009	0.192	−0.078	0.059	0.909	0.651
	(5.258)	(0.118)	(0.215)	(0.463)	(0.443)	(0.043)	(0.235)	(0.197)	(0.643)	
Larceny	−10.796	−0.049	−0.276	2.267	1.214	0.107	0.186	0.573	—	0.551
	(3.784)	(0.095)	(0.201)	(0.526)	(0.577)	(0.053)	(0.284)	(0.279)		
Auto Theft	−22.294	−0.097	−0.162	3.182	1.380	0.129	0.147	0.435	1.062	0.676
	(4.959)	(0.076)	(0.138)	(0.532)	(0.568)	(0.050)	(0.275)	(0.258)	(0.799)	
All Offenses	−10.267	−0.388	−0.546	1.917	1.061	0.194	0.037	0.159	1.044	0.696
	(4.040)	(0.136)	(0.201)	(0.433)	(0.420)	(0.041)	(0.215)	(0.207)	(0.611)	

[a]Between parentheses is the standard error of the estimate. Degrees of freedom: 39 (38 if ln *Age* is part of the equation).

TABLE 9 2SLS—(Unweighted[a]) Estimates[b] Including Unemployment and Labor Force Participation of Young Age Groups in 1960 (Labor Force Participation Variable in Error)

Crime Category	Intercept	$\ln \hat{P}_i$	$\ln T_i$	$\ln W$	$\ln X$	$\ln NW$	$\ln U$	$\ln LF$	$\ln Age$
Murder	0.824	−2.124	−0.710	−0.763	−1.043	0.202	−0.151	−1.510	2.072
	(11.122)	(0.771)	(0.308)	(1.210)	(1.262)	(0.161)	(0.563)	(0.615)	(1.597)
Rape	−5.019	−0.759	0.094	0.090	−0.816	0.021	0.286	−0.851	1.430
	(6.101)	(0.150)	(0.139)	(0.679)	(0.668)	(0.071)	(0.308)	(0.253)	(0.892)
Assault	−18.300	−0.932	−0.927	1.686	1.216	0.190	−0.132	−0.162	3.403
	(8.566)	(0.238)	(0.414)	(0.913)	(0.988)	(0.145)	(0.466)	(0.437)	(1.366)
Robbery	−11.541	−1.373	−0.272	1.338	0.563	0.271	−0.634	−0.793	—
	(6.818)	(0.273)	(0.282)	(0.999)	(0.970)	(0.089)	(0.495)	(0.395)	
Burglary	0.542	−0.792	−1.026	0.739	1.052	0.223	−0.306	−0.136	—
	(4.177)	(0.209)	(0.298)	(0.577)	(0.507)	(0.050)	(0.275)	(0.243)	
Larceny	−10.332	−0.096	−0.321	2.222	1.284	0.107	0.214	0.487	—
	(4.125)	(0.191)	(0.256)	(0.551)	(0.628)	(0.054)	(0.410)	(0.301)	
Auto Theft	−17.596	−0.169	−0.229	2.967	1.610	0.131	0.052	0.401	—
	(3.683)	(0.112)	(0.140)	(0.526)	(0.584)	(0.051)	(0.289)	(0.275)	
All Offenses	−3.930	−1.207	−1.328	0.994	1.168	0.212	−0.129	−0.481	1.386
	(6.098)	(0.357)	(0.402)	(0.694)	(0.589)	(0.057)	(0.307)	(0.373)	(0.863)

[a]The reduced form variables are: constant, ln *Age*, *Dummy*, ln *Ed*, ln Exp_{59}, ln *X*, ln $(Q_i/N)_{59}$, ln *LF*, ln *Males*, ln *NW*, ln *N*, ln *SMSA*, ln T_i, ln *U*, ln *W*. The equations are identified with the following variables: *Dummy*, ln *Ed*, ln Exp_{59}, ln $(Q_i/N)_{59}$, ln *Males*, ln *N*, ln *SMSA* and, if ln *Age* is not part of the equation, also with ln *Age*.

[b]Between parentheses is the standard error of the estimate. Degrees of freedom: 39 (38 if ln *Age* is part of the equation).

TABLE 10 2SLS[a] (Weighted[b]) Estimates[c] Including Unemployment and Labor Force Participation of Young Age Groups in 1960 (Labor Force Participation Variable in Error and Incorrect Weighting Scheme)

Crime Category	Intercept	$\ln \hat{P}_i$	$\ln T_i$	$\ln W$	$\ln X$	$\ln NW$	$\ln U$	$\ln LF$	$\ln Age$
Murder	−7.284	−0.852	−0.042	0.457	0.860	0.501	−0.324	−0.822	1.293
	(4.903)	(0.330)	(0.126)	(0.506)	(0.539)	(0.063)	(0.264)	(0.419)	(0.761)
Rape	−10.347	−0.842	−0.375	0.886	0.147	0.047	0.209	−0.576	2.043
	(5.356)	(0.128)	(0.181)	(0.612)	(0.596)	(0.074)	(0.270)	(0.384)	(0.791)
Assault	−13.696	−0.749	−0.968	1.745	1.271	0.438	−0.389	−0.167	1.344
	(7.907)	(0.211)	(0.481)	(0.851)	(0.900)	(0.133)	(0.414)	(0.617)	(1.210)
Robbery	−12.158	−1.400	−0.419	1.522	1.099	0.294	−0.748	−0.920	—
	(6.029)	(0.197)	(0.269)	(0.868)	(0.784)	(0.087)	(0.380)	(0.525)	

Burglary	−2.949	−0.661	−1.051	1.486	1.978	0.256	−0.033	0.334	—
	(3.554)	(0.117)	(0.230)	(0.475)	(0.422)	(0.054)	(0.214)	(0.301)	
Larceny	−12.074	−0.280	−0.483	2.413	1.749	0.137	0.103	−0.033	—
	(4.902)	(0.155)	(0.321)	(0.607)	(0.589)	(0.069)	(0.336)	(0.487)	
Auto Theft	−16.185	−0.367	−0.231	2.661	1.937	0.115	−0.315	0.177	—
	(3.511)	(0.096)	(0.143)	(0.484)	(0.471)	(0.056)	(0.231)	(0.341)	
All Offenses	−2.718	−0.930	−1.053	1.392	1.745	0.262	−0.169	0.004	—
	(3.657)	(0.165)	(0.241)	(0.479)	(0.415)	(0.052)	(0.210)	(0.310)	

[a]The reduced form variables are: constant, ln *Age*, *Dummy*, ln *Ed*, ln Exp_{59}, ln *X*, ln $(Q_i/N)_{59}$, ln *LF*, ln *Males*, ln *NW*, ln *N*, ln *SMSA*, ln T_i, ln *U*, ln *W*. The equations are identified with the following variables: *Dummy*, ln *Ed*, ln Exp_{59}, ln $(Q_i/N)_{59}$, ln *Males*, ln *N*, ln *SMSA* and, if ln *Age* is not part of the equation, also with ln *Age*.
[b]In order to induce homoscedasticity, all variables in the regression, including the constant, are multiplied with $\sqrt{N}$, with *N* the state population size in 1960.
[c]Between parentheses is the standard error of the estimate. Degrees of freedom: 39 (38 if ln *Age* is part of the equation).

TABLE 11 2SLS[a] (Weighted[b]) Estimates[c] (Corrected)

Crime Category	Intercept	$\ln \hat{P}_i$	$\ln T_i$	$\ln W$	$\ln X$	$\ln NW$
Murder	0.337	−0.863	−0.086	0.170	1.104	0.533
	(3.757)	(0.346)	(0.126)	(0.527)	(0.562)	(0.064)
Rape	−2.143	−0.824	−0.351	0.594	0.558	0.091
	(4.706)	(0.134)	(0.189)	(0.637)	(0.589)	(0.074)
Murder and Rape	2.130	−0.796	−0.342	0.161	0.605	0.286
	(3.599)	(0.119)	(0.108)	(0.491)	(0.458)	(0.054)
Assault	−7.775	−0.708	−0.950	1.667	1.698	0.473
	(5.853)	(0.191)	(0.416)	(0.804)	(0.796)	(0.125)
Robbery	−12.621	−1.225	−0.346	1.901	1.376	0.342
	(5.766)	(0.171)	(0.255)	(0.811)	(0.736)	(0.079)
Burglary	−3.001	−0.675	−1.069	1.489	2.012	0.244
	(3.525)	(0.114)	(0.227)	(0.472)	(0.418)	(0.053)
Larceny	−11.373	−0.332	−0.546	2.305	1.763	0.140
	(4.586)	(0.134)	(0.290)	(0.612)	(0.577)	(0.068)
Auto Theft	−14.857	−0.414	−0.249	2.595	2.063	0.101
	(3.619)	(0.099)	(0.147)	(0.505)	(0.485)	(0.055)
Larceny and Auto Theft	−10.260	−0.535	−0.614	2.244	2.152	0.155
	(3.839)	(0.125)	(0.215)	(0.524)	(0.513)	(0.059)
Crimes against the Person	−1.123	−0.781	−0.483	0.391	0.590	0.386
	(4.222)	(0.118)	(0.143)	(0.565)	(0.501)	(0.076)
Property Crimes	−6.809	−0.757	−0.874	1.945	2.121	0.239
	(3.124)	(0.122)	(0.205)	(0.429)	(0.387)	(0.049)
All Offenses	−2.168	−0.937	−1.063	1.383	1.779	0.261
	(3.581)	(0.156)	(0.237)	(0.471)	(0.408)	(0.050)

[a]The reduced form variables are: constant, $\ln Age$, *Dummy*, $\ln Ed$, $\ln Exp_{59}$, $\ln X$, $\ln (Q_i/N)_{59}$, $\ln Males$, $\ln NW$, $\ln N$, $\ln SMSA$, $\ln T_i$, $\ln W$, $\ln U_{35-39}$. The equations are identified with the following variables: $\ln Age$, *Dummy*, $\ln Ed$, $\ln Exp_{59}$, $\ln (Q_i/N)_{59}$, $\ln Males$, $\ln N$, $\ln SMSA$, $\ln U_{35-39}$.

[b]In order to induce homoscedasticity, all variables in the regression, including the constant, are multiplied with $\sqrt{N}$, with N the state population size in 1960.

[c]Between parentheses is the standard error of the estimate. Degrees of freedom: 41.

TABLE 12 OLS—(Unweighted) Estimates[a] Including Unemployment and Labor Force Participation of Young Age Groups in 1960 (Corrected)

Crime Category	Intercept	$\ln P_i$	$\ln T_i$	$\ln W$	$\ln X$	$\ln NW$	$\ln U$	$\ln LF$	$\ln Age$	R^2
Murder	−0.162	−0.393	−0.515	0.148	0.370	0.470	0.046	1.366	1.175	0.836
	(7.009)	(0.186)	(0.178)	(0.713)	(0.702)	(0.078)	(0.366)	(0.971)	(0.958)	
Rape	−3.820	−0.413	0.087	0.550	−0.104	0.166	0.481	1.522	0.680	0.641
	(6.017)	(0.105)	(0.137)	(0.645)	(0.625)	(0.064)	(0.315)	(0.839)	(0.843)	
Assault	−20.948	−0.359	−0.267	2.101	1.098	0.469	−0.129	−0.737	2.533	0.856
	(6.403)	(0.103)	(0.209)	(0.676)	(0.683)	(0.085)	(0.353)	0.954)	(0.936)	
Robbery	−19.995	−0.667	0.025	2.762	1.430	0.368	−0.005	0.230	—	0.782
	(5.509)	(0.161)	(0.232)	(0.752)	(0.780)	(0.077)	(0.427)	(1.207)		
Burglary	−7.393	−0.412	−0.590	1.468	0.917	0.198	−0.026	0.485	0.966	0.655
	(4.420)	(0.106)	(0.213)	(0.469)	(0.442)	(0.044)	(0.245)	(0.615)	(0.611)	
Larceny	−5.033	−0.192	−0.440	1.711	1.060	0.141	0.431	1.968	—	0.534
	(4.081)	(0.073)	(0.197)	(0.525)	(0.568)	(0.055)	(0.294)	(0.781)		
Auto Theft	−20.493	−0.200	−0.152	2.873	1.203	0.137	0.259	1.263	1.402	0.674
	(5.303)	(0.069)	(0.138)	(0.559)	(0.572)	(0.051)	(0.290)	(0.794)	(0.769)	
All Offenses	−9.090	−0.432	−0.532	1.741	0.930	0.199	0.095	0.624	1.172	0.700
	(4.187)	(0.116)	(0.201)	(0.437)	(0.422)	(0.041)	(0.224)	(0.589)	(0.582)	

[a]Between parentheses is the standard error of the estimate. Degrees of freedom: 39 (38 if ln *Age* is part of the equation).

TABLE 13 OLS—(Weighted[a]) Estimates[b] Including Unemployment and Labor Force Participation of Young Age Groups in 1960 (Corrected)

Crime Category	Intercept	$\ln P_i$	$\ln T_i$	$\ln W$	$\ln X$	$\ln NW$	$\ln U$	$\ln LF$	$\ln Age$	R^2
Murder	−5.415	−0.328	−0.130	0.542	1.068	0.553	−0.214	0.095	1.032	0.947
	(4.946)	(0.139)	(0.111)	(0.491)	(0.501)	(0.058)	(0.239)	(0.792)	(0.675)	
Rape	−9.145	−0.590	−0.224	1.080	0.314	0.182	0.391	1.339	1.455	0.957
	(5.258)	(0.094)	(0.160)	(0.577)	(0.558)	(0.067)	(0.253)	(0.831)	(0.707)	
Assault	−24.374	−0.299	−0.151	2.654	1.384	0.598	−0.276	−1.846	1.677	0.985
	(5.562)	(0.075)	(0.219)	(0.608)	(0.624)	(0.079)	(0.285)	(0.937)	(0.792)	
Robbery	−22.629	−0.939	−0.287	3.015	1.973	0.335	−0.473	−1.274	—	0.977
	(5.159)	(0.132)	(0.232)	(0.706)	(0.691)	(0.079)	(0.331)	(1.119)		
Burglary	−1.714	−0.549	−0.881	1.383	1.702	0.270	0.078	1.506	—	0.995
	(3.660)	(0.094)	(0.205)	(0.469)	(0.424)	(0.053)	(0.205)	(0.683)		
Larceny	−16.034	−0.125	−0.238	2.767	1.659	0.123	−0.123	−0.284	—	0.989
	(4.577)	(0.076)	(0.238)	(0.577)	(0.578)	(0.069)	(0.295)	(0.919)		
Auto Theft	−15.135	−0.275	−0.153	2.560	1.622	0.143	−0.249	1.009	—	0.992
	(4.028)	(0.067)	(0.132)	(0.518)	(0.468)	(0.054)	(0.225)	(0.799)		
All Offenses	−9.004	−0.544	−0.596	1.977	1.574	0.239	−0.092	0.437	0.468	0.997
	(4.054)	(0.101)	(0.183)	(0.421)	(0.391)	(0.047)	(0.187)	(0.614)	(0.533)	

[a]In order to induce homoscedasticity, all variables in the regression, including the constant, are multiplied with $\sqrt{N}$, with N the state population size in 1960.
[b]Between parentheses is the standard error of the estimate. Degrees of freedom: 39 (38 if ln *Age* is part of the equation).

TABLE 14 2SLS—(Unweighted[a]) Estimates[b] Including Unemployment and Labor Force Participation of Young Age Groups in 1960 (Corrected)

Crime Category	Intercept	$\ln \hat{P}_i$	$\ln T_i$	$\ln W$	$\ln X$	$\ln NW$	$\ln U$	$\ln LF$	$\ln Age$
Murder	6.151	−1.283	−0.726	−0.538	−0.152	0.335	0.046	1.146	0.831
	(9.613)	(0.572)	(0.257)	(0.988)	(0.940)	(0.127)	(0.463)	(1.236)	(1.230)
Rape	2.449	−0.779	0.024	−0.254	−0.626	0.065	0.563	1.530	0.649
	(7.260)	(0.177)	(0.159)	(0.794)	(0.741)	(0.082)	(0.363)	(0.964)	(0.968)
Assault	−22.336	−1.059	−1.116	2.079	1.668	0.092	−0.381	−2.196	3.421
	(9.533)	(0.271)	(0.412)	(1.005)	(1.032)	(0.174)	(0.530)	(1.493)	(1.420)
Robbery	−15.911	−1.604	−0.458	1.730	1.160	0.204	−1.009	−3.228	—
	(7.656)	(0.386)	(0.357)	(1.085)	(1.069)	(0.118)	(0.676)	(2.023)	
Burglary	0.779	−0.738	−0.969	0.769	1.043	0.228	−0.220	0.386	—
	(4.098)	(0.172)	(0.277)	(0.532)	(0.497)	(0.050)	(0.272)	(0.694)	
Larceny	−2.151	−0.418	−0.718	1.541	1.519	0.160	0.681	2.269	—
	(4.753)	(0.135)	(0.257)	(0.591)	(0.670)	(0.062)	(0.349)	(0.882)	
Auto Theft	−12.084	−0.435	−0.308	2.428	1.717	0.149	0.257	2.122	—
	(4.765)	(0.117)	(0.160)	(0.621)	(0.667)	(0.059)	(0.328)	(0.967)	
All Offenses	−3.446	−0.970	−1.171	1.178	1.213	0.225	−0.013	0.402	1.005
	(5.593)	(0.237)	(0.335)	(0.580)	(0.537)	(0.052)	(0.283)	(0.471)	(0.731)

[a]The reduced form variables are: constant, $\ln Age$, *Dummy*, $\ln Ed$, $\ln Exp_{59}$, $\ln X$, $\ln (Q_i/N)_{59}$, $\ln LF$, $\ln Males$, $\ln NW$, $\ln N$, $\ln SMSA$, $\ln T_i$, $\ln U$, $\ln W$. The equations are identified with the following variables: *Dummy*, $\ln Ed$, $\ln Exp_{59}$, $\ln (Q_i/N)_{59}$, $\ln Males$, $\ln N$, $\ln SMSA$ and, if $\ln Age$ is not part of the equation, also with $\ln Age$.

[b]Between parentheses is the standard error of the estimate. Degrees of freedom: 39 (38 if $\ln Age$ is in the equation).

TABLE 15 2SLS[a] (Weighted[b]) Estimates[c] Including Unemployment and Labor Force Participation of Young Age Groups in 1960 (Corrected)

Crime Category	Intercept	ln $\hat{P}_i$	ln T_i	ln W	ln X	ln NW	ln U	ln LF	ln Age
Murder	−5.455	−0.527	−0.109	0.500	1.031	0.539	−0.257	−0.142	0.977
	(5.078)	(0.277)	(0.117)	(0.506)	(0.516)	(0.061)	(0.251)	(0.861)	(0.697)
Rape	−4.486	−0.839	−0.393	0.457	−0.073	0.117	0.344	1.357	1.594
	(5.911)	(0.129)	(0.182)	(0.658)	(0.620)	(0.076)	(0.276)	(0.904)	(0.771)
Assault	−20.096	−0.810	−1.055	2.332	1.809	0.334	−0.597	−2.683	1.566
	(8.401)	(0.212)	(0.455)	(0.910)	(0.939)	(0.149)	(0.439)	(1.423)	(1.178)
Robbery	−17.191	−1.420	−0.489	2.094	1.669	0.252	−0.878	−2.721	—
	(6.152)	(0.199)	(0.274)	(0.854)	(0.804)	(0.094)	(0.398)	(1.353)	
Burglary	1.149	−0.702	−1.063	1.031	1.644	0.290	0.050	1.575	—
	(3.927)	(0.112)	(0.222)	(0.501)	(0.439)	(0.056)	(0.212)	(0.706)	
Larceny	−11.998	−0.336	−0.566	2.421	1.905	0.126	0.141	−0.467	—
	(5.586)	(0.153)	(0.328)	(0.666)	(0.650)	(0.075)	(0.361)	(1.012)	
Auto Theft	−9.722	−0.495	−0.222	1.933	1.649	0.147	−0.187	1.826	—
	(4.964)	(0.111)	(0.152)	(0.629)	(0.529)	(0.061)	(0.255)	(0.951)	
All Offenses	−1.214	−0.943	−1.058	1.235	1.625	0.277	−0.127	0.536	—
	(4.090)	(0.159)	(0.240)	(0.513)	(0.445)	(0.055)	(0.215)	(0.716)	

[a]The reduced form variables are: constant, ln *Age*, *Dummy*, ln *Ed*, ln Exp_{59}, ln X, ln $(Q_i/N)_{59}$, ln LF, ln *Males*, ln NW, ln N, ln *SMSA*, ln T_i, ln U, ln W. The equations are identified with the following variables: *Dummy*, ln *Ed*, ln Exp_{59}, ln $(Q_i/N)_{59}$, ln *Males*, ln N, ln *SMSA* and, if ln *Age* is not part of the equation, also with ln *Age*.
[b]In order to induce homoscedasticity, all variables in the regression, including the constant, are multiplied with $\sqrt{N}$, with N the state population size in 1960.
[c]Between the parentheses is the standard error of the estimate. Degrees of freedom: 39 (38 if ln *Age* is part of the equation).

TABLE 16 OLS (Weighted[a]) Estimates[b]: North-South Dummy or *SMSA* Included in the Crime Function

Crime Category	$\ln P_i$	$\ln T_i$	*Dummy* (South = 1)	$\ln P_i$	$\ln T_i$	ln *SMSA*
Murder	−0.357 (0.132)	−0.050 (0.108)	0.364 (0.166)	−0.403 (0.138)	−0.138 (0.102)	−0.064 (0.035)
Rape	−0.591 (0.110)	−0.189 (0.170)	0.057 (0.205)	−0.596 (0.101)	−0.205 (0.169)	−0.040 (0.041)
Assault	−0.283 (0.079)	−0.091 (0.243)	0.256 (0.229)	−0.277 (0.080)	−0.165 (0.234)	−0.023 (0.046)
Murder and Rape	−0.601 (0.100)	−0.271 (0.104)	0.108 (0.158)	−0.628 (0.092)	−0.297 (0.096)	−0.068 (0.031)
Robbery	−0.873 (0.143)	−0.228 (0.231)	0.067 (0.259)	−0.853 (0.124)	−0.224 (0.233)	0.002 (0.050)
Burglary	−0.560 (0.097)	−0.875 (0.210)	0.200 (0.153)	−0.554 (0.100)	−0.910 (0.212)	−0.027 (0.033)
Larceny	−0.130 (0.071)	−0.276 (0.233)	−0.046 (0.205)	−0.148 (0.073)	−0.294 (0.229)	0.028 (0.043)
Auto Theft	−0.251 (0.067)	−0.193 (0.141)	−0.074 (0.168)	−0.278 (0.068)	−0.177 (0.132)	−0.055 (0.036)
Burglary and Robbery	−0.658 (0.101)	−0.669 (0.177)	0.192 (0.146)	−0.639 (0.102)	−0.682 (0.179)	−0.021 (0.032)
Larceny and Auto Theft	−0.256 (0.068)	−0.349 (0.174)	−0.041 (0.164)	−0.260 (0.068)	−0.331 (0.164)	−0.015 (0.033)
Crimes against the Person	−0.580 (0.090)	−0.290 (0.133)	0.243 (0.178)	−0.584 (0.088)	−0.361 (0.124)	−0.058 (0.035)
Property Crimes	−0.517 (0.090)	−0.602 (0.177)	0.086 (0.136)	−0.517 (0.090)	−0.618 (0.175)	−0.017 (0.029)
All Offenses	−0.572 (0.102)	−0.619 (0.179)	0.131 (0.136)	−0.563 (0.101)	−0.639 (0.178)	−0.019 (0.028)

[a]In order to induce homoscedasticity, all variables in the regression, including the constant, are multiplied with $\sqrt{N}$, with N the state population size in 1960.

[b]Between parentheses is the standard error of the estimate. Degrees of freedom: 40.

TABLE 17 2SLS (Weighted[a]) Estimates: Effect of Different Reduced Form Specifications[b]—Basic Model

Crime Category	Reduced Form 1[c]		Reduced Form 2[d]		Reduced Form 3[e]	
	$\ln \hat{P}_i$	$\ln T_i$	$\ln \hat{P}_i$	$\ln T_i$	$\ln \hat{P}_i$	$\ln T_i$
Murder	−0.863	−0.086	−0.996	−0.072	−1.525	−0.018
	(0.346)	(0.126)	(0.406)	(0.136)	(0.686)	(0.188)
Rape	−0.824	−0.351	−1.012	−0.477	−0.869	−0.381
	(0.134)	(0.189)	(0.177)	(0.221)	(0.146)	(0.196)
Murder and Rape	−0.796	−0.342	−0.850	−0.355	−0.886	−0.365
	(0.119)	(0.108)	(0.128)	(0.112)	(0.135)	(0.115)
Assault	−0.708	−0.950	−1.103	−1.652	−0.777	−1.073
	(0.191)	(0.416)	(0.349)	(0.713)	(0.212)	(0.457)
Robbery	−1.225	−0.346	−1.313	−0.375	−1.264	−0.359
	(0.171)	(0.255)	(0.185)	(0.268)	(0.177)	(0.261)
Burglary	−0.675	−1.069	−0.883	−1.317	−0.728	−1.131
	(0.114)	(0.227)	(0.147)	(0.269)	(0.120)	(0.234)
Larceny	−0.332	−0.546	−0.394	−0.635	−0.427	−0.681
	(0.134)	(0.290)	(0.159)	(0.324)	(0.170)	(0.340)
Auto Theft	−0.414	−0.249	−0.420	−0.252	−0.601	−0.334
	(0.099)	(0.147)	(0.101)	(0.148)	(0.146)	(0.183)
Larceny and Auto Theft	−0.535	−0.614	−0.535	−0.614	−0.658	−0.739
	(0.125)	(0.215)	(0.125)	(0.216)	(0.159)	(0.257)
Crimes against the Person	−0.781	−0.483	−0.810	−0.499	−0.896	−0.549
	(0.118)	(0.143)	(0.123)	(0.146)	(0.137)	(0.158)
Property Crimes	−0.757	−0.874	−0.790	−0.908	−0.873	−0.992
	(0.122)	(0.205)	(0.128)	(0.211)	(0.143)	(0.229)
All Offenses	−0.937	−1.063	−0.946	−1.073	−1.047	−1.185
	(0.156)	(0.237)	(0.159)	(0.239)	(0.179)	(0.264)

[a]In order to induce homoscedasticity all variables in the regression, including the constant, are multiplied with $\sqrt{N}$, with N the state population size in 1960. Between parentheses is the standard error of the estimate. Degrees of freedom: 41.

[b]The crime equation contains the following variables: constant, $\ln P_i$, $\ln T_i$, $\ln W$, $\ln X$, $\ln NW$ (see also Table 11).

[c]The reduced form variables are: constant, ln *Age*, *Dummy*, ln *Ed*, ln Exp_{59}, ln X, ln $(Q_i/N)_{59}$, ln *Males*, ln *NW*, ln *N*, ln *SMSA*, ln T_i, ln *W*, ln U_{35-39}. These two columns correspond to Table 11.

[d]The reduced form used is as in footnote *c* above, but after omitting the following three variables: ln Exp_{59}, ln U_{35-39}, and ln *Males*.

[e]The reduced form used is as in footnote *c* above, but after omitting the following three variables: ln *SMSA*, ln *Ed*, and ln *N*.

TABLE 18 2SLS[a] (Weighted[b]) Estimates[c]—Vermont Omitted

Crime Category	$\ln \hat{P}_i$	$\ln T_i$
Murder	−0.893 (0.361)	−0.081 (0.130)
Rape	−0.832 (0.135)	−0.359 (0.190)
Murder and Rape	−0.808 (0.119)	−0.342 (0.108)
Assault	−0.716 (0.190)	−0.945 (0.414)
Robbery	−1.235 (0.174)	−0.336 (0.259)
Burglary	−0.560 (0.120)	−0.924 (0.229)
Larceny	−0.325 (0.136)	−0.522 (0.300)
Auto Theft	−0.415 (0.100)	−0.242 (0.149)
Larceny and Auto Theft	−0.535 (0.126)	−0.602 (0.219)
Crimes against the Person	−0.785 (0.117)	−0.468 (0.141)
Property Crimes	−0.755 (0.123)	−0.862 (0.207)
All Offenses	−0.931 (0.156)	−1.037 (0.236)

[a]The crime equation contains the following variables: constant, $\ln P_i$, $\ln T_i$, $\ln W$, $\ln X$, $\ln NW$. The reduced form variables are: constant, $\ln Age$, $Dummy$, $\ln Ed$, $\ln Exp_{59}$, $\ln X$, $\ln (Q_i/N)_{59}$, $\ln Males$, $\ln NW$, $\ln N$, $\ln SMSA$, $\ln T_i$, $\ln W$, $\ln U_{35-39}$. The equation is identified with the following variables: $\ln Age$, $Dummy$, $\ln Ed$, $\ln Exp_{59}$, $\ln (Q_i/N)_{59}$, $\ln Males$, $\ln N$, $\ln SMSA$, $\ln U_{35-39}$.

[b]In order to induce homoscedasticity, all variables in the regression, including the constant, are multiplied with $\sqrt{N}$, with N the state population size in 1960.

[c]Between parentheses is the standard error of estimate. Degrees of freedom: 40.

TABLE 19 2SLS[a] (Weighted[b]) Estimates[c]—Basic Model, Identified by ln Exp_{59} and ln $(Q_i/N)_{59}$

Crime Category	All States		Vermont Omitted		Omitting Utah, Vermont, and Wisconsin	
	ln $\hat{P}_i$	ln T_i	ln $\hat{P}_i$	ln T_i	ln $\hat{P}_i$	ln T_i
Murder	−2.944 (1.749)	0.129 (0.370)	−2.961 (1.773)	0.141 (0.379)	−2.812 (1.848)	0.149 (0.406)
Rape	−1.347 (0.274)	−0.699 (0.304)	−1.350 (0.276)	−0.704 (0.306)	−1.399 (0.313)	−0.541 (0.310)
Murder and Rape	−1.119 (0.182)	−0.424 (0.140)	−1.121 (0.182)	−0.420 (0.139)	−1.164 (0.230)	−0.385 (0.157)
Assault	−0.968 (0.287)	−1.412 (0.598)	−0.955 (0.280)	−1.367 (0.582)	−0.834 (0.229)	−1.263 (0.507)
Robbery	−1.584 (0.244)	−0.465 (0.319)	−1.599 (0.250)	−0.451 (0.326)	−1.440 (0.226)	−0.576 (0.312)
Burglary	−0.884 (0.146)	−1.317 (0.268)	−0.666 (0.147)	−1.051 (0.254)	−0.599 (0.131)	−1.107 (0.226)
Larceny	−1.554 (0.943)	−2.287 (1.502)	−1.570 (0.966)	−2.353 (1.583)	−1.704 (1.046)	−2.735 (1.797)
Auto Theft	−0.880 (0.241)	−0.460 (0.260)	−0.877 (0.242)	−0.449 (0.263)	−0.866 (0.246)	−0.472 (0.267)
Larceny and Auto Theft	−1.052 (0.311)	−1.135 (0.440)	−1.052 (0.315)	−1.128 (0.449)	−0.992 (0.286)	−1.144 (0.426)
Crimes against the Person	−1.072 (0.174)	−0.651 (0.188)	−1.063 (0.169)	−0.627 (0.183)	−1.020 (0.165)	−0.662 (0.189)
Property Crimes	−1.082 (0.192)	−1.205 (0.288)	−1.079 (0.194)	−1.193 (0.293)	−0.962 (0.149)	−1.250 (0.244)
All Offenses	−1.249 (0.230)	−1.407 (0.327)	−1.241 (0.229)	−1.376 (0.326)	−1.017 (0.285)	−1.056 (0.441)

[a]The crime equation contains the following variables: constant, ln P_i, ln T_i, ln W, ln X, ln NW. The equation is identified by the exclusion of ln Exp_{59} and ln $(Q_i/N)_{59}$.

[b]In order to induce homoscedasticity, all variables in the regression, including the constant, are multiplied with $\sqrt{N}$, with N the state population size in 1960.

[c]Between parentheses is the standard error of estimate. Degrees of freedom: All States—41; Vermont omitted—40; omitting Utah, Vermont, and Wisconsin—38.

TABLE 20 2SLS[a] (Weighted[b]) Estimates[c]—Basic Model + LF, Age, and U, Identified by ln Exp_{59} and ln $(Q_i/N)_{59}$

	All States		Vermont Omitted		Omitting Utah, Vermont, and Wisconsin	
Crime Category	ln $\hat{P}_i$	ln T_i	ln $\hat{P}_i$	ln T_i	ln $\hat{P}_i$	ln T_i
Murder	−3.611 (2.648)	0.219 (0.520)	−3.562 (2.593)	0.213 (0.514)	−4.455 (4.493)	0.378 (0.866)
Rape	−1.196 (0.219)	−0.634 (0.258)	−1.205 (0.222)	−0.644 (0.262)	−1.258 (0.250)	−0.503 (0.272)
Murder and Rape	−1.064 (0.177)	−0.407 (0.143)	−1.069 (0.176)	−0.411 (0.143)	−1.093 (0.219)	−0.385 (0.173)
Assault	−0.922 (0.253)	−1.254 (0.533)	−0.917 (0.250)	−1.232 (0.528)	−0.855 (0.226)	−1.244 (0.509)
Robbery	−1.701 (0.273)	−0.612 (0.330)	−1.709 (0.278)	−0.599 (0.337)	−1.460 (0.230)	−0.756 (0.296)
Burglary	−0.862 (0.139)	−1.214 (0.264)	−0.735 (0.137)	−1.050 (0.251)	−0.685 (0.120)	−1.159 (0.225)
Larceny	−0.943 (0.521)	−1.584 (0.952)	−0.959 (0.537)	−1.634 (1.012)	−1.316 (0.786)	−2.432 (1.531)
Auto Theft	−0.995 (0.293)	−0.399 (0.312)	−0.993 (0.294)	−0.376 (0.313)	−0.967 (0.294)	−0.431 (0.326)
Larceny and Auto Theft	−1.121 (0.370)	−1.385 (0.567)	−1.122 (0.375)	−1.375 (0.576)	−1.079 (0.342)	−1.495 (0.567)
Crimes against the Person	−1.009 (0.160)	−0.602 (0.189)	−1.005 (0.157)	−0.592 (0.185)	−0.969 (0.151)	−0.683 (0.205)
Property Crimes	−1.038 (0.188)	−1.193 (0.299)	−1.037 (0.189)	−1.178 (0.302)	−0.945 (0.141)	−1.348 (0.251)
All Offenses	−1.224 (0.233)	−1.363 (0.338)	−1.219 (0.232)	−1.333 (0.337)	−0.974 (0.287)	−0.978 (0.463)

[a] The crime equation contains the following variables: constant, ln P_i, ln T_i, ln W, ln X, ln NW, ln U, ln LF, ln Age. The equation is identified by the exclusion of ln Exp_{59} and ln $(Q_i/N)_{59}$.

[b] In order to induce homoscedasticity, all variables in the regression, including the constant, are multiplied with $\sqrt{N}$, with N the state population size in 1960.

[c] Between parentheses is the standard error of the estimate. Degrees of freedom: All States—38; Vermont omitted—37; omitting Utah, Vermont, and Wisconsin—35.

TABLE 21 2SLS[a] (Weighted[b]) Estimates[c]—Enlarged Model, Identified by ln Exp_{59} and ln $(Q_i/N)_{59}$

Crime Category	All States		Vermont Omitted		Omitting Utah, Vermont, and Wisconsin	
	$\ln \hat{P}_i$	$\ln T_i$	$\ln \hat{P}_i$	$\ln T_i$	$\ln \hat{P}_i$	$\ln T_i$
Murder	−2.440 (1.229)	0.488 (0.416)	−2.440 (1.253)	0.488 (0.424)	−2.975 (1.936)	0.679 (0.685)
Rape	−1.270 (0.245)	−0.450 (0.248)	−1.286 (0.250)	−0.457 (0.252)	−1.339 (0.273)	−0.294 (0.280)
Murder and Rape	−1.110 (0.184)	−0.228 (0.140)	−1.122 (0.187)	−0.229 (0.142)	−1.192 (0.235)	−0.113 (0.205)
Assault	−0.925 (0.295)	−1.140 (0.574)	−0.922 (0.295)	−1.135 (0.575)	−0.834 (0.259)	−1.170 (0.551)
Robbery	−1.674 (0.281)	−0.528 (0.333)	−1.676 (0.285)	−0.525 (0.340)	−1.535 (0.273)	−0.662 (0.334)
Burglary	−0.776 (0.122)	−0.826 (0.226)	−0.619 (0.130)	−0.692 (0.216)	−0.590 (0.120)	−0.871 (0.212)
Larceny	−1.018 (0.558)	−1.370 (0.855)	−1.025 (0.567)	−1.351 (0.884)	−1.172 (0.683)	−1.712 (1.119)
Auto Theft	−0.791 (0.175)	−0.289 (0.230)	−0.793 (0.178)	−0.280 (0.236)	−0.782 (0.179)	−0.321 (0.256)
Larceny and Auto Theft	−0.878 (0.236)	−0.842 (0.355)	−0.880 (0.239)	−0.832 (0.365)	−0.831 (0.220)	−0.929 (0.371)
Crimes against the Person	−1.150 (0.221)	−0.425 (0.215)	−1.148 (0.220)	−0.413 (0.214)	−1.133 (0.231)	−0.436 (0.268)
Property Crimes	−0.899 (0.141)	−0.739 (0.230)	−0.897 (0.143)	−0.721 (0.234)	−0.837 (0.118)	−0.967 (0.226)
All Offenses	−1.113 (0.210)	−0.885 (0.287)	−1.104 (0.208)	−0.847 (0.286)	−0.857 (0.304)	−1.053 (0.498)

[a]The crime equation contains the following variables: constant, ln P_i, ln T_i, ln W, ln X, ln NW, ln U, ln LF, ln Age, ln $SMSA$, ln $Males$, ln Ed, $Dummy$, and ln N. The variable ln P_i is endogenous. The equation is identified by the exclusion of the following two variables: ln Exp_{59} and ln $(Q_i/N)_{59}$.

[b]In order to induce homoscedasticity, all variables in the regression, including the constant, are multiplied with $\sqrt{N}$, with N the state population size in 1960.

[c]Between parentheses is the standard error of the estimate. Degrees of freedom: All States—33; Vermont omitted—32; omitting Utah, Vermont, and Wisconsin—30.

TABLE 22 2SLS[a] (Weighted[b]) Estimates[c]—Basic Model, Identified by ln Exp_{59}

Crime Category	All States		Vermont Omitted		Omitting Utah, Vermont, and Wisconsin	
	$\ln \hat{P}_i$	$\ln T_i$	$\ln \hat{P}_i$	$\ln T_i$	$\ln \hat{P}_i$	$\ln T_i$
Murder	−0.492	−0.124	−0.497	−0.123	−0.310	−0.187
	(1.421)	(0.180)	(1.488)	(0.192)	(1.150)	(0.188)
Rape	−0.771	−0.316	−0.753	−0.306	−0.766	−0.295
	(0.556)	(0.404)	(0.547)	(0.398)	(0.468)	(0.261)
Murder and Rape	−0.830	−0.350	−0.797	−0.339	−0.881	−0.378
	(0.795)	(0.228)	(0.755)	(0.216)	(0.653)	(0.127)
Assault[d]	3.882	7.216	3.992	7.383	3.174	6.114
	(10.992)	(19.614)	(11.871)	(21.056)	(7.319)	(13.541)
Robbery	−4.223	−1.336	−4.162	−1.260	−4.258	−1.100
	(7.471)	(2.664)	(7.290)	(2.509)	(7.363)	(1.783)
Burglary	−0.445	−0.793	−0.441	−0.782	−0.515	−1.011
	(0.163)	(0.265)	(0.165)	(0.267)	(0.142)	(0.232)
Larceny	−1.441	−2.127	−1.445	−2.169	−1.557	−2.508
	(0.882)	(1.402)	(0.898)	(1.468)	(1.007)	(1.713)
Auto Theft	−0.616	−0.341	−0.841	−0.949	−0.654	−0.383
	(0.239)	(0.205)	(0.205)	(0.273)	(0.251)	(0.218)
Larceny and Auto Theft	−0.940	−1.022	−0.938	−1.013	−0.999	−1.151
	(0.326)	(0.429)	(0.330)	(0.437)	(0.357)	(0.481)
Crimes against the Person	−1.256	−0.758	−1.242	−0.730	−1.280	−0.793
	(0.608)	(0.398)	(0.594)	(0.386)	(0.610)	(0.378)
Property Crimes	−0.845	−0.964	−0.841	−0.950	−0.929	−1.216
	(0.204)	(0.270)	(0.205)	(0.273)	(0.202)	(0.278)
All Offenses	−1.021	−1.156	−1.015	−1.128	−1.069	−1.115
	(0.266)	(0.340)	(0.265)	(0.338)	(0.436)	(0.579)

[a]The crime equation contains the following variables: constant, ln P_i, ln T_i, ln W, ln X, ln NW. The equation is identified by the exclusion of ln Exp_{59} only.

[b]In order to induce homoscedasticity, all variables in the regression, including the constant, are multiplied with $\sqrt{N}$, with N the state population size in 1960.

[c]Between parentheses is the standard error of estimate. Degrees of freedom: All States—41; Vermont omitted—40; omitting Utah, Vermont, and Wisconsin—38.

[d]This equation is unstable, possibly due to multicollinearity.

TABLE 23 2SLS[a] (Weighted[b]) Estimates[c]—Basic Model +*LF*, *Age*, and *U*, Identified by ln Exp_{59}

Crime Category	All States		Vermont Omitted		Omitting Utah, Vermont, and Wisconsin	
	$\ln \hat{P}_i$	$\ln T_i$	$\ln \hat{P}_i$	$\ln T_i$	$\ln \hat{P}_i$	$\ln T_i$
Murder	−4.012[d]	0.261[d]	−13.494[d]	1.265[d]	−0.622	−0.167
	(249.566)	(26.528)	(3221.25)	(341.358)	(5.534)	(0.797)
Rape	−1.281	−0.692	−1.270	−0.688	−1.183	−0.474
	(0.696)	(0.523)	(0.689)	(0.519)	(0.550)	(0.322)
Murder and Rape	−0.974	−0.380	−0.961	−0.379	−0.970	−0.386
	(0.485)	(0.191)	(0.471)	(0.187)	(0.493)	(0.156)
Assault[e]	—	—	—	—	—	—
Robbery	−1.490	−0.528	−1.495	−0.515	−1.488	−0.763
	(0.560)	(0.353)	(0.569)	(0.357)	(0.560)	(0.330)
Burglary	−0.583	−0.873	−0.582	−0.863	−0.621	−1.084
	(0.139)	(0.245)	(0.140)	(0.246)	(0.125)	(0.224)
Larceny	−1.474	−2.455	−1.473	−2.507	−1.592	−2.926
	(0.847)	(1.527)	(0.854)	(1.591)	(0.973)	(1.888)
Auto Theft	−0.825	−0.329	−0.827	−0.310	−0.843	−0.383
	(0.350)	(0.279)	(0.353)	(0.280)	(0.367)	(0.301)
Larceny and Auto Theft	−1.008	−1.248	−1.008	−1.237	−1.061	−1.471
	(0.352)	(0.528)	(0.356)	(0.537)	(0.380)	(0.602)
Crimes against the Person	−1.091	−0.655	−1.086	−0.644	−1.078	−0.751
	(0.402)	(0.312)	(0.395)	(0.306)	(0.394)	(0.320)
Property Crimes	−0.853	−0.989	−0.852	−0.975	−0.899	−1.293
	(0.179)	(0.270)	(0.180)	(0.272)	(0.162)	(0.262)
All Offenses	−1.060	−1.178	−1.060	−1.155	−0.965	−0.968
	(0.247)	(0.335)	(0.247)	(0.335)	(0.382)	(0.548)

[a]The crime equation contains the following variables: constant, ln P_i, ln T_i, ln W, ln X, ln NW, ln U, ln LF, ln Age. The equation is identified by the exclusion of ln Exp_{59} only.

[b]In order to induce homoscedasticity, all variables in the regression, including the constant, are multiplied with $\sqrt{N}$, with N the state population size in 1960.

[c]Between parentheses is the standard error of estimate. Degrees of freedom: All States—38; Vermont omitted—37; omitting Utah, Vermont, and Wisconsin—35.

[d]This equation is unstable, possibly due to multicollinearity.

[e]Possibly due to multicollinearity, the results obtained for assault were nonsensical.

TABLE 24 2SLS[a] (Weighted[b]) Estimates[c]—Enlarged Model, Identified by ln Exp_{59}

Crime Category	All States		Vermont Omitted		Omitting Utah, Vermont, and Wisconsin	
	$\ln \hat{P}_i$	$\ln T_i$	$\ln \hat{P}_i$	$\ln T_i$	$\ln \hat{P}_i$	$\ln T_i$
Murder[d]	2.178	−0.482	2.074	−0.462	0.963	−0.365
	(19.940)	(4.207)	(18.994)	(4.019)	(12.214)	(3.250)
Rape	−2.979	−1.240	−2.921	−1.212	−1.691	−0.368
	(6.972)	(3.276)	(6.787)	(3.189)	(1.618)	(0.488)
Murder and Rape	−2.709	−0.411	−2.619	−0.399	−1.444	−0.052
	(9.521)	(1.156)	(8.970)	(1.088)	(1.418)	(0.418)
Assault[d]	3.851	5.754	3.892	5.812	4.170	6.220
	(17.263)	(25.004)	(17.997)	(26.057)	(18.698)	(27.734)
Robbery	−1.109	−0.357	−1.112	−0.354	−1.224	−0.617
	(0.507)	(0.288)	(0.514)	(0.294)	(0.475)	(0.282)
Burglary	−0.416	−0.547	−0.416	−0.535	−0.485	−0.797
	(0.148)	(0.225)	(0.149)	(0.227)	(0.130)	(0.214)
Larceny	−1.231	−1.637	−1.237	−1.619	−1.348	−1.950
	(0.680)	(1.036)	(0.691)	(1.069)	(0.796)	(1.298)
Auto Theft	−0.650	−0.246	−0.654	−0.238	−0.660	−0.286
	(0.202)	(0.197)	(0.206)	(0.203)	(0.202)	(0.222)
Larceny and Auto Theft	−0.862	−0.828	−0.865	−0.820	−0.898	−0.990
	(0.279)	(0.373)	(0.284)	(0.383)	(0.296)	(0.432)
Crimes against the Person	−2.546	−1.006	−2.546	−0.990	−2.349	−0.718
	(3.759)	(1.637)	(3.797)	(1.642)	(2.975)	(0.916)
Property Crimes	−0.739	−0.626	−0.743	−0.611	−0.797	−0.936
	(0.154)	(0.208)	(0.156)	(0.213)	(0.148)	(0.228)
All Offenses	−1.043	−0.824	−1.049	−0.800	−0.783	−0.985
	(0.282)	(0.321)	(0.283)	(0.324)	(0.452)	(0.577)

[a]The crime equation contains the following variables: constant, ln P_i, ln T_i, ln W, ln X, ln NW, ln U, ln LF, ln Age, ln $SMSA$, ln *Males*, ln *Ed*, *Dummy*, and ln N. The equation is identified by the exclusion of ln Exp_{59}.

[b]In order to induce homoscedasticity, all variables in the regression, including the constant, are multiplied with $\sqrt{N}$, with N the state population size in 1960.

[c]Between parentheses is the standard error of estimate. Degrees of freedom: All States—33; Vermont omitted—32; omitting Utah, Vermont, and Wisconson—30.

[d]This equation is unstable, possibly due to multicollinearity.

TABLE 25 2SLS[a] (Weighted[b]) Estimates—Log-Linear Model[c]

Crime Category	Intercept	$\hat{P}_i$	T_i	W	X	NW
Murder	−1.204	−2.007	−0.00163	0.000262	8.991	0.0500
	(1.421)	(0.735)	(0.000920)	(0.000126)	(3.436)	(0.00797)
		[−0.929]	[−0.251]	[1.376]	[1.744]	[0.505]
Rape	−1.001	−1.920	−0.0119	0.000430	8.894	0.00767
	(1.652)	(0.436)	(0.00630)	(0.000157)	(3.898)	(0.00960)
		[−0.779]	[−0.460]	[2.259]	[1.725]	[0.0776]
Murder and Rape	0.248	−1.954	−0.00524	0.000308	7.237	0.0306
	(1.232)	(0.314)	(0.00144)	(0.000116)	(2.905)	(0.00667)
		[−0.846]	[−0.432]	[1.618]	[1.404]	[0.309]
Assault	−0.452	−9.309	−0.00921	0.000530	8.841	0.0512
	(3.927)	(5.935)	(0.0243)	(0.000371)	(8.819)	(0.0242)
		[−0.879]	[−0.238]	[2.784]	[1.715]	[0.518]
Robbery	−0.983	−10.010	−0.0114	0.000652	12.428	0.0290
	(2.072)	(1.763)	(0.00747)	(0.000202)	(4.890)	(0.0106)
		[−1.476]	[−0.453]	[3.425]	[2.411]	[0.293]
Burglary	3.661	−27.977	−0.0443	0.000349	10.741	0.0294
	(1.300)	(5.641)	(0.0111)	(0.000122)	(2.810)	(0.00825)
		[−0.949]	[−0.996]	[1.834]	[2.083]	[0.297]

Larceny	0.188	−9.828	−0.0224	0.000662	11.530	0.0152
	(1.174)	(5.685)	(0.0151)	(0.000116)	(3.095)	(0.00815)
		[−0.288]	[−0.424]	[3.478]	[2.237]	[0.154]
Auto Theft	0.542	−11.773	−0.00404	0.000539	9.580	0.0118
	(1.275)	(4.718)	(0.00804)	(0.000136)	(2.913)	(0.00708)
		[−0.410]	[−0.078]	[2.832]	[1.858]	[0.119]
Larceny and Auto Theft	2.729	−37.124	−0.0408	0.000425	12.917	0.0269
	(1.785)	(13.243)	(0.0189)	(0.000185)	(4.158)	(0.0118)
		[−1.153]	[−0.770]	[2.233]	[2.506]	[0.272]
Crimes against the Person	2.309	−6.656	−0.00853	0.000313	5.695	0.0362
	(2.839)	(1.835)	(0.00455)	(0.000271)	(6.330)	(0.0159)
		[−1.167]	[−0.542]	[1.644]	[1.105]	[0.366]
Property Crimes	3.714	−33.512	−0.0367	0.000432	12.261	0.0322
	(1.412)	(7.858)	(0.0121)	(0.000139)	(3.120)	(0.00954)
		[−1.201]	[−0.865]	[2.270]	[2.378]	[0.325]
All Offenses	4.230	−24.992	−0.0390	0.000440	10.268	0.0356
	(1.460)	(5.854)	(0.0117)	(0.000132)	(3.117)	(0.00928)
		[−1.177]	[−1.038]	[2.312]	[1.992]	[0.360]

[a] The model $\ln (Q_i/N) = \alpha_0 + \alpha_1 P_i + \alpha_2 T_i + \alpha_3 W + \alpha_4 X + \alpha_5 NW + \mu$ with $\ln (Q_i/N)$ and P_i endogenous. The reduced form variables are: constant, *Age*, *Dummy*, *Ed*, Exp_{59}, *X*, Males, *NW*, *N*, *SMSA*, U_{35-39}, *W*, $(Q_i/N)_{59}$, and T_i. The equations are identified with the following variables: *Age*, *Dummy*, *Ed*, Exp_{59}, $(Q_i/N)_{59}$, *Males*, *N*, *SMSA*, and U_{35-39}.

[b] In order to induce homoscedasticity, all variables in the regression, including the constant, are multiplied with $\sqrt{N}$, with *N* the state population size in 1960.

[c] Between parentheses are the standard errors of the estimate; between brackets are the elasticities calculated at the mean value of the right-hand-side variables. Degrees of freedom: 41.

APPENDIX D: FIGURES

The horizontal scale in all the figures in this appendix represents the code numbers of the states. These are:

Code	*State*	*Code*	*State*
1	Alabama	25	Nebraska
2	Arizona	26	Nevada
3	Arkansas	27	New Hampshire
4	California	28	New Mexico
5	Colorado	29	New York
6	Connecticut	30	North Carolina
7	Delaware	31	North Dakota
8	Florida	32	Ohio
9	Georgia	33	Oklahoma
10	Idaho	34	Oregon
11	Illinois	35	Pennsylvania
12	Indiana	36	Rhode Island
13	Iowa	37	South Carolina
14	Kansas	38	South Dakota
15	Kentucky	39	Tennessee
16	Louisiana	40	Texas
17	Maine	41	Utah
18	Maryland	42	Vermont
19	Massachusetts	43	Virginia
20	Michigan	44	Washington
21	Minnesota	45	West Virginia
22	Mississippi	46	Wisconsin
23	Missouri	47	Wyoming
24	Montana		

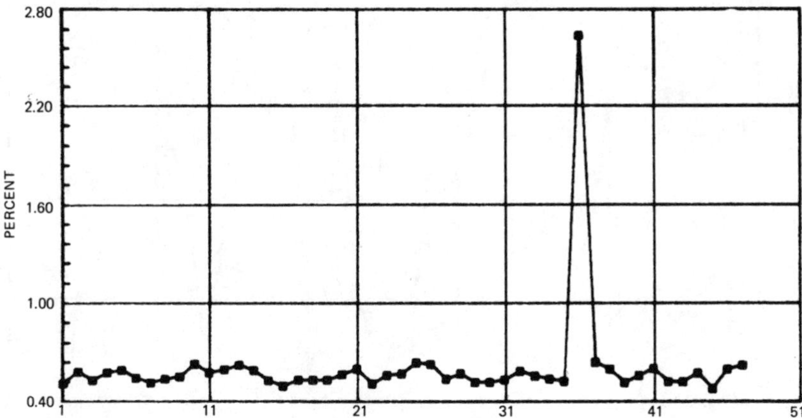

FIGURE 1 LF: labor force participation rate (uncorrected).

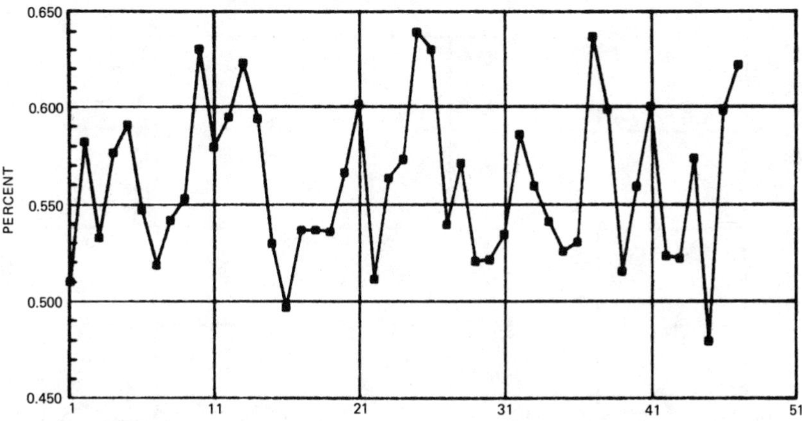

FIGURE 2 LF: labor force participation rate (corrected).

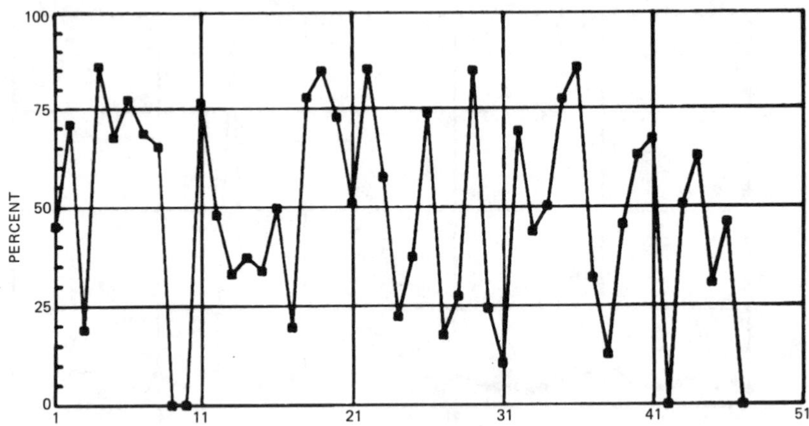

FIGURE 3 SMSA: percentage of population living in standard metropolitan statistical areas.

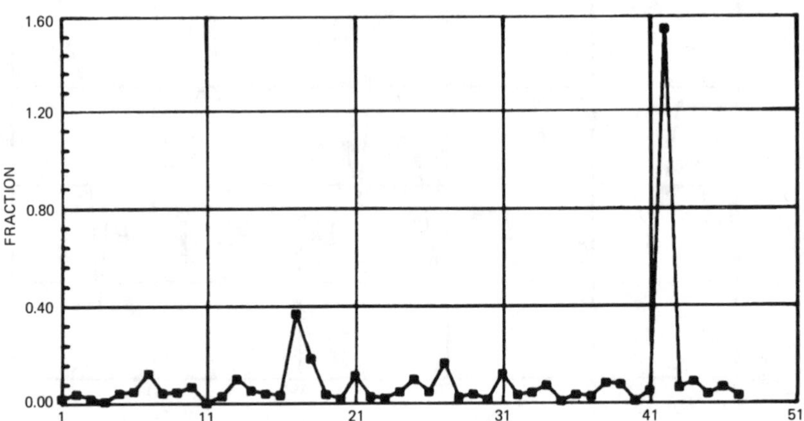

FIGURE 4 Probability of imprisonment for assault.

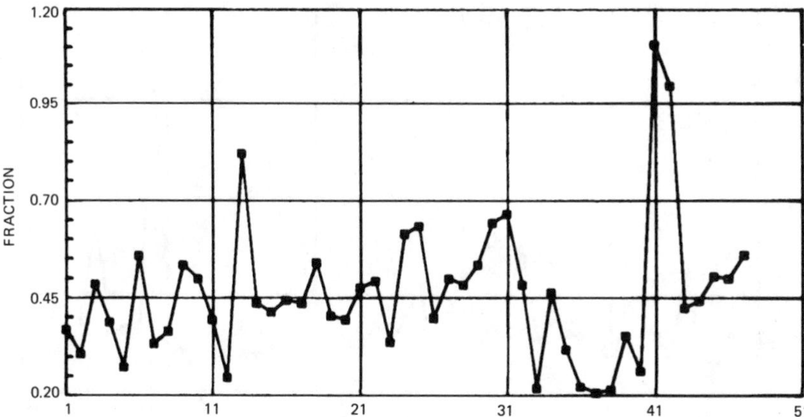

FIGURE 5 Probability of imprisonment for murder.

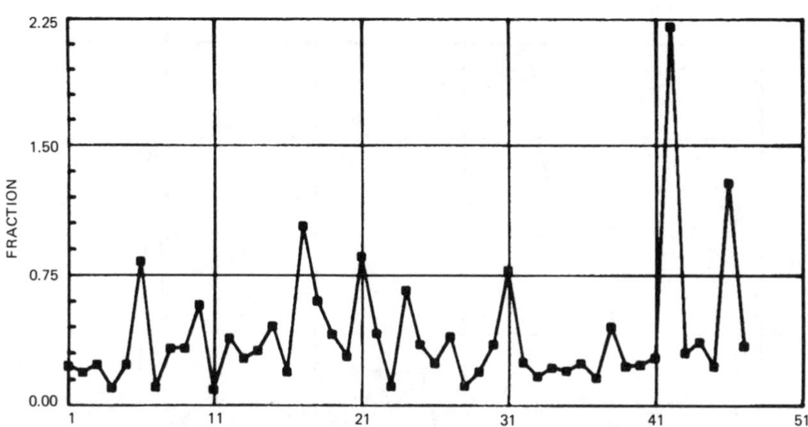

FIGURE 6 Probability of imprisonment for rape.

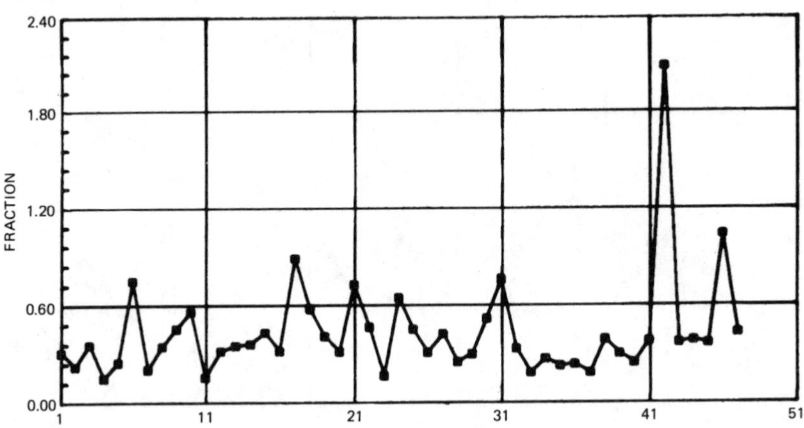

FIGURE 7 Probability of imprisonment for murder and rape.

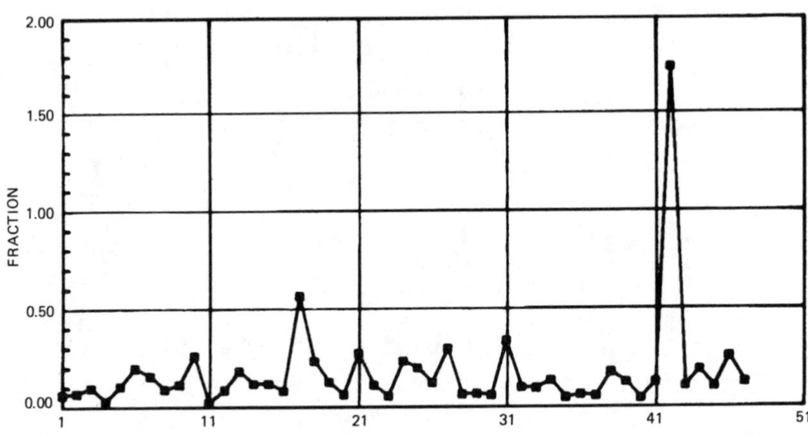

FIGURE 8 Probability of imprisonment for crimes against the person.

APPENDIX E: DATA

The data given in this appendix have been obtained by exponentiating the logarithmic transformed data. Therefore, some rounding errors were encountered.

The symbols used are those given in Appendix B. Also, the first page of Appendix D should be consulted for the code numbers. The remaining pages contain the data on the crime rate (R.), lagged crime rate (L.), probability of imprisonment (P.), and the time served (T.). The second part of each of these four symbols refers to the particular crime involved:

ALL:	All Offenses	M.RP:	Murder and Rape
ASS:	Assault	MUR:	Murder
AU:	Auto Theft	PROP:	Property Crime
BUR:	Burglary	PSON:	Crime against the Person
LAR:	Larceny	RAPE:	Rape
L.AT:	Larceny and Auto Theft	ROB:	Robbery

AGE

1	15.1001	14.3006	14.1994	13.6004
5	14.1004	12.0999	12.7	13.0998
9	15.7006	14.0006	12.4	13.4006
13	12.7994	13.5001	15.2001	14.1994
17	14.3006	13.5001	12.9994	12.4996
21	12.6	15.7006	13.1998	13.0998
25	12.9994	13.0998	13.5001	15.2001
29	11.8995	16.5999	14.0006	12.4996
33	14.6993	12.6	12.3	15.0008
37	17.7006	13.3005	14.9006	14.4993
41	14.7996	14.1004	16.1998	13.6004
45	13.9002	12.6	12.9994	

DUMMY

1	1.	0.	1.	0.
5	0.	0.	1.	1.
9	1.	0.	0.	0.
13	0.	0.	1.	1.
17	0.	1.	0.	0.
21	0.	1.	0.	0.
25	0.	0.	0.	0.
29	0.	1.	0.	0.
33	1.	0.	0.	0.
37	1.	0.	1.	1.
41	0.	0.	1.	0.
45	1.	0.	0.	

ED

1	9.10023	11.3	8.90043	12.0999
5	12.0999	11.	11.0995	10.9004
9	8.99978	11.8	10.5003	10.7995
13	11.3	11.7001	8.6998	8.80042
17	11.	10.3999	11.5999	10.7995
21	10.7995	8.90043	9.60035	11.5999
25	11.5999	12.0999	10.9004	11.1998
29	10.6995	8.90043	9.29986	10.9004
33	10.3999	11.8	10.2001	10.0001
37	8.6998	10.3999	8.80042	10.3999
41	12.1996	10.9004	9.89965	12.0999
45	8.80042	10.3999	12.0999	

EXP

1	5.77016	10.3202	4.5299	14.85
5	10.8602	11.7705	8.24	11.4799
9	6.47987	7.14991	12.0504	7.54964
13	6.69995	6.24013	5.68028	8.13032
17	6.56991	12.2595	12.8302	11.2898
21	7.44022	4.68001	8.65987	7.82012
25	6.29024	15.9698	6.89986	8.24989
29	16.6299	5.78981	5.52012	8.95042
33	6.26012	9.69975	9.69005	10.8504
37	5.77016	5.12997	6.10007	8.18988
41	7.24999	5.62995	7.52026	9.50959
45	4.58	10.5698	9.04037	

EXP.59

1	5.61028	9.48964	4.36012	14.1102
5	10.0503	11.5098	7.93037	10.8797
9	6.19969	6.78015	11.5502	7.07028
13	6.02008	6.12023	5.33987	7.73999
17	6.31988	11.5098	12.8494	10.5202
21	6.71001	4.38987	8.30037	7.27977
25	5.7002	14.2906	7.09011	7.62018
29	15.6802	5.44991	5.44991	8.14008
33	6.37	9.68037	8.69024	9.82962
37	5.59011	4.65993	5.40001	7.44989
41	6.59031	5.38006	7.00974	9.63979
45	4.06982	9.65041	9.09023	

LF

1	0.510431	0.582707	0.533061	0.577088
5	0.591402	0.547491	0.51897	0.542298
9	0.553258	0.631713	0.58012	0.595282
13	0.624153	0.594818	0.529978	0.497018
17	0.537138	0.53716	0.536489	0.56689
21	0.602119	0.51156	0.564108	0.573739
25	0.640568	0.631132	0.539998	0.571432
29	0.521018	0.52143	0.534539	0.586349
33	0.559708	0.54162	0.525992	0.53089
37	0.638151	0.59929	0.515499	0.559831
41	0.601018	0.523489	0.52227	0.57425
45	0.479668	0.598811	0.623242	

MALES

1	95.0022	101.2	96.902	99.4048
5	98.5043	96.3994	98.1994	96.902
9	95.4975	102.904	96.602	97.2029
13	97.2029	98.6028	98.6028	95.6026
17	97.6998	97.7976	93.4008	98.5043
21	98.396	96.1971	95.2972	103.804
25	98.396	107.104	96.4958	101.799
29	93.8033	97.3001	104.501	96.3994
33	97.2029	98.9981	94.8029	96.3994
37	97.3975	102.401	95.2972	98.1013
41	99.8032	96.7955	99.6038	101.2
45	96.7955	98.8991	104.899	

N

1	32.6714	13.0202	17.8606	157.166
5	17.5403	25.3505	4.45978	49.5212
9	39.429	6.66987	100.806	46.6186
13	27.5802	21.7911	30.3805	32.5703
17	9.69005	31.0097	51.4906	78.2337
21	34.1411	21.7802	43.1983	6.74971
25	14.1102	2.84995	6.07025	9.50959
29	167.821	45.5586	6.31988	97.0572
33	23.2801	17.69	113.194	8.59001
37	23.8289	6.81005	35.6696	95.8035
41	8.91023	3.90009	39.6702	28.5312
45	18.6007	39.5197	3.29993	

NW

1	30.0992	10.2001	21.9003	7.99967
5	2.99996	4.39998	13.9002	17.9
9	28.5998	1.50001	10.6005	5.90028
13	1.	4.6002	7.20014	32.1014
17	0.599997	16.9998	2.4	9.39991
21	1.2	42.3005	9.19997	3.59988
25	2.6	7.69984	0.4	7.9003
29	8.90043	25.3988	2.00001	8.19972
33	9.50008	2.10001	7.59963	2.4
37	34.9005	4.00002	16.5007	12.6
41	1.89999	0.200008	20.801	3.59988
45	4.89983	2.4	2.20001	

SMSA

1	45.2997	71.4002	19.1002	86.4962
5	67.9995	77.6025	68.903	65.6016
9	0.099999	0.099999	76.8995	48.1008
13	33.1983	37.4011	34.1001	49.8989
17	19.6996	78.2023	85.1998	73.0979
21	51.3005	85.9014	57.89	22.5989
25	37.5998	74.2027	17.7006	27.5995
29	85.4986	24.5988	10.6005	69.4981
33	43.8994	50.4005	77.898	86.2026
37	32.2011	12.7	45.8007	63.4023
41	67.4981	0.099999	50.9019	63.0987
45	30.9014	46.2981	0.099999	

U

1	0.108392	0.096097	0.094043	0.102499
5	0.090754	0.083919	0.096656	0.079389
9	0.081106	0.09951	0.077027	0.083417
13	0.077181	0.077104	0.092153	0.11624
17	0.113915	0.089421	0.078004	0.130081
21	0.101571	0.096743	0.083201	0.142146
25	0.070172	0.101632	0.079516	0.103478
29	0.092098	0.071884	0.13497	0.104895
33	0.075562	0.101693	0.123836	0.087187
37	0.075888	0.098539	0.086061	0.087799
41	0.083643	0.107174	0.07316	0.110825
45	0.135187	0.077918	0.112748	

U_{35-39}

1	4.10005	3.59988	3.29993	3.90009
5	2.00001	2.89997	3.8	3.50013
9	2.79995	2.4	3.50013	3.09999
13	2.5	2.7	4.29994	4.70018
17	3.50013	3.40008	3.40008	5.80025
21	3.29993	3.40008	3.20016	4.20006
25	2.10001	4.10005	2.20001	2.79995
29	3.59988	2.6	4.00002	4.29994
33	2.4	3.50013	4.99981	3.8
37	2.79995	2.7	3.50013	3.09999
41	2.00001	3.69988	2.7	3.69988
45	5.29996	2.5	4.00002	

W

1	3937.1	5568.05	3184.02	6725.76
5	5780.24	6887.07	6196.87	4722.06
9	4207.82	5259.02	6566.26	5798.19
13	5069.01	5294.9	4050.92	4271.84
17	4873.17	6308.79	6272.31	6256.02
21	5573.06	2883.9	5127.12	5402.95
25	4861.97	6735.86	5635.83	5371.17
29	6370.92	3956.04	4530.1	6170.9
33	4619.77	5892.29	5718.72	5589.25
37	3821.12	4250.96	3948.93	4883.9
41	5898.77	4889.77	4964.16	6224.82
45	4571.97	5925.97	5876.99	

X

1	0.261192	0.194407	0.249699	0.167395
5	0.173705	0.125795	0.168099	0.205893
9	0.238998	0.1736	0.170095	0.171804
13	0.206202	0.189607	0.2635	0.246893
17	0.166294	0.165497	0.135498	0.165995
21	0.195401	0.276208	0.226502	0.175608
25	0.196204	0.152103	0.139206	0.21509
29	0.153893	0.236502	0.199808	0.163197
33	0.232608	0.166194	0.157804	0.152896
37	0.253701	0.225102	0.250599	0.227592
41	0.143704	0.169908	0.224495	0.161605
45	0.2491	0.171307	0.160301	

R.ALL

1	791.318	1634.51	577.611	1969.43
5	1233.61	681.502	963.334	1554.64
9	856.111	704.579	1673.71	849.289
13	511.323	663.879	797.674	945.676
17	539.099	929.271	750.47	1224.76
21	742.186	438.605	1215.85	968.356
25	523.219	1993.21	342.201	1215.97
29	1043.05	695.896	372.71	754.081
33	1072.34	922.789	653.407	1272.07
37	830.56	565.777	825.839	1150.56
41	880.069	542.398	823.036	1029.99
45	455.183	508.111	849.119	

R.ASS

1	123.396	119.403	57.5987	118.997
5	40.0008	21.6001	21.501	106.901
9	98.7015	14.7996	126.204	36.1003
13	8.60033	29.0001	50.5013	78.6966
17	10.7995	88.5972	19.4005	94.8029
21	10.2995	65.8975	60.6003	24.2012
25	16.4003	50.5013	4.89983	88.7036
29	73.5011	184.694	5.20021	32.9009
33	35.4988	26.0001	49.2003	19.1998
37	100.605	15.8997	50.2998	110.598
41	25.7002	4.6002	102.197	15.4005
45	34.5014	16.3006	37.9019	

R.AU

1	87.3044	338.39	45.9981	326.588
5	213.791	129.697	161.305	187.598
9	147.393	100.003	353.294	159.605
13	75.9975	87.1996	124.499	190.395
17	117.801	184.104	211.093	177.505
21	136.702	48.2985	184.805	243.496
25	125.399	391.897	57.8007	256.39
29	177.505	77.9993	67.9995	134.599
33	193.098	130.699	120.602	308.709
37	104.7	86.6	121.498	162.195
41	158.793	86.9036	120.097	158.001
45	69.4009	104.397	114.801	

R.BUR

1	349.813	685.467	272.598	910.506
5	569.922	333.386	552.802	807.062
9	392.094	301.388	577.726	428.118
13	231.204	353.683	371.111	387.3
17	245.501	366.391	309.204	589.397
21	349.289	204.691	595.201	396.391
25	231.505	913.515	182.6	434.502
29	335.896	258.501	198.006	344.399
33	523.376	405.694	295.096	510.505
37	376.004	247.894	462.71	596.692
41	410.387	242.112	346.298	487.505
45	234.206	198.601	299.885	

R.L.AT

1	269.589	753.328	205.203	820.571
5	528.689	311.5	339.917	540.99
9	321.212	365.001	738.484	342.51
13	256.288	254.5	331.093	417.214
17	268.191	424.41	395.282	451.195
21	351.215	137.896	450.519	509.179
25	250.911	933.835	146.306	634.984
29	580.39	218.11	160.501	327.602
33	453.82	447.51	265.098	724.876
37	311.407	285.402	271.999	394.217
41	415.382	290.79	331.989	488.09
45	165.108	280.788	446.214	

R.LAR

1	182.308	414.884	159.206	493.983
5	314.914	181.799	178.591	353.4
9	173.799	264.992	385.214	182.893
13	180.296	167.302	206.603	226.807
17	150.4	240.303	184.196	273.691
21	214.498	89.604	265.709	265.709
25	125.499	541.91	88.4998	378.607
29	402.905	140.106	92.4992	193.002
33	260.708	316.809	144.503	416.214
37	206.706	198.8	150.506	231.991
41	256.595	203.894	211.897	330.102
45	95.6983	176.408	331.391	

R.M.RP

1	20.9995	22.1005	17.4005	22.1005
5	17.2999	5.7002	15.0008	18.6996
9	19.4005	9.60035	22.4996	8.99978
13	4.29994	7.9003	12.0999	16.8998
17	6.69995	12.6	6.19969	16.5999
21	3.59988	15.2001	18.9007	11.
25	6.49999	21.4002	5.40001	19.1002
29	9.19997	17.6	2.7	9.10023
33	20.2996	11.8	10.9004	3.29993
37	22.5989	7.49998	13.9002	18.0005
41	7.79982	2.6	17.1998	7.9003
45	8.60033	4.10005	11.8	

R.MUR

1	12.4	6.00024	8.50028	3.90009
5	4.20006	1.59999	6.69995	10.6005
9	11.8995	2.4	4.89983	4.29994
13	0.599997	2.89997	6.69995	8.30037
17	1.7	5.40001	1.4	4.29994
21	1.2	10.0001	4.39998	3.90009
25	2.3	8.80042	1.29999	7.20014
29	2.89997	10.0001	0.499999	3.20016
33	7.49998	2.4	2.6	1.
37	13.1998	2.10001	8.50028	8.60033
41	1.	0.299992	10.0001	2.10001
45	4.39998	1.29999	4.79992	

R.PROP

1	646.906	1492.94	502.603	1828.41
5	1176.27	654.192	926.765	1428.96
9	737.968	680.209	1524.93	804.162
13	498.398	626.971	735.095	850.139
17	521.599	828.072	724.876	1113.43
21	728.291	357.487	1136.26	933.182
25	500.296	1921.38	331.889	1108.21
29	960.256	493.588	364.782	712.087
33	1016.48	885.011	593.3	1249.63
37	707.402	542.398	761.583	1021.98
41	846.576	535.178	703.593	1006.67
45	412.114	487.7	799.431	

R.PSON

1	144.402	141.5	75.0009	141.104
5	57.3	27.3004	36.4995	125.6
9	118.096	24.4004	148.695	45.1008
13	12.8997	36.8996	62.6022	95.6026
17	17.5	101.2	25.6002	111.397
21	13.9002	81.1014	79.5034	35.1984
25	22.8992	71.9017	10.2995	107.802
29	82.6984	202.31	7.9003	42.0013
33	55.8015	37.7997	60.0994	22.4996
37	123.199	23.3992	64.1998	128.599
41	33.4985	7.20014	119.403	23.3011
45	43.099	20.3993	49.6998	

R.RAPE

1	8.60033	16.0997	8.90043	18.1996
5	13.0998	4.10005	8.30037	8.10029
9	7.49998	7.20014	17.6	4.70018
13	3.69988	4.99981	5.40001	8.60033
17	4.99981	7.20014	4.79992	12.3
21	2.4	5.20021	14.4993	7.10004
25	4.20006	12.6	4.10005	11.8995
29	6.29969	7.59963	2.20001	5.90028
33	12.7994	9.39991	8.30037	2.3
37	9.39991	5.40001	5.40001	9.39991
41	6.79984	2.3	7.20014	5.80025
45	4.20006	2.79995	6.99993	

R.ROB

1	27.5004	54.201	24.7989	97.3001
5	77.7034	9.29986	34.1001	80.8989
9	24.6999	13.8004	208.805	33.5991
13	10.9004	18.8008	32.9009	45.5996
17	7.9003	37.3003	20.3993	72.7988
21	27.799	14.9006	90.6042	27.5995
25	17.9	74.0026	2.99996	38.6985
29	44.0004	16.9998	6.29969	40.1009
33	39.299	31.8011	33.0989	14.1994
37	19.9994	9.10023	26.8993	31.0997
41	20.801	2.3	25.2999	31.0997
45	12.7994	8.30037	53.298	

L.ALL

1	750.32	1500.27	558.917	1635.82
5	1184.17	630.87	869.223	1386.03
9	807.788	657.602	1284.85	775.882
13	467.08	629.987	751.897	701.976
17	478.617	893.816	708.111	1077.18
21	593.3	420.397	1018.82	863.678
25	448.317	1915.82	470.502	1170.17
29	962.564	652.884	336.905	656.879
33	863.16	819.423	655.895	1058.17
37	772.012	597.707	821.473	1026.9
41	827.079	366.61	768.315	957.955
45	456.779	428.504	762.117	

L.ASS

1	111.097	93.5971	51.3005	107.404
5	38.7992	25.5005	21.2	116.106
9	101.697	18.6996	91.3958	30.9014
13	8.39973	29.3004	45.3995	46.6
17	12.0999	87.8033	19.4005	89.3982
21	8.10029	82.9967	75.8987	17.8
25	12.7	38.6985	4.79992	58.7975
29	75.8001	182.199	5.40001	31.3998
33	32.2011	21.7998	54.0009	27.0991
37	113.795	14.0006	56.1991	106.997
41	25.8989	2.6	102.105	14.0006
45	31.5004	15.7998	51.5009	

L.AU

1	96.3994	378.115	53.2022	286.689
5	227.102	103.296	171.297	181.708
9	141.698	113.5	281.998	154.996
13	70.0984	80.3025	139.198	161.499
17	102.802	191.502	209.6	175.792
21	115.804	41.0011	170.699	193.098
25	102.596	317.793	73.5967	319.514
29	164.104	71.4002	59.6981	126.697
33	138.297	123.804	116.501	264.595
37	83.4961	100.303	135.694	167.603
41	159.206	75.0984	120.001	170.
45	75.3015	106.399	114.801	

L.BUR

1	321.887	572.378	264.701	718.812
5	539.693	314.191	462.617	701.135
9	351.215	275.311	445.011	382.298
13	219.708	325.903	341.894	283.298
17	219.796	320.794	287.493	509.994
21	271.7	179.092	468.811	351.286
25	202.593	958.625	279.5	418.593
29	302.506	254.195	174.6	287.407
33	391.584	360.9	308.493	442.792
37	343.608	253.991	437.817	489.997
41	368.485	208.096	346.298	445.991
45	225.09	178.895	300.185	

L.L.AT

1	271.103	765.631	199.497	713.869
5	516.306	273.308	348.417	488.481
9	304.387	344.812	594.309	325.805
13	225.405	241.701	324.407	323.209
17	232.293	432.811	379.1	401.698
21	290.586	127.702	385.793	458.793
25	212.597	786.977	173.799	641.173
29	532.19	184.491	147.895	295.007
33	397.184	398.099	248.589	565.212
37	278.495	306.403	287.091	380.391
41	404.884	152.796	331.989	462.71
45	177.097	243.691	446.616	

L.LAR

1	174.705	387.494	146.306	427.22
5	289.195	170.	177.097	306.801
9	162.699	231.296	312.311	170.801
13	155.306	161.402	185.193	161.693
17	129.502	241.29	169.508	225.902
21	174.793	86.704	215.099	265.709
25	110.002	469.186	100.203	321.694
29	368.116	113.103	88.1994	168.292
33	258.889	274.294	132.105	300.606
37	195.	206.108	151.396	212.81
41	245.697	77.7034	212.003	292.686
45	101.799	137.304	331.789	

L.M.RP

1	21.2	20.3993	18.1996	21.9003
5	17.1998	4.39998	11.3	18.6996
9	24.0011	7.40015	16.6999	8.80042
13	4.39998	8.39973	12.0999	12.0999
17	5.80025	11.4995	5.7002	15.4994
21	3.29993	16.8004	15.4994	11.8995
25	8.30037	24.9008	5.7002	14.5997
29	9.19997	17.1004	4.20006	8.6998
33	17.7006	10.5003	11.7001	2.99996
37	20.899	8.30037	13.6004	18.8008
41	8.99978	1.80001	16.0997	8.10029
45	10.3999	4.20006	11.3	

L.MUR

1	12.8997	5.20021	10.3999	3.29993
5	5.40001	1.29999	4.10005	10.2001
9	13.4006	2.3	4.5001	3.40008
13	1.4	2.4	5.29996	5.7002
17	1.50001	4.39998	1.2	4.20006
21	1.	11.3999	5.80025	4.00002
25	2.79995	7.79982	2.7	6.00024
29	2.99996	8.90043	0.499999	3.20016
33	6.69995	2.20001	2.5	0.900001
37	12.1996	2.10001	6.99993	9.60035
41	1.	0.499999	8.80042	1.89999
45	4.39998	1.1	4.29994	

L.PROP

1	618.131	1386.17	489.41	1506.43
5	1128.22	600.883	836.729	1251.25
9	682.116	631.628	1176.74	736.198
13	454.092	592.529	694.575	643.293
17	460.817	794.49	683.072	972.334
21	581.785	320.698	927.414	833.889
25	427.391	1852.15	459.988	1096.74
29	877.608	453.593	327.308	616.773
33	813.3	787.135	590.282	1028.03
37	637.21	575.305	751.823	900.995
41	792.11	362.201	703.593	935.892
45	415.092	430.394	800.39	

L.PSON

1	132.304	114.	69.4981	129.295
5	56.0027	29.9012	32.4987	134.801
9	125.7	26.0991	108.105	39.702
13	12.7994	37.7015	57.5009	58.6977
17	17.9	99.2954	25.1008	104.899
21	11.3999	99.8032	91.3958	29.6986
25	20.9995	63.5992	10.5003	73.3983
29	85.0042	199.298	9.60035	40.1009
33	49.8989	32.301	65.7	30.0992
37	134.693	22.3003	69.7976	125.801
41	34.9005	4.39998	118.203	22.1005
45	41.9006	19.9994	62.8028	

L.RAPE

1	8.30037	15.2001	7.79982	18.6007
5	11.8	3.09999	7.20014	8.50028
9	10.6005	5.09979	12.1996	5.40001
13	2.99996	6.00024	6.79984	6.40001
17	4.29994	7.10004	4.5001	11.3
21	2.3	5.40001	9.69975	7.9003
25	5.49974	17.1004	2.99996	8.60033
29	6.19969	8.19972	3.69988	5.49974
33	11.	8.30037	9.19997	2.10001
37	8.6998	6.19969	6.6002	9.19997
41	7.99967	1.29999	7.30019	6.19969
45	6.00024	3.09999	6.99993	

L.ROB

1	25.1008	48.202	25.1989	73.8031
5	72.1971	13.4006	25.7002	61.6023
9	26.4988	11.4995	137.401	28.1009
13	8.99978	24.9008	28.3011	36.8001
17	8.6998	40.8988	16.5007	60.6003
21	19.4997	13.9002	72.7988	23.8003
25	12.1996	106.602	6.69995	36.8996
29	42.9012	14.9006	4.79992	34.4015
33	24.5007	28.1009	33.1983	19.9994
37	15.1001	14.9006	26.8993	30.6
41	18.6996	1.29999	25.2999	27.1995
45	12.8997	7.79982	53.5974	

P.ALL

1	0.084602	0.029599	0.083401	0.015801
5	0.041399	0.034201	0.0421	0.040099
9	0.071697	0.044498	0.016201	0.031201
13	0.045302	0.0532	0.0691	0.052099
17	0.076299	0.119804	0.019099	0.034801
21	0.0228	0.089502	0.0307	0.041598
25	0.069197	0.041698	0.036099	0.038201
29	0.0234	0.075298	0.041999	0.042698
33	0.049499	0.040799	0.0207	0.0069
37	0.045198	0.053998	0.047099	0.038801
41	0.0251	0.088904	0.054902	0.0281
45	0.056202	0.046598	0.052802	

P.ASS

1	0.0226	0.043101	0.0233	0.0105
5	0.047	0.052897	0.125005	0.0465
9	0.0491	0.070701	0.0039	0.0333
13	0.101703	0.057	0.044401	0.036301
17	0.371398	0.187196	0.039999	0.020101
21	0.116799	0.031401	0.024101	0.0491
25	0.099103	0.048602	0.166693	0.026101
29	0.039601	0.0189	0.121202	0.037202
33	0.047198	0.073903	0.0106	0.0364
37	0.029599	0.083301	0.079198	0.0109
41	0.052403	1.5556	0.0643	0.0913
45	0.039	0.068303	0.032001	

P.AU

1	0.0491	0.0325	0.065802	0.0085
5	0.033101	0.018201	0.030599	0.0364
9	0.087598	0.027	0.0072	0.022199
13	0.0749	0.051602	0.054498	0.0184
17	0.0289	0.019799	0.0059	0.0252
21	0.016901	0.097999	0.0232	0.021301
25	0.0362	0.050102	0.0085	0.052099
29	0.01	0.088602	0.032601	0.037299
33	0.020199	0.035901	0.0091	0.0008
37	0.0309	0.017001	0.041798	0.018
41	0.019099	0.056	0.029399	0.0297
45	0.0248	0.028799	0.1029	

P.BUR

1	0.0628	0.018701	0.0708	0.0081
5	0.029101	0.025699	0.036502	0.025499
9	0.060199	0.041798	0.0136	0.024299
13	0.0224	0.038898	0.044498	0.051401
17	0.055899	0.057602	0.011599	0.019799
21	0.013101	0.062599	0.022199	0.035098
25	0.054199	0.027201	0.0307	0.022999
29	0.011799	0.078402	0.0304	0.0316
33	0.040498	0.0307	0.0156	0.008
37	0.0323	0.0362	0.0211	0.0299
41	0.0186	0.0434	0.042299	0.017799
45	0.0491	0.034701	0.035402	

P.L.AT

1	0.079803	0.0221	0.070397	0.0061
5	0.0242	0.0133	0.021801	0.0258
9	0.044299	0.0246	0.0048	0.019
13	0.037501	0.035402	0.055498	0.028699
17	0.040401	0.071999	0.0061	0.0304
21	0.0163	0.088204	0.023899	0.024699
25	0.0345	0.031902	0.0101	0.029801
29	0.0111	0.058601	0.025599	0.0251
33	0.039199	0.023499	0.0085	0.0006
37	0.027201	0.0335	0.050701	0.028201
41	0.012699	0.038801	0.031201	0.024101
45	0.0384	0.018701	0.042801	

P.LAR

1	0.094496	0.013699	0.071697	0.0045
5	0.018101	0.0098	0.0138	0.020199
9	0.0076	0.023799	0.0027	0.016201
13	0.021701	0.026901	0.056101	0.037399
17	0.0494	0.112096	0.0063	0.0338
21	0.015801	0.083001	0.024399	0.027901
25	0.032699	0.0188	0.0112	0.0147
29	0.011599	0.041798	0.020501	0.016599
33	0.0532	0.0184	0.0081	0.0006
37	0.0254	0.040701	0.057902	0.035299
41	0.0088	0.031401	0.0322	0.021301
45	0.048301	0.0128	0.021899	

P.M.RP

1	0.312985	0.226502	0.36009	0.154201
5	0.248304	0.756903	0.209004	0.351587
9	0.458699	0.562502	0.161395	0.322195
13	0.35289	0.364182	0.4348	0.320588
17	0.8906	0.5765	0.411799	0.317112
21	0.731703	0.469701	0.166693	0.648599
25	0.456498	0.311486	0.4242	0.254107
29	0.303189	0.5194	0.764701	0.334105
33	0.188209	0.272695	0.229099	0.2414
37	0.189191	0.392201	0.306512	0.251503
41	0.385698	2.10001	0.375401	0.387701
45	0.371101	1.044	0.435901	

P.MUR

1	0.369502	0.307709	0.486801	0.389602
5	0.274008	0.561002	0.333304	0.366191
9	0.537299	0.499999	0.3947	0.247511
13	0.823501	0.437499	0.4146	0.4444
17	0.437499	0.541702	0.4054	0.395201
21	0.476199	0.4954	0.338612	0.615402
25	0.636399	0.4	0.499999	0.485299
29	0.536499	0.642499	0.666697	0.485498
33	0.218406	0.465101	0.31851	0.222195
37	0.207008	0.214295	0.354304	0.263105
41	1.1111	1.	0.4253	0.442599
45	0.506202	0.499999	0.562502	

P.PROP

1	0.072898	0.021899	0.076002	0.0096
5	0.031701	0.022299	0.035299	0.029299
9	0.059701	0.032801	0.012399	0.0237
13	0.0343	0.041798	0.055001	0.0441
17	0.050002	0.073498	0.0128	0.027299
21	0.016201	0.077398	0.0264	0.031101
25	0.049302	0.035	0.025299	0.030101
29	0.015801	0.075103	0.0321	0.0335
33	0.0424	0.029599	0.0155	0.0046
37	0.031201	0.036301	0.0352	0.0325
41	0.0184	0.043101	0.041598	0.0229
45	0.0485	0.0281	0.040901	

P.PSON

1	0.064803	0.071697	0.101601	0.033002
5	0.107604	0.199408	0.159502	0.092098
9	0.116205	0.263791	0.027701	0.0909
13	0.185909	0.122996	0.1199	0.086397
17	0.568002	0.235793	0.130798	0.0643
21	0.276402	0.113302	0.057902	0.236289
25	0.200609	0.126806	0.301586	0.066298
29	0.068797	0.062399	0.340003	0.1015
33	0.0985	0.136	0.050297	0.066997
37	0.058901	0.182391	0.128401	0.044498
41	0.130406	1.75001	0.109099	0.192492
45	0.104999	0.261505	0.128003	

P.RAPE

1	0.231309	0.196204	0.238998	0.103498
5	0.240196	0.835003	0.1081	0.332505
9	0.333304	0.583302	0.097004	0.3917
13	0.274501	0.321101	0.460101	0.200709
17	1.0417	0.602697	0.413702	0.289993
21	0.864201	0.419601	0.114796	0.666697
25	0.355902	0.249999	0.4	0.115003
29	0.197899	0.356508	0.7857	0.251704
33	0.170606	0.222907	0.201493	0.249999
37	0.164392	0.459498	0.232004	0.240797
41	0.278705	2.22221	0.306603	0.367512
45	0.230801	1.2936	0.34781	

P.ROB

1	0.132496	0.059499	0.178298	0.052502
5	0.101297	0.199209	0.151299	0.089896
9	0.253599	0.054302	0.0356	0.065102
13	0.209297	0.182903	0.168807	0.123304
17	0.194796	0.245293	0.159693	0.068797
21	0.0547	0.1821	0.066198	0.091401
25	0.193709	0.170606	0.4444	0.114098
29	0.107496	0.238401	0.249999	0.118304
33	0.104999	0.103003	0.069697	0.082003
37	0.073402	0.129005	0.120706	0.136997
41	0.129704	0.555598	0.168301	0.085803
45	0.168099	0.186504	0.056801	

T.ALL

1	26.2011	25.2999	24.3006	29.9012
5	21.2998	20.9995	20.6993	24.5988
9	29.4001	19.5994	41.6	34.2984
13	36.2993	21.501	22.7008	26.0991
17	19.1002	18.1996	24.9008	26.401
21	37.5998	37.0994	25.1989	17.6
25	21.9003	22.1005	28.4999	25.8006
29	36.7009	28.3011	21.7998	30.9014
33	25.5005	21.6997	37.4011	44.0004
37	31.6995	16.6999	27.3004	29.3004
41	30.0001	12.1996	31.9989	30.0001
45	32.5996	16.6999	16.0997	

T.ASS

1	27.5995	20.3993	22.7008	34.1991
5	21.501	16.4003	13.0998	21.2998
9	23.3992	16.0002	45.2997	40.1009
13	29.4001	26.7999	25.7002	22.4996
17	11.9999	12.4	21.6997	25.7002
21	27.799	27.8992	37.4985	28.7001
25	26.3008	16.3006	12.3	29.3004
29	31.3998	27.3988	18.3	28.1009
33	15.8997	19.5994	26.999	63.803
37	26.3008	23.9005	29.0001	38.2981
41	38.7992	13.5001	21.7998	37.4985
45	35.4988	18.9007	14.3996	

T.AU

1	22.2002	18.3	7.99967	22.3003
5	9.89965	16.6999	10.0001	20.9995
9	20.2996	18.9993	33.7001	24.9008
13	27.0991	24.5988	13.3005	17.7006
17	10.0001	12.1996	17.1004	17.6
21	23.3011	22.2002	18.5005	7.49998
25	20.3993	18.3	16.9998	25.0006
29	29.3004	15.2001	18.6996	24.2012
33	23.9005	12.0999	26.0001	23.5
37	7.9003	25.0006	27.0991	19.4997
41	28.4999	7.99967	19.4997	23.2011
45	29.4001	15.4005	17.4005	

T.BUR

1	22.7008	20.2003	23.5	26.8993
5	16.5007	17.2999	14.9006	23.5989
9	26.999	16.3006	30.7995	29.7997
13	34.6016	21.2998	18.4009	22.8009
17	15.4994	18.9007	20.2003	22.2002
21	25.2999	27.3004	20.899	13.9002
25	21.4002	16.6999	21.2998	22.4009
29	33.7001	22.4009	16.3006	25.3988
33	21.2998	18.9007	32.4014	24.7989
37	29.5003	14.3006	29.4001	25.7002
41	24.3006	13.0998	30.1987	26.0001
45	25.0006	16.6999	15.2001	

T.L.AT

1	20.899	18.9993	15.4005	22.7008
5	12.6	16.6999	10.2995	19.9994
9	20.2996	18.0998	31.8998	25.3988
13	26.401	20.6993	12.8997	18.0998
17	10.6005	11.0995	16.9998	18.9007
21	24.7989	21.2	16.3006	10.9004
25	18.5005	17.9	5.7002	23.9005
29	27.1995	16.0997	19.1002	23.5
33	15.8997	14.1004	27.0991	22.1005
37	16.5007	15.4994	20.2996	19.9994
41	27.5995	6.99993	23.0992	23.5
45	27.8992	15.3007	16.6999	

T.LAR

1	20.6002	20.2996	17.4005	23.2011
5	16.0002	16.8004	10.9004	19.1002
9	20.6002	17.7006	27.3988	26.0001
13	25.2999	16.8998	12.7	18.3
17	10.9004	10.9004	16.8998	19.4997
21	25.8989	20.6002	14.7996	13.3005
25	16.4003	16.9998	16.9998	21.1006
29	26.401	17.1998	19.5994	22.4996
33	13.7001	15.7006	28.1009	20.6993
37	21.7998	13.8004	16.4003	20.2003
41	26.4988	6.29969	25.0006	23.7006
45	27.3004	15.2001	15.6005	

T.M.RP

1	78.5001	86.2974	64.0011	67.3027
5	79.5034	65.7987	80.6001	61.1971
9	95.2019	36.5983	126.697	99.0971
13	122.095	73.2003	87.6981	64.3026
17	55.902	56.7014	65.3005	71.4002
21	101.099	101.504	83.196	62.2028
25	98.2977	56.098	74.4033	77.7968
29	138.795	92.601	50.6987	133.7
33	124.499	69.7	65.3985	96.902
37	166.801	71.9017	92.2959	66.5997
41	101.697	49.6998	73.6998	68.903
45	85.3961	27.6991	102.197	

T.MUR

1	89.604	139.798	75.6033	93.7002
5	198.006	222.294	109.596	74.4033
9	106.901	126.204	196.999	178.306
13	272.19	139.7	114.4	78.6022
17	303.809	77.2001	185.991	140.597
21	354.391	122.904	117.202	101.301
25	163.4	65.0984	206.706	97.6998
29	216.61	111.598	235.993	217.892
33	214.305	118.404	115.7	250.51
37	207.203	283.496	100.003	65.2026
41	208.701	210.103	84.5041	97.3975
45	94.8029	97.6022	181.	

T.PROP

1	25.5005	21.2998	21.6997	29.6986
5	17.9	18.0005	17.2999	23.8003
9	26.2011	17.8	36.8001	32.7991
13	32.9998	23.5989	19.4997	23.0992
17	14.3006	18.6007	21.9991	22.8992
21	28.1994	26.701	23.3011	13.7001
25	23.0001	18.0998	19.9994	24.4004
29	35.3006	22.1005	18.4009	27.6991
33	22.1005	18.6996	33.8995	26.701
37	25.1989	14.7996	27.9999	26.999
41	29.6008	10.5003	31.5004	27.0991
45	29.0001	16.8998	19.1002	

T.PSON

1	63.4023	52.8998	56.7014	58.3991
5	61.7998	55.4011	49.4024	44.1018
9	69.7976	33.1983	116.898	81.8018
13	88.4025	56.3003	69.2	49.7993
17	38.0994	25.8989	55.3015	59.1987
21	78.1008	84.9022	68.6966	57.3975
25	72.7988	45.3995	58.102	62.0972
29	83.8978	74.597	43.099	103.4
33	91.3958	50.9987	58.7975	81.5976
37	109.104	57.0028	61.701	60.6973
41	82.3024	29.0001	47.4986	59.0982
45	70.5979	25.8989	85.4986	

T.RAPE

1	38.9002	45.8007	36.2993	45.7001
5	32.4014	19.1998	7.99967	36.8001
9	53.3994	42.3005	50.8002	78.6022
13	44.7997	19.5994	41.3015	27.8992
17	23.3011	36.4011	27.799	35.3996
21	32.9009	41.6	44.7997	40.6988
25	30.7012	55.4011	23.7006	31.8998
29	45.5996	45.2997	16.5999	38.9002
33	43.7985	47.5984	40.1009	35.4988
37	63.1998	32.1014	66.1021	48.202
41	38.0005	25.0006	41.4008	49.2003
45	59.6981	15.8997	14.3006	

T.ROB

1	70.0984	37.1997	34.5014	40.6013
5	29.6008	23.9005	36.4995	31.3998
9	36.4011	38.6019	45.5996	68.903
13	57.0997	40.6013	44.7012	34.6986
17	28.5998	43.099	27.5995	35.7983
21	49.4024	48.2985	41.4008	26.0991
25	40.2013	21.501	30.4992	30.9014
29	47.6985	39.0015	24.3006	40.1009
33	53.1012	32.7008	43.6019	34.9983
37	39.5	12.1996	56.0027	50.9019
41	48.701	18.9993	56.4977	46.4
45	53.298	23.0001	48.2985	

The Deterrent Effect of Capital Punishment: An Assessment of the Estimates

LAWRENCE R. KLEIN, BRIAN FORST, *and* VICTOR FILATOV

While the very thought of death as a legal penalty may be repugnant to many people, it generally seems to be tolerated under circumstances in which a sufficiently large number of innocent lives are spared. There has been little or no objection, for example, to the killing of persons caught in the act of hijacking airplanes. This is not precisely the same as the execution of a convicted murderer, but it may suggest nonetheless that most people might prefer capital punishment if it were known that executions deterred a sufficiently large number of homicides.

Of course, no one can reasonably claim to know exactly how many homicides would, in fact, be prevented as the result of an execution. The existence of data on executions and homicide does, however, provide an opportunity to estimate the average number of homicides that were deterred (or encouraged) by an execution. Such estimates have indeed been made.

Estimates of this sort ordinarily go no further than graduate seminars and scholarly journals. Estimates of the deterrent effect of capital punishment, however, have been introduced as evidence before the United States Supreme Court.[1] Hence, the empirical aspect of the issue has quite literally become a matter of life or death—certainly for death row inmates and quite possibly for potential victims.

Lawrence R. Klein is Benjamin Franklin Professor of Economics and Finance, Department of Economics, University of Pennsylvania; Brian Forst is Director of Research, Institute for Law and Social Research, Washington, D.C.; and Victor Filatov is a graduate student, Department of Economics, University of Pennsylvania.

[1]*Fowler v. North Carolina,* Case No. 73-7031, U.S. Supreme Court term beginning in October 1974; also five cases (Nos. 74-6257, 75-5394, 75-5491, 75-5706, and 75-5844) in the 1975 term.

It is the primary purpose of this paper to review the prominent analyses that have been done in this area of inquiry. These studies are by no means in agreement. We then address the major methodological issues raised by these studies, with emphasis on a time-series analysis by Isaac Ehrlich that has become a subject of particular controversy. We conclude with an assessment of the suitability of presenting available estimates as a basis for judicial or legislative decisions about capital punishment.

I. A REVIEW OF THE LITERATURE

Theories about the deterrent value of punishment are two centuries old at the very least. A much earlier belief in the deterrence theory may be suggested by the especially public nature of executions and lesser punishments in imperial Rome, medieval Europe, and elsewhere. Cesare Beccaria, who argued against capital punishment in the 18th century in *Dei Delettie Dele Pene,* was nonetheless among the first to reason: "It is better to prevent crimes, than to punish them." Jeremy Bentham argued later in the same century in *The Rationale of Punishment* that punishments should be designed to discourage greater "evil," under the premise that each person behaves according to a "felicific calculus."

A. THE WORK OF THORSTEN SELLIN

A paucity of data and limited computational capabilities prevented empirical tests of the deterrence theory of punishment until the 1950s. The first important statistical investigation of the deterrent effect of punishment, by Thorsten Sellin (1959), focused on the death penalty. Sellin's study is significant also because it provided no support for the deterrence hypothesis.

Sellin's method consisted primarily of comparing homicide rates over time between contiguous states, some with statutes permitting executions, others with laws abolishing capital punishment. He attempted to control for other factors by matching states that were as nearly alike as possible except for the legal status of capital punishment. Sellin concluded:

> Within each group of states having similar social and economic conditions and populations, it is impossible to distinguish the abolition state from the others. . . . The inevitable conclusion is that executions have no discernable effect on homicide death rates (p. 34).

Sellin's study has been both praised and criticized for its simplicity. Baldus and Cole (1975) regard it as a study that provides a more reliable basis for drawing inferences about the deterrent effect of capital punishment than a more recent study that was "statistically more sophisticated" (p. 173). The Solicitor General of the United States (Bork *et al.* 1974), on the other hand, has faulted Sellin's work for its failure "to hold constant factors other than the death penalty that might influence the rate of murders" (p. 37).

Sellin's analysis has been criticized also by Peck (1976) for its essentially subjective selection of states under comparison and its failure to separate the deterrent effect of executions on homicides from the reverse effect of changes in homicides on the demand for executions.

B. THE WORK OF ISAAC EHRLICH

Perhaps the strongest attempt at refutation of Sellin's work has come from Isaac Ehrlich, who writes that "the statistical methods used by Sellin and others to infer the nonexistence of the deterrent effect of capital punishment do not provide an acceptable test of such an effect and consequently do not warrant such inferences" (1975a, p. 398). Ehrlich has criticized Sellin's analysis along several lines, including those by the Solicitor General and Peck cited above (Ehrlich 1975a, pp. 411, 415; 1975b, pp. 221-224). Ehrlich adds that Sellin's analysis is flawed by its having ignored the extent of use of capital punishment in those states where it had not been abolished—he criticizes Sellin for drawing strong conclusions from the similarity of homicide rates in retentionist states and adjacent abolitionist states when, in fact, many of Sellin's retentionist states rarely used capital punishment (1975b, pp. 222-223).[2]

Ehrlich also formulated an elaborate theory, following that of Gary Becker. This theory "emphasizes the interaction between offense and defense—the supply of and the (negative) social demand for murder" (1975a, p. 398). A fundamental element of this analysis is that it "rests on the presumption that offenders respond to incentives" (p. 415). Ehrlich's theory leads eventually to his asserting that the deterrent effect of executions "must be identified empirically through appropriate simultaneous equation estimation techniques" (p. 406).

[2]This criticism may be too strong, since the perception of the risk of execution in a retentionist state that only rarely uses capital punishment may greatly exceed that in an abolitionist state, even though the relative frequencies of execution are similar in the two states—identically zero in one and nearly zero in the other.

His first empirical test of this theory is based on a regression analysis of aggregate United States data for the individual years 1932-1970.[3] This analysis is extraordinary at least insofar as it employs a vast array of manipulations: to create values of missing data, to test alternative time-lag structures, to reduce bias or efficiency loss associated with autoregressive disturbances, to avoid undefined values of the independent variable of central interest, and to test alternative systems of simultaneity.[4] An end product of this exercise is the statement (Ehrlich 1975a, p. 398):

> In fact, the empirical analysis suggests that on the average the tradeoff between the execution of an offender and the lives of potential victims it might have saved was of the order of magnitude of 1 for 8 for the period 1933-67 in the United States.

Ehrlich arrives at this conclusion by way of his "murder supply function:"

$$\frac{Q}{N} = kP_a^{\alpha_1} P_{c/a}^{\alpha_2} P_{e/c}^{\alpha_3} U^{\beta_1} L^{\beta_2} Y_p^{\beta_3} A^{\beta_4} \exp(v_1), \tag{1}$$

where Q/N is the homicide rate, k is a constant, P_a is the probability of apprehension, $P_{c/a}$ is the conditional probability of conviction of murder given apprehension, $P_{e/c}$ is the probability of execution given conviction, U is the unemployment rate of the civilian labor force, L is the labor force participation rate of the adult civilian population, Y_p is an estimate of real per capita income, A is the proportion of the residential population in the age-group 14-24, and v_1 is the disturbance term (pp. 406, 408). He finds data for the construction of each variable in equa-

[3] A second empirical test reported by Ehrlich (1975b, p. 217) but not yet published is based on two cross-sectional analyses of the United States—one using 1940 state data and the other using 1950 data.

[4] Specifically, values of missing data were produced via auxiliary regressions (Ehrlich 1975a, pp. 409, 412), using both linear and geometric interpolation techniques; alternative time lags were produced under linear and nonlinear distributed lag regressions (p. 408); the coefficient of serial correlation was estimated by way of the Cochrane-Orcutt iterative procedure (p. 410), with associated parameters estimated via Ray Fair's nonlinear three-round estimation procedure (p. 406); the arbitrarily selected number 1 was used to replace the observed value 0 in three instances in which Ehrlich took the logarithm of the probability of execution variable (p. 409); and the conditional probability of execution variable was treated alternatively as predetermined and endogenous (pp. 408, 410). The parameters of primary interest result from his regressing modified first differences of murder rates, in natural logarithms, on corresponding modified first differences of selected variables (p. 410).

tion (1) toward the estimation of α_3, the elasticity of the murder rate with respect to the conditional probability of execution.

C. ASSESSMENTS OF EHRLICH'S ANALYSIS

Ehrlich's study received considerable attention once it was introduced to the Supreme Court, by the Solicitor General of the United States, as evidence in support of capital punishment (Bork *et al.* 1974, pp. 35-38). It is surely accurate to state that Ehrlich's analysis has become controversial and has been attacked on several different fronts.

Passell and Taylor (1975) were among the first to criticize Ehrlich's regression estimates. They attempted to replicate his findings and were unable to do so up to rounding errors, although they have come close in most cases. They discovered nonetheless that their own estimates of the effect of changes in the execution rate on the homicide rate were quite sensitive to whether the regression equation was log linear or linear

$$\frac{Q}{N} = b_o + b_1 \cdot P_a + b_2 \cdot P_{c/a} + b_3 \cdot P_{e/c} + \cdots \quad (2)$$

as in eq.(1). In particular, they obtained a significant negative relationship between Q/N and $P_{e/c}$ (i.e., the appearance of a deterrent effect of executions on homicides) under Ehrlich's multiplicative form and a positive insignificant relationship under an additive model (pp. 6-8). They reported also that the finding of a deterrent effect did not hold up when the years after 1962 were excluded from the analysis (pp. 5, 21, 22).

A second attempt to replicate Ehrlich's work was reported by Bowers and Pierce (1975). Like Passell and Taylor, they obtained a much stronger appearance of a deterrent effect under the log-linear form than under the linear form (pp. 199-205). Also like Passell and Taylor, they obtained results consistent with the deterrence hypothesis only when data from the latter half of the 1960's were included in the analysis (pp. 197-202). Nor were Bowers and Pierce able to replicate Ehrlich's findings precisely. In addition, Bowers and Pierce faulted Ehrlich for his choice of data sources (pp. 187-189), specifically with respect to his use of FBI rather than Vital Statistics data.

D. CROSS-SECTIONAL ANALYSES

Sellin's study of selected pairs of states and Ehrlich's time-series analysis of aggregate United States data represent two fundamentally different empirical approaches to the testing of the hypothesis that capital punishment deters homicide. Regional effects are explicitly accounted for in Sellin's work and ignored in the time-series analysis. Ehrlich's time-series study, on the other hand, attempts to isolate a pure deterrent effect of capital punishment by controlling explicitly for the effects of other variables, including alternative sanction variables; by accounting for simultaneity among the offensive and defensive aspects of homicide; and by measuring the magnitude of the execution rate, under several alternative constructions. The advantages cited here of each of these studies appear at the same time to be weaknesses of the other.

A recent study by Peter Passell (1975) has attempted to overcome these weaknesses by applying econometric techniques to cross-state data. This general approach provides the potential for a more thoroughly controlled estimate of the effect of changes in executions on homicides not only by way of the existence of large inter-regional variation in several of the included variables, the incorporation of a regional dummy variable, and a corresponding reduction in aggregation bias, but also by way of the opportunity to include a term-of-imprisonment variable, which is not available in time-series. We shall say more about this potentially important substitute sanction for capital punishment in a following section on omitted variables.

Passell tested the deterrence hypothesis using a model similar to those put forward by Becker and Ehrlich.[5] He reported separate results based on 1950 data for 41 states and 1960 data for 44 states (Passell, p. 66), using both ordinary least squares (OLS) and two-stage least squares (2SLS) estimation techniques (pp. 69-77), for both the linear and log-linear models (pp. 69-73), and using alternative constructions of the execution rate variable (pp. 77-78). Passell found five variables to be related systematically to the homicide offense rate: the homicide conviction rate, the average term of incarceration for convicted murderers, poverty, age, and racial migration. He summarized his findings for the execution rate variable as follows: "Students of capital punishment must look elsewhere for evidence confirming deterrence. We know of

[5]See Becker 1975, pp. 176-179; Ehrlich 1973, pp. 524-543; Ehrlich 1975a, pp. 398-406; and Passell 1975, pp. 64-66.

no reasonable way of interpreting the cross-section data that would lend support to the deterrence hypothesis'' (p. 80).[6]

These cross-section results provide a useful complement to the aggregate national time-series analysis. By analogy with econometric analysis in more conventional economic settings, this is a common procedure. We often look at given problems from the point of view of cross-section analysis in econometrics. In the present context, state-to-state variation in homicide rates and execution rates are suggested with a similar or possibly amplified set of other variables, and it is necessary to think through the parametric specification as well as the classification of variables into endogenous and exogenous categories.

Sellin's analysis (1959) is, in effect, a cross-section analysis, but it is not a parametric regression analysis, and it is not multivariate to the degree needed for comparison with the time-series results. Sellin's findings, however, together with Passell's, prompt us to contrast the cross-section and time-series cases.

The failure of these cross-section studies to find a significant negative deterrent effect is similar to discrepancies that have arisen in econometric investigations of consumer spending. In national time-series samples, there is evidence of significant positive association, at the margin, between an index of consumer attitudes and spending on durable goods; but in cross-section samples, with family-to-family variation, this same effect cannot readily be found. This lack of correspondence between the time-series and cross-section findings has always cast some doubt on the validity of the former. It has also been the case that significant time-series effects have not always carried over from sample to extrapolation. There have been serious enough reversals in appraisals of the macro-economy through methods based on time-series that we may be led by analogy to mistrust the policy extrapolation of Ehrlich's time-series results in the absence of cross section as well as other confirmations of his findings.

[6]We find no serious problems with the Passell paper. The analysis appears fairly straightforward, with generally adequate robustness tests. It does not address the potential problem of heteroscedasticity, a not uncommon problem in cross-sectional analyses, and reports only unweighted regression results. This could have distorted the estimated standard errors of the regression coefficients, but ought not to have altered the positive sign for the execution rate variable. We have not attempted to check Passell's calculations, and so cannot attest to their accuracy. Isaac Ehrlich has also analyzed cross-state data and reports having found once again that capital punishment deters murder (1975b, p. 217). We do not explore the differences between Passell's cross-state results and Ehrlich's, prior to the publication of Ehrlich's paper. One cannot help but be puzzled, however, that two apparently similar approaches would yield such strikingly different findings.

II. THE EHRLICH MODEL AND SOME METHODOLOGICAL ISSUES

The deterrence problem examined in Ehrlich's time-series analysis is not strictly an econometric problem, and the methods used are not strictly econometric. There are various analogies to econometrics, but references to the methods of econometrics should not be used in support of the findings, and it should be remarked that the analogy to econometric method is not fully implemented—that being a strong reservation about some of the conclusions that are drawn.

Ehrlich's problem is one of generalized regression. The use of nonexperimental data and the attempt to deal with simultaneity give some superficial resemblances to econometrics. Ehrlich (1975a, p. 399) lays out a model of rational behavior for:

> . . . analysis of the incentive to commit murder and other crimes against the person by explicitly incorporating into the model the uncertainties associated with the prospective punishments for crime.

His theoretical model is much like that used to derive specifications for demand and supply functions in the economic analysis of consumption and production. In that respect, we find his theory strongly contrived, i.e., set up in an essentially imitative way vis à vis the design of economic theory that is used to generate specifications of econometric models. We have doubts about the insight that this approach is likely to bring to an understanding of criminal behavior. There is much to be said for an investigation that links together economic, criminological, and other sociological aspects of behavior, but this is not to suggest that the analysis start from some rational utility analysis of criminal behavior that is designed to look like the standard model of rational utility analysis of economic behavior.

A much more fruitful approach would seem to be the methodology used in the smoking-cancer link studies. These do not attempt to lock the analysis into a utility calculus or some other limited set of specifications. In using such a technique, greater scope could be given to the exploration of effects of other variables, possibly subjective in character, to allow for emotional behavior and other social phenomena.

Apart from all the trappings of a utility theory of the incentive to commit murder, Ehrlich specifies a fairly common aggregative model, with no formal bridge between the microcosmic utility analysis and national supply function. The aspects of this function that resemble econometrics are:

1. Some of the variables are interdependent; the empirical estimates of probabilities of arrest, conviction given arrest, and execution given conviction are assumed to be mutually dependent
2. Other variables are assumed to be exogenous, or independent
3. The stochastic part of the murder supply function is assumed to be serially correlated, following a first-order autoregressive process

Econometric models are generally designed so that they consist of some mutually dependent (endogenous) variables and some independent (exogenous) variables. The equations of such models are usually assumed to be linear in unknown parameters with additive stochastic parts that satisfy a first-order autoregressive process.

This is the substance of the econometrics of the model specification. The economic variables of the model are classified in the exogenous set and contribute nothing to the interdependence of the model that is usually characteristic of econometric systems. An interesting research challenge nowadays is to integrate economic and sociological systems with mutual feedback or interdependence between the sociological (or criminological) variables and the economic variables. Such an approach is lacking in the Ehrlich model; he assumes that economic factors affect criminal behavior but that criminal factors do not affect economic behavior through the economic variables that he has selected. This is certainly a drawback to the generality of his approach.

Given the specification of the single equation—some interdependent variables and autoregressive errors—Ehrlich followed the latest and best econometric practice in estimating the parameters of the equation. These generalized regression methods would be recommended whether the model were an econometric one or not, as long as it had the structure specified above by Ehrlich.

The two-stage least squares method used by Ehrlich takes account of the interdependence aspect, while the serial correlation adjustment takes account of the autoregressive aspect. None of the estimated autoregressive parameters is very large, and some are quite small. In such circumstances, the autoregressive corrections are superfluous and may even lead to poorer estimates if used when they are not needed. This aspect of best econometric practice might well have been avoided in several cases, at least. The two-stage type of estimator is all right for the problem but probably contributes much less to the claimed superiority of Ehrlich's estimates than the reader may be brought to believe.

In fact, the real contribution to the strength of Ehrlich's statistical findings lies in the simple graph of the upsurge of the homicide rate after 1962, coupled with the fall in the execution rate in the same period. The whole statistical story lies in this simple pairing of these observations and not in the theoretical utility model, the econometric type specification, or the use of best econometric method. Everything else is relatively superficial and dominated by this simple statistical observation.

A. OMITTED VARIABLES

This leaves us with the question: Did the decline and eventual ending of executions during the 1960's cause some portion of the sharp increase in the homicide rate, or would the homicide rate have increased at least as much anyway?

To address this question, we can first acknowledge the obvious, that ending the practice of capital punishment in the 1960's does not constitute a controlled experiment from which one can safely draw conclusions about deterrence by observing only homicides and executions. Factors other than the ending of capital punishment surely affected the homicide rate during this period. Ehrlich's use of explanatory factors other than the execution probability in equation (1) is an explicit recognition of this fact. What may be less obvious is that the omission of factors other than those used by Ehrlich to "control" his analysis may have contributed to his finding a negative relationship between the homicide rate and the execution probability.[7] Some of the factors omitted by Ehrlich have, in fact, been found previously to affect crime rates.

For example, Ehrlich himself found in an earlier (1973) study that long prison sentences, the conventional alternative to capital punishment, serve as an effective crime deterrent. This factor was omitted from Ehrlich's time-series analysis because of the unavailability of data. To the extent that his previous analysis is correct and to the extent that the length of prison sentences declined during the 1960's, Ehrlich's attributing the increase in homicides to the elimination of capital punishment could be erroneous.

We do find evidence that the actual time served in prison, both for homicides and for other offenses that often result in homicide, did indeed decline in the 1960s. Based on *National Prisoner Statistics*

[7]We are grateful to Isaac Ehrlich and William Landes for reminding us that some of the omitted variables may have worked to understate the estimated deterrent effect of capital punishment. We refer here to the *net* effect of the omission of all other factors on the deterrence estimates.

figures for the 33 states that reported in both 1960 and 1970, we find that 46.8 percent of the prisoners released in 1960 who had been convicted of homicides had served at least 5 years; only 35.8 percent of those released in 1970, imprisoned for the same offenses, had served that long. The computer that printed out a significant negative regression coefficient for Ehrlich's execution variable might not have done so had it known that terms of incarceration for murders became more lenient during the 1960's.

Other factors omitted from Ehrlich's regression model also appear to have contributed to the increase in the homicide rate during this period. One of these is the availability of guns. The contribution of handguns to the murder upsurge of the 1960's has been indicated in a study by Newton and Zimring (1969). Phillips, in addition, has reported that from 1961 to 1970 the rate of murders with firearms increased from 2.5 to 6.1 per 100,000 persons (Phillips 1973). It is likely that increased gun possession may partly follow a relaxation in punishment, but gun possession is sure to have grown during the period for other reasons as well, such as the increased availability of inexpensive foreign models.

The importance of the omitted variables problem may be seen in another way. Crime increased generally during the 1960's. Some of the increase is no doubt due to factors measured by Ehrlich and some to yet other factors. It is sobering to note that while the FBI reported murders and non-negligent manslaughters to have increased by 74 percent from 1960 to 1970, burglaries increased by 142 percent, auto thefts by 183 percent, and larcenies ($50 and over) by 245 percent. Of these four crime categories, the only one potentially deterrable by capital punishment is the one that showed the most modest gain, even though executions came to a halt by 1967. This suggests to us that the strength of Ehrlich's statistical relationships between executions and homicides depends significantly on changes during this recent decade in variables omitted from the analysis, variables that would explain the increase in crime generally.[8]

[8]That Ehrlich's time series results depend upon the inclusion of the years since 1964 is clearly due to temporal heterogeneity, rather than to the loss of degrees of freedom in excluding the recent years. Ehrlich has reported results that indicate that his deterrence estimates are not weakened by the exclusion of the eight observations, 1933 through 1940 (Ehrlich 1975a, p. 410). He also indicated that the deterrent effect disappears when data from the six years 1964 through 1969 are excluded from the analysis (Ehrlich 1975b, p. 217).

B. NEGATIVE BIAS IN THE EXECUTION MEASURE

Ehrlich indicates in a footnote (1975a, p. 207) that he calculated his execution rate variable, $P_{e/c}$ as

$$P_{e/c} = \frac{E}{\hat{C}} = \frac{E}{Q \cdot P_a \cdot P_{c/a}} \tag{3}$$

where $\hat{C}$ is the estimated number of convictions, Q is the reported number of murders and non-negligent manslaughters, and P_a and $P_{c/a}$ are as defined in equation (1).

The use of Q both as the numerator of the homicide rate and as part of the denominator of the execution rate could have biased Ehrlich's estimate of the regression coefficient for $P_{e/c}$ toward the appearance of a deterrent effect. It is immediately apparent that any errors in the measurement of the true number of homicides could cause Q/N and $P_{e/c}$ to move in opposite directions. Sources of error in Ehrlich's measure of Q, based on FBI homicide statistics, have been thoroughly discussed by Hindelang (1974, pp. 2-5).[9]

What may not be so apparent is the magnitude of this bias, even for small errors in the measurement of homicides. If the homicide rate were in fact totally insensitive to changes in the execution rate, measurement errors even as small as those caused by Ehrlich's having used a homicide series rounded to the nearest 10 murders would have biased his estimate of this key relationship toward a negative unit elasticity.[10] That Ehrlich has estimated elasticities for $P_{e/c}$ considerably nearer to zero than to -1 could be regarded as evidence that the true elasticity is positive, indicating a counterdeterrent effect of capital punishment.

One might suspect that this bias would be diminished under constructions of $P_{e/c}$ that do not use current values of Q directly. In fact, not all of Ehrlich's constructions of $P_{e/c}$ use the immediate values of

[9]For example, some murders and non-negligent manslaughters are never discovered, others are not reported to local authorities as such, local jurisdictions may define these terms differently, and some jurisdictions do not report to the FBI.

[10]This can be seen by solving for values of E that force $P_{e/c}$ to be constant, such as the mean value Ehrlich computes for $P_{e/c}$ (which happens to be 0.0259, but any constant will do), and then adding a random disturbance term (distributed normally with mean zero) to Q in both the homicide rate and the execution rate. Under certain conditions worked out by Daniel Nagin (in this volume), the random disturbance terms will cause each k percent increase (or decrease) in $P_{e/c}$ to correspond with a k percent decrease (or increase) in Q/N, giving an elasticity of -1.

Q.[11] To test whether this bias is lessened when the current value of Q is not used directly to form the denominator of $P_{e/c}$, we have tested the effect of adding noise to Q in amounts that average 2 percent of Q, distributed normally, and use these values within the structure of Ehrlich's equation (6), from Table 3 (1975a, p. 410).[12] Equation (6) uses $P_{e/c}$ constructed as an endogenous variable, so that current values of Q are not used directly in the estimate here. The result of this exercise is an estimated elasticity of -1.01 for the execution rate variable, which is consistent with our prediction of the previous paragraph.

This is by no means the only source of bias produced by Ehrlich's method of estimating values for $P_{e/c}$. We have found that another source of bias results from his having P_a and $P_{c/a}$ comprise part of the denominator of $P_{e/c}$ and having them serve also as separate explanatory variables. If these variables were all measured with perfect accuracy, they would be correlated with one another at least to the extent that they are substitute sanctions within the criminal justice system. They will surely be artificially correlated due to measurement errors, under Ehrlich's construction of $P_{e/c}$.[13]

We find that if P_a and $P_{c/a}$ were both measured with a mean random error as small as 2 percent, a deterrence elasticity of -0.05 would be produced even if, in fact, no relationship existed between the homicide rate and the conditional execution probability. If Ehrlich's estimates were accurate in every other respect, this bias alone would lead one to conclude that his estimates provide no support to the deterrence hypothesis. While it is often the case that measurement errors bias the regression coefficient toward zero, we have here a situation in which

[11]Ehrlich has informed us through correspondence that concern about this bias was a primary motivation for these alternative constructions.

[12]This test consisted of using the basic data that produced a replication of equation (6), up to rounding errors; using the values of Q, P_a, and $P_{c/a}$ in this data and solving for values of E, for each observation, such that $P_{e/c}$ would equal its mean value, .0259; setting E equal to these solved values, a sufficient condition for producing artificially the circumstance of no effect of $P_{e/c}$ on Q/N; adding 2 percent mean noise to Q in both $P_{e/c}$ and Q/N to get new values of $P_{e/c}$ and Q/N; forming the endogenous counterpart to these revised values of $P_{e/c}$; and reestimating equation (6) with this counterpart and the original data for the other variables in the model.

[13]Errors are indeed evident. For example, Ehrlich created artificial values for $P_{c/a}$ for the years 1933, 1934, 1935, and 1961, for which data were missing. Errors are indicated also by visual inspection. It is not easy to explain, for instance, how factors other than measurement error could have caused the true probability of conviction given arrest for murder to have increased from 0.258 to 0.496 from 1936 to 1939. In addition, evidence has been presented by Bowers and Pierce (1975) that the FBI's estimates of arrests and convictions are based on nonrandom samples, with response rates that vary considerably over the period 1933 to 1969 (pp. 190-191).

errors in three crucial variables—Q, P_a, and $P_{c/a}$—all appear to work in such a way as to bias the coefficient of $P_{e/c}$ negatively.[14]

C. ALTERNATIVE MODELS

A more complete theoretical model specification ought to go in two directions:

1. Imbed the murder decision in a more general model of criminal behavior
2. Integrate the economic and sociological or criminological variables into a more general model of behavior

The criminal who commits murder may also have a propensity to commit other crimes. On the occasion of carrying out a criminal act, the final murder decision may be quite impulsive, but the criminal may weigh the penalty associated with a more serious crime against that associated with a less serious crime. A plausible mode of behavior may be one in which armed robbery will be carried out without murder if at all possible because the penalty, without murder, is less severe; therefore, murder will be committed only in an act of desperation. In such a situation, the murder decision depends not only on penalties associated with homicide but also with other lesser crimes. In this case, we write:

$$Q/N = f(P_a, P_{c/a}, P_{e/c}, \ldots q_a, q_{c/a}, \ldots)$$

where q_a and $q_{c/a}$ are probabilities of arrest and conviction given arrest associated with other crimes. There may be several such arguments in f.

The model is incomplete not only with respect to other variables affecting the murder decision but also with respect to the behavior of the law enforcement system. The whole point of casting the problem in a simultaneous equations mode is to consider jointly the actions of all the decision makers involved. If Q/N and $P_{e/c}$ are to be mutually dependent, the decision of the judicial system (subject to public opinion and many other factors) about the rules for the invocation of the death penalty must be simultaneously modeled. It is plausible to suggest that decisions about $P_{e/c}$ depend on the frequency of homicide and many

[14]Although we have not explicitly estimated the extent to which small errors in the measurement of P_a and $P_{c/a}$ also bias the elasticities Ehrlich estimates for these variables, due to multicollinearity with $P_{e/c}$, we are led by this analysis to question his estimates of these elasticities, too.

other factors—notably society's ethical and moral values. We might write

$$P_{e/c} = g(Q/N, S, \ldots)$$

where S stands for societal values. Other variables, too, enter the g-function, but the whole process is not investigated by Ehrlich.

This means that the use of the two-stage-least-squares method as an estimation procedure might start from quite a different reduced form expression. Many exogenous variables in the system (S, for one) are candidates for inclusion. Without careful investigation, the problem is pretty much open at this stage. Ehrlich could argue, of course, that he has selected a subset of the relevant exogenous variables and consequently has obtained consistent estimates, but that is hardly an adequate stand in a small-sample situation such as the one at hand. There are, undoubtedly, significant small-sample biases associated with omission of relevant exogenous variables from the entire model.

In addition, variables representing other arrest/conviction rates could have been included as endogenous variables. These variables may not be readily measured with decent accuracy, but there is a way around this complication—namely, to introduce frequency of occurrence of other crimes in place of their penalty rates. In the theory of demand in economics, we may use the whole price vector as arguments or develop "mixed demand functions" with own penalties (prices) and other crime rates (quantities) as the arguments. In two-stage estimations for such an enlarged system, the reduced forms should include the specific exogenous variables from the behavioral equations associated with the other crimes.[15] It is quite evident that Ehrlich has only scratched the surface in serious model building and has a long way to go in order to establish his results as definitive.

Economic variables affect crime rates. It makes good sense to include labor force participation, income, and unemployment rate in the equation for Q/N. The same is true of police and other government

[15]There is an additional justification for including the rate or frequency of other crimes—doing so is likely to reduce the distortions produced by omitted variables. We have noted earlier that if the factors that caused crime generally to increase during the period on which Ehrlich's deterrence finding depends had been included, the estimated deterrent effect might have been quite different. The rate at which other crimes are committed might serve as a useful proxy for these factors.

expenditures. But do crime rates—the murder rate in particular—have an impact on the economy? Ehrlich assumes that they do not, but we think otherwise. For example, an increase in crime rates might cause a wave of business closures and could thereby increase unemployment rates. There is little doubt that police expenditures are influenced by Q/N. Although, in a purely formal sense, police expenditures for the previous year are used in Ehrlich's model, the exogeneity of such a variable cannot be established by a dating mechanism alone. At the macro level, there are many avenues for establishing relationships between crime rates and the unemployment rate. Crime of all sorts, including homicide, can impede the smooth functioning of the economy and thus affect unemployment or labor force participation.

Students of econometrics ought to learn very early that significant economic conclusions can rarely be drawn from estimates of single equations, much less from single parameters. Partial analysis is all right for giving empirical content to some piece of economic structure, but it is hardly ever adequate to the problem of policy formation. In the present case, where very serious national legal policy is being considered, it would be a travesty of model building to use only part of the necessary analysis to come to strong conclusions about a complete system problem. The problem being considered is serious enough that there is no compelling reason to try to draw a conclusion in a hurry from premature analysis.

In a separate paper critically examining Ehrlich's work, Passell and Taylor (1975) introduce the important distinction between a structural equation and the reduced form of a system. They also show that the relevant coefficient within the single equation is not simply the coefficient of execution given conviction, because the dependent variable, the number of murders, appears also in the denominator of another dependent explanatory variable—namely, the arrest rate. The partial variation of murders, Q, with respect to execution, E, can go either way, i.e., positive or negative—large or small—depending on the joint variation of the arrest rate with the execution rate. That, however, is the whole point of simultaneous equation construction and estimation. It is extremely important to examine covariation between Q and E through the workings of complete system solutions and not through examination of isolated parameters or isolated equations. Ehrlich estimates an unrestricted reduced form regression to cope with this problem, but his reduced form is not derived from complete system construction and is not the appropriate equation through which to examine the total effect of E on Q.

III. THE EMPIRICAL RESULTS

An important issue in the debate over Ehrlich's findings has been the matter of replicability. The degree to which other investigators have been able to reproduce Ehrlich's results has been substantial, but not quite satisfying, in the sense that they have found approximately the same numerical estimates of coefficients, but not exactly the same. The discrepancies cannot be safely attributed to round-off error, the use of different computer programs (for the same estimators), or the use of different hardware. We are happy to report, however, that we can reproduce Ehrlich's main results up to round-off error, using his own data series, which he has kindly made available to one of the present authors. Other investigators have approximated some of his statistical series but have not used identical data, and results with fairly small samples (fewer than 35 observations in the present case) are often sensitive to small numerical changes in data.

For example, Ehrlich's equation (1) (Table 3) compares with our estimate as follows:

$$\Delta^*Q/N =$$

$$\begin{array}{l} -3.176 - 1.553\Delta^*\hat{P}^o_a - 0.455\Delta^*\hat{P}^o_{c/a} - 0.039\Delta^*PXQ_1 - 1.336\Delta^*L \\ -3.238 - 1.537\Delta^*\hat{P}^o_a - 0.457\Delta^*\hat{P}^o_{c/a} - 0.039\Delta^*PXQ_1 - 1.341\Delta^*L \end{array}$$

$$\begin{array}{l} + 0.630\Delta^*A + 1.481\Delta^*Y_p + 0.067\Delta^*U - 0.047\Delta^*T \\ + 0.633\Delta^*A + 1.481\Delta^*Y_p + 0.067\Delta^*U - 0.047\Delta^*T \end{array}$$

The top row of coefficients is taken from Ehrlich's Table 3, while the figures in the bottom row are taken from our computer sheets. The discrepancy in the constant term is associated with a slight difference in the origin for chronological time. The variables have the same meaning as in Ehrlich's article—namely, all are measured as natural logarithms except T and all are modified first differences, i.e., autoregressive transformations of the original variables, measured in logarithmic units. Similar results have been obtained for Ehrlich's equations (2) and (6) as well.

These coefficients are all the same, except for round-off error, as Ehrlich's, but his estimate of the residual variance is high. He reports the square root of this estimate as 0.052, while we calculate it as 0.047. The t-statistics associated with his estimated coefficients should have been correspondingly larger. His arguments about statistical significance—not magnitude of effect—are, therefore, weaker than they should be.

We cannot emphasize enough that the fact that we replicated his results in itself gives no support to his conclusions.[16] This replication serves only to ensure that our sensitivity tests are valid. If we did not perform these tests on an accurate replication of Ehrlich's data and methodology, we would have no assurance that the tests were really isolating the effects of specific model perturbations on the findings.

A. TEMPORAL HETEROGENEITY

It was remarked earlier that the major statistical contribution to Ehrlich's results on the strength of the deterrent effect of capital punishment (i.e., execution by implementation of the death sentence) on the occurrence of homicides was the rise in the murder rate since 1962, coupled with the falling off in the implementation of capital punishment. It is possible to argue, in line with Ehrlich's findings, that the former was produced by the latter. But if the death penalty were really a basic deterrent, it should have acted as such in other periods as well, taking into account the whole range of variables being considered. The principal argument against changing the sample to investigate only the period up to 1962 is that valuable statistical observations are lost—not simply the observations that make the case, but observations that contribute in a general way to the overall number of degrees of freedom, which are precious and in short supply for analysis of the problem at hand.

Other investigators, particularly Passell and Taylor, have also made calculations dealing with the possibility that Ehrlich's results would not stand up in sample variations that dealt differently with the period after 1962. It is worthwhile reporting our own, however, since we are closer to a replication of Ehrlich's primary result, having the advantage of working with his own data set. We find that the truncated sample, 1935-1962, leads to a slightly smaller and statistically insignificant coefficient of the crucial execution variable. Our result is for the specification in Ehrlich's equation (6).

[16]Ehrlich has regarded previous replications as strong support of the deterrence hypothesis. He writes, for example (1975b, p. 210):

> First and foremost, the Bowers and Pierce work, however inadvertently, has lent considerable strength to the case for the deterrent effect of capital punishment, because their application of the theory and econometric methods outlined in my paper over the entire period considered in my analysis produces results quite similar to my own.

This opinion assumes that Ehrlich's theory and empirical methods produce accurate estimates of the deterrence effect, which, of course, begs the basic issue addressed by those who have attempted to replicate his results.

$$\Delta^*Q/N = \underset{(2.089)}{-6.891} - \underset{(0.424)}{0.358\Delta^*\hat{P}^o_a} - \underset{(0.084)}{0.304\Delta^*\hat{P}^o_{c/a}} - \underset{(0.048)}{0.046\Delta^*P\hat{X}Q_1}$$

$$- \underset{(0.550)}{2.514\Delta^*L} + \underset{(0.160)}{0.280\Delta^*A} + \underset{(0.208)}{0.951\Delta^*Y_p}$$

$$+ \underset{(0.017)}{0.029\Delta^*U} - \underset{(0.008)}{0.036\Delta^*T}$$

$$R^2 = 0.967 \quad SE = 0.027 \quad \hat{\rho} = 0.015 \quad D = 1.59$$

The corresponding estimates of the key coefficient ($\Delta^*P\hat{X}Q_1$) in Ehrlich's equation (6) is −0.059 with a *t*-ratio of −1.73. It appears, therefore, that the deterrent effect does not show up as significantly in the period before 1962 as in the whole period that combines both pre- and post-1962 values for within-sample contrast.

It is not as though the combination of pre- and post-1962 data accounted for the significance of the coefficient of the execution variable at all, for it has had a sharp relationship after 1962. If we combine both parts of the sample together, into one overall equation specification with a "dummy" variable *D* to designate the period 1963-1969 separately, we get

$$\Delta^*Q/N = \underset{(3.483)}{-6.343} - \underset{(0.073)}{0.305D} - \underset{(0.679)}{0.655\Delta^*\hat{P}^o_a} - \underset{(0.119)}{0.317\Delta^*\hat{P}^o_{c/a}}$$

$$- \underset{(0.055)}{0.059\Delta^*P\hat{X}Q_1} - \underset{(0.054)}{0.099\, D\Delta^*P\hat{X}Q_1} \underset{(0.903)}{-2.214\Delta^*L}$$

$$+ \underset{(0.234)}{0.412\Delta^*A} + \underset{(0.279)}{1.141\Delta^*Y_p} + \underset{(0.026)}{0.045\Delta^*U} - \underset{(0.010)}{0.040\Delta^*T}$$

$$R^2 = 0.909 \quad SE = 0.045 \quad \hat{\rho} = -0.148 \quad D = 1.52$$

This equation suggests that the significance of the coefficient of the execution variable falls (from $t = -1.73$ to $t = -1.07$) if intercept and slope dummy variables are introduced to take account of differences in sample phases, but there are two difficulties with the interpretation of this result:

1. The coefficients of *D* are negative, indicating that in the later period there was a lower propensity to commit murder than in the earlier period. This appears to be counter-intuitive
2. The serial correlation coefficient estimated to account for non-

randomness among residual variation is negative, while it is generally expected that it would be positive

This experimental calculation, thus, is inconclusive because as an overall equation estimate it is not entirely plausible.

B. INTRODUCTION OF OTHER CRIMES

Equally important, in comparison with our investigation of robustness under changes in Ehrlich's sample period, is our consideration of alternative specifications, the most relevant being the joint consideration of other related crimes. We have introduced a measure of a crime index (excluding homicide). This index covers six crimes: rape, robbery, aggravated assault, burglary, larceny-theft, and auto theft. Data on frequency of such crimes are taken from the Uniform Crime Reporting Section of the FBI and are weighted in an average measure by using estimates of seriousness estimated by Wolfgang *et al.* (1972). The weights are, respectively, 0.390, 0.135, 0.227, 0.092, 0.060, and 0.095.

The basic equation, corresponding to Ehrlich's (1), with an index of other crime, CR, added as an endogenous variable, gives the result

$$\begin{aligned}\Delta^* Q/N = \underset{(4.020)}{-6.243} &- \underset{(0.931)}{0.468}\Delta^*\hat{P}^o_a - \underset{(0.151)}{0.342}\Delta^*\hat{P}^o_{c/a} - \underset{(0.023)}{0.025}\Delta^* PXQ_1 \\ &+ \underset{(0.298)}{0.436}\Delta^*\hat{C}R - \underset{(0.860)}{1.216}\Delta^* \mathrm{L} + \underset{(0.315)}{0.425}\Delta^* A + \underset{(0.375)}{1.148}\Delta^* Y_p \\ &+ \underset{(0.035)}{0.038}\Delta^* U - \underset{(0.013)}{0.056}\Delta^* \mathrm{T} \\ R^2 = 0.901 \qquad SE &= 0.045 \qquad \hat{\rho} = 0.341 \qquad D = 1.36\end{aligned}$$

A number of coefficients change statistical status in this estimate, particularly in becoming insignificant, although many of the main features of Ehrlich's equation remain invariant. Nevertheless, the key estimate, for the coefficient of $\Delta^* PXQ_1$, becomes insignificant, as well as dropping in point value. The coefficient of CR, on the other hand, has a slightly lower associated t-ratio than the original estimate of the coefficient of PXQ_1. The result suggests a form of complementarity, not necessarily in the strict sense, between homicide and other criminal acts. For given values of the other variables being considered, the homicide rate is positively associated with a broad crime rate. We do not want to argue in any confident manner about the discovery or uncovering of an alternative effect, but we do argue very strongly that there is sufficient evidence in favor of alternative specifications and alternative judgments about the deterrent effect of the death penalty that one is not justified in drawing policy conclusions from Ehrlich's results.

It is possible to push the present line of investigation a bit further by attempting to distinguish between violent crime (other than homicide) and property crime. The violent category consists of rape, robbery, and aggravated assault among the six listed above. In this case, the effect is even more dramatic. The coefficient of violent crime is very strong and statistically significant, while the deterrent effect of the death penalty practically vanishes:

$$\Delta^*Q/N = \underset{(5.196)}{-0.047} + \underset{(1.093)}{0.331}\Delta^*\hat{P}^o_a - \underset{(0.233)}{0.096}\Delta^*\hat{P}^o_{c/a}$$

$$+ \underset{(0.034)}{0.005}\Delta^*PXQ_1 + \underset{(0.424)}{1.099}\Delta^*V\hat{C}R - \underset{(1.210)}{1.124}\Delta^*L$$

$$- \underset{(0.512)}{0.008}\Delta^*A - \underset{(0.788)}{0.405}\Delta^*Y_p - \underset{(0.062)}{0.052}\Delta^*U - \underset{(0.016)}{0.040}\Delta^*T$$

$$R^2 = 0.723 \qquad SE = 0.066 \qquad \hat{\rho} = 0.566 \qquad D = 1.85$$

The intercorrelation of violent crimes with homicide is so strong that it dominates the relationship to the extent of "crowding out" other effects. This result indicates that there is a complicated interrelationship among various types of crime and that a more detailed system of relationships, sorting out these associations, needs to be worked out before we can feel confident of having found the underlying structure of criminal behavior, particularly homicidal behavior.

In the case of property crime, the use of an index of its occurrence in the basic equation shows so little net effect that it has practically no influence on the estimated coefficients for Ehrlich's specification. It appears to be a case of strongly interrelated aspects of violent criminal behavior that is involved.

C. LINEAR SPECIFICATION

Finally, in our examination of alternative specifications, we have looked (following Passell and Taylor as well as others) at a linear as opposed to a log-linear equation. It is worthwhile repeating this exercise here because we have been able to replicate Ehrlich's results, up to round-off error, with his data. As the others have found, the effect of the death penalty variable on the homicide rate is not significant in a linear form equation with the same variables that Ehrlich used. There is nothing in the statistical nature of our results to lead one to prefer a logarithmic specification, and there is certainly no *a priori* theoretical reason for using a log-linear instead of a straight linear regression. Using the same two-stage least squares estimator, with correction for autoregressive errors, we compute from a "search" algorithm for values of $\hat{\rho}$,

$$\begin{aligned}\Delta^*Q/N = {} & \underset{(0.057)}{0.191} - \underset{(0.000412)}{0.000579}\Delta^*\hat{P}^o_a - \underset{(0.000197)}{0.000517}\Delta\hat{P}^o_{c/a} \\ & - \underset{(0.01070)}{0.000439}\Delta^*PXQ_1 - \underset{(0.076)}{0.256}\Delta^*L + \underset{(0.055)}{0.184}\Delta^*A \\ & + \underset{(0.000019)}{0.000116}\Delta^*Y_p + \underset{(0.000178)}{0.000325}\Delta^*U - \underset{(0.000511)}{0.00317}\Delta^*T\end{aligned}$$

$$R^2 = 0.930 \qquad SE = 0.00225 \qquad \hat{\rho} = 0.245 \qquad D = 1.72$$

As Passell and Taylor emphasize, the principal change in this estimate in comparison with Ehrlich's equation (1) is that the coefficient of PXQ_1 has fallen to insignificance. Ehrlich (1975b, p. 219) reports a linear equation and reaches a different conclusion about the significance of the estimated coefficient of Δ^*PXQ_1, but his estimated value of $\hat{\rho}$ apparently does not produce a (global) minimum sum of squared residuals.[17]

IV. CONCLUSION

The building and use of statistical models of structural relationships in the field of criminal behavior, human capital, and the broader interface between sociological and economic relationships is in its infancy.

[17]We searched over values of ρ between −0.6 and +0.4 in increments of 0.0005. The surface is quite flat over the interval. Double-precision computer calculations on our IBM 370/168 provided standard error estimates—for the second-stage regression equation—of 0.019422 and 0.0019401, with Ehrlich's $\hat{\rho}$ equal to −0.119 and our $\hat{\rho}$ equal to +0.2445, respectively.

Many results look very promising, suggestive, and provocative. We might well classify this research effort as being at the stage that econometric modeling reached in the 1940's and 1950's. A great deal of further painstaking developmental work was necessary to build up econometrics to the point at which the numerical findings ceased to be just interesting from an academic viewpoint and became applicable in public policy analysis. We believe that current results must undergo the same kind of testing and scholarly scrutiny over a period of years before they are ready to be used in an application as serious as the one that is associated with the use of the death penalty.

In the first instance, application might be made to general questions of public policy in the field of criminology—such questions as budgetary allocations for police work, deployment of police personnel, or use of training programs. But it seems unthinkable to us to base decisions on the use of the death penalty on Ehrlich's findings, as the Solicitor General of the United States has urged (Bork *et al.* 1974, pp. 32-39). They simply are not sufficiently powerful, robust, or tested at this stage to warrant use in such an important case. They are as fragile as the most tentative of econometric estimates of parameters, and we know full well how uncertain such results are under extrapolation. It is not that Ehrlich's estimates are demonstrably wrong; it is merely that they are too uncertain and must, at best, be interpreted as tentative at this stage.

There is nothing wrong with Ehrlich's particular numerical findings. His arithmetic is correct; his formulation is imaginative; but application to the most serious of issues is premature. In short, we see too many plausible explanations for his finding a deterrent effect other than the theory that capital punishment deters murder.

Following is a list of reasons that Ehrlich's results cannot be used at this time to pass judgment on the use of the death penalty.

1. The conclusion is being drawn on the basis of the estimate of a single parameter in a single equation. It is standard econometric practice to make policy application judgment on the basis of complete system solutions (simulations). Ehrlich must specify and build his interrelated system before he can try to draw policy conclusions from his work. He may not necessarily come to different conclusions, but there is no way of knowing this in advance.

2. The estimate of the coefficient of the execution variable is not significantly negative if the sample is truncated at 1962, an index of other crimes is introduced in the equation, or the equation is specified in linear form.

3. The absolute value of the estimate of the coefficient of the execution variable may be upwardly biased in an absolute sense, as a result of measurement error.
4. The partial effect of execution on homicides, if computed with allowance for the fact that homicides are used to estimate the arrest rate, is not necessarily significantly negative.
5. Cross-sectional analyses have produced results that are not consistent with the hypothesis that capital punishment deters homicide.

Sellin, Ehrlich, Passell, and others are to be congratulated on opening up a fascinating area of research with much scholarly potential. It remains to pursue this line of research to the point at which it can be used in the future for making important contributions to legal policy. The deterrent effect of capital punishment is definitely not a settled matter, and this is the strongest social scientific conclusion that can be reached at the present time.

REFERENCES

Baldus, D. C., and Cole, J. W. L. (1975) A comparison of the work of Thorsten Sellin and Isaac Ehrlich on the deterrent effect of capital punishment. *Yale Law Journal* 85(2):170-86.

Becker, G. S. (1975) Crime and punishment: an economic approach. *Journal of Political Economy* 78(2):169-217.

Bork (Solicitor General) *et al.* (1974) *Fowler v. North Carolina,* U.S. Supreme Court case no. 73-7031. Brief for U.S. as *amicus curiae*:32-39.

Bowers, W. J., and Pierce, G. L. (1975) The illusion of deterrence in Isaac Ehrlich's research on capital punishment. *Yale Law Journal* 85(2):187-208.

Ehrlich, I. (1973) Participation in illegitimate activities: a theoretical and empirical investigation. *Journal of Political Economy* 81(3):521-65.

Ehrlich, I. (1975a) The deterrent effect of capital punishment: a question of life and death. *American Economic Review* 65(3):397-417.

Ehrlich, I. (1975b) Deterrence: evidence and inference. *Yale Law Journal* 85(2):209-27.

Hindelang, M. J. (1974) The Uniform Crime Reports revisited. *Journal of Criminal Justice* 2(1):1-17.

Newton, G. D., and Zimring, F. E. (1969) *Firearms and Violence in American Life*. Staff report to the National Commission on the Causes and Prevention of Violence. Washington, D.C.: U.S. Government Printing Office.

Passell, P. (1975) The deterrent effect of the death penalty: a statistical test. *Stanford Law Review* 28(1):61-80.

Passell, P., and Taylor, J. B. (1975) The Deterrent Effect of Capital Punishment: Another View. Discussion paper 74-7509. Columbia University Department of Economics.

Peck, J. K. (1976) The deterrent effect of capital punishment: a comment. *Yale Law Journal* 85(3):359-67.

Phillips, L. (1973) Crime control: the case for deterrence. Pages 65-84 in S. Rottenberg, ed., *The Economics of Crime and Punishment*. Washington, D.C.: American Enterprise Institute for Public Policy Research.

Sellin, T. (1959) *The Death Penalty*. Philadelphia: American Law Institute.

Wolfgang, M. E., Figlio, R. M., and Sellin, T. (1972) *Delinquency in a Birth Cohort*. Chicago: University of Chicago Press.

On the Feasibility of Identifying the Crime Function in a Simultaneous Model of Crime Rates and Sanction Levels

FRANKLIN M. FISHER *and* DANIEL NAGIN

I. INTRODUCTION

In recent years, considerable social science research activity has been directed toward empirically estimating the deterrent impact of criminal sanctions. With few exceptions, the analyses have found a negative and often statistically significant association between crime rates and sanction measures such as clearance rates,[1] interpretable as a measure of probability of apprehension given crime; the ratio of imprisonments to crimes, interpretable as a measure of probability of imprisonment given crime; and time served in prison, a measure of severity of punishment given imprisonment (e.g., Gibbs 1968; Ehrlich 1973; and Sjoquist 1973).

While these negative associations are consistent with the hypothesis that deterrence exists at a measurable level, several reviews (Green-

Franklin M. Fisher is Professor of Economics, Department of Economics, Massachusetts Institute of Technology, and Daniel Nagin is Assistant Professor of Policy Sciences, Institute of Policy Sciences and Public Affairs, Duke University.

NOTE: Contributions by Daniel Nagin were partially supported by PHS research grant no. 1 RO1 MH 28437-01 from the National Institute of Mental Health, Center for Studies of Crime and Delinquency.

[1]The clearance rate is the proportion of reported crimes that are eventually "solved." In general, crimes are solved by the arrest of a suspect.

berg 1977; Gibbs 1975; and Nagin, in this volume) have questioned these results on several grounds. The key issues raised by Nagin are:

1. The processes underlying the generation of data on crimes and sanctions offer alternative explanations for the observed inverse association between crime and sanctions. Variations, either across jurisdictions or over time, in police practices in the recording of offenses reported to them by the public or in the subsequent unfounding[2] of recorded offenses may in themselves generate an inverse association between published crime rates and any sanction variable using published counts of crime in its denominator (e.g., clearance rate, prison commitments per crime). Jurisdictions that record fewer reported crimes and/or unfound more recorded crimes will tend to have lower crime rates and higher measures of such sanction rates. Overt manipulation of clearance and crime reports will serve to generate an even larger negative association between crime rates and the clearance rate. High clearance rates and low crime rates are used as indicators of an effective police department. Police departments may use their discretion not to record or to unfound a reported offense to manipulate reductions in published crime rates. Concurrently, by offering suspects leniency if they admit to previously unsolved crimes, the police can also inflate clearance rates. The negative association between clearance rates and crime rates may simply reflect the varying intensity across jurisdictions with which such practices occur.

Similarly, the observed inverse association between prison commitments per crime and the crime rate may also be a reflection of the plea bargaining process. Plea bargaining will have the effect of understating in published statistics the actual number of prison commitments for more serious offenses because the commitments will be recorded for a less serious offense (e.g., assault charges may be disposed of as disorderly conduct). If plea bargaining is more prevalent in judicial systems that are overcrowded by increased crime, an inverse association between commitments per reported crime (a measure of probability of imprisonment) and crime rates will be induced that is not a reflection of deterrence.

2. The inverse association between crime and sanctions also re-

[2]An offense is said to be "unfounded" when (a) circumstances following the report show that no crime actually occurred (e.g., a reported theft is in fact a case of misplaced property) or (b) there is good reason to believe that no crime occurred (e.g., it is suspected that an offense is reported merely to implicate another individual in wrongdoing).

flects, at least in part, incapacitation effects rather than deterrent effects. In places where the probability of imprisonment is larger and/or time served is longer, a greater proportion of the criminal population will be incarcerated, *ceteris paribus*. The crime rate will thereby be reduced by physically restraining a greater proportion of the criminal element from committing crimes.

3. Motivated by a belief that crimes and sanctions mutually affect one another, many recent analyses have postulated simultaneous systems in which crime is presumed to affect sanctions and sanctions are presumed to affect crime. To separate empirically the mutual effects, *a priori* restrictions must be imposed on the behavior of the system. These restrictions have taken the form of selectively excluding significant exogenous variables from one equation in the system while including them in one or more of the other equations in the system. The restrictions are made on the assumption that a variable has a direct causal effect on the dependent variable in the equation in which it is included but has no direct effect on the dependent variable in the equation from which it is excluded. If these exclusions are seriously in error, then the estimated coefficients are as unsuitable for inferring the effect of sanctions on crime as those estimated by nonsimultaneous estimation procedures. The restrictions used to identify the crime-generating function are often implausible, consequently raising serious doubts as to the interpretability of the estimated parameters.

The purpose of this paper is to pursue the identification problem raised in (3) by addressing the question of whether it is possible to identify and estimate the deterrent effects of sanctions under a maintained hypothesis that crimes and sanctions mutually affect one another.

When two factors x and y are simultaneously related, a regression of y on x and x on y cannot tell us the magnitude of the respective effects of x on y and y on x, since their mutual effects on each other will be confounded in both of the respective regression coefficients. For example, one cannot estimate the causal effect of price, P, on quantity demanded, q_D, by simply regressing q_D on P because P also affects the quantity supplied, q_S, which in equilibrium equals q_D. Statistical procedures exist that provide methods for identifying and estimating the mutual effects of simultaneously related variables provided certain conditions are satisfied. It can be shown, however, that if those conditions are not satisfied, then there is no way the effects can be estimated. Before discussing these methods, we shall first discuss the reasons for believing that crime affects sanctions as well as that sanctions affect crime.

Economists have argued that for a given level of resources devoted to the criminal justice system (CJS), increased crime rates saturate the resources of the CJS. The effect of the over-utilization of CJS resources is a reduction in the level of sanctions delivered per crime, S. Specifically, if we define a relationship $S = h(C,E)$ that defines S as a function of crime rate, C, and CJS resources, E, then the resource saturation hypothesis would predict that $\partial h/\partial C < 0$ and $\partial h/\partial E > 0$.

A specific example of the resource saturation hypothesis is a predicted negative effect of crime rate on the clearance rate, holding E constant. Although the police will clear more crimes in absolute terms when crime rates increase, the percentage cleared (i.e., the clearance rate) will decrease (Figure 1).

The resource saturation hypothesis is explored in analyses done by Avio and Clark (1974), Carr-Hill and Stern (1973), and Ehrlich (1973). In each of these analyses the structural equation defining sanction level showed a negative and significant association of crime rate with the dependent variable, sanction level. However, because of problems related to identification of the sanction functions (in addition to those related to the identification of the crime function), their results indicating a negative effect of crime on sanctions must be regarded as tentative.

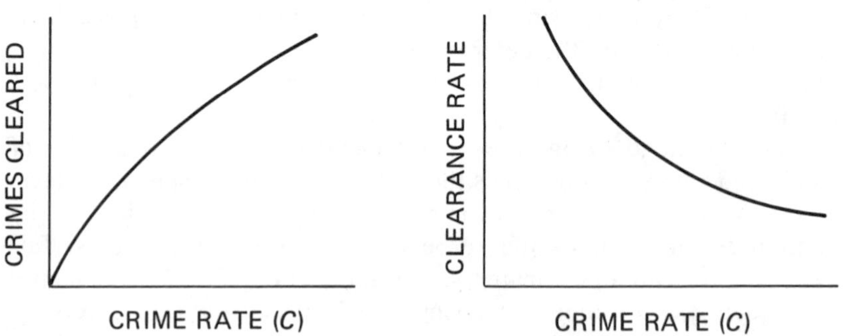

FIGURE 1 Relationship between number of crimes cleared and clearance rate per crime for a fixed level of resources under the assumption of decreasing marginal productivity for police resources.

Blumstein and Cohen (1973) and Blumstein *et al.* (1976) have offered still another reason for believing that crime rates will negatively affect sanctions. They have hypothesized that society is willing to deliver only a limited amount of punishment. As crime rates increase, a relatively constant level of punishment is maintained by adjusting the standards defining criminal behavior, reducing the probability of sanctions being imposed or the severity of sanctions imposed or all of these. This might involve a general reduction in sanctions in response to an overall increase in crime or a more selective response that is limited to specific crimes. While Blumstein, Cohen, and Nagin have provided empirical support for the "limits on punishment" hypothesis, their results are also tentative and require further investigation.

Both the "resource saturation" and "limits on punishment" hypotheses predict a negative effect of crime on sanctions. Some have argued the plausibility of increased crime rates causing a toughening of sanctions. This hypothesis is raised, for example, by Forst[3] and Avio and Clark (1974). Empirical evidence supporting this position is scant.[4] Avio and Clark (1974) observed a positive association between crime rate and sentence length. The enactment of the New York Repeat Offender Law and the Massachusetts Gun Law also support the "toughening" position.[5]

The possibility of simultaneity between crime and sanctions, no matter what its cause, raises serious obstacles to empirical analysis and requires that simultaneous estimation be used to estimate the deterrent impact of sanctions in the simultaneous association of crime and sanctions. The separation of the two effects cannot be achieved unless *a priori* assumptions about the specific nature of the simultaneous relationship are invoked. These assumptions, which are called "identification restrictions," are the keystone of simultaneous equation estimation, for data alone are not sufficient for estimating the structural parameters of a simultaneous system "no matter how extensive and complete those observations may be" (Fisher 1966, p. 2).

In the next section, the identification problem will be discussed and its basic role in simultaneous equation estimation illustrated.

[3]Private communication.

[4]However, to the extent that identification problems arise, empirical evidence either way must be viewed with caution.

[5]While this evidence is consistent with the "toughening" hypothesis, in each case the sanction pertains either to sentences or to statutory definition. It is not clear that these official declarations materially alter the level of sanctions actually delivered (e.g., actual time served). If criminals react primarily to cues on actual sanctions, then the "toughening" hypothesis would require evidence of a positive effect of crime on actual sanctions.

II. THE IDENTIFICATION PROBLEM

Simultaneous estimation procedures were developed because classical regression techniques are inadequate for estimating the structural equations in a simultaneous system. In particular, when two variables x_t and y_t are simultaneously determined as indicated by the system (1) shown below (such variables are referred to as endogeneous), then a simple regression of y_t on x_t will generate a biased and inconsistent[6] estimate of b, the parameter defining the direct effect of x_t on y_t, and likewise a regression of x_t on y_t will generate a biased and inconsistent estimate of d, the parameter defining the direct effect of y_t on x_t:

$$y_t = a + bx_t + \epsilon_t \quad (1a)$$

$$x_t = c + dy_t + u_t \quad (1b)$$

The respective regression coefficients are not consistent estimates of the structural parameters b and d because the mutual interaction of x_t and y_t makes it impossible to assume that either is independent of the stochastic disturbances ϵ_t and u_t. Since ϵ_t influences y_t, and since y_t influences x_t, it cannot be the case that x_t and ϵ_t are uncorrelated. Hence a regression of y_t on x_t will confound the effect of x_t on y_t with that of ϵ_t on y_t and will not produce a consistent estimate of b.[7]

[6]An estimator is said to be consistent if its probability limit exists and is the true parameter value. Intuitively, this is similar to saying that with a sufficiently large sample the parameter can be estimated with high probability with any desired precision. An estimator that is inconsistent will also, generally, be biased. The converse is often not the case.

[7]The respective covariances of x_t with ϵ_t and y_t with u_t can be shown to be:

$$\sigma_{x\epsilon} = \frac{1}{1-bd}\,[d\sigma_\epsilon^2 + \sigma_{u\epsilon}]$$

$$\sigma_{yu} = \frac{1}{1-bd}\,[b\sigma_u^2 + \sigma_{u\epsilon}]$$

where:

$\sigma_{x\epsilon}$ = covariance of x_t and ϵ_t
σ_{yu} = covariance of y_t and u_t
σ_ϵ^2 = variance of ϵ_t
σ_u^2 = variance of u_t
$\sigma_{u\epsilon}$ = covariance of u_t and ϵ_t

Since $\sigma_{x\epsilon} = 0$ and $\sigma_{yu} = 0$ are respectively necessary conditions for regression to produce consistent estimates of b and d, regression is an inappropriate estimation technique.

Indeed, in the present case, not only will ordinary regression techniques produce inconsistent parameter estimates, but no consistent estimator of those parameters exists. *There is no consistent way to estimate them from the data.* The problem can be seen in Figure 2 which presents the non-stochastic components of equations (1a) and (1b).

Because x_t and y_t mutually affect one another, we will observe only a single equilibrium point (x_o,y_o). (If the stochastic terms were introduced, then the equilibrium points would be scattered about $[x_o,y_o]$.) This single equilibrium point does not provide sufficient information for estimating either of the two equations, (1a) and (1b), that produced it. For example, the equilibrium (x_o,y_o) could just as well have been generated by the system shown in Figure 3.

Indeed, there are an infinite number of such systems that could have generated (x_o,y_o). There is no way to use the data to distinguish the true system from the others. Algebraically, this amounts to observing that any linear combination of equations (1a) and (1b) will produce an identical equilibrium (x_o,y_o). There is no way of distinguishing the true (1a) or (1b) from any such linear combination.

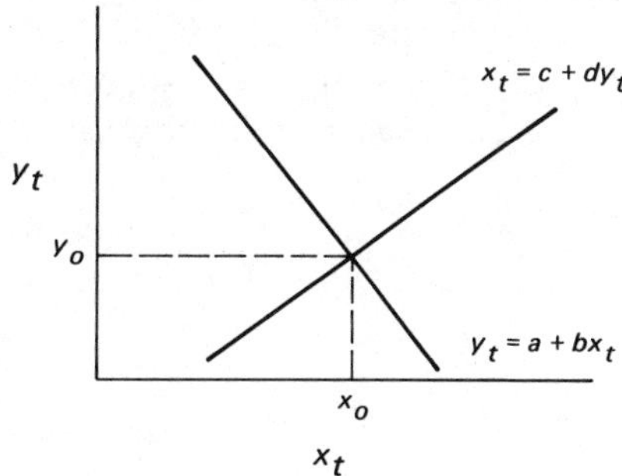

FIGURE 2 A simplified model of a simultaneous relationship between two variables.

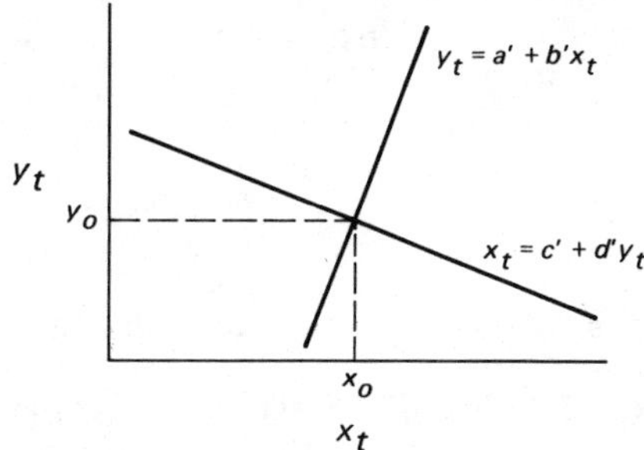

FIGURE 3 Example of an alternative system that generates the same equilibrium point as shown in Figure 2.

Nevertheless, estimating structural equations involving simultaneously related variables is often possible.[8] Under certain conditions, discussed below, simultaneous estimation procedures do provide methods for consistently estimating the true structural equations that generated the observed associations among the simultaneously related variables. However, the true system must satisfy these conditions if the identification problem just exemplified is to be avoided and consistent estimation is to be possible.

The necessary conditions for estimating the true structural equations involve the imposition of *a priori* assumptions about the behavior of the system. Most commonly, these take the form of assuming that variables whose values are determined outside the system ("exogenous variables") or values of endogenous variables determined in prior periods ("predetermined variables") directly affect one or more of the endogenous variables but not all of them. Such restrictions aid in the identification of the structural equation from which the exogenous or predetermined variable is excluded. The exclusion of a variable from one or more equations, however, does not aid in the identification of the structural equations that do include that variable.

To illustrate how such exclusions can identify a structural equation, consider again system (1). As the system is specified, neither equation is identified and neither can be estimated consistently by any method. As indicated earlier, the impossibility of estimating the system is a reflection of there being an infinite set of equation systems that could generate (x_o, y_o).

Suppose, however, that an exogenous variable, T_t, is suspected to have an effect on y_t, but is *known* to have no effect on x_t. Eq. (1a) could then be re-specified as:

$$y_t = a + bx_t + fT_t + \epsilon_t \qquad \text{(1a')}$$

Additionally, assume for concreteness that $f < 0$.[9]

In Figure 4, the non-stochastic component of (1a′) is presented as a function of x_t for three different values of T_t. Consistent with the assumption that $f < 0$, Figure 4 shows that for any given value of x_t, y_t is smaller for larger values of T_t.

[8]Ordinary least squares regression, however, remains inconsistent even though consistent estimators exist.

[9]An assumption of $f > 0$ would do just as well; an assumption, however, of $f = 0$ would leave both equations unidentified as before.

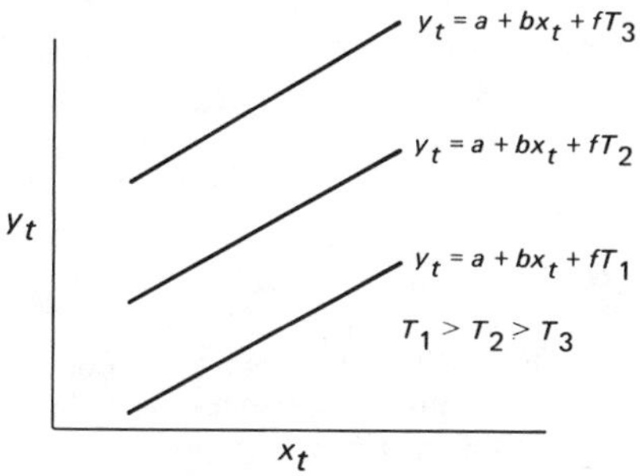

FIGURE 4 y_t as a function of x_t and an exogenous variable, T_t.

In Figure 5, eq. (1b) is superimposed on (1a′) for the different values of T_t. The three points where (1a′) and (1b) intersect indicate the equilibrium values of x_t and y_t for the three different values of T_t.

If these three equilibrium points were observed and connected, then the structural equation (1b) for x_t would be *uniquely* determined. Note, however, that (1a′), the structural equation for y_t, is still not identified; no variables included in (1b) are excluded from (1a′).

The fact that (1a′) is not identified can be seen in Figure 6, where an alternative set of structures for y_t would generate identical equilibrium values of x_t and y_t. Again, there are an infinite number of versions of (1a′) that would generate the observed equilibria; however, there is only a single version of (1b), the true one, that could do so.

It is important to stress, however, that the identification of (1b) is predicated on f, the coefficient of T_t, being different from zero. If f were equal to zero, the situation would revert to that in Figure 2; a single equilibrium point (x_o, y_o) would be observed; and (1b) would no longer be identified.[10]

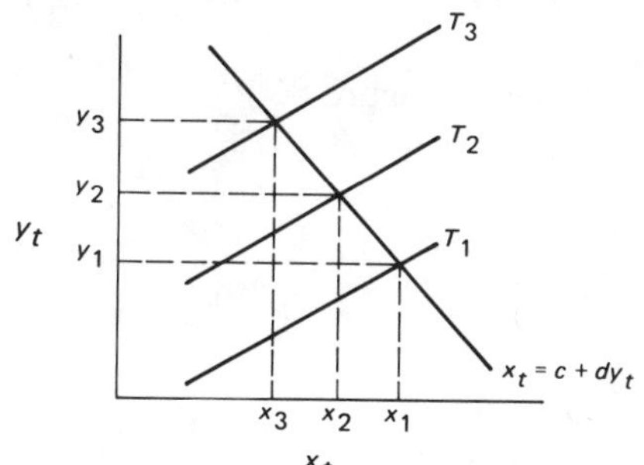

FIGURE 5 The identifying role of an exogenous variable, T_t, in a simplified model of a simultaneous relationship between two variables.

[10]If f is nearly equal to zero, then (1b) is still identified but there will be very little movement in the equilibrium over variations in T_t. Thus, it may be very difficult in practice to estimate (1b).

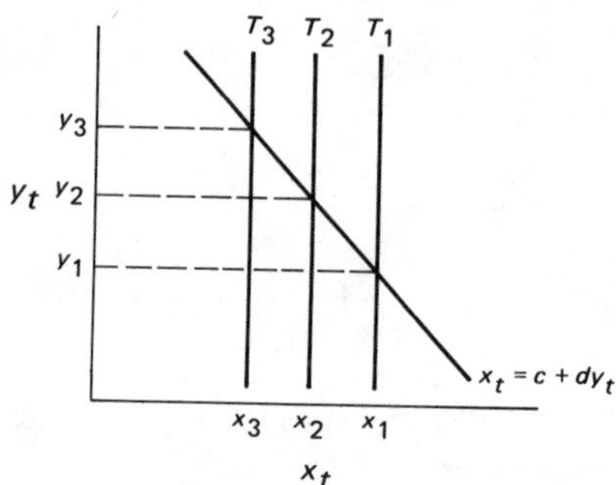

FIGURE 6 An alternative set of y_t functions that generates the same equilibrium points as shown in Figure 5.

When more than two variables simultaneously affect one another, the conditions for identification become somewhat more complicated (see Fisher 1966). Before outlining these conditions, a simplified model of the simultaneous relationship between crime and clearance rates will be examined to illustrate the importance of proper identification for making correct causal inferences.

Suppose, in system (1), x_t is the clearance rate in period t, and y_t is the crime rate in period t. Also, suppose that unbeknownst to us, clearance rates do not in fact affect crime rate (i.e., $b = 0$), but increased crime rates do decrease clearance rates (i.e., $d < 0$). Under the assumption of $b = 0$, a graphical characterization of the unobserved (and as was shown unidentifiable) system is given in Figure 7.

Suppose, however, that the average sentence in period t, T_t, *does* affect crime rates, with longer sentences reducing the crime rate. Thus, the augmented specification of the crime rate equation would be as in equation (1a′), which is repeated below:

$$y_t = a + bx_t + fT_t + \epsilon_t \qquad (1a')$$

The presumed effect of T_t on y_t is illustrated in Figure 8.

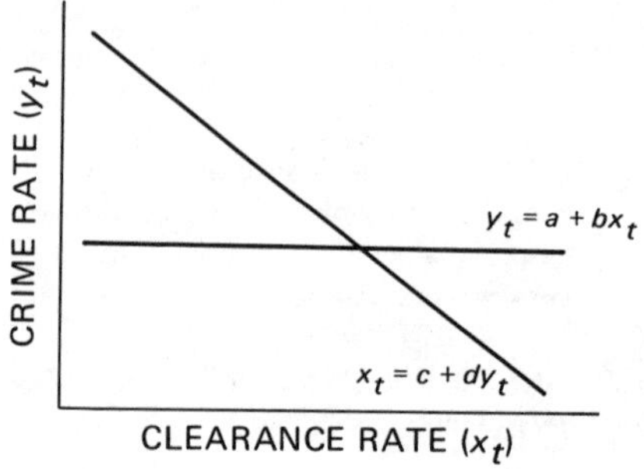

FIGURE 7 A simplified model of the relationship between crimes and sanctions in which sanctions do not affect crimes but crimes do affect sanctions.

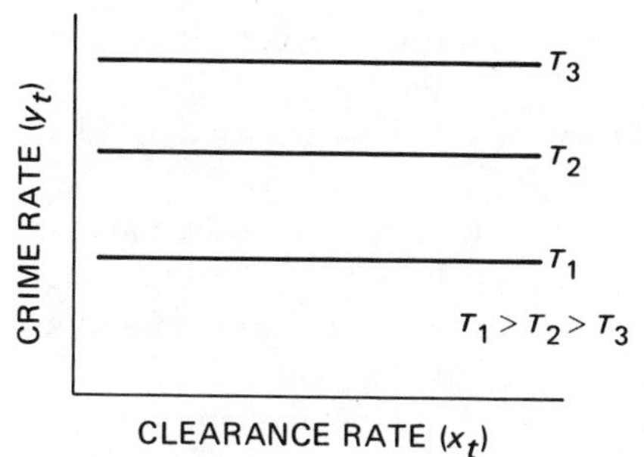

FIGURE 8 The crime rate as a function of the clearance rate and the average sentence (T_t).

In Figure 9, the clearance rate function is superimposed on the crime functions in Figure 8. As was shown previously, the *clearance rate function* is now identified. By connecting the observed intersections in Figure 9, the exact specification for the clearance rate function can be determined. The *crime function,* however, remains unidentified and it will remain unknown and unknowable to us that, indeed, higher clearance rates do not deter crime.

Suppose, however, it were arbitrarily assumed that sentence, T_t, affected clearance rates and not crime rates. Then the mechanics of simultaneous estimation would have allowed an equation for the crime rate to be estimated. That equation, however, would be identical to the one obtained by drawing a line through the equilibrium values of x_t and y_t. Thus, the estimated relation would actually be the relationship describing the effect of crime rate on clearance rates and not clearance rate on crime rates, and so would be completely wrong. In this case, we would conclude that clearance rates have a deterrent effect on crime when in fact they have none.

The very real possibility of making erroneous causal inferences when a model is identified through erroneous assumptions underscores the point that identification is not a minor technical point of estimation. If an equation is not identified, one cannot estimate it. If one tries to do so

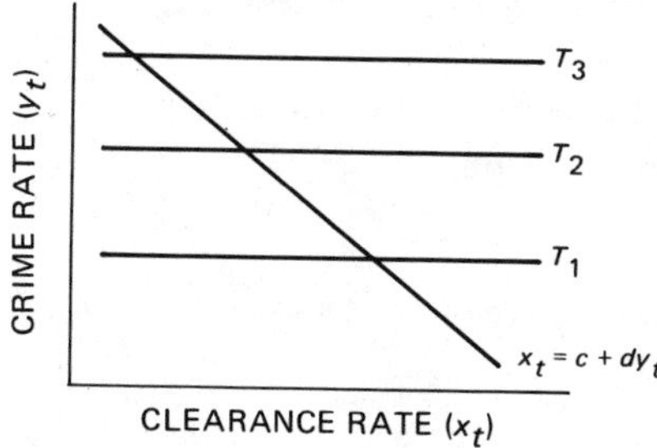

FIGURE 9 The identifying role of average sentence (T_t) in a simplified model of the relationship between crime and sanctions.

using false restrictions to identify the equation, one can draw completely erroneous conclusions from the estimated relationship.

It is thus essential that when exclusion restrictions are used for identification, the restrictions must be carefully justified on the *a priori* grounds that the excluded variables do not directly affect the value of the endogenous variable on the left side of the equation from which they are excluded. If a variable is excluded from an equation merely to facilitate estimation, then the coefficient estimates will remain inconsistent and thus unsuitable for inference about the behavior of the system. Moreover, identifying restrictions must be assumed *a priori* and the nature of the problem is such that restrictions needed to identify can never be tested using data generated by the model under investigation.[11]

In analyzing the mutual association of crime and sanctions, the possibility of making erroneous causal inferences about the causal effect of sanctions on crime is particularly high. Since there are good reasons for believing that crime has a negative causal effect on sanctions, we would expect to observe a negative association in the data between crime and sanctions even if sanctions do not deter crime. Such negative associations are well documented in the deterrence literature (e.g., Ehrlich 1973; Sjoquist 1973; Tittle 1969). Having observed the negative association, we are left with the delicate problem of determining the extent to which it is produced by the negative deterrent effect of sanctions on crime as opposed to the negative effect of crime on sanctions (if the latter effect is indeed negative).[12]

In view of the importance of the identification problem, we shall review some of the restrictions that have been used by some authors to identify the crime functions so that the validity of their findings on the deterrent effect of sanctions can be put into perspective. When evaluating the validity of such restrictions, one should keep in mind that crime-function restrictions presume that the variables involved affect either sanctions, police expenditures per capita (a variable commonly hypothesized to be simultaneously related to crime), or other endogenous variables included in the model, but do not directly affect the crime rate itself.

Ehrlich (1973) identified his crime function by excluding from it (but including elsewhere in his model) the following variables:

[11]However, other data generated in other ways (by experiment, for example) can be so used.

[12]Indeed, in a complex model, such an observed negative association could occur even if neither direct effect is negative because of relations among the disturbance terms.

1. The crime rate lagged one period
2. Police expenditures per capita lagged one period
3. Unemployment rate of civilian males aged 35-39
4. Percent of males aged 14-24
5. Percent of population living in SMSAS
6. Males per female
7. A southern regional variable
8. Mean years of schooling of population over age 25
9. Total population.[13]

In Carr-Hill and Stern (1973), the crime function is identified by excluding:

1. Total population
2. Proportion of reported crimes that are violent
3. A measure of the proportion of the population that is middle class.

Avio and Clarke (1974) estimate a model in which crime rates, clearance rates, and police expenditures per capita are simultaneously determined. The crime function is identified by excluding:

1. Population density
2. The total population
3. Police expenditures lagged one period
4. Motor vehicle registration per capita lagged one period
5. Crimes against persons lagged one period.

In all these papers, identification of the crime function relies on the exclusion of socioeconomic variables (SES) and lagged endogenous variables from the crime function. It is difficult to imagine any plausible argument for the exclusion of the SES variables. Intercorrelation among these SES and demographic correlates of crime makes it difficult to determine which among them do have a causal association with crime, but it is simply not plausible to assume that such SES variables do not have a direct effect on crime, while also assuming that each does directly affect either sanctions or police expenditures per capita.[14]

[13]In his Ph.D. dissertation, Ehrlich (1970) estimated a crime function that includes the above unemployment, age, and education variables and found a negative and generally significant association between crime rate and sanctions. This crime function was identified in part by the exclusion of the remaining variables listed above, a different but still apparently arbitrary set of identification restrictions.

[14]Indeed, Ehrlich's own theoretical model specifies that unemployment in particular does have such an effect.

Further, two of the analyses also use the exclusion of lagged endogenous variables to identify the crime function. For the estimation procedures employed, the use of such restrictions to identify rests crucially upon an assumption of no serial correlation in the stochastic disturbance terms in the equations, because these estimation procedures treat lagged endogenous variables as uncorrelated with current disturbances. If current and lagged disturbances are correlated, this assumption cannot be true. (This point will be discussed in greater detail below.) While methods exist to handle serial correlation, the analyses discussed do not use such methods. There are cogent reasons, which will also be discussed, for believing (a) the assumption of no serial correlation to be incorrect and (b) there is positive serial correlation in the disturbances for the type of data used in these analyses.

Assuming that crime and sanctions are simultaneously related, our conclusion is that it is most unlikely that the authors mentioned have successfully identified and consistently estimated the deterrent effect of sanctions. Consequently, one can have little confidence that the estimated sanctions coefficients are consistent. Moreover, the magnitude of the inconsistency seems likely to be substantial since the restrictions used to identify seem unlikely to be even approximately correct (see Fisher 1961). Consequently, the resulting parameter estimates cannot be used for causal interpretation.

A crucial question is then: Can the crime function ever plausibly be identified, i.e., can we ever hope to find variables that influence sanctions but have no direct effect on crimes? This question, which is the central topic of this paper, is the focus of the next section. The question of the feasibility of identifying the crime function requires an appreciation of some more generalized identification concepts. Thus, before we turn to the topic of feasibility, we shall develop these concepts.

III. SOME MORE GENERALIZED IDENTIFICATION CONCEPTS

The prior discussion has focused on the requirements for identifying the structural equations in a system where only two variables are simultaneously related. We shall now generalize to a situation where M variables simultaneously affect one another.

Suppose we specify the interrelationship of the M variables by:

$$\begin{aligned}
y_1 &= a_{12}y_2 + a_{13}y_3 + \ldots + a_{1M}y_M + b_{11}x_1 \\
&\qquad + b_{12}x_2 + \ldots + b_{1N}x_N + \epsilon_1 \\
y_2 &= a_{21}y_1 + a_{23}y_3 + \ldots + a_{2M}y_M + b_{21}x_1 \\
&\qquad + b_{22}x_2 + \ldots + b_{2N}x_N + \epsilon_2 \qquad (2) \\
&\cdot \\
&\cdot \\
&\cdot \\
y_M &= a_{M1}y_1 + a_{M2}y_2 + \ldots + a_{MM-1}y_{M-1} + b_{M1}x_1 \\
&\qquad + b_{M2}x_2 + \ldots + b_{MN}x_N + \epsilon_M
\end{aligned}$$

where:

y_i = the ith endogenous variable ($i = 1, \ldots, M$)
a_{ik} = the coefficient defining the magnitude of the direct ("causal") effect of y_k on y_i
x_j = the jth non-endogenous variable ($j = 1, \ldots, N$)
b_{ij} = the coefficient defining the magnitude of the jth, non-endogenous variable's direct effect on y_i
ϵ_i = the stochastic component of the ith structural equation.

As was shown previously, when variables are simultaneously related, the empirical observations of the system's behavior, no matter how well measured or extensive they may be, are not sufficient for consistently estimating the structural relationships. Consider the first structural equation in system (2). Estimation of the relationship would require generating $M - 1 + N$ parameter estimates. However, the limits of empirical information are such that only N independent pieces of information can be obtained from the data to estimate the $N + M - 1$ parameters of this equation. This corresponds to the fact that only the N non-endogenous variables, the x_j, can be varied independently. The M endogenous variables, the y_i, are determined (except for stochastic effects) once the x_j are set. If there were no stochastic effects, we could think of performing experiments (or having nature perform them for us) by setting the values of the x_j and observing the effect on the y_i. There would be, however, only N independent ways of setting the N non-endogenous x_j, and further experiments would be redundant.

In the stochastic case, the corresponding fact is that we are entitled to assume (at most) that each of the N non-endogenous x_j is uncorrelated with the disturbances, ϵ_i, and in particular with the disturbance from the first equation, ϵ_1. The y_i cannot be so uncorrelated.

If $M = 1$ so that there were no simultaneity, then these N zero correlations would suffice to allow the consistent estimation of the first (and only) equation by ordinary regression. In that case, only exogenous variables would appear on the right side of that equation and the N zero correlations would satisfy the necessary conditions for ordinary regression to generate a consistent estimator—namely, that the regressors be uncorrelated with the disturbance. Where $M > 1$ and there is simultaneity, these N zero correlations are not enough to recover the $M - 1 + N$ parameters of the first equation.

Another way of putting it is to say that analysis of the data can at most only tell us about the full effects (direct and indirect) of the x_j on the y_i (from the "reduced form" in which the equations are solved for the y_i only in terms of the x_j and ϵ_i). The direct effects of the x_j on the y_i (the b_{ij}) and the direct effects of the y_i on each other (the a_{ik}) cannot be recovered from the data without at least $M - 1$ additional independent pieces of information for each equation.[15] Such additional information must come from outside, *a priori* considerations.[16]

The situation is completely isomorphic to the logical impossibility of finding a unique solution to a system of linear equations in $M + N - 1$ unknowns, when only N independent equations are available. A unique solution can only be obtained if $M - 1$ additional independent equations, comparable to our restrictions, are imposed. The identification restrictions in simultaneous equation estimation provide the $M - 1$ additional restrictions that sufficiently augment the empirical information to allow the estimation of the structural equation.

The $M - 1$ additional equations in the system of linear equations in $M + N - 1$ unknowns are as important in specifying a unique solution as the N original equations. Similarly, the identification restrictions are as important in the determination of the coefficients as the observational information.

The additional $M - 1$ restrictions can be (but need not be) generated by assuming that $M - 1$ of the parameters in the equation are zero. The $M - 1$ restrictions could be generated if we assumed $a_{1i} = 0$ ($i = 2, \ldots, M$), which is to assume that y_1 is *not* simultaneously related to any of the other y_i's. Since the x_i's are assumed to be uncorrelated with ϵ_1, the coefficients of the first equation could then be consistently estimated by ordinary least squares.

Suppose, however, that we conclude that *a priori* considerations allow us only to assume that $(M - 1) - k$, *where* $0 \leq k < M - 1$, of the

[15]This is a necessary but not sufficient condition for identification. For a full discussion see Fisher (1966).

[16]See Fisher (1966) for a complete discussion.

a_{1i}'s are zero. We must still estimate $k + N$ parameters, which can still not be done using only the N pieces of empirical information available.[17] The additional k pieces of information can be generated if *a priori* considerations would allow us to assume plausibly that k of the N non-endogenous x_j do not enter the first equation but do enter one or more of the other equations (i.e., k of the $b_{1j} = 0$ but $b_{1j} \neq 0$ for some $i \neq 1$). By assuming that k of the b_{1j} are zero, it becomes unnecessary to estimate them. Thus the N pieces of empirical information can be used to estimate the remaining N parameters consistently. It must be emphasized, however, that the remaining N parameters will only be consistently estimated if the *a priori* considerations that led to the assumptions that $M - 1 - k$ of the a_{1i}'s and k of the b_{1j}'s were zero are correct.[18] Thus, any empirical conclusion hinges critically on the validity of those *a priori* premises.

When only $M - 1$ restrictions can be imposed and the equation in question is identified, it is said to be "just identified." This terminology derives from the fact that if we can generate only $M - 2$ restrictions, then the equation will not be identified (i.e., unidentified). Being short only a single restriction means that there exists more than one, and in general an infinite number of equations that are consistent with the data. All such equations are observationally equivalent to the true one. Thus, it must be remembered that from the perspective of the existence of a consistent estimator, one is no better off having $M - 2$ restrictions than zero restrictions. In either case, no consistent estimator will exist and no causal inference can be made about the equation for y_1. In some of the models to be examined in the next section, this point will return to haunt us.

Sometimes it is also possible to generate more than $M - 1$ restrictions and to identify the equation in more than one way. In such instances, the equation is said to be "over-identified" and, since we have more than N pieces of information to estimate less than N parameters, estimation, of course, remains possible.

Before turning to the next section on the feasibility of identifying the crime function, several important points must be made. In order of importance, they are: First, if an equation is just identified, then the restrictions used to identify it cannot be tested with the data being analyzed. The untestability of the restrictions follows from the fact that a model cannot even be estimated unless we assume they are true;

[17]In the earlier discussion, $M = 2$ and $k = 0$; thus, we needed only one identification restriction.

[18]Fisher (1961) shows that the magnitude of the inconsistency in parameter estimates is directly related to the degree of "correctness" of the identification restrictions.

[e.g., the clearance rate's specification (1b) cannot be estimated unless we assume that T_t does not enter (1b). Since we cannot estimate (1b) if T_t does enter it, then we cannot test whether it should enter (1b).]

A related point follows when a model is over-identified, that is, when there are alternative ways to just-identify it. One can estimate the model under a variety of subsets of just-identifying restrictions, with each of the resulting model estimates being contingent upon the validity of the just-identifying subset used. If one has little or no faith in the validity of any one of the subsets, then even if one gets the same results under each subset (for example, sanctions do not deter crime), then one cannot conclude that those results are valid.

Second, any additional restrictions beyond a set of $M - 1$ just-identifying ones can be tested. Those tests are, however, contingent upon the validity of the $M - 1$ just-identifying restrictions. If one has faith in the validity of these $M - 1$ restrictions, then one can have faith in the validity of the empirical tests of the additional over-identifying restrictions. But, if one has little faith in the validity of the just-identifying restrictions, one can have only little faith in the validity of the test of the remaining restrictions. One implication of this point is that if one generates a set of over-identifying restrictions—but in this set there does not exist a subset of just-identifying restrictions whose validity is unquestionable (or nearly so)—one cannot gain a valid test of the set of restrictions by exhaustively testing each restriction under the assumption that the remaining ones are correct.[19]

IV. ON THE FEASIBILITY OF IDENTIFYING THE CRIME FUNCTION

In this section, we shall examine the central issue of this paper: Can the crime function be plausibly identified? We shall proceed by first examining the simplest model in which a single crime type and sanction type are simultaneously related. Several categories of just-identifying restrictions, none of which are mutually exclusive, will be analyzed for their strengths and weaknesses. The single-crime-type, single-sanction-type model overly simplifies the real phenomenon of multiple crime types and multiple sanction types. However, to date no analyses have attempted to estimate models in which more than one crime and sanction type are simultaneously related. More important for our pur-

[19]There do exist methods for testing an entire set of over-identifying restrictions symmetrically; however, such tests are not very strong as indications of which restrictions are incorrect. See Fisher (1966, Chapter 6).

poses, such simple models will serve to highlight the strengths and weaknesses of some different categories of just-identifying restrictions. These points will remain valid in analyzing more complex models.

We shall then consider the more complex but more realistic models in which (a) a single crime type is simultaneously related to multiple sanction types and (b) multiple crime types and a single sanction type are simultaneously related. We shall not consider under a separate heading the most complex model in which multiple crime and sanction types are simultaneously related because the problematic feasibility of identifying such a model will become clear from the discussion of the preceding two model types. The principal focus of our discussion will be the identification of simultaneous models. The mutual association of crime and sanctions may, however, occur with time lags rather than simultaneously. In the Appendix we shall point out the difficulties with results based upon path models, which are a specific class of lagged models, and then discuss the difficulties likely to be encountered in estimating more general classes of lagged models.

None of the models that will be discussed will explicitly include SES variables. While SES variables should indeed be included in a specification of the crime function, we do not envisage the exclusion of SES variables being plausibly used as identification restrictions. Such exclusions would have to be predicated upon *a priori* considerations that allow one to assume that the excluded SES factor directly affects some other endogenous variable in the system but not crime. Currently we simply do not have a sufficiently well-developed and validated theory of the socioeconomic factors affecting crime and sanctions plausibly to assume that some SES factor can be excluded from the crime-generating model but included elsewhere in the system. Some new insight in this regard would, of course, be very useful.

The absence of explicit consideration of SES effects should not be interpreted as indicating that we believe these effects to be inconsequential; their effects are undoubtedly substantial, but the mechanism of their operation is simply not understood well enough plausibly to employ SES variables as identification restrictions. Thus, our discussion omits SES variables only for expositional convenience. Most models would include such variables, at least in the crime function. However, it is the exclusion of such variables from the crime function (but not from other equations) that would aid identification.[20]

[20]Naturally, no model is likely to include all relevant SES variables. Omitted SES effects become part of the disturbance terms. We shall later discuss at length the behavior of omitted SES factors on these stochastic components of the model since appropriate specification of such behavior is crucial to making consistent estimates of the parameters.

A. SINGLE-CRIME-TYPE, SINGLE-SANCTION MODELS

1. Models Using Expenditures as an Identifying Omitted Variable

Suppose we specify the following model:

$$C_t = f(S_t) + \epsilon_t^1 \tag{3a}$$

$$S_t = h(C_t, E_t) + \epsilon_t^2 \tag{3b}$$

where:

$f(S_t)$ and $h(C_t, E_t)$ are linear functions[21]
C_t = crime rate in t
S_t = sanctions per crime in t
E_t = criminal justice system (CJS) expenditures in t
ϵ_t^i = stochastic error ($i = 1,2$) whose properties are to be discussed.

In this model, which is also characterized by the flow chart in Figure 10, C_t is determined by S_t, and S_t is determined jointly by C_t and E_t. The CJS expenditures variable, E_t, enters the equation for S_t under the theory that increased resources devoted to the CJS, as measured by E_t, will decrease the resource saturation effect of any given level of crime, C_t (i.e., $\partial h/\partial E_t > 0$). As noted earlier, the resource saturation theory is one of the primary theories underlying simultaneous models of crimes and sanctions.

In this system, there are two endogenous variables, C_t and S_t. The crime equation includes one right-side endogenous variable, S_t. Estimation of eq. (3a) will thus require that one identification restriction be imposed. [Within the context of the identification rules laid out in the previous section, $M = 2$ and therefore we need $M - 1 = 1$ restriction to identify eq. (3a).]

In this system, E_t is not included in the crime function. This exclusion, which can be used to provide the necessary single identifying restriction to estimate eq. (3a), is predicated upon the theory that E_t affects crime only insofar as it affects the capability of the CJS to deliver sanctions. For sanctions delivered by the courts (e.g., conviction, im-

[21]In this analysis, we assume for simplicity that all functions are linear. Nonlinearities in the sanctions function can aid in identification, but only if one is sure of the functional form of the nonlinearity and sure that similar nonlinearities are not present in the crime equation. Such precise information on functional forms is seldom available and is certainly not so in this case. (See Fisher, 1966, Chapter 5, for extended discussion.)

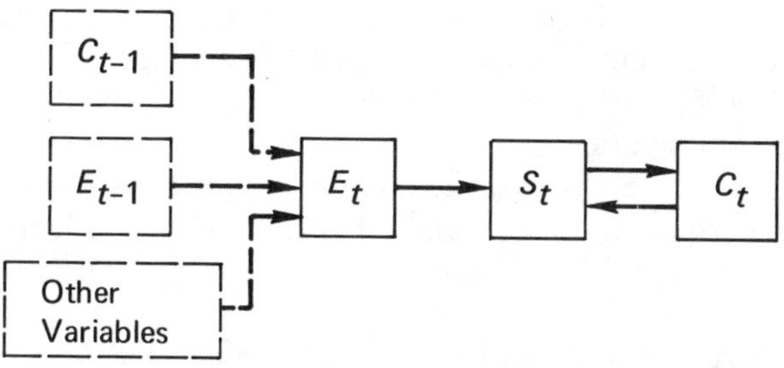

FIGURE 10 Diagram of model using expenditures as an identifying variable. The possibility that C_{t-1}, E_{t-1}, and other variables affect expenditures at t but are omitted from the crime equation does not aid in the identification of the latter. This is because these variables do not appear anywhere in the sanctions-crime loop and have no effect captured beyond taking expenditures as exogenous to that loop. Another way of putting it is that the omission of such variables from the crime equation does not help to distinguish it from the sanctions equation since the variables do not appear in that equation either.

prisonment) or regulated by corrections (e.g., time served in prison), such an assumption seems reasonable. However, if E_t is police expenditures and S_t is defined as the clearance rate, then the assumption that E_t has no direct effect on C_t is suspect.

The level of police expenditures is likely to influence the visibility of police, since in two identical communities, the one with greater expenditures is likely to have a larger police force. Police visibility may have an independent deterrent effect beyond S_t, where S_t is measured by clearance rate, because the potential criminal's perception of apprehension probability (which is the "true" measure of S_t we are seeking when S_t refers to police-delivered sanctions) undoubtedly derives from multiple cues from his environment. A potential criminal cannot observe the actual apprehension probability, but rather can only measure it roughly. One such measure is the frequency with which he and fellow criminals with whom he has contact experience apprehension. Perhaps this frequency can be approximated by the clearance rate. The criminal's perception of apprehension probability, however, does not have to be based solely upon these undoubtedly inaccurate frequency estimates. He is likely, in making his estimate of apprehension probability, to react to additional cues from the environment—such as the intensity of the police presence.

To the extent that police visibility provides an independent cue of apprehension probability and thus acts as an independent direct deterrent distinct from the indirect effect of an increased police presence on clearance rates and hence on crime, then E_t should appear directly in the equation for C_t. Such an appearance, however, would leave the crime function unidentified.

Putting such considerations aside and presuming the exclusion of E_t from the crime equation to be valid, that exclusion will identify the crime equation if either of the following statements is true:

1. Expenditures are fully exogenous. To assume that E_t is exogenous is to assume that neither C_t nor S_t in the current period or in prior periods affects E_t. An assumption of exogeneity seems untenable because it is likely that the level of crime affects the level of expenditures, at least across jurisdictions and probably over time. The observed positive association between police expenditures per capita and crime rate provides some evidence for the likelihood of such an effect (see, for example, McPheters and Strong 1975).
2. Expenditures are influenced only by lagged crime rates and are therefore predetermined, although not fully exogenous. This seems more reasonable than does full exogeneity. Due to the governmental budgeting cycle, the level of E_t is specified before the beginning of period t. That level, although probably influenced by the crime rate, is influenced by rates in prior periods, for example, C_{t-1}. Thus, E_t is a predetermined variable.[22]

Granting that E_t is predetermined, a further crucial assumption must be made about the behavior of the stochastic components, ϵ_t^i. We must specify the behavior of these stochastic terms over time. We could assume that the errors are independent over time, or we could make a less restrictive assumption that they are serially correlated. For example, we might assume that they follow a first-order autoregressive process, characterized by:

$$\epsilon_t^i = \rho_i \epsilon_{t-1}^i + \delta_t^i \quad (4)$$

where:

ρ_i = a parameter
δ_t^i = non-serially correlated disturbance term.

[22]It should be noted that if C_t does influence E_t directly, perhaps because the budget is adjusted in t in reaction to C_t, then E_t becomes determined simultaneously with C_t and S_t, and the crime function is no longer identified even if E_t does not appear in it. Some additional restrictions involving a nonendogenous variable are necessary.

Such assumptions about the serial relationships among the ϵ_t^i are critical for identification. In our previous discussion on the limits of the empirical information in a simultaneous system, we stated that the maximum number of independent pieces of empirical information available for consistently estimating each structural equation was N, where N equals the number of non-endogenous variables in the system. This was because of the assumption that there are N non-endogenous variables that are uncorrelated with the stochastic disturbances and thus that can be varied independently. If that assumption fails for J_1 of the non-endogenous variables, then the number of pieces of empirical information for consistently estimating each structural equation is reduced to N-J_1. In effect, an additional J_1 of the variables become endogenous.

When using predetermined variables for identification, the possibility that the disturbances are serially correlated must be given special consideration. If the ϵ_t^i are serially correlated [for example, a first-order autoregressive process as in eq. (4)], then the predetermined variables will necessarily be correlated with at least some of the stochastic components. In particular, E_t will be correlated with ϵ_t^1 because ϵ_t^1 is correlated with ϵ_{t-1}^1 and E_t is a function of C_{t-1}, which is in turn a function of ϵ_{t-1}^1.

When serial correlation among the disturbances is thought to be present, estimation still remains possible if one correctly specifies the specific structure of the presumed serial correlation. If one is not certain of the specific structure of the serial correlation, and one rarely is, then the less restrictive the assumption the better. For example, the first-order autoregressive assumption is less restrictive than assuming no serial correlation because the latter will occur for the special case of all the ρ_i zero. However, if the model is estimated under an assumption of no serial correlation, then the possibility of serial correlation of some specific type cannot be tested. Even less restrictive assumptions about the nature of the serial correlation (higher-order processes, for example) can be made, but some specific assumptions must be made.

Excepting a capital punishment analysis by Ehrlich (1975), all simultaneous analyses have employed estimation methods that generate consistent estimates only when there is no serial correlation of any kind among the disturbances. If the exclusion of a predetermined variable is used as an identification restriction, as with E_t in the model under consideration, the validity of using that restriction when using these methods turns on the assumption of no serial correlation. If the assumption is incorrect, then the parameter estimates will be inconsistent.

The assumption of no serial correlation among the disturbances is not only fundamental in cases like this; it reflects implicit assumptions about real effects stemming from factors influencing crime or sanctions that are captured in the disturbances because they are not explicitly included in the model. Deciding whether the assumption of no serial correlation can plausibly be maintained thus requires consideration of such factors.

In the crime function shown in eq. (3a), the variables not explicitly included would include all SES variables that affect crime. However, this is because of the simplistic nature of eq. (3a) adopted for expositional purposes. As already remarked, in practice, if eq. (3a) were to be estimated, some SES variables would be explicitly included. Nevertheless, some part of the stochastic disturbance, ϵ_t^1, would still consist of SES effects. It is impossible to include all the SES variables influencing crime both because we do not know all of them or cannot measure them and because there are likely to be many of them, each with a small effect. In addition, if included SES variables affect crime in ways only approximated by our choice of functional form in eq. (3a), then departures from that approximation influence the disturbance term.

From this perspective on the factors generating ϵ_t^1, is it reasonable to assume no serial correlation in ϵ_t^1? The answer, we believe, is no. Many of the SES variables influencing ϵ_t^1 change only gradually over time. Thus, if the realized values of these variables in period t are such that the disturbance is positive in period t, it is likely that their realized values in period $t+1$ will lead to a positive disturbance as well. Hence we should expect positive serial correlation in ϵ_t^1. One possible characterization might be the first-order autoregressive process shown in eq. (4), with $\rho_1 > 0$.

When using data with a cross-sectional component, the most common type of data utilized in deterrence analyses, the likelihood of serial correlation is particularly high because there is likely to be particularly wide variation in the values of excluded variables across the sampling units (usually states). Put simply, locations whose actual crime rate is higher than predicted by the systematic part of the equation in one year are likely to remain so in the next year.

The implausibility of an assumption of no serial correlation requires that estimation be done under a less restrictive assumption about the serial correlation of the stochastic terms if inconsistency is to be avoided. We shall not address the question of what sort of assumption on the nature of the serial dependence is plausible. The question deserves further attention, but it can be said that the less restrictive the assumption, the better. One possibility, given enough data, would be to allow for an autoregressive relationship of order γ, where:

$$\epsilon_t^i = \sum_{j=1}^{\gamma} \rho_{ij}\epsilon_{t-j} + \delta_t^i \tag{5}$$

Estimation under any assumption of serial dependence, however, requires the use of data with a time-series component. For example, the γth order autoregressive assumption would require that the time-series component in the data be at least $\gamma + 1$ periods. Pure cross-sectional data cannot be used.

To summarize, we conclude that the exclusion of the expenditures variable cannot be used plausibly to identify the crime function, at least with cross-sectional data. To do so at best requires the very implausible assumption of serial independence in the stochastic components. To estimate a model under any assumption of serial dependence requires time-series data and thereby precludes the possibility of using only cross-sectional data.

Moreover, as we have seen, the use of the expenditures restriction, no matter what one assumes about the nature of the serial dependence, hinges upon the assumption that E_t does not directly affect crime. If S_t and E_t are defined in terms of court-related activities only, this seems plausible. If E_t and S_t pertain to the police, however, then the assumption that E_t does not directly influence C_t is questionable. Expenditures on police will be closely linked to the visibility of police in the community, and police visibility may indeed be a very important factor in deterring crime. Further, if expenditures on courts and expenditures on police vary together, then one may simply be fooling oneself about identification in specifying and estimating a model in which E_t relates only to courts.

2. *Models Using Prison Cell Utilization*

In the system shown below, C_t is again a function of S_t and S_t is a function of C_t. Additionally, S_t is specified to be a function of prison-cell utilization, U_t, defined to be the ratio of the prison population in t, P_t, to total prison cells in t, K_t.

$$C_t = f(S_t) + \epsilon_t^1 \tag{6a}$$

$$S_t = h(C_t, U_t) + \epsilon_t^2 \tag{6b}$$

where:

P_t = the prison population in period t
K_t = prison cell capacity in period t
$U_t = P_t/K_t$

As before, SES variables are omitted for expositional convenience. To our knowledge, no deterrence investigation has included U_t in the equation for sanctions. The rationale for its inclusion again involves a resource utilization argument and, indeed, this model can be taken as a simple example in which the resource saturation hypothesis is made explicit. As prisons become increasingly crowded, pressure will be exerted to reduce utilization, U_t. In the short term (*e.g.*, a year) this reduction can only be accomplished through a reduction in prison population, P_t, since expansion of existing cell capacity, K_t, would require considerably more time.[23]

One recent example of this effect of resource saturation at work is Federal Judge Frank Johnson's order to the Alabama Corrections Department to release a sufficient number of prisoners to alleviate prison overcrowding (see *Criminal Justice Bulletin* 1976). Judge Johnson's order resulted in the reduction of both the probability of imprisonment given conviction and time served given imprisonment.

In this single-sanction and single-crime-type model with only two endogenous variables, identification of the crime function requires that one restriction be imposed; the absence of U_t, prison cell utilization in t, from eq. (6a) provides the necessary restriction. To see this, consider a log-linear specification of eqs. (6a-b):

$$\ln C_t = B_o + B_1 \ln S_t + \epsilon_t^1 \qquad (6a')$$

$$\ln S_t = \gamma_o + \gamma_1 \ln C_t + \gamma_2 \ln \left(\frac{P_t}{K_t}\right) + \epsilon_t^2$$

$$= \gamma_o + \gamma_1 \ln C_t + \gamma_2 \ln P_t - \gamma_2 \ln K_t + \epsilon_t^2 \qquad (6b')$$

In addition, if we specifically define S_t to be the probability of imprisonment given a crime and assume that an imprisoned individual is incarcerated for a single period,[24] P_t will be:

[23]To the degree that crime does influence K_t by leading to more prison cell construction, that effect is longer-term, perhaps 5 to 10 years.

[24]This model is clearly an oversimplification. In general, prison terms are often considerably longer than a year, so that the prison population is not solely a function of the current values of C_t, S_t, and N_t but also depends on past incarcerations. This makes no essential difference to the points under discussion, however, save that past incarcerations could be used as an omitted predetermined variable in identifying the crime function under the assumption of no serial correlation.

$$P_t = C_t S_t N_t \tag{6c}$$

$$\ln P_t = \ln C_t + \ln S_t + \ln N_t \tag{6c'}$$

where:

N_t = total population in t[25]

Substituting eq. (6c′) in eq. (6b′) and rearranging terms:

$$\ln S_t = \frac{\gamma_0}{1-\gamma_2} + \frac{\gamma_1 + \gamma_2}{1-\gamma_2} \ln C_t + \frac{\gamma_2}{1-\gamma_2} \ln (N_t/K_t) + \frac{\epsilon_t^2}{1-\gamma_2} \tag{6b''}$$

The exclusion of ln (N_t/K_t) from eq. (6a′) provides the necessary restriction for identification.[26]

The validity of this identification procedure hinges upon the assumption that U_t does not directly affect crime. This assumption will fail if potential criminals have information on crowding in prisons and view the level of U_t as a partial measure of the severity of punishment. If, indeed, U_t has such an effect, then it should be included in the crime equation and the exclusion of N_t/K_t cannot be used validly to identify the crime function.

3. Inertia Model: Lagged Sanctions

In the system shown below, the equation for S_t includes S_{t-1}. Its inclusion could be argued on the grounds that sanctioning practice, being bound by tradition, will adjust slowly to changes in the crime rate or indeed to any other factors influencing sanctions. As a result, S_t will be

[25]The variable N_t is entered because C_t is expressed as crimes per capita, while P_t is the total number of prisoners.

[26]It might appear that we might separate ln (N_t/K_t) into two variables by writing ln (N_t/K_t) = ln N_t − ln K_t and then use the exclusion of both ln K_t and ln N_t from the crime equation to achieve not merely identification but over-identification. This apparent achieving of something for nothing does not succeed, however. Perhaps the easiest way to see this is to observe that the restrictions stating that both ln K_t and ln N_t do not appear in the crime equation can be written equivalently as the restriction that the coefficient of ln K_t in that equation is zero plus the restriction that the coefficient in that equation of (−ln N_t) is equal to that of ln K_t. This latter restriction, however, is also satisfied in the sanctions equation and hence does not help at all in telling the two apart; if we used only that restriction we would not have identification. (This is an example of the fact referred to in a previous footnote that counting restrictions provides only a necessary, not a sufficient condition for identification.) To put it another way, ln K_t and ln N_t do not independently affect ln C_t and ln S_t. There is only one piece of useful information to be gained from using them, not two.

influenced by sanctions in prior periods, assumed for illustration to be represented sufficiently by S_{t-1}. Since S_{t-1} does not appear in the crime equation, the crime function is identified with some assumption on the nature of the serial dependence of the ϵ_t^i.

$$C_t = f(S_t) + \epsilon_t^1 \tag{7a}$$

$$S_t = h(C_t, S_{t-1}) + \epsilon_t^2 \tag{7b}$$

While this rationale for including S_{t-1} in the specification of S_t is highly plausible, it is not plausible at the same time to exclude S_{t-1} from the crime equation. To do so assumes that potential criminals are not influenced by sanctions in prior periods. Such an assumption has little plausibility as a crucial identifying restriction, since it implies that historical sanction levels have no influence on perceptions of current sanctions even though they do influence current sanctions themselves.

For example, suppose a rational criminal has information indicating that a certain offense was not being prosecuted as vigorously as it had been previously. Should he disregard his information on sanction levels in prior periods and base his decision solely upon the new information on sanctions? There are several reasons that a rational criminal might still continue to consider prior information on sanctions.

First, unlike stock market prices, daily quotations of sanction levels are not available and the information that is available derives from very uncertain sources, including the criminal's own experience, the experience of his criminal peers, news reports, or even the published statistics utilized by deterrence researchers. When current information is poor, considering information from the past, even if it is also uncertain, is very sensible in making estimates of the current status.

Second, even if current information on a variable is good, information on prior levels provides important information on the stability or trend of the sanction over time. If, for example, potential criminals are not risk neutral, then they will want information on the distribution of potential sanctions. Prior periods may provide such useful information. Moreover, past information on sanctions may provide useful information on trends in sanctions that may also be of value to a rational criminal.

In view of the implausibility of assuming that S_{t-1} affects S_t but not C_t, we do not believe that identification can be validly achieved in this way.

B. A SINGLE-CRIME-TYPE, MULTIPLE-SANCTION MODEL

Our focus has been on simple models in which only a single sanction and single crime type are simultaneously related. We now turn to a model in which a single crime type is simultaneously related to several sanction types.

In this model we attempt to capture some of the interrelationships between crime and the CJS subsystems—police, courts, and corrections. These interrelationships derive from a model of the CJS put forward by Blumstein and Larson (1969) that characterizes the CJS as a flow process. A very simplified version of their conceptualization is shown in Figure 11.

Society generates crime, which is an input into the first of the pictured subsystems—the police. The police arrest suspects, some of whom are charged, while others are subsequently released without charge. The charged individuals are inputs to the courts subsystem. The courts in turn adjudicate the charges and some of those charged

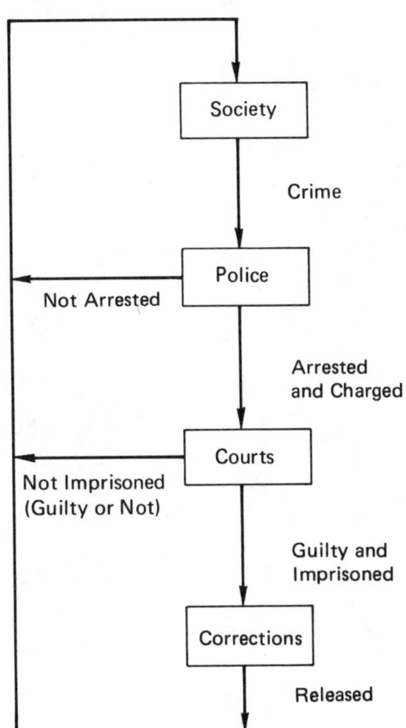

FIGURE 11 A simplified flow model of the criminal justice system.

are found guilty and imprisoned and turned over to the corrections subsystem. Others are not imprisoned, either because the charges do not lead to indictment or, if indicted, the indictment is dismissed or the defendant is acquitted—or, possibly, the defendant is convicted but not imprisoned. Finally, those individuals who are imprisoned are subsequently released to society either on parole or after having served their sentence.

The actions of each of the subsystems have implications for the possible penalties confronting a potential criminal; similarly, the amount of crime in the society has implications for the magnitudes of the flows through the subsystems.

In the models to be discussed, we attempt to capture these interrelationships between crimes and sanctions. Let us introduce the following notation:

C_t = total crimes in t
P_t^A = probability of apprehension and charge given a crime in t
$P_t^{G|A}$ = probability of conviction given charge in t
$P_t^{I|G}$ = probability of imprisonment given conviction in t
T_t = time served in period t
E_t^{Po} = police expenditures in t
E_t^J = judicial expenditures in t
E_t^{Pr} = prison expenditures in t
A_t = number of charges in t
G_t = number of convictions in t
I_t = number of imprisonments in t
U_t = prison utilization in period t
μ_t, ϵ_t^i, ν_t^i = random disturbances

$$C_t = f(P_t^A, P_t^{G|A}, P_t^{I|G}, T_t) + \mu_t \quad (8a)$$

$$P_t^A = g_1(E_t^{Po}, C_t) + \epsilon_t^1 \quad (8b)$$

$$P_t^{G|A} = g_2(E_t^J, A_t) + \epsilon_t^2 \quad (8c)$$

since $A_t = P_t^A C_t$ (ignoring sampling variation)

$$P_t^{G|A} = g_2(E_t^J, P_t^A C_t) + \epsilon_t^2 \quad (8c')$$

$$P_t^{I|G} = g_3(E_t^{Pr}, G_t, U_t) + \epsilon_t^3 \quad (8d)$$

since $G_t = P_t^{G|A} P_t^A C_t$

$$P_t^{I|G} = g_3(E_t^J, P_t^{G|A}P_t^A C_t, U_t) + \epsilon_t^3 \tag{8d'}$$

$$T_t = g_4(E_t^{Pr}, U_t) + \epsilon_t^4 \tag{8e}$$

$$E_t^{Po} = h_1(C_{t-1}, E_{t-1}^{Po}) + \nu_t^1 \tag{8f}$$

$$E_t^J = h_2(A_{t-1}, E_{t-1}^J) + \nu_t^2 \tag{8g}$$

$$E_t^{Pr} = h_3(U_{t-1}, E_{t-1}^{Pr}) + \nu_t^3 \tag{8h}$$

A crucial feature of this model is the distinction among the different types of sanctions. By differentiating among such sanctions as the probability of apprehension and charge, the probability of conviction given charge, the probability of imprisonment given conviction, and time served given imprisonment, the effect of each type of sanction can, at least theoretically, be measured. Different categories of sanctions are possible or greater refinement in the number of sanction types could be made. The crucial point, however, is that, *a priori,* there are good reasons for believing that the magnitude of the deterrent effect associated with each sanction type may be different. For example, the disutility of a conviction given charge is likely to be greater than the disutility associated with charge, since the stigma of conviction is greater than that associated with only being charged.

The likelihood of differential deterrent effects associated with different sanctions has both important technical implications for estimation and significant policy implications. For the purpose of estimation, if two types of sanctions, for example P^A and $P^{G|A}$, have different effects, then it is inappropriate to estimate a single parameter for the conglomerate effect of $P^G = P^A P^{G|A}$. Further, from a policy perspective, we would not want to aggregate the two, since it may be useful to know the relative magnitudes of the separate effects. By comparing effects with costs, we can determine where resources should be allocated. If, for example, identical increases in expenditures on police and courts would achieve the same percent increase in P_t^A and $P_t^{G|A}$, respectively, then crime reduction would be pursued more efficiently by allocating the additional expenditures to the sanction with the larger deterrent effect.

The second crucial feature of the system, which has significant implications for estimation, is the simultaneous relationship of C_t with each of the sanction variables, due perhaps to resource saturation considerations. Thus, given police resources, E_t^{Po} (which are themselves affected by the number of past crimes), the probability of arrest, P_t^A, depends on the current number of crimes, C_t, facing the police.[27] Further, although C_t only affects P_t^A directly, the levels of C_t also affect the workload of the courts and corrections subsystems "downstream" from the police. The probability of conviction given charge, $P_t^{G|A}$, is likely to be affected by the workload of the courts, A_t, but A_t will be determined by the product of C_t and P_t^A. Since C_t is also hypothesized to be affected by $P_t^{G|A}$, $P_t^{G|A}$ and C_t will be simultaneously related.

Similarly, the probability of imprisonment given conviction, $P_t^{I|G}$ is affected by G_t, the number of convictions in t. Since G_t is the product of C_t, P_t^A, and $P_t^{G|A}$, $P_t^{I|G}$ is simultaneously related to C_t. Time served, T_t, and $P_t^{I|G}$ are also hypothesized to be affected by the utilization of prison capacity, U_t, because we expect utilization to have its predominant effect on judges and parole boards who most directly control the size of the prison population. Since U_t is affected by the size of the prison population, which is just the number of currently imprisoned criminals (and thus depends on C_t, P_t^A, $P_t^{G|A}$, and $P_t^{I|G}$), T_t will also be simultaneously related to C_t.

As the model is specified, none of the sanctions is in a direct simultaneous relationship with any other (e.g., P_t^A directly affects $P_t^{G|A}$, but $P_t^{G|A}$ does not directly affect P_t^A). In terms of the problem of identifying the crime function, the validity of this assumption about the interrelationship among the sanctions is not relevant; the model could be generalized to allow such direct simultaneous relationships without altering our conclusion about the identifiability of the crime function (8a).

The crime rate, C_t, is determined by four sanction variables, all of which are presumed to be simultaneously related to C_t. Therefore, at least four independent restrictions are necessary to identify the crime function. Four such restrictions are provided by the exclusion of E_t^{Po}, E_t^J, E_t^{Pr}, and U_t (prison cell utilization).

The requirements for plausibly using these restrictions to identify the crime function have already been discussed. The key issues are worth restating. Since the expenditures variables are predetermined rather than exogenous [eqs. (8f)-(8g)], it is dangerous to assume no serial correlation in the ϵ_t^i. Some more general assumptions about the nature of that serial dependence are necessary; whatever the explicit assumption, data with a time-series component will be needed. The restrictions involving the exclusion of the police expenditure variable, E_t^{Po},

[27]In earlier sections, C_t was crimes per capita. Defining C_t as total crime instead of the crime rate would not affect our conclusion for this model; all state variables to be discussed, A_t, G_t, E_t^{Po}, E_t^J and E_t^{Pr} could be normalized by total population and thereby be redefined as rates.

and U_t are particularly vulnerable to criticism, since being a measure of the intensity of the police presence in the community and the severity of punishment, respectively, it can be argued convincingly that each should also be included in the crime function. However, since the four restrictions are just-identifying and thereby necessary for estimation, we cannot test the validity of the restrictions involving E_t^{Po} and U_t, even assuming away the serial correlation problem just discussed.

In this multiple-sanction model, identification of the crime function requires the joint use of both the expenditures and cell-capacity identification restrictions, whereas in the one-sanction models, either one was sufficient to just-identify. The necessity of using both categories of restrictions to identify the crime function points to still another problem. As the number of endogenous sanctions increases, the difficulties in identifying the crime functions increase also. In the context of a multiple-crime-type model, which will be discussed next, this difficulty can become fatal to identification.

C. A MULTIPLE-CRIME-TYPE, SINGLE-SANCTION MODEL

Our discussion thus far has been limited to the consideration of single-crime-type models. We now consider the problem of identifying each of the crime equations in a multiple-crime-type model. A multiple-crime-type formulation is of interest because each crime type will incrementally impact a single set of CJS resources. An examination of their joint effect has important implications for identification.

A two-crime-type, single-sanction characterization of such a phenomenon is given below, along with the model's equivalent flow diagram, in Figure 12.

$$C_t^1 = f_1(S_t^1) + \epsilon_t^1 \tag{9a}$$

$$C_t^2 = f_2(S_t^2) + \epsilon_t^2 \tag{9b}$$

$$S_t^1 = g^1(E_t, C_t^1, C_t^2, S_t^2) + \epsilon_t^3 \tag{9c}$$

$$S_t^2 = g^2(E_t, C_t^1, C_t^2, S_t^1) + \epsilon_t^4 \tag{9d}$$

$$E_t = h(E_{t-1}, C_{t-1}^1, C_{t-1}^2) + \epsilon_t^5 \tag{9e}$$

where:

C_t^i = crimes of type i per capita in t

S_t^i = sanctions per crime of type i in t

E_t = CJS expenditures in t.

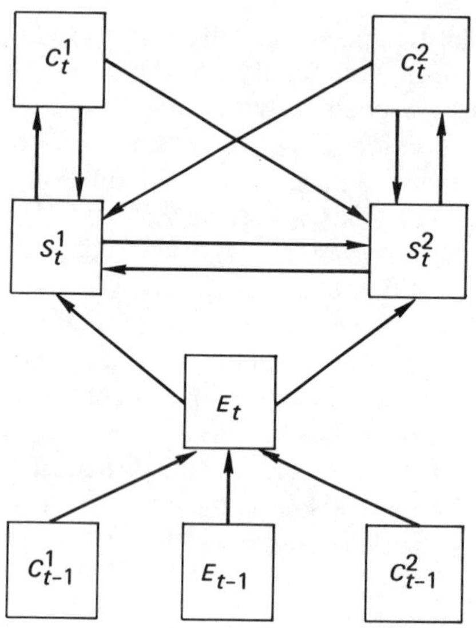

FIGURE 12 Flow diagram of multiple-crime-type, single-sanction model.

As indicated by eqs. (9c) and (9d), S_t^i is a function of total resources available to the CJS (E_t), the demands placed on these resources by each of the crime inputs (C_t^i, $i = 1,2$), and the level of the sanction imposed for the other crime type. The resource saturation theory would predict that increases in E_t would act to increase S_t^i ($\partial g^i/\partial E_t > 0$), increases in the prevalence of either crime type would act to reduce S_t^i ($\partial g^i/\partial C_t^j < 0$, $j = 1,2$) and increases in S_t^j would decrease S_t^i, $i \neq j$ ($\partial g^i/\partial S_t^j < 0$) because the additional resources required to increase S_t^j would be drawn from those used to maintain S_t^i.

Alternative theories of the effects of crime on sanctions might make different predictions, but the crucial point is that sanctions for each crime type are influenced by the level of both types of crime, because each crime type impacts the common set of CJS resources.

Considering eqs. (9a)-(9d) as the simultaneous system and treating E_t as predetermined by eq. (9e), the number of endogenous variables, M, is 4. Hence, at least three restrictions are necessary for the identification of each crime function. One such restriction is provided by the exclusion of E_t from eqs. (9a) and (9b) under assumptions outlined previously. A second is provided by the assumption that crime of one type has no direct effect on crime of the other type. The final restriction necessary for identification of each crime function, however, rests additionally upon the assumption that sanctions for one crime type do not influence the level of crime for the other crime type (e.g., S_t^1 does not affect C_t^2). In the context of property crimes, (e.g., larceny and burglary), the possibility of such a cross-effect is quite conceivable and is indeed consistent with the basic principle that underlies the deterrence hypothesis—namely, that behavior is influenced by incentives.

If such cross-effects exist, then the two crime functions become:

$$C_t^1 = f^1(S_t^1, S_t^2) + \epsilon_t^1 \qquad (9a')$$

$$C_t^2 = f^2(S_t^1, S_t^2) + \epsilon_t^2 \qquad (9b')$$

These more general versions of the two crime functions are no longer identified; there are now only two, not three restrictions on them. Since estimation requires the imposition of three identification restrictions on each crime equation, identification would require that an additional restriction be imposed. For this simple two-crime-type, single-sanction model, the prison cell utilization identification might also be imposed.

This, however, is really only an illusory solution to the identification problem in a multi-crime-type setting. The addition of still another crime type (e.g., robbery) with S_t^3 affecting C_t^1, C_t^2 and C_t^3, and C_t^3 being affected by S_t^1, S_t^2, and S_t^3 would increase the number of endogenous variables *(M)* by two (C_t^3 and S_t^3) but would increase the number of restrictions on each crime equation by only one (because C_t^3 does not directly affect C_t^1 or C_t^2). Hence we would have moved from a just-identified case of $M = 4$ with three restrictions to one of $M = 6$ with only four restrictions, and identification would fail. In general, identification of the crime functions in a multi-crime, single-sanction model seems even more difficult than in the single-crime-type case.

The difficulties in finding sufficient restrictions become even more acute when multiple sanctions are introduced into the model. If, for example, S_t^i were divided into the four sanction types discussed in the single-crime-type, multiple-sanctions model and the sanctions for each of the three crime types all had cross-effects on the other crime types, the number of endogenous variables would be 15. Thus, 12 identification restrictions would be required to estimate each of the crime functions, in addition to the automatic restrictions that only one type of crime appears in each such function.

In general, a model with *n* crime types and *m* sanction types would require $n \times m$ non-automatic restrictions to identify the crime functions. Hybrid versions of the model would require fewer additional restrictions. For example, one might plausibly assume that cross-effects only exist among subsets of crime types (perhaps distinguishing between property and violent crimes). From a practical perspective, however, such an approach offers little help since, for example, even a two-sanction model for the four index property crimes (i.e., robbery, burglary, larceny, and auto theft) would require eight non-automatic restrictions to identify each of the separate crime functions.

In view of the difficulty in generating plausible restrictions, the estimation of the generalized multi-crime-type, multi-sanction model including cross-effects of the sanctions does not appear feasible. To the extent that the generalized model is viewed as the only plausible characterization of the simultaneous association between crime and sanctions, an argument as to the impossibility of valid identification is even more compelling than in the case of the simplified models discussed earlier.

The apparent infeasibility of identifying the generalized model hinges upon the assumption that the sanctions for C_t^i directly affect C_t^j. It may be that such cross-effects are, at most, very weak. The difficulty is that, using aggregate, non-experimental data, we cannot test for this. Moreover, a model estimated simply assuming no cross-effects would always remain suspect for having assumed that cross-effects are not operating.

V. CONCLUSION

Identification is the *sine qua non* of all estimation and especially of simultaneous equation estimation. It establishes the feasibility of determining the structure of a system from the data generated by that system. Without identification, estimation is logically impossible.

Researchers who have employed simultaneous estimation techniques to study the deterrent effect of sanctions on crime have failed to recognize fully the importance of this issue. The restrictions that they (implicitly or explicitly) use to gain apparent identification have little theoretical or empirical basis.

In this paper we have examined a variety of plausible approaches to the identification of the crime functions in a system in which crime rates and sanction levels are simultaneously related. Our conclusions with regard to the feasibility of identification, while not wholly negative, are certainly soberly cautious. In particular, it appears very doubtful that work using only aggregate cross-sectional data can ever succeed in identifying and consistently estimating the deterrent effect of punishment on crime. If we are to know that effect and, particularly, if we are to rely on that knowledge for policy purposes, that knowledge must come from analyses of a different sort. In particular, analyses using aggregate non-experimental data must have a time-series component in the data (i.e., pure time-series or a time-series, cross-section), and the estimation procedures must account for the possibility of serial correlation in the stochastic components of the specification.

TECHNICAL NOTE: LAGGED MODELS OF THE MUTUAL ASSOCIATION OF CRIME AND SANCTIONS

The principal focus of this paper is the estimability of simultaneous models of crime and sanctions. In a simultaneous formulation, the mutual interaction is assumed to occur contemporaneously during the period of observation. For an observation period of a given length, a necessary requirement for a phenomenon to be simultaneous is that the impact of the actions taken by the system's actors (e.g., criminals and the CJS) be transmitted sufficiently fast so that each actor can react to the actions of the other actors within the observation period. Thus, a critical parameter is the length of the observation period. If the period is sufficiently short, then any mutual association can be modeled as non-simultaneous, whereas, if the period is sufficiently long, all such associations can be made simultaneous. In the context of the mutual association of crimes and sanctions, in which observations are generally made annually, the association is simultaneous if within a 1-year period potential criminals receive cues on the current level of sanctions being delivered by the CJS and if the level of crime in the current period also works to influence the sanctions delivered by the CJS.

If information does not flow this quickly, an alternative characterization of the mutual association involves lags. In the single-crime-type, single-sanction model, such a characterization could take the form

$$C_t = a + bS_{t-1} + \epsilon_t \tag{10a}$$

$$S_t = c + dC_{t-1} + \mu_t \tag{10b}$$

If the parameters of this model are to be estimated consistently by regression, the disturbances, ϵ_t and μ_t, must not be serially correlated.[28]

[28]The parameters of one of the equations could be consistently estimated if there is not serial correlation in that equation's disturbance. In general, however, if ϵ_t and μ_t are correlated either with their own past values or with each others' past values, consistency will not be present. In such general cases, the covariances of S_{t-1} and C_{t-1} with ϵ_t and μ_t will be complex expressions involving both the serial correlation behavior of ϵ_t and μ_t and their covariance.

In our prior discussion, we elaborated upon the reasons for believing that there is, in fact, serial correlation. Hence, we would have very little confidence in any causal inferences drawn from parameter estimates that are generated by ordinary least squares.

Our pessimism about using regression is reinforced by the fact that in the simplest case, where there is only serial correlation in ϵ_t, the serial correlation will result in an over-estimate of the deterrent effect of sanctions. Suppose that ϵ_t follows a first-order autoregressive process with parameter ρ. Let σ^2 denote the variance of ϵ_t. Additionally, assume that $d < 0$ (i.e., increases in C_{t-1} decrease S_t). Under these plausible conditions, if $\epsilon_{t-2} > 0$, then C_{t-2} will be larger than predicted by the structural component of eq. (10a). This larger-than-predicted value of C_{t-2} will drive down the value of S_{t-1}, since $d < 0$. In addition, since $\epsilon_{t-2} > 0$, ϵ_t will tend to be positive because cov $(\epsilon_t, \epsilon_{t-2}) = \rho^2\sigma^2 > 0$. With $\epsilon_t > 0$, C_t would be larger than that predicted by the structural component of eq. (10a). We would then observe large values of C_t being associated with small values of S_{t-1}, even if $b = 0$. This negative association, however, would drive the estimate of b to a negative value.

Attempts to analyze models of the type given by eqs. (10a) and (10b) have been limited to the sociological literature on deterrence (Logan 1975, and Tittle and Rowe 1974). In these analyses, S_t is defined as arrests per crime. Tittle and Rowe found a negative and often significant path coefficient between S_{t-1} and C_t, a result that is consistent with the deterrence hypothesis, while Logan found no such association.

The path coefficient estimate of the association between S_{t-1} and C_t is estimated in a way that is analytically equivalent to regression estimation of b in the model shown in eq. (10a). Therefore, these path coefficients suffer from all the ambiguities that we have discussed.

Models in which the mutual association between crime and sanctions occurs with a lag, however, are attractive because they offer an intuitively attractive characterization of this mutual association. Information on the sanctioning behavior of the CJS is probably transmitted very slowly through the kinds of cues that have been discussed. An assumption that information lag on sanctions is greater than a year may, therefore, be plausible in most instances.[29] Under such an assumption that C_t is a function of sanctions in prior periods, we could maintain the assumption that C_t affects S_t [e.g., C_{t-1} is replaced by C_t in eq. (10b)],

[29]In specific instances where official statements are published announcing changes in sanctioning practice (e.g., the case in which the District Attorney of San Francisco announced that prostitution would no longer be prosecuted), the assumption of a 1-year lag would be untenable.

and the model would remain non-simultaneous—but there would still be a catch. For such a model to be consistently estimated by ordinary regression, there not only must be no serial correlation, but also ϵ_t and μ_t must be uncorrelated.

Thus, whatever the specific nature of the model employing a lagged structure, estimation must use methodologies that allow for the possibility of serial correlation and non-zero covariance in the stochastic terms if the estimated coefficients are to be plausibly regarded as an estimate of the causal effect of sanctions on crime.

REFERENCES

Avio, K., and Clarke, S. (1974) Property Crime in Canada: An Econometric Study. Prepared for the Ontario Economic Council.

Blumstein, A., and Cohen, J. (1973) A theory of the stability of punishment. *Journal of Criminal Law and Criminology* 64(2):198-207.

Blumstein, A., and Larson, R. (1969) Models of a total criminal justice system. *Operations Research* 17(2):199-232.

Blumstein, A., Cohen, J., and Nagin, D. (1976) The dynamics of a homeostatic punishment process. *Journal of Criminal Law and Criminology* 67(3):317-34.

Carr-Hill, R. A., and Stern, H. H. (1973) An econometric model of the supply and control of recorded offenses in England and Wales. *Journal of Public Economics* 2(4):289-318.

Criminal Justice Bulletin (1976) Alabama Prison. Newsletter published by Anderson Editorial Services, Cincinnati.

Ehrlich, I. (1970) Participation in Illegitimate Activities: An Economic Analysis. Doctoral dissertation, Columbia University.

Ehrlich, I. (1973) Participation in illegitimate activities: a theoretical and empirical investigation. *Journal of Political Economy* 81(3):521-67.

Ehrlich, I. (1975) The deterrent effect of capital punishment: a question of life and death. *American Economic Review* 65(3):397-417.

Fisher, F. M. (1961) On the cost of approximate specification in simultaneous equation estimation. *Econometrica* 29(2):139-70.

Fisher, F. M. (1966) *The Identification Problem in Econometrics*. New York: McGraw-Hill Book Company.

Gibbs, J. B. (1968) Crime, punishment and deterrence. *Southwestern Social Science Quarterly* 48(4):515-30.

Gibbs, J. B. (1975) *Crime, Punishment and Deterrence*. New York: American Elsevier.

Greenberg, D. (1977) Crime, deterrence research, and social policy. In Stuart Nagel, ed., *Modeling the Criminal Justice System*. Los Angeles: Sage Publications.

Logan, C. (1975) Arrest rates and deterrence. *Social Science Quarterly* 56(3):376-89.

McPheters, L., and Stronge, W. B. (1974) Law enforcement expenditures and urban crime. *National Tax Journal* 27(4):633-44.

Sjoquist, D. (1973) Property crime and economic behavior: some empirical results. *American Economic Review* 83(3):439-46.

Tittle, C. (1969) Crime rates and legal sanctions. *Social Problems* 16(Spring):408-28.

Tittle, C., and Rowe, A. (1974) Certainty of arrest and crime rates: a further test of the deterrence hypothesis. *Social Forces* 52(4):455-62.

Prospects for Inference on Deterrence through Empirical Analysis of Individual Criminal Behavior

CHARLES F. MANSKI

This paper explores the possibilities for inferring the impact of deterrence policies through the observation and analysis of individual criminal behavior.

While society's ultimate interest in deterrence policies may be in their impact on aggregate crime rates, such policies directly influence individual criminal behavior. To study deterrence at the level of individual decision making is therefore natural. To date, almost all empirical analyses of deterrence have been based on macro models of crime commission and have used aggregated crime rate, socioeconomic, and demographic statistics as their data. The macro approach, it is now generally recognized, suffers from deep logical problems that make clear interpretation of empirical findings difficult to achieve. Empirical analysis of individual criminal behavior avoids these problems—hence, the practical interest in this approach. Unfortunately,

---

Charles F. Manski is Associate Professor of Economics, School of Urban and Public Affairs, Carnegie-Mellon University.

NOTE: This paper is a considerably revised version of a paper prepared for the conference convened by the National Research Council's Panel on Research on Deterrent and Incapacitative Effects. I have benefited from discussions with Alfred Blumstein and Daniel Nagin and from the opportunity to discuss the ideas contained herein at the conference and at a seminar at the Hoover Institution. All opinions and conclusions expressed in this paper are mine alone.

individual-level analysis of criminal decision making has its own difficulties, which are basically operational rather than conceptual.

Section I is an overview of the issues that make empirical analysis of individual criminal behavior appealing in the abstract but troublesome in practice. The primary problem hindering individual-level analysis is data availability. A secondary problem exists with respect to the structuring of realistic and tractable behavioral models. These two concerns are examined in some detail in Sections II and III, respectively. Section IV summarizes the prospects for obtaining useful evidence on deterrence from studies of individual criminal behavior.

I. OVERVIEW

DETERRENCE AND CRIME RATES

Deterrence policy might be characterized as an attempt to balance society's desire for lower crime rates with the resource costs of doing so, the constitutional requirements of due process, and a punishment suited to the crime. By lowering the attractiveness of criminal activities, deterrence policies seek to channel individual decisions away from such activities, thus lowering the aggregate rate of crime commission. The actual impact of any policy on crime rates, however, can be difficult to assess. Two distinct forces create this problem.

First, an individual's reaction to shifts in deterrence policies can be quite complex. For example, an increase in efforts to deter a particular type of crime may induce the individual not to stop his criminal activities but to shift them to other crime types. That is, deterrence policies can have crime substitution effects as well as crime rate effects. As another example, an increase in the severity of sentences may lead persons committing crimes to resist apprehension more strongly, thus inducing additional crimes. In particular, a person facing capital punishment, if caught, can be expected to resist capture by whatever means he can. A comprehensive analysis of deterrence policies requires one to cope with such behavioral complexities.

Second, determination of the impact of a deterrence policy on aggregate crime commission is not simply a matter of adding up isolated effects across individuals. While the individual may view his environment as exogenous, the aggregate crime rates for crimes of different types are endogeneous variables in a system in which criminals seek opportunities of the various crime types and potential victims seek, through collective and private action, to dissuade the criminals. To determine the ultimate effect of a deterrence policy on crime rates, one should model the behavior of all the actors in the system and appropriately characterize their interactions. In particular, crime rate determination might be treated as an equilibration process.

This paper concerns itself with issues that arise in empirically modeling the possibly complex manner in which deterrence policies may influence individual criminal behavior. It does not address the larger question of empirically modeling the ultimate, equilibrium impact of deterrence policies on aggregate crime rates.

THE ATTEMPT TO INFER DETERRENT EFFECTS FROM MACRO CRIME MODELS

To date, almost all empirical analyses of deterrence have been based on macro models of crime commission and aggregated crime data. (In particular, see Carr-Hill and Stern 1973, Ehrlich 1973, 1975, and Forst 1976, among others. A fairly complete listing of macro studies is given in this volume.) Both the logical foundations and operational aspects of the macro studies have recently been subjected to intense scrutiny. (See the papers by Fisher and Nagin, Klein *et al.*, Vandaele, and Nagin in this volume, Passell and Taylor 1976, and Peck 1976 for reviews of portions of the literature, and see this entire volume for a comprehensive overview.) Given the extensive critiques available, it is necessary here only to state the two fundamental problems with macro studies that particularly motivate interest in individual-level analysis of deterrence.

First, aggregate crime rates are determined within a system whose actors include criminals, victims, and the various organs of the criminal justice complex—the police, courts, prisons, etc. Attempts to model the interplay of these actors realistically at the macro level inevitably conclude that the decisions of the actors are so directly interdependent and they share so many common exogeneous determinants that the effects of deterrence policies on aggregate crime rates cannot easily, if at all, be isolated within a macro model. That is, within such a model, realistic prior assumptions sufficient to identify a deterrent effect are not generally available.

Second, in the absence of considerable homogeneity in the decision rules and circumstances of individual criminals, the aggregation of individual criminal behavior over the population implies no simple macro function adequately capturing the behavior of that population. That individual criminals are homogeneous enough in their behaviors to justify the existence of a macro crime function of the type commonly assumed in the literature is *a priori* unlikely and, at any rate, can be verified only through individual-level analysis.

EMPIRICAL ANALYSIS OF INDIVIDUAL CRIMINAL BEHAVIOR: CONCEPTUAL ADVANTAGES

The advantages of individual-level analysis of criminal behavior for the study of deterrence are in counterpoint to the problems inherent in the macro approach.

First, because any individual can generally influence only negligibly the level of aggregate criminal opportunities and the operation of the criminal justice system, it is realistic to model the individual criminal as acting within a recursive system in which the aggregated decisions of other actors influence his own behavior, but not vice versa. Given such a recursive structure, deterrent effects are in principle identifiable through examination of individual criminal behavior.

Second, in contrast to the *ad hoc* reasoning on which direct specification of a macro crime function must be based, there exists substantial, if conflicting, behavioral theory and observation to guide model selection when the individual is the unit of analysis. Moreover, given a model of individual criminal behavior, the appropriate function characterizing population behavior, both in and out of equilibrium, can be derived by explictly aggregating the individual decisions predicted by the model.

These conceptual advantages of individual-level analysis are, of course, not specific to the context of criminal behavior. Rather, they are expressions of general arguments in favor of empirically modeling behavior at the level at which it occurs.

EMPIRICAL ANALYSIS OF INDIVIDUAL CRIMINAL BEHAVIOR: OPERATIONAL PROBLEMS

Beginning with Becker (1968) and continuing through Ehrlich (1973) and Block and Heinecke (1973) among others, economists have produced a succession of theoretical models of individual criminal behavior. In the decade since Becker awoke professional interest in the economics of crime, almost no attention has been given to the empirical analysis of such behavior.[1] This contrast between the theoretical

[1]Attempts at individual-level empirical analysis within limited contexts have been made by Weimer and Stonebraker (1975) and Witte (1976). The empirical analysis performed in Ehrlich (1973) is at the macro level and is only marginally related to the theoretical individual-choice model he develops in the same paper.

and empirical literatures is striking, particularly since theoretical models, by their nature, may suggest the existence of a deterrent effect but can provide no evidence as to its magnitude. The question of existence, it seems fair to say, is relatively uncontroversial. The crucial policy matter of magnitude is inherently an empirical issue.

The absence of empirical work on individual criminal behavior derives primarily from the lack of suitable data. However the criminal's decision problem is theoretically structured and whatever form of decision rule the criminal is assumed to use, empirical analysis of criminal choice requires that one be able to characterize the alternatives available to each of an appropriate sample of individuals and specify what choices each one makes.

The only readily available data on individual criminal behavior have been contained in the "rap sheets," (individual criminal histories) maintained by the criminal justice system for individuals with existing criminal records.[2] These files, which record arrests, dispositions of cases, and limited individual demographic data, are of very limited use in behavioral modeling. In particular, because rap sheets can only report those crimes resulting in an arrest, these files provide a systematically biased sample of crimes actually committed and no data at all characterizing the opportunities, both criminal and legitimate, that an individual has available but does not select. If empirical analysis of criminal behavior is to be pursued, alternative data sources, less accessible than rap sheets, will have to be developed.

A secondary problem hindering empirical research has been the absence of satisfactory econometric models of criminal behavior. Perhaps because lack of data has made empirical behavioral modeling seem impractical, the existing theoretical models of criminal choice have not been developed with empirical application in mind. These models, while insightful, are too idealized and abstract from too much of the criminal decision problem to serve as useful bases for empirical work. If empirical criminal choice analysis is to be pursued, appropriate econometric choice models must be developed, not only for their direct application but also to guide the process of data collection.

The prospects for remedying the data and the modeling problems confronting empirical analysis of criminal behavior are not clear. Section II below explores some potentially useful but as yet untested data sources and elaborates on the uses and limitations of rap sheet data.

[2]While public use data files are not generally maintained, rap sheet data in various forms have been made available by the FBI and some state agencies to a number of researchers for studies of crime commission. Some of the sources used are described in Cohen (in this volume).

Section III then discusses the features econometric models of criminal behavior should have and introduces a new modeling approach that may prove useful in practice.

II. DATA NEEDS AND SOURCES

DATA REQUIREMENTS FOR BEHAVIORAL MODELING

The data requirements for empirical behavioral modeling can be described only in the context of a specified behavioral model and an inferential procedure. If we adopt the usual economic approach, in which behavior is manifested by choice from a given choice set, or, more generally, a time path of choices from a sequence of such sets, and where inference is predicated on the observation of revealed preferences, two general if fairly obvious principles for data collection can be asserted.

First, as stated earlier, the data should, for each decision maker in an appropriate sample, be sufficient to characterize the decision maker, his available alternatives, and his actual decisions. It should be emphasized that for empirical choice analysis it is as important to know what alternatives are available but not chosen as to identify the chosen alternatives. In attempting to use for choice analysis data sets originally collected for other purposes, researchers often find that such data sets specify in great detail what people do but give no information about what they could have done. To perform the analysis, the researcher must then deal with a sometimes difficult missing data problem.[3]

Second, I have referred to the need for an "appropriate sample" of decision makers. Part of the specification of a behavioral model must be a definition of the population of decision makers to which the model applies. Given a specified population, data may be collected using any sampling process, as long as two conditions are met. First, the sam-

[3]In a neoclassical choice context, in which the choice set is fully determined by knowledge of commodity prices and consumer income, the missing data problem is easily handled. In discrete choice contexts, in which choice sets usually differ in complex ways among decision makers, the problem can be quite serious. The prevailing "fix" is for the analyst to make a point prediction of the available alternatives, thus imputing a choice set to the decision maker. Kohn et al. (1976) provide an example of choice set imputation in a study of students' educational choices. Lerman and Ben-Akiva (1975) use a different imputation procedure in a study of transportation choices. A theoretically more satisfactory but considerably less practical solution to the missing data problem would be for the analyst to predict a probability distribution of choice sets and, integrating over this distribution, make unconditional inferences on behavior.

pling process should be informative. In particular, if inferences are to be based on the distribution of point estimates of parameters, the relevant parameters should be estimable under the sampling process used. Second, the analyst should have enough prior knowledge of the sampling process to be able to specify a proper inferential procedure. It is too often forgotten in econometric work that the statistical properties of an estimator depend on the sampling process by which observations are drawn from the population as well as on the economic process governing the population.[4]

Within the context of the modeling of criminal behavior, some additional guidance for data collection beyond the above general principles can be offered.

First, anyone can commit a crime. Hence, the relevant decision-making population for a study of criminal behavior should be the entire population of an area and not some *a priori* specified "criminal element." To analyze criminal behavior effectively, it will usually be essential to sample from the full population rather than only the subpopulation known to have previously committed a crime.[5]

Second, the decision to engage in criminal activities is a temporarily recurrent one, not a single irrevocable act. Over time, people can move in and out of criminal activities or among criminal activities of different types. It follows that in modeling criminal behavior, longitudinal data will be useful for some purposes and crucial for others.

[4]In the context of linear models, the literature on "limited dependent variables" has made the dependency of estimator properties on the sampling process clear. See for example Tobin (1958) and Hausman and Wise (1977), in which it is shown that ordinary least squares estimation is inconsistent if the sampling process conditions draw on the value of the dependent variable. In the context of discrete choice models, the literature on "choice-based sampling" demonstrates this same dependency. In particular, see Manski and Lerman (1977), in which it is proved that a familiar maximum likelihood estimator is inconsistent if the sampling process conditions draw on the identities of chosen alternatives.

[5]I say "usually" rather than "always" because there do exist circumstances, rarely achieved in practice, in which prior information about the characteristics of the decision-making population allows the analyst to draw inferences about population behavior given a sample of known criminals only. A sample consisting only of known criminals is a "choice-based sample" in that decision makers are drawn into the sample based on their past choice of a criminal career. Estimation in choice-based samples is possible under realistic informational conditions, if at least some individuals selecting each available alternative are included in the sample. Thus, non-criminals as well as criminals must be included in the sample. A random sample of the population is not required to make estimation feasible. See Manski and McFadden (1977) for a detailed examination of estimation in choice-based samples.

Finally, the criminal's decision problem may be structured in a variety of distinct ways. For example, some of the existing theoretical models of criminal behavior regard the decision problem as one of time allocation, without reference to the actual commission of criminal acts. Other studies view the criminal instantaneously deciding whether or not to commit a given crime and make no reference to a time allocation decision. Clearly, the data one wishes to collect depend on the way one wishes to model the criminal decision problem.

In the remainder of this section, three alternative data sources on criminal behavior will be examined in light of the above discussion. These sources are, in order of consideration, self-reports, criminal justice system records, and victimization surveys.

DATA SOURCES: SELF-REPORTS OF CRIMINAL BEHAVIOR

In principle, self-reports of criminal behavior, obtained through survey instruments, provide by far the most comprehensive source of data on individual criminal behavior. In particular, self-report surveys can give direct data on committed crimes not resulting in an arrest and information about the criminal and legitimate alternatives available to but not chosen by individuals. They can provide in great detail perceptual data, such as subjective probabilities of arrests and convictions for crimes of different types, as well as individual background data. The potential comprehensiveness of the self-report data obtainable for each sampled individual is complemented by the flexibility that the analyst has in principle in selecting a sample. In particular, self-reports may provide the only viable mechanism for sampling individuals not engaged in criminal activities and for whom, consequently, criminal justice system records can provide no data.

If trained as an economist, one's temptation may be to dismiss out of hand analyses based on criminal self-reports. The incentives to report criminal activity inaccurately plus the frailty of human memory, it will be said, make self-report data too inaccurate to be useful. Such a judgment should be withheld, at least temporarily, for several reasons.

First, substantial experience with self-report surveys in the sociological literature has produced numerous instructive failures and some apparent successes. Certainly, a considerable amount has been learned [see Reiss (1973) for an interesting overview of this literature].

Second, it should be recognized that self-report data need not be objectively correct in order to be usable. What is necessary is that responses be systematically related to the "truth" and that it be possible to determine the nature of this relationship. For example, if it were known that respondents tend to underestimate frequency of crime commission in a systematic way, then reported frequencies could be blown up to their true values *ex post facto*.

The third and most compelling reason for interest in self-reports is the inherent limitations in alternative data sources. It can be seen that criminal justice system records and victimization survey results (the only other data sources apparent to me) are both fairly restricted in the sampling processes possible and in the information obtainable for each sampled individual. Given this fact, self-reports may provide the only vehicle for the study of many aspects of criminal behavior.

Because there now is considerable uncertainty about the meaningfulness of self-reported crime data, it is premature to recommend acceptance of self-reports as a data strategy for studying criminal behavior. If self-report surveys are eventually to be used in empirical deterrence analysis, some modifications to existing survey practices will be required.

A good example of current practice is a recent Rand Corporation survey of repetitively violent offenders. [See Petersilia *et al.* (1977) for a description of the survey and an analysis of the results.] This study consists of in-depth interviews with a small number of persons (50) convicted on robbery charges and subsequently imprisoned. The survey asks for extensive personal background data and a history of crimes committed, arrests, and convictions by crime type. It also records subjective arrest expectations and asks the respondent to make some hypothetical choices.

Ignoring problems with the way some questions are worded, the Rand survey, like others before it, is inadequate for deterrence analysis on two grounds, both remediable. First, the survey seeks no information on the environments in which crimes were and were not committed. In particular, alternative criminal and legitimate alternatives available to the individual but not selected are not identified. Second, limitation of the respondents to convicted felons makes it impossible to use the study to ask why some people pursue criminal careers and others do not. For that purpose, administration of the survey to a broader cross-section of the population would be necessary.

DATA SOURCES: CRIMINAL JUSTICE SYSTEM RECORDS

The data available from the criminal justice system regarding individual criminal behavior takes two forms. First there are the individual criminal histories or rap sheets mentioned earlier. Second, there are some less accessible but possibly more useful data on plea and sentence bargaining decisions. The two data forms are different enough to warrant separate discussions.

Individual Criminal Histories

Rap sheets, it will be recalled, record arrests, disposition of cases, and limited demographic data for individuals with known criminal histories. The use of such data to analyze criminal behavior is problematic for a number of distinct reasons.

First, the behavioral modeler's concern is with crimes committed, and rap sheets record arrests, not crimes. The use of arrest records as a proxy for crimes committed is possible only if the arrest process is *a priori* known or otherwise can be disentangled from the crime commission process. To see why, consider a person with attributes s arrested for a crime of type γ during some time period. Let Q denote the deterrence policies in effect at the time of the crime and arrest. The probability of observing such an arrest can be written as

$$P(\gamma \text{ arrest}/s,Q) = P(\gamma \text{ crime}/s,Q)\, P(\gamma \text{ arrest}/\gamma \text{ crime}, s,Q)$$

where it is assumed for simplicity that false arrests do not occur and where determinants of the probabilities other than s and Q have been suppressed.

The problem is that the crime commission probability $P(\gamma \text{ crime}/s,Q)$, reflecting criminal behavior, and the conditional arrest probability $P(\gamma \text{ arrest}/\gamma \text{ crime},s,Q)$, reflecting police action, may both depend nontrivially on the same variables s and Q. For example, a person's criminal skill can be expected to affect his crime commission probability positively and his conditional arrest probability negatively. The density of police patrols should negatively influence crime commission and positively influence the arrest rate on committed crimes.[6]

Clearly, without further information, any attempt to analyze observed arrests as a function of personal characteristics s and deterrence policies Q will confound criminal behavior with police action. In other words, in the absence of prior assumptions, the two structural proc-

[6]The statement that increased density of police patrols will increase the arrest rate of committed crimes must be interpreted in a *ceteris paribus* sense only. If crimes differ in the ease with which arrests are made and if police vigilance dissuades the commission of easily arrestable crimes more than it does other crimes, then an increase in police patrols may move the mix of crimes committed toward those for which arrests are difficult. Hence, we may observe a negative relation between police efforts and arrest rates.

esses jointly determining arrests cannot be identified relative to one another.

The only way to use rap sheets to study deterrence is to make enough prior assumptions about the arrest process to render the crime commission process identifiable. For a few crime types, such as draft evasion and bail jumping, almost all offenses result in the issuance of an arrest warrant, if not actual capture, so crime commission can be properly inferred from criminal justice system records (see for example the study of draft evasion by Blumstein and Nagin 1977). More generally, however, little is known about the arrest process, so that realistic identifying assumptions cannot be made. In the operations research literature modeling crime commission as a stochastic process, it is conventionally assumed that conditional arrest probabilities given crime commission are not affected by deterrence policies and do not vary systematically across individuals (see for example Shinnar and Shinnar 1975 and the review by Cohen in this volume). These assumptions are not substantiated in this literature and seem quite unrealistic.

If the identification problem in arrest records can be suitably resolved, other difficulties still confront the use of such data to study criminal behavior. For one thing, rap sheets can provide no information about criminal and legitimate opportunities available to but not selected by the sampled individuals. Another problem, referred to earlier, is that the sampling process generating observations excludes non-criminals. Finally, the personal attributes recorded for sampled individuals are generally limited to demographic characteristics.

The above problems severely restrict the potential usefulness of rap sheet data for deterrence analysis. Such data may find application in circumstances in which the arrest process can be *a priori* specified, the criminal's choice set can be successfully imputed by the analyst, data on the behavior of non-criminals are available from other sources, and the personal characteristics relevant to decision making are basically demographic ones. One should expect to find these circumstances only rarely.

Plea and Sentence Bargaining Decisions

An important issue in deterrence policy concerns the relative deterrent effects of high arrest and conviction probabilities on one hand and long sentences given conviction on the other. Interestingly, data on plea and sentence bargaining decisions may be able to shed light on this question.

Consider the arrested person offered a plea bargain by the district attorney. His choice between pleading guilty to a reduced charge and pleading innocent to a higher charge is essentially a choice between a certain conviction with a relatively low sentence and an uncertain conviction with a longer sentence. A similar trade-off between probability of conviction and sentence length is faced in a sentence bargaining situation. What this suggests is the use of observations on plea and sentence bargaining decisions to infer the relative weights that criminals give to conviction probabilities and sentences, and hence the relative effectiveness of each in deterring crime.

Fortunately, criminal justice system data on plea and sentence bargain decisions can be quite good. As a concrete example, in Alameda County, California, the District Attorney's office routinely records all offers of plea bargains, defendants' responses, ultimate case dispositions, and defendants' criminal background data. These records also include prosecutors' subjective probabilities of conviction if the case goes to trial. Assuming that defendants' subjective probabilities coincide with those of prosecutors', these data provide a solid base for analysis of plea bargaining and, ultimately, for inference of deterrence.[7] A paper by Weimer and Stonebraker (1975) has already opened up this fertile source. Most district attorney's offices do not keep as organized or extensive a set of records as does the Alameda County office. There would, however, appear to be no fundamental reason preventing analogous, or even more sophisticated, systems from being instituted elsewhere.

Obviously, analysis of plea and sentence bargaining decisions cannot illuminate all aspects of criminal behavior. Even where such analysis appears useful in principle, operational problems may make inference difficult. In particular, if the interaction of the arrested person and the district attorney is really one of bargaining, that is, gaming, behavioral analysis will be complicated by the absence of a pre-specified choice set and the presence of strategic elements in decisions. Another potential problem regards the transfer of inferences based on plea bargaining decisions to forecast aspects of crime commission decisions. Conceivably (although I think unlikely), criminals weigh conviction probabilities against sentences differently in the two contexts. In exploring the use of plea and sentence bargaining data for deterrence analysis, one should keep these possible difficulties in mind. Nevertheless, such explorations seems quite worthwhile.

[7]When the defendant has an experienced lawyer, it is plausible to assume that defense and prosecution subjective probabilities will coincide. In other situations, however, such coincidence of opinions seems harder to justify.

DATA SOURCES: VICTIMIZATION SURVEYS

Self-reports of criminal activity and criminal justice system records would appear to be the only data sources allowing direct investigation of individual criminal behavior. In this section, I would like to suggest a somewhat indirect approach, but one which may be useful in deterrence analysis. This involves the use of victimization surveys.

Consider, for concreteness, the set of gasoline stations in a given metropolitan area. A victimization survey of these stations would indicate the frequency with which each was robbed or burglarized in a given interval of time and the conditions under which each incident took place.

If we imagine a population of potential gas station robbers and burglars living in the area, it is reasonable to assume that each such criminal could conceivably "hit" any of the area's stations. In general, the number and locations of the attempts each criminal does make will depend on personal characteristics and on the characteristics of the available alternatives. In particular, we might expect that the criminal's decisions are determined in part by the "take" at each station, the quality of the private protective system each station possesses, and the extent of local police surveillance.

This suggests that a gasoline station victimization survey can reveal aspects of the structure of criminal behavior. Specifically, observation of the relative frequencies of crimes at stations characterized by different takes and different protective systems should indicate something about the reward-risk trade-offs criminals make and the deterrent value of alternative protective systems.[8] Because victimization surveys cannot usually provide the attributes of individual offenders, it should not be expected that individual criminal decision functions will be estimable from such data. An "average" decision function for the population, however, may be estimable.

Determination of exactly how victimization surveys can be used fruitfully in deterrence analysis will require considerable further thought. Beyond the gas station example, such surveys would appear useful in studying the determinants of bank robberies, home burglaries, and muggings, among other crime types.

[8]Note that the take and the security of a given station can vary over the day and the week. Hence, reports of the timing of different incidents at a single station can also provide useful information on criminal behavior.

III. MODELING CONCERNS AND APPROACHES

Successful empirical analysis of criminal behavior requires the development of econometric models that are at the same time behaviorally realistic and operationally practical. In selecting a model specification, the analyst must appropriately structure the decision problems individuals face over time and specify the decision rules they use. Some important concerns in specifying an econometric model of criminal behavior are discussed below, and a behaviorally appealing and potentially practical modeling approach follows.

THE DIMENSIONS OF MODEL SPECIFICATION

Structuring the Criminal Decision Problem

Within the theoretical economic literature on criminal behavior, the criminal decision problem has been posed in two distinct ways.[9] Some authors, including Becker (1968), Ehrlich (1973) and Block and Heinecke (1973), view the individual facing a time allocation decision in which some available activities are legitimate and others criminal. Essentially, these authors simply extend the conventional labor-leisure model so as to distinguish among different forms of labor, some of which society labels criminal.

In the second approach, typified by Allingham and Sandmo (1972), Kolm (1973), and Singh (1973), it is assumed that at some moment the individual faces a set of criminal opportunities, one of which is the "null option" of not committing a crime. Crime commission in these models is an instantaneous event, separate from any time allocation the individual may make.[10]

Both conceptualizations capture important aspects of criminal behavior, but neither by itself suffices. The time allocation models recognize the search and planning activities that precede the commission of premeditated crimes and characterize the professional criminal. These models do not, however, provide any description of how time spent in such activities relates to the number of crimes actually committed. The criminal opportunities models recognize that the actual commission of most crimes consumes very little time and hence crime commission

[9]In preparing this section, I have benefited from an insightful review of the literature by Heinecke (1976).

[10]The models in the literature make the restrictive assumption that all consequences associated with a criminal act are monetary, so that the criminal decision problem falls formally within portfolio theory. This aspect of the literature is irrelevant here.

may realistically be often treated as a timeless event.[11] Such models do not, however, describe how the individual's criminal opportunity set arises. In particular, the role of past planning and search activities in creating present criminal opportunities is ignored.

Clearly, realistic modeling of criminal behavior requires a synthesis of the time allocation and crime commission approaches. The individual's allocation of time among criminal and non-criminal activities will naturally depend in part on the kinds of opportunities he expects criminal activity will yield. Conversely, the actual criminal opportunities the individual has available at any moment will depend in part on the past effort he has expended in seeking out and planning crimes. A model of criminal behavior should therefore explain both time allocation and crime commission decisions and appropriately incorporate the linkages between them.[12]

Specifying the Individual's Decision Rule

With the criminal decision problem structured, the substance of a behavioral model is the decision rule assumed to govern choice. Because the analyst's specification of a rule must be context-specific, I shall limit myself to a brief remark about the "economic" model of criminal behavior and its empirical representation.

[11]Actually, most crimes are legally defined as timeless events. In some cases, such as murder, robbery, forgery, and theft, such a definition is natural. In other cases, such as speeding, price fixing, and the operation of a brothel, crime commission has an inherent time dimension. Here it might be preferable to make part of the definition of an offense its duration.

[12]In some contexts, it may be reasonable simply to assume that the number of crimes committed is proportional to the time allocated to criminal activity, thus effectively condensing the two decisions into one. Unfortunately, such an assumption will often be unrealistic, because individuals may vary in their search and planning skills and because the time devoted to planning per crime may vary with deterrence policies.

While the time allocation decision often constitutes the aspect of criminal behavior most closely tied to crime commission itself, other dimensions of behavior certainly exist. For example, there are decision problems involving the choice of accomplices, the choice of weapons, and the amount of monetary expenditure for crime-related purposes. Moreover, where crimes are not premeditated, the time allocation aspect of behavior will itself be irrelevant.

Because the legal system defines so many different forms of crime and because criminal behavior has so many dimensions, to attempt to capture all crime-related decisions within a single model seems hopeless. One might as easily try to capture all of human behavior. Inevitably, empirical modeling will require the development of models confining their domains to restricted classes of crime types and dimensions of criminal behavior.

An economic model of crime is simply one in which criminal decisions are consistent with a preference ordering. Usually it is assumed that this ordering can be described through a utility function.[13] In empirical applications, in which not all factors influencing behavior can generally be observed, a natural representation of maximizing behavior is a random utility model—that is, a model in which utilities are treated as random variables and behavior is expressed in choice probabilities. Random utility models of aspects of criminal behavior are developed below.

Modeling Criminal Behavior Over Time

Earlier, it was noted that, over time, the individual faces a succession of criminal decision problems and that a decision to engage in criminal activities is not an irrevocable act. Given this fact, it is clear that an empirical model of criminal behavior should aim to describe the time path of criminal choices, not simply behavior at one instant.

Modeling the dynamics of criminal decision making poses two distinct issues, one behavioral and the other observational. First, there is the behavioral matter of how the individual actually deals with decision making over time. Does he, at each decision moment, formulate a hypothetical optimal time path of future behavior based on his present knowledge and circumstances, or does he act more myopically?[14] How do realizations of uncertain events modify the individual's circumstances, particularly his expectations? These questions must be addressed by the analyst in specifying the decision rule that the individual is assumed to use at each moment.

If, for every decision moment, the analyst could specify the individual's decision rule and choice set with certainty, the analyst could perfectly predict the time path of individual behavior simply by applying the posited choice model recursively over the succession of decision moments.[15] Unfortunately, as pointed out earlier, some factors

[13]Much of the theoretical economic literature on criminal behavior imposes the very stringent requirement that all consequences of criminal actions are describable in monetary terms and that utility is a function of money alone. This restriction is, of course, in no way necessary to an economic model of crime.

[14]If the individual does, in the manner of dynamic programming, select an optimal behavioral path at a given decision moment, this path is only hypothetical because realizations of presently uncertain events may lead him to modify the path over time. The hypothetical and actual behavioral paths should be expected to coincide only in a world of perfect information.

[15]This presumes that the sequence of decision moments is specified exogenously. See below for a discussion of alternative approaches in specifying this sequence.

influencing behavior will generally be unobserved in empirical applications. This fact produces the second issue in dynamic modeling—namely, how unobserved factors should be represented.

In a static context, unobserved factors may be treated as random variables. In a dynamic model, with entire time paths of relevant factors unobserved, it is necessary to treat such factors as random functions of time. The analyst's problem is to specify those random functions in a concurrently realistic and tractable manner.

Historically, empirical analyses of individual behavior over time have usually handled this specification problem in unacceptable ways. One approach has been to assume that the unobserved factors are drawn once and thereafter remain fixed over time, while a second has been to assume independent drawings at each decision moment. If, as seems realistic, unobserved factors generally are positively but not perfectly correlated over time, then the former approach will tend to underpredict and the latter to overpredict the extent to which behavior fluctuates over time. Recently, some authors have developed more palatable stochastic specifications, but at some cost in behavioral interpretability (see in particular Bass *et al.* 1976, Ginsberg 1971, Heckman and Willis 1975, Hausman and Wise 1976, and Levy 1976). The model introduced below attempts to achieve an acceptable stochastic specification while retaining an explicit behavioral derivation.

A DYNAMIC RANDOM UTILITY APPROACH TO MODELING CRIMINAL BEHAVIOR

The issues to be faced in specifying an empirical model of criminal behavior become sharpened when one actually attempts to frame such a model. Existing modeling approaches, we have noted, do not adequately recognize the linkage between time allocation and crime commission decisions nor the essential dynamic character of criminal behavior. I have therefore sought to develop a more satisfactory approach, the basic elements of which are described below.

The econometric choice model introduced here is a dynamic generalization of the static random utility models that have increasingly been found useful in empirical choice analysis. After laying out the model in abstract terms, I indicate how it may be applied to analyze time allocation and crime commission decisions. The section concludes with some remarks on the stochastic process models of crime commission prevalent in the operations research literature.

Dynamic Random Utility Models

The conventional static random utility model presumes a population of decision makers T, each member of which must select an alternative from a finite choice set C. With each decision maker $t \in T$ and alternative $i \in C$ there are associated attribute vectors s_t and x_i, respectively. It is assumed that for each decision maker $t \in T$, choice from the set C is consistent with maximization of a utility function $U_{ti} = U(s_t, x_i)$ over $i \in C$.

Some components of the attribute vectors x and s are observed by the analyst; the rest are unobserved. Hence, utilities are themselves not directly observable, and so perfect predictions of choice are not possible. However, if the unobserved attributes are considered a drawing from some probability distribution, then utilities, being functions of those attributes, are random variables. Therefore, probabilistic predictions of choice are possible. In particular, the probability that t chooses i is, assuming indifference among alternatives occurs with probability zero, simply $P_r(U_{ti} \geqslant U_{tj}$, all $j \in C)$. As expressed above, the random utility model has been studied and applied by numerous authors. (See Luce and Suppes 1965 and McFadden 1976 for reviews of parts of the literature.)

Conceptually, generalization of the static random utility model to one of choice over time is quite straightforward. Let each decision maker in T be required to select an alternative from C at every moment in an ordered set of decision moments M.[16] Let s_{tm} and x_{im} now be dated attribute vectors for $m \in M$ and let $U_{tim} = U(s_{tm}, x_{im})$. Assume that the time paths of some components of x and s are observed by the analyst; the rest are unobserved. If the time path of the unobserved components is considered a drawing from a probability distribution of paths, then utilities are random functions of time. The probability that t chooses i during some set of decision moments $M_o \subseteq M$ is, ignoring indifference, $P_r(U_{tim} \geqslant U_{tjm}$, all $j \in C$, $m \in M_o)$. More generally, if c_{tm} designates the alternative selected by t at moment m, the probability distribution of choice paths $(c_{tm}, m \in M)$ can be derived from the distribution of utility paths.

In empirical applications of the static random utility model, it is usually assumed that for each $t \in T$, the utilities U_{ti}, $i \in C$ have the form

[16]The set M may be countable, in which case we have a discrete time model or a continuum, in which case a continuous time model results. However M is specified, it is important that it be exogenous rather than determined within the decision process itself.

$U_{ti} = z_{ti} \cdot \Theta + \epsilon_{ti}$, where $z_{ti} = z(s_t, x_i)$ is a vector of functions of observed attributes, $(\epsilon_{ti}, i \in C)$ is a drawing from a multivariate distribution $F_t(\varphi)$, and Θ and φ are parameter vectors to be estimated from the sample data.[17] The obvious dynamic generalization of this specification is to let $U_{tim} = z_{tim} \cdot \Theta + \epsilon_{tim}$ where $z_{tim} = z(s_{tm}, x_{im})$ and where $(\epsilon_{tim}, i \in C, m \in M)$ is a drawing from a multivariate stochastic process. Just as in the static literature an important concern has been to find realistic yet tractable distributional specifications for the disturbances, in the dynamic context it will be important to find appropriate stochastic process specifications. Work on this problem is now in its early stages.[18]

Application to the Time Allocation and Crime Commission Decisions

The dynamic random utility approach offers an appealing vehicle for modeling both the time allocation and crime commission aspects of criminal behavior.

Consider first the time allocation problem. Let C be a set of activities or uses of time, including criminal search and planning activities, legitimate employment, and leisure activities. For concreteness, let M, the set of decision moments, be an interval on the real line so that decisions are updated continuously. At each moment $m \in M$, the individual must, we assume, select exactly one activity from C. Decision making, we assume, does not itself consume time. The individual's selected activity path determines his time allocation over the interval M. In particular, his allocation of time to criminal activities is simply that subset of M in which he selects a criminal activity. If the choice of an activity at every moment is consistent with utility maximization, and if, in the manner described earlier, utilities are treated as observationally random functions of time, then the individual's time allocation process is described by a dynamic random utility model.

Figure 1 illustrates how an individual's realized time path of utilities determines his activity path and hence his time allocation. The figure

[17]For example, the assumption that the disturbances are independently identically distributed following a Weibull distribution leads to the conditional logit model of McFadden (1973). If the disturbances are specified multivariate normal, a multinomial probit model results. See Albright *et al.* (1977), among other sources.

[18]Certainly, two specifications which should usually be avoided are the one in which ϵ_{tim} is fixed over $m \in M$ and the one in which each decision moment brings a temporally independent drawing. Historically, attempts to apply static random utility models to analyze inherently temporal behavior have of necessity made one or the other of these extreme assumptions.

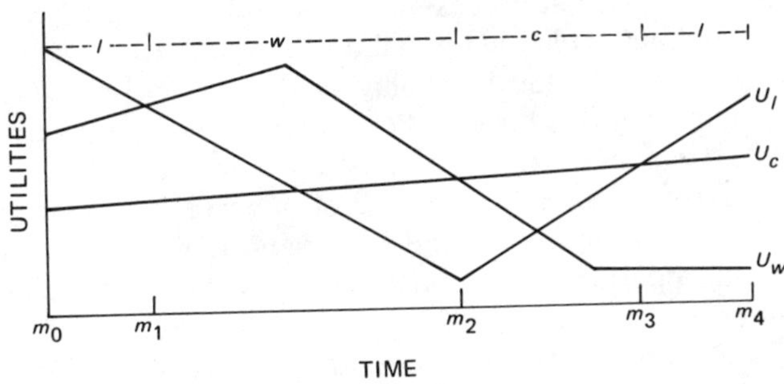

FIGURE 1 Activity utilities and choices.

depicts a situation in which the individual must, at every moment, select among three activities, criminal (c), work (w) and leisure (l). His time allocation, determined by the identity of the activity maximizing utility at each moment, gives the intervals $[m_0,m_1)$ and $[m_3,m_4)$ to leisure, $[m_1,m_2)$ to work, and $[m_2,m_3)$ to criminal activity.[19] Note that, as drawn, the utility time paths are everywhere continuous functions of time. In practice, it will often be desirable to allow discontinuities at certain decision moments. For example, if there exist transitional costs in switching among activities, discontinuities can be expected at the switch points. A different source of discontinuities appears in modeling crime commission decisions, to which subject we now turn.

Suppose that the generation of criminal opportunities can be described by a birth and death process. That is, every so often a new criminal opportunity appears and has some life span over which its characteristics may vary. An opportunity may go out of existence in one of two ways: either it is "used up" by the individual as he commits the relevant crime, or, unused by him, it ends in some other manner at some time.

Given the above process, the individual will at every moment have available some population of opportunities. While the size and character of this population will generally vary with time, we shall suppose that one alternative is always available. This is the "null option" of committing no crime. Assume now that at every moment the individual must select exactly one opportunity. If, as before, his choices over time are consistent with utility maximization and if utilities are again treated as random functions of time, then a dynamic random utility model describes crime commission behavior.

[19]The intervals are made half open to resolve the ambiguity in choice that occurs at points of transition among activities.

The crime commission process is illustrated in Figure 2. In the figure, the null option's utility is normalized to equal zero always. Opportunity 1 is born before the beginning of the time period M and dies unused. Opportunity 2 is born and eventually is used, the crime being committed at moment m_2. There exists a time interval between the death of opportunity 1 and emergence of opportunities 3, 4, and 5, in which only the null option is available. Opportunity 4 is used at moment m_4 and opportunities 3 and 5 still exist as the time period of observation ends.

How our models of time allocation and crime commission relate to each other remains to be specified. Consider the crime commission model. It should be expected that both the birth rate of criminal opportunities and the evolution of their characteristics over time will depend in part on the amount of time the individual has allocated to criminal search and planning activities. Thus, past time allocation decisions help determine the criminal opportunity sets faced and hence may influence crime commission decisions. Note that present crime commission decisions may also be influenced by past crimes committed. In particular, the outcome of past attempted crimes may affect the individual's wealth, criminal record, and perceived probabilities of arrest and conviction. And these factors may in turn affect present crime commission decisions. Similar forces will in general make present time allocation decisions a function of both past crime commission and time allocation choices.

Some Remarks on Stochastic Process Models of Crime Commission

In the econometric model of crime commission described above, the temporal nature of the criminal decision problem and the analyst's limited information make crime commission appear to follow a stochastic process. At present, the manner in which different structural as-

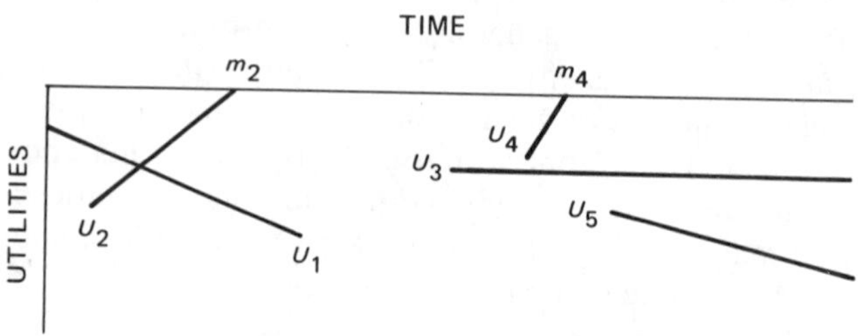

FIGURE 2 Crime commission utilities and choices.

sumptions translate into stochastic process properties for crime commission is unknown. In particular, it is not known whether realistic structural assumptions yielding convenient stochastic processes exist.

A number of authors, working in the operations research tradition, have directly formulated stochastic process models of crime commission. For example, Blumstein and Greene (1976) construct a career length-crime rate model in which the length of a criminal career is *gamma* distributed in the population and the crime rate for an active criminal is *Poisson* distributed, independent of his career length. Other models describe transitions among crime types. For example, an estimated "crime switch" matrix may form the basis for a Markov model of crime commission. (See Blumstein and Larson 1969, Avi-Itzhak and Shinnar 1973, and Shinnar and Shinnar 1975 for further examples of stochastic process models of crime. Cohen, in this volume, reviews the relevant literature.)

The existing stochastic process models offer a variety of analytically convenient forms for the description of crime commission. Unfortunately, these models are, in their present form, decidedly nonbehavioral. Not only are they derived from no behavioral model, but their parameters are treated as physical constants. Criminals, it is assumed, behave essentially like light bulbs.[20]

From the perspective of deterrence analysis, the above suggests two things. First, it would be of interest to ask what structural assumptions, if any, would yield stochastic process models of the forms found in the operations research literature. Where a match can be made, the given stochastic process model will be interpretable as a reduced form for the underlying behavioral model. Moreover, the parameters of the stochastic process model will be functionally determined by parameters of the relevant behavioral model. Hence, study of the stochastic process model may be useful in recovering the behavioral model.

Second, ignoring any formal behavioral-stochastic process model relations, the convenient analytical forms of the stochastic process models can be exploited by directly specifying the parameters of these models to be functions of behaviorally relevant variables. For example, the crime rate for decision maker t at moment m might be assumed *Poisson* with parameter

$$\lambda_{tm} = \lambda(Q_m, s_{tm}, \rho)$$

[20]In fairness to the authors working in this literature, it should be noted that they do not claim that stochastic process models are relevant to deterrence analysis. Rather, their interest has centered on the impact of incapacitation policies on the crime rate, holding deterrent policies constant. For this purpose, only a descriptive model of criminal action is necessary.

where Q_m is a vector characterizing deterrence policies, economic conditions, and the like and ρ is a parameter vector. The empirical problem would then be to estimate the pseudo-behavioral parameters ρ. In non-crime contexts, *ad hoc* approaches to behavioral analysis like the one suggested here have been used by Ginsberg (1971) and Heckman and Willis (1975).

IV. CONCLUSIONS

Overall, the prospects for useful inference on deterrence through empirical analysis of individual criminal behavior seem decidedly mixed. Because the data likely to be available for such analysis have limitations and because criminal behavior can be so complex, the emergence of a definitive behavioral study laying to rest all controversy about the behavioral effects of deterrence policies should not be expected. On the other hand, data capable of illuminating important aspects of criminal behavior are obtainable and realistic, tractable behavioral models can be developed. The prospects for a piecemeal accumulation of useful evidence on deterrence are therefore good.

In thinking about modeling criminal behavior, it is natural to ask whether the paradigm of economic—that is, rational—man can in fact be successfully applied in this context. I obviously believe so. There do exist, however, two respects in which modeling criminal behavior differs in degree from the typical economic modeling problem. First, acquiring suitable data for modeling criminal behavior seems to be a more difficult task than is usually the case. Second, because the deterrence issue is so sensitive and because empirical evidence may play a role in judicial decisions as well as legislative policy formation, the desired standard of proof sought in empirical analyses of crime is higher than that found acceptable in most other contexts.[21] For this reason, researchers should be quite cautious in the performance and interpretation of empirical work on criminal behavior.

[21]The most notable recent example of a role played by empirical analysis in judicial deliberation is the advancement by the U.S. Solicitor General in the case *Fowler v. North Carolina* of the results in Ehrlich (1975) as an argument in favor of finding capital punishment constitutional. In its opinion, the U.S. Supreme Court (wisely, I think) declared that this evidence was too uncertain to influence their decision on the capital punishment issue (see Bork 1975 and U.S. Supreme Court 1975).

REFERENCES

Albright, R., Lerman, S., and Manski, C. (1977) The Multinomial Probit Estimation Package: Features and Operational Tests. Cambridge Systematics, Inc.

Allingham, M., and Sandmo, A. (1972) Income tax evasion: a theoretical analysis. *Journal of Public Economics* 1(314):323-38.

Avi-Itzhak, B., and Shinnar, R. (1973) Quantitative models in crime control. *Journal of Criminal Justice* 1:185-217.

Bass, F., Jeuland, A., and Wright, G. (1976) Equilibrium stochastic choice and market penetration theories: derivations and comparisons. *Management Science* 22(10): 1051-63.

Becker, G. (1968) Crime and punishment: an economic approach. *Journal of Political Economy* 78(2):189-217.

Block, M., and Heinecke, J. (1973) The allocation of effort under uncertainty: the case of risk averse behavior. *Journal of Political Economy* 81(2):376-85.

Blumstein, A., and Greene, M. (1976) The Distribution of the Length of Criminal Careers. Unpublished paper. School of Urban and Public Affairs, Carnegie-Mellon University.

Blumstein, A., and Larson, R. (1969) Models of a total criminal justice system. *Operations Research* March/April.

Blumstein, A., and Nagin, D. (1977) The deterrent effect of legal sanctions on draft evasion. *Stanford Law Review* 28(2):241-75.

Bork, R. H. (Solicitor General) *et al.* (1974) Fowler v. North Carolina, U.S. Supreme Court case no. 73-7031. Brief for U.S. as *amicus curiae*:32-39.

Carr-Hill, R., and Stern, N. (1973) An econometric model of the supply and control of recorded offenses in England and Wales. *Journal of Public Economics* 2(4):289-318.

Ehrlich, I. (1973) Participation in illegitimate activities: a theoretical and empirical investigation. *Journal of Political Economy* 81(3):521-67.

Ehrlich, I. (1975) The deterrent effect of capital punishment: a question of life and death. *American Economic Review* 65(3):397-417.

Forst, B. (1976) Participation in illegitimate activities: further empirical findings. *Policy Analysis* 2(3):477-92.

Ginsberg, R. (1971) Semi-Markov processes and mobility. *Journal of Mathematical Sociology* 1:233-62.

Hausman, J., and Wise, D. (1976) The evaluation of results from truncated samples: the New Jersey Income Maintenance Experiment. *Annals of Economic and Social Measurement* 5(4):421-46.

Hausman, J., and Wise, D. (1977) Social experimentation, truncated distributions, and efficient estimation. *Econometrica* 45(4):919-38.

Heckman, J., and Willis, R. (1975) A Beta-Logistic Model for the Analysis of Sequential Labor Force Participation by Married Women. Working paper No. 112. Washington, D.C.: National Bureau of Economic Research.

Heinecke, J. (1976) Economic Models of Criminal Behavior: Implications and Shortcomings. Technical report EMCRD-1-76. Center for the Econometric Studies of Crime and the Criminal Justice System, Hoover Institution, Stanford University.

Kohn, M., Manski, C., and Mundel, D. (1976) An empirical investigation of factors influencing college going behavior. *Annals of Economic And Social Measurement* 5(4):391-420.

Kolm, S. (1973) A note on optimum income tax evasion. *Journal of Public Economics* 2(3):265-70.

Lerman, S., and Ben-Akiva, M. (1976) A disaggregate behavioral model of auto ownership. *Transportation Research Record* 569:34-55.

Levy, F. (1976) How Big is the American Underclass? Unpublished paper. Graduate School of Public Policy, University of California, Berkeley.

Luce, R., and Suppes, P. (1965) Preference, utility and subjective probability. In R. Luce, R. Bush, and E. Galanter, eds., *Handbook of Mathematical Psychology*. Vol. 3. New York: John Wiley.

McFadden, D. (1973) Conditional logit analysis of qualitative choice behavior. In Zarembka, ed., *Frontiers in Econometrics*. New York: Academic Press.

McFadden, D. (1976) Quantal choice analysis: a survey. *Annals of Economic and Social Measurement* 5(4):363-90.

Manski, C., and Lerman, S. (1977) The estimation of choice probabilities from choice based samples. *Econometrica* 45:(8).

Manski, C., and McFadden, D. (1977) Alternative Estimators and Sample Designs for Discrete Choice Analysis. Unpublished paper. Department of Economics, University of California, Berkeley.

Passell, P., and Taylor, J. (1976) The deterrence controversy: reconsideration of the time series evidence. In H. Bedau and C. Pierce, eds., *Capital Punishment*. New York: AMS Press.

Peck, J. (1976) The deterrent effect of capital punishment: a comment. *Yale Law Journal* 86:359-67.

Petersilia, J., Greenwood, P., and Lavin, M. (1977) Criminal Careers of Repetitively Violent Offenders. Report No. R-2144-DOJ. Santa Monica, Rand Corp.

Reiss, A., Jr. (1973) Survey of Self-Reported Delicts. Unpublished paper. Department of Sociology, Yale University.

Shinnar, R., and Shinnar, S. (1975) The effects of the criminal justice system on the control of crime: a quantitative approach. *Law and Society Review* 9(4):581-611.

Singh, B. (1973) Making honesty the best policy. *Journal of Public Economics* 2(3):257-64.

Tobin, J. (1958) Estimation of relationships for limited dependent variables. *Econometrica* 1(26):24-36.

U.S. Supreme Court (1975) Opinion on Fowler v. North Carolina. Case no. 73-7031.

Weimer, D., and Stonebraker, M. (1975) Sentencing Patterns, DA Policy and the Decision to Go to Trial. Unpublished paper. Graduate School of Public Policy, University of California, Berkeley.

Witte, A. D. (1976) Testing the Economic Model of Crime on Individual Data. Unpublished paper. Department of Economics, University of North Carolina.

APPENDIX

CONFERENCE ON DETERRENT AND INCAPACITATIVE EFFECTS

July 19–20, 1976

Invitees

*KURT BAIER, Department of Philosophy, University of Pittsburgh

*GARY BECKER, Department of Economics, University of Chicago

MICHAEL BLOCK, Hoover Institution, Stanford, California

C, P ALFRED BLUMSTEIN, School of Urban and Public Affairs, Carnegie-Mellon University

JAN CHAIKEN, RAND Corporation, Santa Monica, California

PS JACQUELINE COHEN, School of Urban and Public Affairs, Carnegie-Mellon University

C DONALD DESKINS, Department of Geography, University of Michigan

*ISAAC EHRLICH, University of Chicago

C EUGENE EIDENBERG, University of Illinois at Chicago Circle

C MALCOLM FEELEY, Yale Law School, Yale University

P FRANKLIN M. FISHER, Department of Economics, Massachusetts Institute of Technology

* unable to attend

C Member, Committee on Research on Law Enforcement and Criminal Justice

P Member, Panel on Research on Deterrent and Incapacitative Effects

PS Panel Staff

NOTE: Affiliations listed are those at the time of the Conference.

BRIAN FORST, Institute for Law and Social Research, Washington, D.C.

C JACK GIBBS, Department of Sociology, University of Arizona

DAVID GREENBERG, Department of Sociology, New York University

PETER GREENWOOD, RAND Corporation, Santa Monica, California

ZVI GRILICHES, Department of Economics, Harvard University

C *CHARLES HERZFELD, International Telephone & Telegraph Corporation

C ROBERT IGLEBURGER, Chief (Retired), Police Department, Dayton, Ohio

LAWRENCE KLEIN, Department of Economics, University of Pennsylvania

C, P GARY KOCH, Department of Biostatistics, University of North Carolina

C SAMUEL KRISLOV, Chairman, Committee on Research on Law Enforcement and Criminal Justice, and Department of Political Science, University of Minnesota

WILLIAM LANDES, Law School, University of Chicago

RICHARD LINSTER, Director, Office of Evaluation, National Institute of Law Enforcement and Criminal Justice

CHARLES MANSKI, School of Urban and Public Affairs, Carnegie-Mellon University

P PAUL MEEHL, Department of Psychology, University of Minnesota

JOHN MONAHAN, Department of Social Ecology, University of California, Irvine

PS DANIEL NAGIN, School of Urban and Public Affairs, Carnegie-Mellon University

FRED NOLDE, Hoover Institution, Stanford University, California

C BERYL RADIN, The LBJ School of Public Affairs, The University of Texas at Austin

P ALBERT REISS, Department of Sociology, Yale University

C SIMON ROTTENBERG, Department of Economics, University of Massachusetts

C RICHARD D. SCHWARTZ, School of Law, State University of New York at Buffalo

REUEL SHINNAR, Department of Chemical Engineering, City University of New York

LESTER P. SILVERMAN, Associate Executive Director, Assembly of Behavioral and Social Sciences

WALTER VANDAELE, Graduate School of Business Administration, Harvard University

ANDREW VON HIRSCH, School of Criminal Justice, Rutgers University

EUGENE WEBB, College of Business, Stanford University

SUSAN O. WHITE, Study Director, Committee on Research on Law Enforcement and Criminal Justice

P JAMES Q. WILSON, John Fitzgerald Kennedy School and Department of Government, Harvard University

C, P *MARVIN E. WOLFGANG, Department of Criminology, University of Pennsylvania

C *COLEMAN YOUNG, Mayor, Detroit, Michigan

HANS ZEISEL, Law School, University of Chicago

P FRANKLIN ZIMRING, Department of Law and the Center for Studies in Criminal Justice, University of Chicago

Agenda

July 19, 1976

ISSUE: ECONOMETRIC ESTIMATION OF DETERRENT EFFECTS

Time	Title of Paper or Discussion[1]	Author	Primary Discussant(s)	Other Discussant(s)
9:00-10:00	General Deterrence: A Review and Critique of Empirical Evidence (not including capital punishment)	Daniel Nagin	Fred Nolde	Michael Block
10:00-11:00	Sensitivity Analysis of Simultaneous Econometric Models	Walter Vandaele	Charles Manski	William Landes Brian Forst
11:00-12:00	Further Analysis of the Deterrent Effect of Capital Punishment	Lawrence Klein Brian Forst Victor Filatov	William Landes	Franklin Fisher
1:30-2:30	On the Feasibility of Identifying the Crime Function in a Simultaneous Model of Crime and Sanctions	Franklin Fisher Daniel Nagin	Zvi Griliches Michael Block	Charles Manski
2:30-3:30	On the Feasibility of Inferring Deterrent Effects from Observation of Individual Criminal Behavior	Charles Manski	William Landes Michael Block	Zvi Griliches Jan Chaiken

ISSUE: OPERATIONAL SIMILARITIES AND DIFFERENCES AMONG POLICIES

Time	Title of Paper or Discussion	Author	Primary Discussant(s)	Other Discussant(s)
3:30-4:30	The Principal Alternative Policies of Imprisonment	Kurt Baier	Andrew von Hirsch	Franklin Zimring Samuel Krislov James Q. Wilson

July 20, 1976

ISSUE: EXPERIMENTAL ESTIMATION OF DETERRENT EFFECT

Time	Paper	Author	Discussants	
9:00-10:30	Policy Experiments in General Deterrence 1970-1975	Franklin Zimring	Hans Zeisel	Albert Reiss
10:30-12:00	Some Possible Experiments		Gary Koch Eugene Webb	Richard Schwartz James Q. Wilson Franklin Zimring

ISSUE: INCAPACITATION AND THE PREDICTION OF CRIMINALITY

Time	Paper	Author	Discussants	
1:30-2:30	Incapacitation: A Review of the Literature	Jacqueline Cohen	Reuel Shinnar David Greenberg	Peter Greenwood Jan Chaiken
2:30-3:30	Approaches to Analysis of Criminal Careers		Peter Greenwood David Greenberg	Reuel Shinnar Albert Reiss
3:30-4:30	The Prediction of Violent Criminal Behavior: A Methodological Critique and Prospectus	John Monahan	Gary Koch	Paul Meehl

[1]The papers were distributed to all participants prior to the Conference and served as the basis for discussion.